From civil strife to civil society

From civil strife to civil society: Civil and military responsibilities in disrupted states

Edited by William Maley, Charles Sampford and Ramesh Thakur

TOKYO • NEW YORK • PARIS

© The United Nations University, 2003

The views expressed in this publication are those of the authors and do not necessarily reflect the views of the United Nations University.

United Nations University Press
The United Nations University, 53-70, Jingumae 5-chome,
Shibuya-ku, Tokyo, 150-8925, Japan
Tel: +81-3-3499-2811 Fax: +81-3-3406-7345
E-mail: sales@hq.unu.edu (general enquiries): press@hq.unu.edu
http://www.unu.edu

United Nations University Office in North America
2 United Nations Plaza, Room DC2-2062, New York, NY 10017, USA
Tel: +1-212-963-6387 Fax: +1-212-371-9454
E-mail: unuona@ony.unu.edu

United Nations University Press is the publishing division of the United Nations University.

Cover design by Andrew Corbett

Printed in Hong Kong

UNUP-1070
ISBN 92-808-1070-7

Library of Congress Cataloging-in-Publication Data

From civil strife to civil society : civil and military responsibilities in disrupted states / edited by William Maley, Charles Sampford and Ramesh Thakur.
    p. cm.
Includes bibliographical references and index.
ISBN 92-808-1070-7
1. Political violence. 2. Conflict management. 3. Civil-military relations.
4. Humanitarian assistance. 5. Peacekeeping forces. 6. Civil society.
7. Democratization. I. Maley, William, 1957– II. Sampford, C. J. G.
(Charles J. G.) III. Thakur, Ramesh Chandra, 1948–
JC328.6 F76 2003
341.5—dc21   2002153957

Contents

Preface and acknowledgements...................................... ix

Introduction.. 1
    William Maley, Charles Sampford and Ramesh Thakur

Part 1: The problem of disrupted states............................. 15

  1 The dimensions of state disruption............................. 17
    Amin Saikal

  2. The international community and disrupted states.............. 31
    Paul F. Diehl

  3. The prevention–intervention dichotomy: Two sides of the
    same coin?... 57
    Simon Chesterman and David M. Malone

Part 2: Challenges for the military in disrupted states............... 81

  4. Managing future chaos: The United States Marine Corps in
    the twenty-first century 83
    Thomas E. Seal

5. Complex emergencies and military capabilities 96
    Frederick M. Burkle, Jr

Part 3: Ending violence 109

6. Violence, sovereignty and conflict resolution................... 111
    Raimo Väyrynen

7. Waging peace and ending violence in the twenty-first
    century.. 132
    Cees de Rover

8. Mercy and justice in the transition period 145
    Helen Durham

Part 4: Reconstituting political order............................... 161

9. Institutional design and the rebuilding of trust................. 163
    William Maley

10. Democracy and democratisation 180
    Reginald Austin

Part 5: Reconstituting legal order 205

11. Rebuilding the rule of law.. 207
    Mark Plunkett

12. Military force and justice 229
    Michael Kelly

Part 6: Reconstituting social order 255

13. The United Nations and social reconstruction in disrupted
    states... 257
    Lorraine Elliott

14. Reconstituting whose social order? NGOs in disrupted
    states... 279
    Fiona Terry

15. Comprehensive security partnerships for refugees............. 300
    Sadako Ogata

Part 7: Transition to civil order 307

16. Disarmament and reintegration of combatants 309
    Samuel M. Makinda

17. Policing civil order 327
    Adrien Whiddett

18. Afterword: Rebuilding the rule of law in the Horn of Africa .. 340
    Martin P. Ganzglass

List of contributors 351

Index 355

Preface and acknowledgements

The problems of disrupted states, and the responsibilities assumed by international civilian and military personnel in attempting to rescue the hapless peoples of such states from the perils which disruption creates, have long occupied the headlines in a range of states. The deployment in Kosovo of NATO forces, together with civilians from many countries under the auspices of a UN mission, is but the latest reminder of how challenging such responsibilities can be. This book seeks to illuminate the nature of these problems and responsibilities, and to identify some of the steps which might be taken to smooth the path from civil strife to civil society.

The book had its origins in two conferences. The first was held in Canberra in July 1999 under the joint sponsorship of the Australian Defence Studies Centre, the University of New South Wales, and the Key Centre for Ethics, Law, Justice, and Governance, Griffith University. It benefited from the active support of the Center of Excellence in Disaster Management and Humanitarian Assistance, Hawaii, and the Defence Legal Office, and backing from Tenix, Compucat, and SGI. The conference formed part of a larger project, financially supported by an Australian Research Council SPIRT grant. The second conference was held at the United Nations University (UNU) in Tokyo in January 2001, entitled "Partners in Humanitarian Crises", and organised jointly by the UNU and the Delegation of the European Commission in Japan.

The chapters of this book represent revised and expanded versions of papers prepared initially for these conferences. The authors have benefited both from the discussions that their individual papers generated and from the comments offered in the plenary sessions. We wish to thank the panellists at these conferences, and the other conference participants, for the rich insights that they were able to supply, and in particular, at the Canberra conference, Ms Sue Downie, Professor José Ramos-Horta, Major-General Sitiveni Rabuka, and Lieutenant-General John Sanderson. In preparing this book, we benefited from the assistance of Associate Professor Anthony Bergin, Ms Sue Brown, and Dr Bob Hall of the Australian Defence Studies Centre, Dr Yeong-Han Cheong of the Key Centre for Ethics, Law, Justice, and Governance, Ms Janet Boileau of the United Nations University Press, and especially Mrs Beverley Lincoln and Mrs Sue Moss of the School of Politics, University of New South Wales. We thank them for their sterling efforts. Finally, Janet Boileau and Gareth Johnston at the UNUP handled a complex manuscript with a high level of expertise.

William Maley, Charles Sampford and Ramesh Thakur
Canberra, Brisbane and Tokyo, November 2002

Introduction

William Maley, Charles Sampford and Ramesh Thakur

Man without law is the lowest of animals – *Aristotle*

As the Western world enters a new millennium, the seemingly settled parameters of a global politics based on the interaction of sovereign states appear increasingly threatened. On the one hand, processes of globalisation, especially in the economic sphere, have limited the freedom of action of those political elites who do not wish to bear the costs of pursuing autarkic policies. The debate between free traders and protectionists, which so marked the politics of democratic states at the beginning of the twentieth century, has for the moment been resolved – in international agreements if not always in the practice of strong states. On the other hand, however, processes of fragmentation have led to the disruption of a significant number of states or proto-states. Whether in Kosovo or East Timor, Somalia or Afghanistan, Cambodia or Bosnia and Herzegovina, Sierra Leone or Zimbabwe, the instrumentalities of the state have been compromised. Yet in a curious twist, another form of globalisation – this time a globalisation based not on market exchange but on a spreading sense that the rule of law, human security, and the ability of ordinary people to change their rulers without bloodshed are all values worth protecting – has drawn what is loosely called "the international community" into the internal affairs of these territories. It is with some key dimensions of that involvement that the essays in this book are concerned.

This involvement marks a significant departure from what one might call the Westphalian ideal. In 1648, the Peace of Westphalia, comprising the Treaties of Münster and Osnabrück, concluded the Thirty Years War by entrenching the state as the principal form of political organisation in Europe. This put an end to the hopes of an undivided Christendom, which is why the Pope denounced the Peace of Westphalia as "null, void, invalid, iniquitous, unjust, damnable, reprobate, inane, and devoid of meaning for all time".[1] Recent works, particularly the writings of Stephen D. Krasner,[2] have challenged the interpretation of the Peace of Westphalia itself as providing the constitutive framework of a system of sovereign states; indeed, the treaties that made up the Peace of Westphalia contained no specific reference to sovereignty.[3] However, few deny that "Westphalia" has become a metaphor for one particular type of world politics, one in which the principal actors are "sovereign states", enjoying the undisputed right to manage their "internal affairs" free from outside interference.

This was of course a predominantly European conception. Indeed, the first Secretary-General of the League of Nations, Sir Eric Drummond, resented the presence of Abyssinia in the League on the grounds that it was not a state fit for membership; in his eyes, it was attempting, as one writer ironically summarised it, "to seek shelter in the League against the legitimate interests of the great powers".[4] The Second World War put paid to most such thinking, not simply because of US President Franklin D. Roosevelt's hostility to colonialism, but also because the evils of the Holocaust killed off the notion of the moral superiority of Europe in general. However, this did not guarantee that the wave of decolonisation in the two decades which followed the establishment of the United Nations in 1945 would establish political units that would fit readily into the Westphalian ideal of statehood. Although it was widely assumed that Westphalian statehood was the natural and desirable end point to which all political communities would evolve, many did not. Herein lie some of the challenges by which the world is still confronted.

The sense of relative stability of the international system in the nuclear age is belied by the change in the number of actors. The United Nations, with 189 member states, has nearly four times as many member states as it had in 1945. Some of these are longstanding, highly institutionalised states, but a great many others reflect the tensions inherent in the notion of *sovereignty*.[5] In one sense, sovereignty refers to the accepted membership by a particular territory in a community of states, marked most notably by diplomatic recognition and by membership of international organisations, of which the United Nations is the most important. This has been labelled "juridical" or "external" sovereignty. In another sense, sovereignty refers to the capacity of the instrumentalities of "the state" to exercise effective control over the particular territory. This has been labelled "empirical" or "internal" sovereignty. These two senses sit, somewhat uncomfortably, alongside a third and more recent sense, "popular sovereignty", which refers to the extent to which a particular pattern of rule embodies the ideal that the ruled should be able to determine *by whom* they are to be ruled. It will immediately be apparent that the connections between these different senses of sovereignty are contingent rather than necessary. Some states which enjoy unquestioned external or juridical sovereignty – Somalia and Afghanistan come readily to mind – suffer from severe deficits in the realm of internal or empirical sovereignty.[6] The reverse can also be true, as demonstrated by such territorial units as Taiwan and the "Turkish Republic of Northern Cyprus". Furthermore, despite a recent wave of democratisation, there are still states with high levels of internal and external sovereignty but low levels of popular sovereignty. As media of communication heighten the capacity of peoples in such states to realise what they are missing, the internal or empirical sovereignty of their rulers may also come under threat, as the Tiananmen Square massacre revealed.

The 1990s have frequently been depicted as the decade in which intrastate conflict entered the agenda of international politics. This was always an exaggeration,[7] as those who recall the Congolese crisis of the early 1960s can affirm, and perhaps a product of particular influences, which could fade as time passes, or be better managed by concerned powers.[8] But it would be as well not to take too sanguine a view of the prospects. Although the United Nations has striven mightily to address these problems, it has not always done so with any great success, as the dead of Rwanda, Srebrenica, and East Timor remind us.[9] Is it possible to develop better diagnoses of the problems of state disruption and of ways in which they might be addressed?

Formulating the issues

Speaking of state *disruption*, rather than of state "collapse", "failure", or "disintegration", is one step towards a more nuanced exploration of the challenges posed by these problems. Terminologies of failure or collapse sound rather too absolute and/or judgemental, and run the risk of detracting from the complexities of the problems with which it may be necessary to deal. In Kosovo, the Yugoslav state neither collapsed nor failed, but rather was effectively ejected through open warfare, allegedly for the betterment of the local residents. In East Timor, the Indonesian state did not fail or collapse; it quit the territory in flames and ashes. The result in East Timor is a proto-state under United Nations tutelage. The result in

Kosovo is an ill-defined form of international "protectorate" pursuant to UN Security Council Resolution 1244 of 10 June 1999. In order to appreciate the range of responsibilities by which the international community can be confronted, it is necessary to consider these kinds of cases as well as those of complete state breakdown, and the middle ground of "quasi-states" in which the instrumentalities of the state are increasingly enfeebled but still constitute a potential partner for international actors.

Speaking of *civil* and *military responsibilities* also carries us further than does simple discussion of "peacekeeping". What one might call "traditional" or "classical" peacekeeping evolved as a creative response to particular needs for confidence-building which the United Nations Charter had not explicitly addressed: hence Secretary-General Dag Hammarskjöld's famous description of peacekeeping as "Chapter Six-and-a-half Operations". The peacekeeping operations of the Cold War era largely involved the deployment of troops under UN authority, with the consent of the combatant parties, mandated to discharge specific confidence-building tasks in a strictly neutral fashion, and to use force only for self-defence.[10] Operations tended not to occur in areas where the vital interests of permanent members of the UN Security Council were engaged, and peacekeeping troops tended to be drawn from the armed forces of "middle powers", some of which rightly took pride in the contributions they made to peacekeeping. With the waning of the Cold War, peacekeeping under UN auspices took a more complex form, with emphasis on the integrated discharge of a range of tasks necessary to restore order in societies that had somehow become dysfunctional. In such "complex", "multidimensional" or "second-generation" peacekeeping, refugee repatriation, the holding of free and fair elections, demining, and movement towards "development" all figured as important responsibilities.[11] None was in itself an entirely new form of activity for the United Nations, but the bundling of the activities to form a comprehensive package was. In all these cases, however, there was at least some reality of consent to the presence of international forces on the territory in point. By contrast, in a case such as Kosovo,[12] the work of the international community is greatly complicated by the lack of any real consent to its activities from a significant party to the dispute, which makes the maintenance of an image of neutrality extremely difficult. Should further such interventions occur, the world will need to learn the skills of building political, legal, social, and civil order in potentially unwelcoming climates.

Speaking of *civil society* highlights the importance of a long-term perspective on what such operations should aim to achieve. In a world of states, it is too easy to conceive the role of peace operations as being simply to reconstitute the instrumentalities of a functioning state, as fast as possible. This, unfortunately, can be a recipe for renewed turmoil as groups struggle to control what may be an important resource, and may do little to foster other mechanisms of governance with much to commend them.[13] The reconstitution of civil society certainly involves the development of appropriate political frameworks, but it also crucially requires the consolidation of the Rule of Law, attention to the material needs of ordinary people, and the beating of swords into ploughshares.

Addressing the issues

Detailed discussion of these elements of the transition from civil strife to civil society makes up the core of this book. Given the vast range of issues that can arise in the context of sociopolitical transitions, the contributions make no claims to being definitive. Rather, they offer explorations of key points, and build foundations upon which further work can be conducted.

Amin Saikal examines various forms that states might take, and notes five different types of disrupted state: those scarred by conflict but still accepted as states; those whose very existence is contested; embryonic states; those being punished for violating international law or norms; and those gripped by strong undercurrents of instability and held together by coercion. He goes on to discuss internal factors that can contribute to disruption: elite fragmentation; ethnic antagonisms; ideological struggle; confessional or sectarian divisions; loss of the revenue base of the state; a specific legitimacy crisis; or separatism. These can be aggravated by external factors: direct foreign intervention, creeping invasion, or unintended destabilisation. He concludes by surveying three abstract models of appropriate international responses to the problems of state disruption.

These issues are taken up more concretely by Paul Diehl. He opens by discussing the range of interests – humanitarian interests, human rights interests, and security interests – which can underpin the various dimensions of international action. He argues that the international community has choices of how to proceed in terms of timing (when), actions (what) and organisation (by whom). Actions can take a diverse range of forms: preventive deployment; humanitarian assistance; pacification; protective services; traditional peacekeeping; sanctions enforcement; election supervision; state/nation building; and arms control verification. In mobilising action, however, a number of difficulties can arise: galvanising action; coordination; coping with the specific perils of internal conflict; and striking the right balance between sustaining action and implementing an exit strategy.

Simon Chesterman and David M. Malone seek to advance the troubled discussion of prevention and intervention by arguing that it is necessary to shift the focus from seeing prevention as an alternative to intervention, to seeing intervention as a consequence of failed prevention. They offer a survey of prevention strategies, both in the abstract and as practised by the United Nations, and argue that humanitarian action is not synonymous with military intervention. Prevention – by now a much-discussed topic[14] – depends not so much on better early warning as on political will. Kosovo was long foreseen as a likely venue for bitter conflict. So were a host of other conflicts on which this book touches. "Last time", said Winston Churchill in his famous 1946 Fulton speech, "I saw it all coming, and cried aloud ... but no one would listen and one by one we were all sucked into the awful whirlpool."[15] Mobilising political will so that the peoples of states can be spared the grief that so often accompanies state disruption remains one of the most troubling issues of our times.

The United States of America, as a globally dominant power, is frequently the target of demands for action to help overcome the problems of state disruption.[16] Thomas E. Seal discusses the roles of the United States Marine Corps as the cutting edge of American power, given its forward presence, multiple capabilities, capacity for rapid response and its historical and cultural affinity for dealing with disrupted states. He argues that a range of constant factors – human nature; the nature of states; the nature of war; geography; national character; and resistance to attempts to disrupt the status quo – shape America's outlook, while variables such as globalisation, migration and urbanisation, and the changing character of military operations create new challenges. He goes on to examine how the Marine Corps has been structured to optimise its capacity to respond to these challenges, noting, however, that there are limits on one's capacity to predict what the future might bring. He concludes by noting some obstacles to civil–military cooperation: a plethora of actors; mission clash; communications problems; and institutional inertia.

The diversity of the challenges posed by state disruption is emphasised by Frederick M. Burkle, Jr, in his discussion of "complex emergencies". The complexity of complex emergencies, he notes, lies in the multifaceted responses which the international community initiates in reacting to the simultaneous emergence of political and social decay, high levels of violence, catastrophic threats to public health, population shifts and competition for resources. After examining the political, legal, socioeconomic and environmental security factors that underpin such emergencies, he goes on to discuss the involvement of Western militaries in responding to what are profound public health crises, and specifically the architecture put in place to attempt an integrated response to the emergency in East Timor.

Observing that civil war is not unique to our times, Raimo Väyrynen notes its disappearance from modern industrialized societies and links it to the decline of interstate wars among them. He finds examples in Latin America and East Asia of various security regimes and limited security communities with mutually reinforcing internal stability and external peace. By symmetric contrast, in Africa, where the informal political and economic map differs substantially from the formal boundaries, the internal and external dimensions of crises are often linked. On the basis of this survey, Väyrynen concludes that the institutionalisation of sovereignty contributes substantially to the internal and external stability of a region through building identity, political authority and legitimacy. In regions that have been ravaged by wars, including disrupted states, the best route to peace may lie, therefore, in the re-establishment of sovereign states whose mutual relations are regulated by international law. This leads Väyrynen to question the merits of external intervention in situations of humanitarian emergency, for it is very difficult to import external solutions to protracted civil wars underwritten by self-sustaining political economies. Efforts to alter the balance of incentives in favour of viable peace accords founder because of the great variety of actors and interests entangled in protracted conflicts.

Cees de Rover too takes up the question of how violence might be brought to an end in those countries wracked by civil strife. Dissatisfied with explanations of violence that simply identify patterns of social differentiation, he draws on Maslow's theory of needs to argue that one must take account of historical developments which create differential access to the resources by which needs can be satisfied. It is therefore important to address economic and social issues as well as civil and political rights if one is seeking a durable end to violence. The current collective security system is unable to do this. International intervention also has its limitations, as NATO's actions over Kosovo demonstrate. A reinvigoration of law is vital, to govern both the circumstances in which intervention can occur and the actual conduct of intervention. Finally, waging war to resolve a conflict can simply entrench the conflict itself. It is necessary also to "wage peace", by bringing parties together with a focus on the well-being of people.

Civil strife has many victims, and an issue which invariably arises as part of the transition to civil society is how the perpetrators of past evils should be held to account. Helen Durham investigates this issue in her chapter. Mercy, she argues, has a role to play in reconstituting society after trauma, but not a foundational role. Justice, on the other hand, has a range of fundamental roles to play – bringing wrongdoers to account; acknowledging the suffering of victims; educating the public as to the evils of the past. She then explores a range of institutional options for meeting the demand for justice. Domestic prosecutions may lack impartiality or legality; Truth and Reconciliation Commissions are an important alternative. But the burden may well fall on the international community, as it did with the famous Nuremberg and Tokyo trials. Some important steps have been taken by the ad hoc International Criminal Tribunals for the Former Yugoslavia and for Rwanda; and the proposed tribunal to try the Khmer Rouge in Cambodia may play a similar role. But the most striking recent development was the adoption in Rome in 1998 of a Statute for an International Criminal Court, which came into existence on 1 July 2002. A key challenge now will be the gathering of evidence, and here there are differences between the roles that can be played by human rights actors, on the one hand, and by humanitarian agencies such as the International Committee of the Red Cross, on the other.

Justice in this sense is concerned with creating a basis for moving forward. This is taken up by William Maley, who discusses more generally the issues of institutional design and the rebuilding of trust. Distinguishing anonymous trust from face-to-face trust, he argues that the breakdown of trust leads to unworkable political communities and disunified political elites. Ways of addressing these problems include the provision of neutral security, the resocialisation of antagonists and the design of institutions to mute the effects of political conflict. Institutional design should not be overlooked, or rushed, and it benefits from expert input. A range of abstract features mark institutions that are likely to be effective, but issues such as the nature of political authority, the distributive capacity of the state and the nature of military power will need to be addressed, as will the question of how new institutions should be legitimated. Architects will need to address questions such as whether power should be apportioned or alternated, and how offices should be structured and their occupants chosen. He concludes by noting that effective institutional design does not offer magic solutions to complex problems, but reduces the risk and costs of political conflict.

Reginald Austin addresses a range of problems associated with democratisation. He notes a growing rhetorical commitment to democracy, but sees this as compromised by the reality of state decay or corruption. The international community, through bodies such as the United Nations, the Commonwealth, and the International Institute for Democracy and Electoral Assistance (IDEA), has been heavily involved in seeking to give practical support to a nascent right to democratic governance. However, "electoral democratisation" is subject to a number of serious limitations. What works in the short term may face problems in the long term, and an appropriate balance between internal and external involvement in the performance of key "democratic" tasks needs to be struck.

The case of Zimbabwe points to the perils of settlements that paper over significant conflicts that need to be addressed. The case of Cambodia points to problems arising from a reluctance to regard democratisation as a comprehensive and ongoing process. Some lessons have been learned from these experiences, but others are yet to be properly absorbed.

Mark Plunkett is concerned with the practicalities of restoring the rule of law in disrupted states. Lawlessness, he notes, is one of the most pressing problems arising from the spread of civil strife, and two broad models are available to assist the reconstruction of a legal system: an enforcement model and a negotiation model. The enforcement model involves the establishment of a functioning criminal justice system and a Criminal Justice Commission to permit both exposure of misdeeds and reintegrative shaming. Plunkett offers a range of specific proposals relating to the staffing, organisation and functioning of such mechanisms of justice delivery. The negotiation model seeks to engage the local population in bringing about fundamental shifts in population consciousness, directed against toleration of impunity for violence. The heart of this model is to be found in two types of work technique: the Rapid Participatory Rule of Law Appraisal and the Rule of Law Participatory Assessment, Monitoring and Evaluation. The former is designed to assess the real needs of locals so that they can be properly addressed; the latter involves the setting of baselines for performance by which the achievements of institutions set up pursuant to the enforcement model can be evaluated. Together, these two models can deliver the foundations for the creation of a new state and ultimate peace.

The particular tasks of external military forces in the delivery of justice in disrupted states are investigated by Michael Kelly. Where peace operations are conducted by the military, it is vital from the earliest phases that appropriate frameworks for the delivery of justice be put in place, lest the legitimacy of the mission be compromised. The law of occupation, as embodied in the Fourth Geneva Convention of 1949, offers an appropriate general regime for such forces. In other circumstances – of pacific occupation by agreement – it is important that the terms of the agreement facilitate an effective approach to the maintenance of public security. In particular, the use of force must be properly regulated: the experience of the Canadian Airborne Regiment Battle Group in Somalia highlights how badly things can go wrong if this need is overlooked. Civil affairs capabilities should be developed by those states that are likely participants in peace operations, but the staff must be flexible and imaginative, rather than committed to the rigid application of "laboratory solutions".

The peoples of disrupted states are typically confronted by daunting social and economic problems, and a range of mechanisms exist by which they might be addressed. Lorraine Elliott examines the performance of the United Nations. Social reconstruction, she argues, must confront issues of human security, taking into account individuals, the rehabilitation of communities and the rebuilding of civil society. It also needs to recognise the roles played by local institutions. In discharging the tasks of social reconstruction, a range of UN agencies are normally involved, but the United Nations has a grim record with respect to operational efficiency, coordination, accountability, transparency and competence. She goes on to consider four specific problem areas in detail: the nature of intervention and consent, which too often is taken to exclude ordinary people; the need for integration of political-military and social humanitarian goals; the need for better coordination of UN programmes and agencies; and the need for long-term support of development activities as part of wider peacebuilding.

Fiona Terry, in her exploration of the activities of non-governmental organisations (NGOs), argues, however, that improved coordination is not a panacea for the problems surrounding humanitarian action. These problems are more fundamental and deeply rooted, arising from the paradox that humanitarian action has the potential to prolong conflict and thus the suffering of its victims. Some NGOs have sought to maintain a strict and complete neutrality, while others have responded with overtly political commitments. Complex emergencies, in Terry's view, are scarcely more complex than in the past; rather, it is the reaction of humanitarian actors that is complicated, because of the diversity of their agendas and objectives. Humanitarian crises have political causes, and governments can too easily wash their hands of responsibility by painting such situations as purely humanitarian, requiring a purely humanitarian response. Civil–military cooperation in disrupted states tends to be complicated by weaknesses in mandates, or by mandates that are poorly focused. This problem is compounded by political expediency and by the push to define "end-states" at which point a mission can be terminated, even at the expense of long-term reconciliation. She concludes that genuine ethical dilemmas surround humanitarian action and that these should be properly debated, rather than smothered by a blanket of conformity.

Sadako Ogata, who had the front-line responsibility for coping with the dramatic upsurge in refugees, reminds us that the right balance has to be struck also between the pressing interests of the most vulnerable and deprived people in the world and the legitimate concerns of states. She notes the paradox that peace operations continue to be country based, reflecting neither the internal nor the regional nature of many contemporary wars. Given compressed time frames and an increasingly congested humanitarian space, she argues for the need for an upgraded "surge capacity" for responding to refugee emergencies, for narrowing the gap between the deployment of humanitarian personnel and security support measures, and for constructing a "ladder of options" that include intermediate security measures pending the deployment of peace operations. Only thus can the security – of refugees, of the communities hosting them, and of the international humanitarian staff assisting them – be enhanced.

Samuel M. Makinda takes up the issue of the disarmament and reintegration of combatants, a problem of fundamental importance in states where the ploughshare is an oddity to soldiers – both adult and child – who know only the sword. He notes that realist, liberal, constructivist and feminist points of departure lead one to investigate the question in quite different ways. Conventional approaches to disarmament have too often been undermined by insufficient attention to vital questions about the states or societies in point, something which Makinda demonstrates with detailed discussion of the situations in Somalia and Cambodia. In Somalia, haphazard disarmament left disarmed groups at the mercy of those that had not disarmed. In Cambodia, the failure to disarm the armed factions left the existing power equation in place in Phnom Penh despite the 1993 vote of the Cambodian people. He concludes by suggesting that a critical perspective which does not take institutions and power relations for granted should augment a problem-solving approach to the disarmament of antagonists. The broader context of political and social reconstruction must be taken properly into account.

Adrien Whiddett discusses the use of police in the transition to civil order. Policing a democracy, he notes, is vastly more arduous than policing a totalitarian state, since the rights of citizens must be properly recognised. Criminal behaviour, in the context of wider world disorder, creates significant challenges for peace operations. Police from middle powers such as Australia have valuable roles to play when such operations are undertaken. In areas as diverse as Cyprus and Cambodia, certain distinctive skills of policing have proved to be effective contributors to order. However, strategies for operations must be properly integrated and graduated; police must be properly trained; and underperformers can seriously impair the efficient discharge of a civilian police contingent's responsibilities.

In conclusion, Martin P. Ganzglass reflects on the problems of rebuilding the rule of law in the Horn of Africa. He surveys the very different experiences of Australians in Somalia and code-drafters in Eritrea, and argues that a new NGO, "Justice Without Borders", might have a useful role to play in filling gaps that the breakdown of the rule of law in disrupted states characteristically causes. Looking at the contemporary cases of Kosovo and East Timor, he offers some suggestions as to how each of these different approaches might have something to offer.

Notes

1. Quoted in Norman Davies, *Europe: A History* (Oxford: Oxford University Press, 1996), p. 568.
2. See Stephen D. Krasner, "Compromising Westphalia", *International Security*, vol. 20, no. 3, Winter 1995-96, pp. 115-151; Stephen D. Krasner, *Sovereignty: Organized Hypocrisy* (Princeton, NJ: Princeton University Press, 1999).
3. See Daniel Philpott, "The Religious Roots of Modern International Relations", *World Politics*, vol. 52, no. 2, January 2000, pp. 206-245 at p. 211; also Derek Croxton, "The Peace of Westphalia of 1648 and the Origins of Sovereignty", *International History Review*, vol. 21, no. 3, September 1999, pp. 569-591.
4. Donald Cameron Watt, *How War Came: The Immediate Origins of the Second World War, 1938-1939* (New York: Pantheon Books, 1989), p. 85.
5. For more detailed discussion, see Daniel Philpott, "Sovereignty: An Introduction and Brief History", *Journal of International Affairs*, vol. 48, no. 2, Winter 1995, pp. 353-368; Michael Barnett, "The New United Nations Politics of Peace: From Juridical Sovereignty to Empirical Sovereignty", *Global Governance*, vol. 1, no. 1, Winter 1995, pp. 79-97; Michael Ross Fowler and Julie Marie Bunck, "What Constitutes the Sovereign State?", *Review of International Studies*, vol. 22, no. 4, October 1996, pp. 381-404; Öyvind Österud, "The Narrow Gate: Entry to the Club of Sovereign States", *Review of International Studies*, vol. 23, no. 2, April 1997, pp. 167-184; Martin van Creveld, *The Rise and Decline of the State* (Cambridge: Cambridge University Press, 1999).
6. Jackson has described these as "quasi-states": see Robert H. Jackson, *Quasi-states: Sovereignty, International Relations and the Third World* (Cambridge: Cambridge University Press, 1990).
7. See Linda B. Miller, *World Order and Local Disorder: The United Nations and Internal Conflicts* (Princeton, NJ: Princeton University Press, 1967); Evan Luard (ed.), *The International Regulation of Civil Wars* (London: Thames & Hudson, 1972).
8. See Ted Robert Gurr, "Ethnic Warfare on the Wane", *Foreign Affairs*, vol. 79, no. 3, May-June 2000, pp. 52-64.
9. See Linda Meivern, "Genocide behind the Thin Blue Line", *Security Dialogue*, vol. 28, no. 3, September 1997, pp. 333-346; Human Rights Watch, *Leave None to Tell the Tale: Genocide in Rwanda* (New York: Human Rights Watch, March 1999); *Report of the Independent Inquiry into the Actions of the United Nations during the 1994 Genocide in Rwanda* (New York: United Nations, 15 December 1999); Human Rights Watch, *The Fall of Srebrenica and the Failure of UN Peacekeeping* (New York: Human Rights Watch, October 1995); *Report of the Secretary-General Pursuant to General Assembly Resolution 53/35: The Fall of Srebrenica* (New York: United Nations, A/54/549, 15 November 1999); William Maley, "The UN and East Timor", *Pacifica Review*, vol. 12, no. 1, February 2000, pp. 63-76.
10. See Arthur Lee Burns and Nina Heathcote, *Peacekeeping by UN Forces: From Suez to the Congo* (New York: Praeger, 1963); Rosalyn Higgins, *United Nations Peacekeeping: Documents and Commentary*, vols. I-IV (Oxford: Oxford University Press, 1969-1981); Alan James, *The Politics of Peacekeeping* (London: Chatto & Windus, 1969); Indar Jit Rikhye, *The Theory and Practice of Peacekeeping* (London: C. Hurst & Co., 1984); *The Blue Helmets: A Review of United Nations Peace-keeping* (New York: Department of Public Information, United Nations, 1990); Alan James, *Peacekeeping in International Politics* (London: Macmillan, 1990); A. B. Fetherston, *Towards a Theory of United Nations Peacekeeping* (London: Macmillan, 1994); Paul F. Diehl, *International Peacekeeping* (Baltimore, MD: Johns Hopkins University Press, 1994).

11. See Donald C. F. Daniel and Bradd C. Hayes (eds), *Beyond Traditional Peacekeeping* (New York: St Martin's Press, 1995); Steven R. Ratner, *The New UN Peacekeeping: Building Peace in Lands of Conflict after the Cold War* (New York: St Martin's Press, 1995); Ramesh Thakur and Carlyle A. Thayer (eds), *A Crisis of Expectations: UN Peacekeeping in the 1990s* (Boulder, CO: Westview Press, 1995); Michael W. Doyle, Ian Johnstone and Robert C. Orr (eds), *Keeping the Peace: Multilateral UN Operations in Cambodia and El Salvador* (Cambridge: Cambridge University Press, 1997); Jarat Chopra (ed.), *The Politics of Peace-Maintenance* (Boulder, CO: Lynne Rienner, 1998); Jarat Chopra, *Peace-Maintenance: The Evolution of International Political Authority* (London: Routledge, 1999); Thomas G. Weiss, *Military–Civilian Interactions: Intervening in Humanitarian Crises* (Lanham, MD: Rowman & Littlefield, 1999); Geoff Harris (ed.), *Recovery from Armed Conflict in Developing Countries: An Economic and Political Analysis* (London: Routledge, 1999).
12. For an exploration of the range of issues involved in the Kosovo case, see Albrecht Schnabel and Ramesh Thakur (eds), *Kosovo and the Challenge of Humanitarian Intervention: Selective Indignation, Collective Action, and International Citizenship* (Tokyo: United Nations University Press, 2000).
13. See James N. Rosenau and Ernst-Otto Czempiel (eds), *Governance without Government: Order and Change in World Politics* (Cambridge: Cambridge University Press, 1992).
14. See, for example, *Preventing Deadly Conflict* (New York: Carnegie Commission on Preventing Deadly Conflict, 1997); Barnett R. Rubin (ed.), *Cases and Strategies for Preventive Action* (New York: Century Foundation Press, 1998).
15. Robert Rhodes James (ed.), *Winston S. Churchill: Speeches 1897–1963*, vol. VII (New York: Chelsea House, 1983), pp. 126–127.
16. See Joseph S. Nye, Jr., *Bound to Lead: The Changing Nature of American Power* (New York: Basic Books, 1990).

Part 1
The problem of disrupted states

1
The dimensions of state disruption

Amin Saikal

One of the most striking features of the post–Cold War world is the dramatic increase in the number of states which in a variety of ways can be classified as *disrupted*. This has constituted a major source of political, social and military turbulence and therefore of potential or actual instability in world politics. Although the causes of disruption have been numerous, stemming from both internal and external factors, the emergence of such states has quite properly rekindled debate on the future of the international system as one made up of an explosive mix of "cohesive" and "disrupted" states.

This chapter has three objectives. The first is to look at variations in the forms of state and forms of state–society interaction, and to outline what constitutes a disrupted as opposed to a cohesive state. The second is to examine the internal and external sources of disruption. The third is to touch on some responses available to the international community, especially in terms of conceiving an appropriate role for the United Nations. To illuminate its discussion the chapter will draw on the examples of a number of states, but with a focus primarily on Afghanistan, Iraq, Lebanon and Pakistan.

Forms of state

As we approach the twenty-first century, debate about the role of states as political and territorial actors, and about their viability as building blocks of a stable post–Cold War international system, has gained potency. We are often warned of the increasing inability of states to cope with growth in social and economic disparities, scarcity and maldistribution of resources, and ethnonationalist demands and conflicts at both sub-national and national levels (as examples of factors pressuring states from "below"), and of internationalisation of forces of the market, finance, mass communications, technological innovation, cross-border migration and environmental challenges (as examples of variables challenging states from "above"). Some scholars have strongly argued that these have not only eroded state sovereignty, with some states fragmenting and losing their sovereignty so that in general the "end of state sovereignty" may be in sight,[1] but also rendered the statist international system somewhat obsolete and ineffective.

By contrast, others have suggested that, although anti-statist forces and disrupted states in the international system have increased in number and, in some cases, reached the point of being "out of control"[2] so that disrupted states have become a main source of instability, this is more a manifestation of adjustments necessary in the transition from Cold War to post–Cold War politics than anything else. They maintain that there are a variety of disrupted states, with some of them even having various "hidden strengths". As such, they contend that statism is still the dominant, functional factor in world politics and that this may remain so for the foreseeable future. Some argue that most of the statist power elites have skilfully managed the forces of globalisation and manipulated them in pursuit of their statist goals.[3]

Whatever the merit of these perspectives, it is clear that today the international system comprises states which range from the extremely cohesive to the highly disrupted. In the 1990s there was a steep rise in the number of disrupted states, in both the political-administrative and territorial meanings of the words, with varying functional capacities. But, before proceeding any further, it is important to state what is generally meant in this paper by a "cohesive" and a "disrupted" state.

Perhaps the most important form of cohesive state is the democratic "Westphalian" state, which is, as Georg Sørensen puts it, a consolidated nation-state with its own structural dynamic and relative autonomy. The relative strength of such a state can be measured by the degree to which it features the rule of law, tolerant pluralism and vigorous civil society, as well as by the extent that the state has the capacity to deliver services and to cope effectively with pressure from above and below. It is generally argued that the strength of this type of state is a normative reflection of the strength of society. Another form of cohesive state, but of somewhat diminishing significance given the transitions to democracy that have marked the past two decades,[4] is the territorial unit ruled by a stable autocracy, either totalitarian or sultanistic in form, marked by an ideologically unified elite and the exercise of non-legitimate forms of domination.

A disrupted state, on the other hand, is what Sørensen refers to as "the post-colonial state"; that is, the unconsolidated state in the periphery, often in an ongoing state of entropy.[5] The degree of disruption within such a territorial unit can be further measured by an assessment of such variables as the personalisation of politics, national divisions, the arbitrary imposition of ideologically driven values and practices, as well as the degree to which the state is incapable of reflecting the complexity of society and managing pressure from above and below. Such a state is also often vulnerable to being physically ruptured, ending up in a situation of open civil conflict, foreign intervention or even occupation, and the collapse of political, administrative and organisational arrangements, with its sovereignty either strained, eroded or divided. Disrupted states need not be suffering from complete state "failure" or "collapse"; rather, they are marked by varying *degrees* of incapacity, some of which can leave the remnants of the state as a significant player with which international actors may need to engage. It follows that disrupted states can come in different forms, of which five have proved to be fairly common.

The first comprises states that have erupted into open conflict but have remained accepted as independent units within the international system, such as Afghanistan since 1978, Lebanon during its recent civil war (1974–1989) and Somalia after the overthrow of the regime of Mohammad Siad Barre. In each case, the standard criteria for the existence of a territorial state[6] had been satisfied at some point in the past, leading to widespread recognition of its distinctiveness. It is these that are most likely to be labelled "failed" or "collapsed" states.[7]

The second form comprises states that are contested by their neighbours in such a way as to thwart their attempts to secure a high level of consolidation. Such disrupted states are often part of the detritus of the breakup of larger autocracies, and the Republic of Bosnia and Herzegovina, admitted to the United Nations on 22 May 1992 but subjected to ongoing and orchestrated challenge from its Serbian neighbour, is a painful contemporary example.

The third form comprises embryonic states, in the form of territories occupied in circumstances of contested legality in which occupying forces are under challenge from local populations: powerful examples can be found in pre-independence Namibia, the Baltic states, East Timor and, to some extent, Kashmir. Here the combination of compromised international legitimacy and contested local control is the key constituent of disruption.

The fourth form comprises states that are being punished for violating either international law or international norms of behaviour and challenging the interests of a major power, as in the cases of Iraq in the wake of its 1990 invasion of Kuwait, or of Yugoslavia over its human rights violations in Kosovo and defiance of the United States and the European Union. Their disruption is reflected in a loss of control of territory or airspace to agents of the international community.

The fifth form comprises states that are not in a situation of open disintegration but are gripped by strong undercurrents of instability and are held together mainly by the military as the most potent uniting force in the country. A prime example of such states is Pakistan, where political and social divisions, lack of a clear sense of national identity, economic decay, a decline in law and order, escalation of violent sectarian and ethnic confrontation, and endemic corruption have seriously undermined the state's structures and governing apparatus. Had it not been for the country's military and security forces as the most important centralising factors, some would argue that Pakistan would have faced disintegration sooner rather than later. It is also in this context that Pakistan's acquisition of a nuclear capability makes the country a peculiarly dangerous state.

Forms of disruption

Of course, the forms of disruption in these territorial units are many and varied, and can be either internal or external or both. The internal causes can be of various types.

First, they can stem from fragmentation of the national elite and breakdown of social order. No country better illustrates this than Somalia, where, following the overthrow of the regime of Mohammad Siad Barre in a popular uprising in the late 1980s, the national elite disintegrated and revolutionary forces lost their unity of purpose and turned their guns on one another along the lines of personality, clan and tribal differences. As the fragile state structures collapsed, no single dominant group could emerge to fill the power vacuum to generate a necessary degree of national cohesion and national order. The overall effect was that Somalia's sovereignty was divided, plunging the country into a long-term state of group conflict – a conflict which continues to this day, and which has defied a series of international efforts to bring it to an end.[8]

Second, disruption can be driven by ethnic antagonisms, which in the absence of a robust state and corrective processes lead to open social conflict.[9] The intensity of conflict may be deeper in the states which are generally characterised as "dual-ethnic" rather than "multi-ethnic". A clear example of this is Rwanda, where in 1994 the conflict between ethnic Tutsis and Hutus resulted in one of the worst cases of genocide in history.[10] Although the violence has been contained, the factors underlying the conflict remain unresolved.

Third, disruption can be a product of ideological struggle, as in the case of Cambodia and Afghanistan. Whereas Cambodia from the late 1970s to the mid-1990s was dominated by a struggle between Marxists of various stripes, as well as more pro-Western forces, Afghanistan was disrupted by contestation between Soviet-backed communists and Islamists in the 1980s.[11] The result in both cases was the incapacity of the state to function as a consolidated whole, to exercise sovereignty over its internationally recognised territory, or to claim the degree of distributive power which could generate a high level of national cohesion.

Fourth, disruption can have confessional or sectarian roots, as in the case of Lebanon during its civil war or Afghanistan after the rise to power of the ultra-orthodox Taliban militia from 1994. The Lebanese civil war had a strong confessional and sectarian dimension underlined by a conflict not only between the Muslim and Christian segments of its population but also within each of these segments along more specific sectarian lines. Although with regard to Afghanistan this dimension was limited to the conflict between the dominant Sunni Taliban and the Shi'ite minority, it nonetheless deepened the problems of Afghanistan as a disrupted state, most notably when the Taliban massacred 2,000 Hazara Shia in August 1998.[12] In this respect, another illustration is Sudan, where the northern Muslim majority has been locked in a protracted violent conflict with the southern Christian and animist minorities, at the cost of rupturing the Sudanese state for years.

Fifth, disruption can arise from collapse of the revenue base of the state, and this may be through loss of foreign aid or domestic sources of income. For example, had it not been for a sharp decline in the mid-1960s in foreign aid, especially from the United States, Afghanistan might not have fallen prey to serious economic difficulties and consequent political disruption in the 1970s. This development was critical in making the country vulnerable to political and social unrest and a Soviet-backed communist takeover, disrupting the country to its foundations.[13] Similarly, the Iraqi state's distributive powers and social and economic programmes might not have been curtailed and it might not have lost control over the country's northern and southern parts, if it were not for its loss of oil revenue in the wake of the UN embargo following Iraq's invasion of Kuwait. Although the imposition of the UN embargo has paradoxically enabled the Iraqi regime to regain some of its political and social control through the distribution of rations, it still does not compensate for the degree of disruption that its loss of full oil revenue has generated.

Sixth, internal disruption can stem from a specific legitimacy crisis, especially through the loss either of traditional mechanisms of legitimation and the ability to institute a viable alternative or of a charismatic leader. This has particularly been true in the case of Afghanistan, where, following the communist coup of 1978, the traditional process of elite settlement and elite legitimation, backed by a Grand Council (Loya Jirgah) representing different social strata, irrevocably broke down, leaving the communists and their successors without any process of legitimation with which a majority of the Afghan population could identify. In respect of the loss of a charismatic leader, the case of Yugoslavia is most notable. The death of President Josip Broz Tito generated a legitimacy crisis, which his successors could not arrest or rectify – a crisis which played a pivotal role in the subsequent disintegration of Yugoslavia and rupture of its core, that is Serbia. The same, to some extent, was true of Ethiopia, where the overthrow in 1974 of the longstanding Emperor Haile Selassie plunged the country into a state of political, economic and ideological disarray for nearly two decades.

Seventh, disruption can also arise from separatism on regional, ethnic and religious grounds. This is illustrated not only by the case of Sudan, but also by the embryonic states of Kosovo and Jammu and Kashmir. Separatism on regional and ethnic grounds also explains the Kurdish struggle for a state of their own, which in relation to Iraq has helped further to weaken the Iraqi state, and in regard to Turkey has resulted in protracted violent unrest in the country's Kurdish-dominated south-east.

Internal sources of disruption are often paralleled, or even driven, by external sources, which are themselves many and varied. They include direct foreign intervention, as in the case of the Soviet invasion of Afghanistan and the Vietnamese invasion of Cambodia; "creeping invasion", as in the case of Pakistan's attempt to gain control over Afghanistan through the Taliban militia;[14] funding of separatism, as in the case of assistance by Iran under the Shah to the Iraqi Kurds,[15] and recently Syria's help to the Kurdish PKK to enable Kurdish secessionism in southeastern Turkey; and unintended destabilisation from events occurring elsewhere, as may arise through refugee flows or increased apprehension on the part of minorities as they witness discrimination against co-ethnics elsewhere.[16] The influx of large numbers of Afghan refugees into Pakistan following the Soviet invasion and the degree of long-term dislocation and resentment that this generated in Pakistan, especially its Northwest Frontier Province, is a case in point.

In almost all cases, the depth and breadth of disruption, as well as the intensity of conflict, prove severe when internal causes are accompanied by external ones. In such situations, disruption can be more enduring and resistant to a viable resolution than is the case otherwise. Afghanistan, once again, provides one of the most potent examples in this respect. Although the causes of disruption initially were rooted in the domestic situation of the country, where the disintegration of the national elite, crisis of legitimacy, mosaic nature of the society and the decline in foreign aid interacted to undermine national stability, it was ultimately the Soviet intervention and the processes of counter-intervention by the international opponents of the USSR that destructured Afghanistan fundamentally.[17] This altered the internal dynamics of the country so much that, more than a decade after the Soviet withdrawal, Afghanistan remained wide open to frequent realignment between internal and external forces determined to maintain the status of the country as a disrupted state for a long time to come. Because the Soviet invasion compromised domestic power structures, Pakistan as the key regional player countering the invasion relied on the changed domestic structures to enforce its own "creeping intervention" following the collapse of Soviet-backed communism in early 1992. As a result, Afghanistan was caught in a spiral where disrupted domestic structures and foreign intervention kept feeding on one another. Furthermore, criminal networks engaged in the narcotics trade had a strong interest in preventing the reconsolidation of effective political structures, as did the terrorists for whom Afghanistan became a base.[18] This changed only when those terrorists finally overplayed their hands on 11 September 2001, triggering a military intervention in Afghanistan by the United States and its allies.

In addition, again in almost all cases, disrupted states end up either with an authoritarian or concealed authoritarian rule, or alternatively as divided and conflict-ridden states, where not only are armed groups pitched against one another for internal reasons of their own, but these groups are helped by outside actors in pursuit of conflicting wider interests. In the latter case, disrupted states become battlefields for proxy wars, with some of these states functioning either partially or fully at the behest of one or more of their neighbours. Afghanistan, Lebanon and Congo, for example, fit the bill well. Until the US intervention, Afghanistan was not only divided between various fighting armed theocratic-ethnic forces, but was also a country where its neighbours were fuelling the conflict, with Pakistan the main protagonist and the dominant influence. Similarly, Lebanon, while possessing a concealed authoritarian rule, maintains its stability at the behest of neighbouring Syria, with Israel occupying its southern part in competition with Syria.[19] In a similar vein, the Democratic Republic of the Congo, where the Kabila regime has turned out to be almost as authoritarian as its brutal predecessor, is as much a victim of internal divisions and conflict as it is a subject of outside interference, with the country's neighbours intervening on behalf of either the Congolese government or the opposition forces. Given the major UN involvement in the Congo from 1960 to 1963,[20] it is bitterly ironic that it again faces disruption of the kind that in other circumstances might prompt demands for humanitarian intervention. The capacity for history to repeat itself never ceases to amaze.

Responding to state disruption

Whatever the forms and causes, disrupted states pose serious humanitarian and non-humanitarian threats in the areas of civil–military relations, both within the state and in the international system. In domestic terms, disruption can blur the distinction between civilian and military spheres of operations and responsibilities, or generate conditions that enable armed organisations, whether armed militias or state military machines, to dominate the civilian sphere. The end result is rule by one or many armed groups along lines of de facto territorial divisions, or by the military as the only organised force capable of holding the state together. Such rule is enforced at the cost of, in the first case, state sovereignty being divided and the civilian sector pulverised and suppressed, or, in the second case, state sovereignty being maintained in a technical sense, but with civil society subjugated to the needs of the military. In either case, international governmental and non-governmental organisations are confronted with serious difficulties and dilemmas in dealing with such states. Any action to help such states would have to be weighed against contradictory consequences and fear of what might come next once the mission was accomplished. For example, an international military intervention in Somalia or, for that matter, Kosovo imports the difficult dilemma of when the military interventionist role will wind back so that competent and acceptable civilian authority can carry the process of state reconstruction forward.

This can involve very difficult and delicate choices. For example, any attempt to assist a state such as Pakistan with positive incentives to retrench the role of the military in politics, heal its national divisions, lift its standard of living and improve its human rights record carries the risk of not only inadvertently helping the military to strengthen further their own position, but also prompting the nuclear-capable military to opt for more foreign policy adventures in relation to either Afghanistan or Kashmir to deflect outside pressure.

In the same vein, the difficulties facing NGOs are no less potent. In the absence of a nationally acceptable authority, their humanitarian operations in a disrupted state can inadvertently help the very organisations and groups responsible for the perpetuation of the disruption.[21] There were several cases of NGOs being accused of inadvertently producing such consequences in Afghanistan, where their operations were skilfully manipulated by the Taliban and their Pakistani backers to enforce their rule rather than enable the Afghan people to determine their own future. International actions in and in relation to disrupted states are also subject to serious problems of geostrategic, political and resource competition and of coordination between the governmental organisations and NGOs and the forces with which they deal in disrupted states. This has been evident as much in Iraq, Somalia and Afghanistan as in Kosovo since the military victory of NATO.

This brings us to perhaps the most difficult questions of all: is the present international system capable of coping effectively with the problems arising from the increasing number of disrupted states, and what forms should the actions of governmental and non-governmental organisations take in helping such states to contain and reverse the negative consequences of disruption? This has engendered a range of prescriptive responses, reflecting differing methodological and ideological perspectives. These responses have been advanced as ways to understand and explain the changes in the role of states and address their consequences. In general, the formulations are premised on an understanding that there is now a definite need either to reorientate or, if possible, to restructure drastically the "statist" international system in order to promote a more viable one in its place, or to retain the statist system but contain the current changes and their consequences in such a way as to make the statist systems work more effectively. The most salient of these formulations can be divided into three clusters.

The first, whose origins can be traced to Kantian views, postulates that the current international system of states and its associated agencies – most importantly the United Nations – have increasingly proved to be inadequate in dealing with inequities in world politics in general, and problems of disrupted states in particular, and emphasises the need for a positive reassessment of the ideas of "global society" and "global federalism".[22] These ideas initially gained some scholarly salience in the 1960s and 1970s to underscore the need for a new and more humane international system. However, they lost much of their gloss in the context of an upsurge in the competitive geopolitics of the later Cold War era, when wider scholarly stress was given to the Hobbesian view of international relations, which characterised the international realm as one of power politics among sovereign states.[23]

A new variant of those earlier ideas has lately emerged. While emphasising that the "world is moving rapidly toward a more integrated economic, cultural and political reality" or "set of circumstances" identified as "geo-governance", this variant seeks the creation of conditions to give rise to what it describes as "humane governance". By this it means "a set of social, political, economic, and cultural arrangements that is committed to rapid" growth of "transnational democracy", "the extension of the primary democratic practices", and "global civil society".[24] It recognises the limitations and difficulties in achieving this goal, but argues in the words of Richard Falk:

> To the extent that global civil society becomes a reality in the imagination and lives of its adherents, the reality of territorial states will often recede in significance even though it may never entirely disappear. In some settings, states under inspired leadership might engender strong loyalties precisely because the outlook is compassionate and globalised.[25]

Furthermore, it stresses that "humane governance" can be achieved without a world government, and proffers it as the most likely course of development. It considers this as the best way to create a new, viable international order, in which states may not disappear altogether but may alter to the point that they will be able to cope with the challenges facing them and live in more peaceful zones of common interests and security. Further, it advocates the strengthening of a reformed United Nations as a truly global body, with the necessary degree of independent authority and operational capacity to deal with world problems, including those of the disrupted states, free of world powers' geostrategic rivalry.

The second cluster of formulations reflects a belief that, parallel to the absence of a better alternative to statism, the conditions are growing for civilisational clashes in world politics.[26] It contends that it is imperative to manage the forces which have emerged to undermine the statist system in such a way as, on the one hand, to accelerate democratisation across the globe, and, on the other, to provide for modifying world political and security systems in ways that would be based on regionalisation of world order[27] within the framework of a regime of checks and balances, derived from theories of balance of power, concert of powers, deterrence and containment.[28] These formulations uphold the position of the United States as the only post-Soviet superpower capable of playing a central role in the creation of such a system in order to ensure its pivotal global status and prevent the rise of any other comparable power. They imply that in this way the United States will not only pre-empt any serious challenge to its own interests, but also prevent any further destabilisation in world politics, without overstretching itself or incurring too many costs. They envisage that the United Nations will remain, more or less, in its present state of existence: that is, playing a peripheral role vis-à-vis the interests of major powers in world affairs, but perhaps picking up the pieces in post-war disrupted contexts such as we are presently witnessing in Kosovo. Formulations of this type have received a great deal of attention since the events of 11 September 2001.

The third cluster of formulations arises from a conviction that, for better or worse, statism is most likely to be dominant in the twenty-first century and that, on the whole, the assertion that there is "post–Cold War chaos" in world politics is more of a myth than reality. It intimates that the efforts of world powers, most importantly the United States, should be not to create a new world order but essentially to reclaim what was created during the Cold War and what emerged in the wake of the breakup of the Soviet Union.[29] Some scholars proffer constructive engagement, diplomacy and regional confidence-building as the means to enhancing security within and between states, and for dealing with challenges facing states and the international system from sub-national sources and the forces of globalisation.[30] It essentially seeks the strengthening of the United Nations and its associated agencies only in this context.

Whereas the proponents of the first formulation wish to see a wider managerial role for the United Nations in the direction of global governance, the second one stresses the need for the United Nations to assume a counselling role. The third tends to favour a role for the United Nations somewhere between management and counselling as the most practical way to enable the organisation to survive challenges confronting it, and yet at the same time achieve a position whereby it would be able to have substantial input in shaping a more peaceful and stable world.[31] Time will tell which of these visions is most likely to be realised.

Whatever other proposals may eventuate, it is clear that disrupted states and the challenges with which they confront the international community are unlikely to go away or diminish. If anything, the contrary may prove to be the case in the twenty-first century. The time has certainly come for urgent, bold actions to address the issue. A failure to do so may lead to the world's becoming a more painful and disturbing place in which to live than was even the case during the dark century to which we have bidden farewell. It is all too clear that there is a need for a concerted, collective approach to the problems of disrupted states. Anything short of such a response, supported by all or most of the major powers under the auspices of the United Nations, is unlikely to have the reach and capacity to manage the problem effectively.

Acknowledgements

An earlier version of this chapter appeared in *Third World Quarterly*, vol. 21, no. 1, February 2000, pp. 39–49.

Notes

1. See Joseph A. Camilleri and Jim Falk, *The End of Sovereignty? The Politics of a Shrinking and Fragmenting World* (Aldershot: Edward Elgar, 1992). On the debate about sovereignty, also see Samuel M. Makinda, "Sovereignty and Global Security", *Security Dialogue*, vol. 29, no. 3, September 1998, pp. 281–292; Martin van Creveld, *The Rise and Decline of the State* (Cambridge: Cambridge University Press, 1999). An important earlier work which sought to raise some of these issues for discussion is Robert H. Jackson, *Quasi-states: Sovereignty, International Relations, and the Third World* (Cambridge: Cambridge University Press, 1990).
2. See Zbigniew Brzezinski, *Out of Control: Global Turmoil on the Eve of the 21st Century* (New York: Collier Books, 1993), especially Parts III–V.
3. For details, see Peter Dauvergne, "Weak States, Strong States: A State-in-Society Perspective", in Peter Dauvergne (ed.), *Weak and Strong States in Asia-Pacific Societies* (Canberra: Allen & Unwin, 1998), pp. 1–10.
4. For a discussion of these transition processes, see Guillermo O'Donnell and Philippe C. Schmitter, *Transitions from Authoritarian Rule: Tentative Conclusions about Uncertain Democracies* (Baltimore, MD: Johns Hopkins University Press, 1986); Giuseppe Di-Palma, *To Craft Democracies: An Essay on Democratic Transitions* (Berkeley and Los Angeles: University of California Press, 1990); Samuel P. Huntington, *The Third Wave: Democratization in the Late Twentieth Century* (Norman, OK: University of Oklahoma Press, 1991); Leslie Holmes, *The End of Communist Power: Anti-Corruption Campaigns and Legitimation Crisis* (New York: Oxford University Press, 1993); Juan J. Linz and Alfred Stepan, *Problems of Democratic Transition and Consolidation: Southern Europe, South America, and Post-Communist Europe* (Baltimore, MD: Johns Hopkins University Press, 1996); Gretchen Casper and Michelle M. Taylor, *Negotiating Democracy: Transitions from Authoritarian Rule* (Pittsburgh, PA: University of Pittsburgh Press, 1996); Richard Rose, William Mishler and Christian Haerpfer, *Democracy and Its Alternatives: Understanding Post-Communist Societies* (Baltimore, MD: Johns Hopkins University Press, 1998).
5. For details, see Georg Sørensen, "A State Is Not a State: Types of Statehood and Patterns of Conflict after the Cold War", in Muthiah Alagappa and Takashi Inoguchi (eds), *International Security Management and the United Nations* (New York: United Nations University Press, 1999), pp. 24–42.
6. See James Crawford, *The Creation of States in International Law* (Oxford: Oxford University Press, 1979).
7. For further discussion, see I. William Zartman, "Introduction: Posing the Problem of State Collapse", in I. William Zartman (ed.), *Collapsed States: The Disintegration and Restoration of Legitimate Authority* (Boulder, CO: Lynne Rienner, 1995), pp. 1–11.
8. On the situation in Somalia, see John Drysdale, *Whatever Happened to Somalia?* (London: HAAN Associates, 1994); Terrence Lyons and Ahmed I. Samatar, *Somalia: State Collapse, Multilateral Intervention, and Strategies for Political Reconstruction* (Washington DC: The Brookings Institution, 1995); Virginia Luling, "Come Back Somalia? Questioning a Collapsed State", *Third World Quarterly*, vol. 18, no. 2, June 1997, pp. 287–302.
9. The genesis of ethnic conflict has been widely discussed in recent years. See Donald L. Horowitz, *Ethnic Groups in Conflict* (Berkeley and Los Angeles: University of California Press, 1995); Ted Robert Gurr, *Minorities at Risk: A Global View of Ethnopolitical Conflict* (Washington DC: United States Institute of Peace Press, 1993); Michael E. Brown (ed.), *Ethnic Conflict and International Security* (Princeton, NJ: Princeton University Press, 1993); Michael Ignatieff, *Blood and Belonging: Journeys into the New Na-*

tionalism (New York: Farrar, Straus & Giroux, 1994); Ted Robert Gurr and Barbara Harff, *Ethnic Conflict in World Politics* (Boulder, CO: Westview Press, 1994); Walker Connor, *Ethnonationalism: The Quest for Understanding* (Princeton, NJ: Princeton University Press, 1994); Milton J. Esman, *Ethnic Politics* (Ithaca, NY: Cornell University Press, 1994); Russell Hardin, *One for All: The Logic of Group Conflict* (Princeton, NJ: Princeton University Press, 1995); and H. D. Forbes, *Ethnic Conflict: Commerce, Culture, and the Contact Hypothesis* (New Haven, CT: Yale University Press, 1997).
10. See *Leave None to Tell the Story: Genocide in Rwanda* (New York: Human Rights Watch, March 1999).
11. On Afghanistan, see Barnett R. Rubin, *The Fragmentation of Afghanistan: State Formation and Collapse in the International System* (New Haven, CT: Yale University Press, 2002). On Cambodia, see MacAlister Brown and Joseph J. Zasloff, *Cambodia Confounds the Peacemakers 1979–1998* (Ithaca, NY: Cornell University Press, 1998).
12. For details, see *Afghanistan: The Massacre in Mazar-i Sharif* (New York: Human Rights Watch, November 1998).
13. Rubin, *The Fragmentation of Afghanistan*, pp. 296–297.
14. For particulars, see William Maley (ed.), *Fundamentalism Reborn? Afghanistan and the Taliban* (New York: New York University Press, 1998), especially the chapters by Amin Saikal, Anthony Davis and Ahmed Rashid; and Ahmed Rashid, *Taliban: Islam, Oil and the New Great Game in Central Asia* (London: I. B. Tauris, 2000).
15. Amin Saikal, *The Rise and Fall of the Shah* (Princeton, NJ: Princeton University Press, 1980), p. 141.
16. For more detailed discussion, see David A. Lake and Donald Rothchild, "Spreading Fear: The Genesis of Transnational Ethnic Conflict", in David A. Lake and Donald Rothchild (eds), *The International Spread of Ethnic Conflict* (Princeton, NJ: Princeton University Press, 1998), pp. 3–32.
17. On these interactions, see Amin Saikal and William Maley, *Regime Change in Afghanistan: Foreign Intervention and the Politics of Legitimacy* (Boulder, CO: Westview Press, 1991).
18. See John K. Cooley, *Unholy Wars: Afghanistan, America and International Terrorism* (London: Pluto Press, 1999).
19. See William Harris, *Faces of Lebanon: Sects, Wars, and Global Extensions* (Princeton, NJ: Markus Wiener Publishers, 1997).
20. See Arthur Lee Burns and Nina Heathcote, *Peacekeeping by UN Forces from Suez to the Congo* (London: Pall Mall Press, 1963).
21. For the most extreme recent version of this argument, see Edward Luttwak, "Give War a Chance", *Foreign Affairs*, vol. 78, no. 4, July–August 1999, pp. 36–44.
22. For early assessment of the ideas, see Richard A. Falk, *This Endangered Planet: Prospects and Proposals for Human Survival* (New York: Vintage Books, 1972).
23. For a discussion of the Hobbesian view, see Hedley Bull, *The Anarchical Society* (New York: Columbia University Press, 1977).
24. Richard Falk, *On Humane Governance: Toward a New Global Politics* (Pennsylvania: Pennsylvania State University Press, 1996), p. 2.
25. Ibid., p. 212.
26. Samuel P. Huntington, "The Clash of Civilizations", *Foreign Affairs*, vol. 72, no. 3, Summer 1993, pp. 29–49. For a more elaborate restatement of Huntington's argument see Samuel P. Huntington, *The Clash of Civilizations and the Remaking of World Order* (New York: Simon & Schuster, 1996).
27. Brzezinski, *Out of Control*, Part 5.
28. See Paul Dibb, *Towards a New Balance of Power in Asia*, Adelphi Paper 295 (Oxford: Oxford University Press, for the International Institute for Strategic Studies, 1995).

29. G. John Ikenberry, "The Myth of Post–Cold War Chaos", *Foreign Affairs*, vol. 75, no. 3, May–June 1996, pp. 79–91.
30. See James L. Richardson, "Asia-Pacific: The Case for Geopolitical Optimism", *The National Interest*, no. 38, Winter 1995, pp. 28–39.
31. See Amin Saikal, "Emerging Powers: The Cases of China, India, Iran, Iraq, and Israel", in Muthiah Alogappa and Takoshi Inoguchi (eds), *International Security Management and the United Nations* (New York: United Nations University Press, 1999), pp. 61–82.

2
The international community and disrupted states

Paul F. Diehl

From a scholarly and practical viewpoint, international responses to threats to peace and security during the Cold War era were relatively simple. The predominant mode of intervention, if it happened at all, was a traditional peacekeeping force, most often organised under the auspices of the United Nations. The standard mission for such a force involved interposition, the separation and monitoring of combatants following a ceasefire. Furthermore, peacekeeping operations required the consent of the host state upon whose territory the peacekeepers would be deployed, and the peacekeeping force was to assume an impartial role in the dispute. Because of superpower tensions in the Security Council, peacekeeping operations were limited in number and geographically confined to areas outside the spheres of influence of either the United States or the Soviet Union.[1]

In the past decade, however, threats to international peace and security have changed dramatically, and the accompanying peacekeeping operations have undergone a simultaneous expansion and reformulation. The number of UN peacekeeping operations beginning since 1989 is more than two and a half times greater than in the previous 40 years. The geographical scope of operations has expanded as well, now including operations in the former superpower bastions of Eastern Europe and the Western hemisphere. The types of conflicts that now prompt international intervention have also changed, shifting away from interstate conflicts to intrastate ones. Of the UN peacekeeping operations deployed since 1989, almost 90 per cent were sent to troubled areas with at least some, if not primary, internal conflict components. With the end of the Cold War and the rise of ethnonationalism, one cannot expect this trend to abate anytime soon. Perhaps most notable has been the expansion in the kinds of missions performed by peacekeeping forces. Among the most dramatic, new missions have been occasioned by the complex emergencies evident in what have been referred to as "failed",[2] "collapsed"[3] or "disrupted" states.

The purpose of this chapter is to provide some starting points for understanding the choices that the international community faces when confronting disrupted states. By the international community, I designate those international organisations, both governmental and non-governmental, and multilateral coalitions of states that act or are considering action in response to or in anticipation of disrupted states. For the purposes of discussion, I exclude unilateral national efforts at addressing the problem, which generally are less likely, less effective and more self-interested than those conducted by the international community.

The analysis begins with a specification of the interests that the international community has in disrupted states. These interests will influence the kinds of responses that are appropriate to the situation as well as the probability that those actions will actually be taken by organisations or collections of states. Following this, there is a review of the key dimensions that define the international community's choices in responding to disrupted states. These include the timing of international actions, the actors selected to perform those functions, and the menu of missions available for these complex emergencies. In conclusion, I present a series of key risks, problems, and barriers that confront the international community in addressing the problems of disrupted states.

There are several caveats to my analysis. First, the empirical evidence on policy options for disrupted states is limited. There have actually been fewer such states thus far than might have been predicted earlier in the 1990s.[4] Accordingly, there are not many empirical referents and there is a tendency to draw lessons from single cases, most prominently from Somalia, and generalise them to other contexts. Although some of this is unavoidable, one must be careful to consider unique contextual factors, in both past and potential operations, in applying those lessons.

Second, we do have some knowledge and experience in many of the component responses to complex emergencies, such as humanitarian assistance, peacekeeping and electoral supervision, to name a few. Yet such knowledge may be limited because previously these responses were done in isolation of one another and not in the context of complex emergencies. It might be argued that a holistic approach to disrupted states and how these components fit together is essential for understanding the effectiveness of international responses.⁵ Thus, we must be cautious in drawing conclusions about options and their problems, recognising that particular combinations of actions may lead to significant difficulties.

Third, I assume that virtually all interventions by the international community in disrupted states will include peacekeeping as a centrepiece around which other elements of the operation evolve. This may not hold for all situations, and indeed peacekeepers may have departed by the time reconstruction activities are in full swing. Nevertheless, peacekeepers will be crucial in the initial intervention, when arresting the crisis is a top priority.⁶ Peacekeepers may also be involved in a variety of nation-building tasks after the crisis abates.

Fourth and finally, I do not directly discuss long-term efforts at economic development carried out in conjunction with the International Monetary Fund, the World Bank and other international financial institutions. This is not to say that such efforts are unimportant in reconstructing disrupted states. Indeed, financial support and technical assistance can be critical in remaking a disrupted state, as was evident in the case of Uganda.⁷ Yet the success of peacekeeping, humanitarian assistance and other shorter-term efforts is largely a prerequisite, laying the necessary groundwork, for later development efforts. Thus, this study concentrates on the immediate and short-term concerns of disrupted states.

International community interests in disrupted states

The complexity of the disrupted states problem means not only that there are multiple dimensions that need to be addressed, but also that there may be a variety of international community interests that arise. Not all interests appear in every situation, because disrupted states encompass a range of problems and there is no prototype. In addition, actions in support of one interest may be problematic or incompatible with actions derived from another interest. Thus, the elucidation of interests is vital in understanding the form, configuration and likelihood of international action.

Humanitarian interests

Often the most pressing concerns for the international community in disrupted states are humanitarian ones. These may include short-term problems with refugees, starvation, housing, sanitation and various health-related concerns. The breakdown of government authority may be a joint outcome with such problems as well as an exacerbating condition. The same causal process leading to humanitarian problems (for example, war, natural disaster) may also contribute to the breakdown of authority. Yet, given state disruption, some of those other problems may be created for the first time and in any case will be exacerbated by the breakdown of government distribution systems for the provision of services.

The international community clearly has a number of interests in alleviating these problems. Most obvious is saving the lives of as many individuals as possible. Supplemental to that goal is providing living conditions that at least meet minimum international standards for the victims of the complex emergency; this includes internally displaced persons as well as refugees.

The international community is interested in these concerns largely for altruistic reasons. Except for refugees, none of these problems has a direct impact on states outside of where they occur. At most, refugees have an impact on the states in the immediate area surrounding the disrupted state. For example, Rwandan refugees have a primary impact on Uganda, Burundi and the Congo (Zaire), but generally not on the rest of the international community. Thus, the response of the international community will primarily be a function of the degree of obligation it feels to respond to any of the humanitarian concerns.

Most humanitarian concerns are conceptualised as relatively short-term problems that can be alleviated by swift action. In fact, disrupted states experienced many of the same problems (albeit in lesser degrees) prior to the breakdown of government authority, and most of the problems will linger well into the future. In principle, the international community should have humanitarian interests before and well after disruption. In practice, the identification of those interests and the moral imperative to act upon them are greatest in times of extreme crisis.

Human rights

A second international concern focuses on human rights within the disrupted state. This is not necessarily a new concern: the international community has an ongoing interest in human rights observation before, during and after the disruption. Yet state disruption occasions some peculiar threats to human rights that go beyond both normal concerns and those related to humanitarian assistance noted above. The breakdown of government order may give freer rein to armed groups and others to commit human rights violations. These include large-scale killings of political opponents, attacks on civilians, torture, rape and a variety of other possible violations. Of course, these may occur without the context of state disruption, but they are facilitated by such a situation. Police and other security forces may not be present to deter or prevent such actions (indeed they may be perpetrators – see below). The criminal justice system may be incapable of dealing with the apprehension and prosecution of such criminals. Furthermore, civil society norms have eroded, such that perpetrators may feel freer to conduct such violations (or any other crime for that matter).

State disruption may involve the disintegration of government structures, but remnants of the security structure still exist and could be well armed. It is often this segment of society that represents the greatest threat to human rights, given its capacity for violence. If these security forces are organised under quasi-governmental structures (for example, militias) and there are strong ethnic or religious tensions, then genocide becomes a significant risk. Continuing problems with Hutu units in Rwanda and Serb units in Bosnia illustrate the death and destruction that can result from unrestrained security forces.

The international community has several specific goals with respect to human rights in disrupted states. First is the immediate cessation of violations to the greatest extent possible. This generally involves some establishment of temporary order for the country or the protection of threatened populations. The second goal is the establishment of order such that future violations of human rights and/or the repetition of past abuses are significantly less likely. Third, and finally, the international community has an interest in promoting the apprehension and prosecution of those responsible for human rights violations, through either national or international adjudicatory mechanisms.

Security interests

Disrupted states are sometimes conceptualised as internal problems, and therefore not within the interest or purview of the international community. Yet disrupted states have the potential to threaten international peace and security, and therefore there are security interests for the international community in general, and for neighbouring states in particular. One risk to international peace and security is that refugees from the disrupted state will cause destabilisation in neighbouring states receiving those refugees. This was certainly the case in the Congo (Zaire), where civil war was exacerbated by the inflow of refugees from Rwanda. The risk of destabilisation is also present in Macedonia as Kosovar refugees threaten to heighten tensions and shift the ethnic balance there.

Military conflict in disrupted states also may spread to neighbouring states, transforming an internal conflict into an internationalised civil one. This kind of conflict has plagued Lebanon for decades. Competing groups may use surrounding states as havens to launch military attacks or receive arms and other support. This makes the neighbouring state vulnerable to attack from opposing forces, and the crossing of international borders for military purposes may become commonplace for attackers and defenders alike. The southern part of Lebanon has been the battleground for almost three decades for various outside forces, including the Israelis, Palestinians and Syrians and their respective allies. A neighbouring state may also see its interests affected by conflict in the disrupted state and choose to intervene directly in the conflict. Even in the absence of widespread conflict, a neighbouring state could act as a predator, taking advantage of the disruption to attack the weakened state and seize disputed territory or other resources.

Although there are several different scenarios, and much depends on the particular context, the international community shares an interest in keeping the conflict confined to the disrupted state and therefore preventing it from becoming an international militarised crisis. The UN arms embargo and the placement of peacekeepers in Macedonia are examples of international efforts to prevent the spread of conflict from Bosnia.

International community responses

Faced with a disrupted state or the prospect of a disrupted state, the international community has a range of choices that are broadly arrayed on three dimensions: timing (when), actions (what) and organisation (by whom). Timing refers to the intersection of when the international community takes action and the phase of the disruption in which the state in question finds itself. Generally the international community may intervene prior to the actual disruption, at different stages during the breakdown, or following the worst manifestations of the disruption process. The policy options or actions for the international community may run the gamut from traditional peacekeeping duties to those involving humanitarian assistance and nation-building. Such options are a function of the requirements of the situation at hand and the timing of the intervention, but generally most of those options are not necessarily mutually exclusive. Finally, there is the question of which organisations will be involved and which will assume leadership roles, with international governmental organisations (IGOs), non-governmental organisations (NGOs), multilateral coalitions of states, or some combination of all three as options. A key concern is matching the particular actions to be taken with the organisation(s) most capable of carrying them out.

Timing

The first consideration is the timing of international intervention in the disrupted state. The timing of third-party intervention is thought to be a key component in conflict management success,[8] although exactly when a conflict is "ripe" for settlement is poorly defined or specified.[9] Cold War peacekeeping was generally characterised by deployment following a ceasefire between disputants, but prior to a final resolution (often indicated by a peace treaty or agreement for elections). More recent international operations have broadened the range of choice for when to intervene. Roughly, there are four different "phases" in which international intervention might occur: pre-disruption, during the disruption process in which armed conflict is occurring, after a ceasefire among warring groups, and following a peace agreement.[10] Each has different implications for the conduct and success of international operations.

The timing of peacekeeping intervention is partly within the control of the authorising agency, but not all disrupted states proceed through all phases or do so in a linear fashion, and the timing of operational deployment may depend on a host of other issues. The timing of the first international intervention is a bit of a misnomer. For most disrupted states, the international community has likely maintained a presence in the country prior to the initial serious threats of breakdown. Non-governmental organisations will have been performing humanitarian assistance and social service functions, perhaps on an ongoing basis for years. Furthermore, international economic institutions, such as the International Monetary Fund and the World Bank, may already be key players in addressing the financial problems that contribute to the disruption process. Nevertheless, the focus here is on the first large-scale and semi-coordinated effort by the international community to deal with a disrupted state. This usually involves peacekeeping forces and other ad hoc responses to what is regarded as a crisis situation.

Deployment of peacekeeping troops and other personnel in the pre-disruption phase, sometimes referred to as preventive deployment, is done in anticipation of state disruption and the outbreak of militarised conflict. The purpose of such action is to deter violence in the area of deployment and to solidify government operations. Preventive deployments may also implicitly suggest that, if violence does occur, the organising agency will respond with greater uses of force to stop the conflict and restore order.

There is strong normative appeal to pre-disruption actions. If they can deter armed attacks and prevent government breakdown, the local citizenry clearly benefit the most. Widespread killing, waves of refugees, and dislocations of the economy are avoided. At the macro level, preventing violent conflict may make it easier to promote conflict resolution in the long run, because the increased hatred and mistrust from war are avoided and the consequences of the armed conflict do not have to be factored into potential settlements. Thus, from a policy-making perspective, early intervention is most desirable. Nevertheless, pre-disruption action presumes a well-developed and effective early warning system that permits the accurate prediction of when and where state disruption is likely, and therefore what international actions should occur. Unfortunately, such a system at the international level does not yet exist and there are significant barriers to its adoption.[11] NGOs, however, may be able to fill part of this gap.[12] Nevertheless, even given accurate early warning, there is also the presumption that the international political will to act on such information also exists. Yet states may be offended by being labelled as sites for potential disruption and armed conflict (especially involving internal conflict) and serious sovereignty issues are raised by early action. Organisations such as the United Nations or others are also notoriously crisis driven and it is difficult to muster political support and resources for problems that are not yet fully manifest. At this writing, perhaps only the original UN operation in Macedonia qualifies as a preventive deployment.

Intervention during the second phase – active breakdown with ongoing military hostilities – is perhaps the most problematic. Indeed, the risk to international humanitarian, human rights and security interests is probably greatest during this phase. The standard peacekeeping force is relatively small in number and lightly armed, especially in comparison with its military counterparts. Thus, it is generally ill equipped to be thrust into the middle of active hostilities; most peacekeeping forces generally do not have the capacity to suppress military conflict and such a force may even be limited in its ability to defend itself. Furthermore, intervention during an ongoing war may jeopardise a peacekeeping force's perceived impartiality or neutrality, an essential ingredient for many international operations. The delivery of humanitarian assistance and the protection of human rights (essentially services to the civilian population) are much more difficult during active warfare than other phases of state disruption. Most prominently, UN peacekeepers attempted to intervene during active fighting in Somalia and Bosnia. By most standards, these efforts were a failure. The peacekeepers were unable to stop the fighting, were involved in several nasty incidents themselves and ultimately were withdrawn well short of their goals. Certainly, the peacekeepers and NGOs can be given credit for delivering humanitarian assistance to needy populations. Yet something of a paradox arises when military forces work in conjunction with NGOs during conditions of active combat. On the one hand, military forces may facilitate humanitarian assistance delivery by NGOs, but at the same time local opposition to the military may contaminate and undermine NGO actions and credibility.[13]

For international intervention during active conflict, it appears that the operation must be coercive and conduct enforcement actions in order to make a meaningful difference in that context.[14] Yet such a force, and more permissive rules of engagement, may blur the distinction between a traditional military or collective security force and a peacekeeping one. Thus, Indian forces in Sri Lanka or Syrian forces in Lebanon represent such an operation, but do not resemble traditional notions of a peacekeeping operation. Furthermore, it seems likely that such operations are more suitable for action by NATO or national military forces than by UN forces or most forces of regional organisations, given their limited military capacity and the political constraints under which they operate.

The most familiar timing of international intervention is following a ceasefire but prior to resolution of the underlying disputes between the hostile parties. This is classical peacekeeping deployment and such forces have a good, albeit far from perfect, record of preventing a renewal of hostilities, in part because the disputants have agreed to stop fighting. Beyond the greater ease of keeping the peace, the financial and troop requirements are significantly less than those required in earlier or later phases of conflict. The local population may benefit from the absence of active fighting, although there is no guarantee that life approaches normalcy during a peacekeeping deployment.

All in all, having a ceasefire in place is quite desirable before intervention, although many conflicts do not offer such a luxury. Obtaining a ceasefire may be particularly problematic in disrupted states. Unlike in interstate conflicts, there are likely to be more than two parties active in the militarised conflict. Furthermore, some of the violence may be the product of armed groups not under the full political control of any clan, militia or organised entity. Thus, negotiations for a ceasefire are likely to be more difficult to coordinate and there is always the risk that some relevant parties will not be included under the ceasefire umbrella.

Even if a ceasefire is achieved, there is still the problem of facilitating conflict resolution such that the forces can be withdrawn and the risk of future war minimised. Peacekeeping after a ceasefire is supposed to facilitate an environment in which resolution is possible. Yet at least one author argues that peacekeeping may have the opposite effect.[15] Peacekeeping may take away much of the time pressure or urgency for settlement and, in the absence of a "hurting stalemate", the status quo may be frozen without any prospects for a peace agreement and therefore the conditions necessary to rebuild society. The UN Peace-keeping Force in Cyprus (UNFICYP) operation, close to completing its fourth decade in Cyprus, is an illustration of how stability may promote complacency. It is unclear where international efforts find the right balance between ensuring stability and sustaining the urgency for settlement.

The world community may no longer wait for conflicts to reach the ceasefire stage before considering international intervention. Yet it is clear that ceasefires are a high priority when intervening in the previous conflict phase, and a peacekeeping operation may rapidly move from phase two (fighting) to phase three (ceasefire). Unfortunately, as the Bosnian and Liberian experiences demonstrate, it is quite possible to oscillate back and forth between these two phases. It is more desirable for intervention to occur after a ceasefire, but clearly the costs of waiting may be high and there is no guarantee that ceasefires will be negotiated, much less hold once in place.

The final phase of conflict, after a peace settlement is achieved, is in some ways the optimal time for international intervention. Yet one must remember that the combatants and the world community may have had to struggle through the other three phases to reach this point. Peacekeepers have been notably successful in supervising democratic elections and facilitating the implementation of peace agreements. The operations in Cambodia[16] and Namibia are examples of operations that led to free and fair elections, with participation rates well above projections and disruptions below what might have been expected. Intervention works well in this phase because some significant conflict resolution has already occurred and the disputants have signed on to a longer-term peace process than a temporary ceasefire.

Intervention after conflict resolution, however, is by no means foolproof. Some agreements, such as the Dayton Accords for Bosnia, are far from comprehensive agreements. In those contexts, the international community may find itself closer to phase three than in an endgame situation. In addition, some tasks (see below) in this stage may be more conducive to international action than others. International observers have a better record of election supervision, for example, than in nation-building. The latest waves of democratisation and ethnic conflicts have produced more opportunities for peacekeepers in this phase. Yet the debacles in Somalia and Bosnia have made states reluctant to assume long-term tasks in nation-building and other post-settlement missions. Finally, success in the tasks of intervention may disappear in the long run, after or sometimes even before the international forces are even withdrawn. Democratic elections in Cambodia and Angola have not proven to promote peace in the long run, no matter how well peacekeepers did their jobs. At this writing, international intervention seems to have had little long-term impact in addressing the fundamental problems of Haiti.[17]

Ideally, international intervention would occur prior to violence, and many situations would never reach any of the three advanced phases of disruption. Yet such actions are the least likely politically. Peacekeeping in its traditional forms seems inappropriate to deployment in active combat, even if the need is arguably the greatest then. The later two phases, after the shooting has stopped, are better designed for international intervention. Still, such phases assume an effective diplomatic process that achieves these conditions, and these phases have pitfalls of

THE INTERNATIONAL COMMUNITY AND DISRUPTED STATES

their own. Of course, it is quite conceivable that international intervention will occur in all four phases.

Actions

Disrupted states represent complex emergencies and therefore multiple courses of action may be appropriate for the international community, depending on the specific situation on the ground and the phase of intervention. In terms of responses with a peacekeeping component, nine different kinds of tasks might be performed by the international community.[18]

1. *Preventive deployment* consists of stationing peacekeeping troops to deter the onset of internal conflict, prevent government breakdown or prevent the spread of war.[19] UN-sponsored troops in Macedonia, deployed in the early 1990s to deter the spread of war in the former Yugoslavia, are an example of this type of non-traditional use of military force. Preventive deployment might occur prior to state disruption or it might occur in a later phase to keep a conflict from spreading to neighbouring territories.

2. *Humanitarian assistance* involves the transportation and distribution of life-sustaining food and medical supplies, in coordination with local and international NGOs, to threatened populations.[20] Operations in Somalia and Bosnia during the 1990s are examples. Humanitarian assistance may be necessary prior to war, under conditions of war or following war.

3. *Pacification* consists of quelling civil disturbances, defeating local armed groups, forcibly separating belligerents and maintaining law and order, especially in the face of significant loss of life, human rights abuses or destruction of property.[21] This appears to be a function that the international community may need to consider no matter what the specific circumstances in disrupted states.

4. *Protective services* include the establishment of safe havens, "no fly" zones and guaranteed rights of passage for the purpose of protecting or denying hostile access to threatened civilian populations or areas of a state. International operations in the 1990s to protect the Kurds in Iraq (Operation Provide Comfort) and the Muslims in Bosnia are consistent with this action. This function primarily serves to protect human rights in the disrupted state and to facilitate the provision of humanitarian assistance; the latter is achieved by mitigating the number of areas needing such assistance or lessening the assistance needed there and by providing safer distribution networks.

5. *Traditional peacekeeping* is the stationing of neutral, lightly armed troops (or unarmed observers) as an interposition force following a

ceasefire to separate combatants and promote an environment suitable for conflict resolution. Traditional peacekeeping may be utilised if there are identifiable ceasefire lines or zones.

6. *Sanctions enforcement* is the use of military troops (air, sea and land) to guard transit points, intercept contraband (for example, arms, trade) or punish a state for transgressions (for example, human rights abuses) defined by the international community or national governments in their imposition of sanctions.[22] In disrupted states, this action is likely to be in conjunction with other actions, and probably designed not to impose economic costs on the disrupted state, but rather to restrict access to arms and other supplies by groups in that state.

7. *Election supervision* consists of the observation and monitoring of a ceasefire, disarmament and a democratic election following a peace agreement among previously warring internal groups; this function may also include the assistance of local security forces.[23] UN operations in Namibia in the late 1980s and in Cambodia in the early 1990s are examples.

8. *State/nation-building* includes the restoration of law and order in the absence of government authority, the reconstruction of infrastructure and security forces, and facilitation of the transfer of power from the interim authority to an indigenous government.[24] The United Nations carried out some of these functions in the Congo in the early 1960s, but it was unable to do so in Somalia after the deployment of forces in the early 1990s. The United Nations has recently pursued such a mission in East Timor.

9. *Arms control verification* includes the inspection of military facilities, supervision of troop withdrawals and all activities normally handled by national authorities and technical means as a part of an arms control agreement.[25]

The choice of mission is clearly conditioned by the situation at hand and the potential reactions of the disputants. Nevertheless, that choice is still primarily within the control of the organising agency, which may choose to take on or bypass certain tasks. Several key issues and implications stem from the choice of mission.

First, it is quite likely that different types of missions will be influenced by different factors. For example, neutrality has been identified as a key factor in traditional peacekeeping and might be important in other monitoring functions. Yet one might expect it to be unrelated (or perhaps even negatively related) to success in missions that help restore civil societies. Furthermore, Dandeker and Gow argue that more coercive missions, what they label "strategic peacekeeping", must maintain support from different audiences, some of those domestic, in the host state and beyond to achieve success.[26] This legitimation is significantly less important in traditional peacekeeping.

Another concern is whether the missions involve tasks suitable for military forces or whether they might be better handled by civilians under the auspices of international organisations or NGOs. Peacekeeping operations were originally designed (number, rules of engagement, and so on) for monitoring ceasefires. Not surprisingly, then, new peacekeeping missions that are closer to this traditional standard tend to be more successful.[27] Arms control verification and election supervision are two examples. With respect to the latter, peacekeepers have a good record in facilitating free and fair elections in Cambodia, Mozambique, El Salvador and elsewhere.[28] Similarly, those peacekeeping operations most different from traditional operations tend to have or are likely to have great difficulties. In large part, this is because the forces are ill designed to carry out the tasks required of them. For example, nation-building is a multifaceted enterprise that cannot be achieved or imposed through the application of military force. Although peacekeeping may provide one of the necessary conditions in the nation-building process (for example, peace), peacekeepers are not necessarily suitable for developing government infrastructure. Highly coercive missions may also be incompatible with peacekeeping philosophy, functions and design.[29] In those cases, operations might be better conducted by standard military forces, which have the training, equipment, size and rules of engagement suitable for coercive missions.[30] Thus, although there is a range of different functions that might be performed by peacekeepers, not all of them are conducive to success.

Another consideration is the compatibility of different missions under the umbrella of one operation. Although one can distinguish between different missions, in practice a given operation may attempt to perform more than one mission, either simultaneously or sequentially. The net effect can be extremely problematic. The attempt to combine pacification efforts with humanitarian assistance efforts in Somalia illustrates such incompatibility of functions, at least when performed by the same operation. One policy implication may be that divergent missions are best handled by different sets of personnel or separate operations. The United Nations has already undertaken to "subcontract" to NGOs and regional organisations many of the tasks involved in complex emergencies.[31] This makes sense given that those other organisations may have greater flexibility and expertise than the United Nations.[32] For example, a prominent role for traditional military forces in pacification and for NGOs in humanitarian assistance, with appropriate coordination between the two, would be preferable to having soldiers attempt both roles simultaneously.

This would also ease the training problems that arise when soldiers are asked to perform divergent duties.[33]

Organisations

The central coordinating agency for most international operations has traditionally been the United Nations (of course, this ignores unilateral national actions). During the Cold War era, there were occasional forays into peacekeeping by regional organisations – for example, the Organization of African Unity (OAU) in Chad, the Organization of American States (OAS) in the Dominican Republic – but these tended to be isolated occurrences amid the dominant pattern of UN-sponsored operations. Although regional efforts are not necessarily more common today, alternatives to UN operations are present on the international agenda. The end of the Cold War left NATO largely without its primary purpose and has led that organisation to consider different roles. Indeed, its actions in Bosnia and Kosovo are the first manifestations of that new focus. Furthermore, US President Clinton proposed the African Crisis Response Initiative (ACRI), which would turn operational responsibility for peacekeeping on that continent over to local states and organisations.

Thus, one decision that faces the global community is which should be the organising agency for a given operation in a disrupted state. To a large extent, this is a manipulable condition, although the practical options may be limited. The range of options is generally confined to the United Nations, an appropriate regional organisation or a multilateral collection of states. NGOs tend to operate semi-autonomously within this environment, although during a major international action they do coordinate with relevant units (for example, the UN High Commissioner for Refugees) of the organising agency. To some extent, however, the greater the coordination involved, the less the NGO autonomy.[34] A related question concerns the structure and control of the operation. These may remain largely in the hands of states, as has been conventional in peacekeeping operations, or international organisations may exercise various degrees of autonomy in the operation.

Does it make a difference if an operation is conducted by the United Nations, a regional organisation or a multilateral grouping? The track record at this stage does not provide definitive conclusions, and the evidence we have is largely drawn from a variety of different peacekeeping operations, some of which do not involve functions that would be carried out in disrupted states. Clearly, United Nations peacekeeping has a decidedly mixed record of success in its 50-plus peacekeeping operations,[35] regardless of the evaluative criteria employed. UN peacekeepers are given great credit for the successful transition to majority rule in

Namibia, for preventing violence on the Golan Heights, and for restoring democratic rule in Haiti. On the other side of the coin, however, are UN failures to stop genocide in Rwanda and Bosnia, and the repeated cease-fire violations in southern Lebanon despite the presence of UN troops there. It is clear that a UN-organised force is no guarantor of success, but neither are such operations inherently doomed to failure.

Of course, all considerations are relative and therefore the viability of UN-organised forces must be considered relative to the alternatives. Comparisons are difficult, however. There are few empirical referents of operations organised by regional organisations or multilateral groupings. With respect to regional organisations, the OAU operation in Chad is generally considered a colossal failure,[36] and the operation in Liberia sponsored by the Economic Community of West African States (ECOWAS) has a mixed record even when viewed in the most favourable light. OAS actions in the Dominican Republic, although helpful in securing order, may be criticised as furthering American hegemony in the region. Similar conclusions can be drawn about Syrian domination of Lebanon facilitated by intervention endorsed by the League of Arab States. Thus, the historical record of regional peacekeeping during the Cold War is sparse and not very encouraging. Not surprisingly, several studies that examined the alleged advantages and disadvantages of regional peacekeeping have concluded that most regional organisations have neither the resources nor the political unity to offer operations superior to those conducted by the United Nations.[37]

The record of NATO in Bosnia since the Dayton Accords perhaps provides a basis for some comparative advantage for regional organisations. NATO forces have largely kept the peace in Bosnia, have facilitated democratic elections and have allowed some Bosnians to return to as normal a life as possible in the circumstances. Peacekeepers have clearly fallen short of goals with respect to promoting lasting peace and apprehending war criminals. Yet NATO's first attempt at peacekeeping is unusual. It is a mission that requires significant military capacity, more toward the coercive end of the scale with respect to peacekeeping and enforcement actions. Thus, the requirements of the operation play to the strengths of NATO and its military might. In contrast, the United Nations lacks the resources and political willingness to carry out such missions. When faced with such challenges in Bosnia and Somalia, it failed miserably.

Multilateral peacekeeping operations are no more numerous than regional ones. It is sometimes difficult to distinguish between a unilateral or multilateral peacekeeping operation and a military intervention. Nevertheless, the Multinational Force and Observers (MFO), a by-product of the Camp David peace process, has quietly served the interests of the world community, Israel and Egypt for 20 years. This indicates that such operations can be successful. Attempts in Africa to respond to crises in the Congo, Sierra Leone and elsewhere are less favourable auguries for multinational peacekeeping, given their overt support of host governments. Whether a multilateral grouping could sustain domestic support (in the home countries of the contributors) over the long haul as demanded by a disrupted state intervention is an open question.

Overall, the United Nations appears superior to other organising alternatives for peacekeeping operations and many of the tasks associated with international intervention in disrupted states. Yet one must be cautious about automatically accepting this. First, there is limited empirical evidence on the viability of alternatives. That few regional or multilateral groupings have undertaken peacekeeping may be prima facie evidence of their unsuitability for peacekeeping tasks, but this may change in the future. Furthermore, a given class of peacekeeping operations may be better organised by regional organisations, namely those with a more coercive mandate. At the present writing, however, only NATO or other European organisations appear to have the structure and military capacity to carry out such operations effectively, and even their applicability to peacekeeping missions is limited.[38] Of course, it is conceivable that the United Nations and regional organisations might undertake joint operations. Yet the empirical evidence for a such a partnership is not encouraging given problems between ECOWAS and the United Nations in Liberia[39] and the United Nations and NATO in Bosnia.[40]

Risks, problems and barriers

Although the international community has a range of options available to it in responding to disrupted states, it faces a number of impediments and difficulties – beyond even those alluded to above. What are labelled here as problems, risks and barriers affect the degree of international response, the success of those responses and the ability of the international community to exit the disrupted state, leaving behind a stable, functioning society. I do not intend the four items listed below to be comprehensive; rather they represent some of the primary challenges facing the international community in responding to disrupted states.

A lack of necessary interest

At the outset of this chapter, I identified three interests for the international community precipitated by state disruption. Yet such interests are not always sufficient to prompt that community to act or to act to the fullest extent of its capabilities. UN Secretary-General Boutros-Ghali chastised the international community in the early 1990s for ignoring the "poor man's war" in Somalia while concentrating its efforts on Bosnia. Boutros-Ghali raises the important point that the international community is more likely to take action, and extensive action in particular, when the national interests of states, specifically the major powers, are directly affected by the state disruption. Accordingly, the international response may be muted if states do not regard what is happening in and around the disrupted state as affecting their national interests.

The late and inadequate response of the international community to Somalia's breakdown and the virtual absence of a response to Rwanda are indicative of the impact of limited national interests. Neither the Western states nor permanent members of the UN Security Council had strong economic or strategic interests in those countries or the surrounding areas. In contrast, the responses by the international community to crises in Kuwait and Bosnia were much swifter and more extensive, owing in large part to their implications for the international oil market and for European regional security, respectively.

When are state interests likely to be sufficient to prompt the necessary response to disrupted states, and can middle powers fill any of the void left by leading states? In addressing the first question, the probability of a concerted international response is increased when state disruption occurs in greater geographic proximity to leading states (whether on a global or a regional level). This necessarily suggests that problems in Europe are more likely to lead to international responses than are problems in Africa or South Asia; unfortunately, disrupted states are more likely in the latter regions. In some cases, however, unilateral actions by the United States or Russia, for example, may pre-empt international action in disrupted states (in Haiti or Georgia, to offer two examples). Significant economic stakes, in the form of trade relationships or resources, will increase international responses. Similarly, the potential spread of the war or threats to key allies of the major powers will also enhance the response.

In an ideal world, all instances of state disruption would prompt commensurate international responses, but in reality the existence and degree of a response, at least one depending on nation-states and the IGOs to which they belong, will be variable. The absence of leading state interests also exacerbates the "public goods" problem and the tendency to "free ride" attendant on any operation for the benefit of the global community; unlike other circumstances, a hegemon or leading state will not step in and shoulder a large burden in providing the public good. Although NGOs are likely to be involved in humanitarian relief regardless of the interests of leading states, the deployment of peacekeepers and the availability of international aid are likely to be a function of how salient the state disruption is seen to be.

There is also some reason to doubt whether middle power states with a history of altruistic service to international interventions (for example, Sweden, Australia and Canada) can compensate for the lack of interest by the major powers. Certainly, such middle power states have contributed disproportionately to peacekeeping operations in the past.[41] Yet such states do not have the political power to ensure that operations are authorised by relevant IGO bodies, such as the UN Security Council. Nor do they necessarily have the military capacity or the resources to lead international operations, especially in the absence of support from the leading states. Nevertheless, they are likely to play critical roles in operations that do receive the blessing of the leading powers in international relations.

Overall, the first hurdle that must be overcome in responding to state disruption is persuading states to authorise, lead and fund international actions. Strong national interests, not merely international ones, must be present to ensure such action – at least for those tasks involving states and IGOs. Without such interests, and it is not clear how one can compel these, the response of the international community to disrupted states will be suboptimal, if indeed there is a response at all.

Problems of coordination

A Cold War peacekeeping operation typically performed one main function – ceasefire monitoring – and this was simply performed by military personnel. In contrast, nowadays the international community may be asked to perform nine or more different tasks (see above). It is also clear that those functions cannot and should not be performed exclusively by peacekeeping troops. Peacekeeping forces may be at the centre of the international response, but numerous other actors will be involved in the operation. These are likely to include: IGOs (and not merely the one that might authorise the peacekeeping force), specialised agencies of IGOs (for example, UNHCR), NGOs (for example, the International Committee of the Red Cross), international legal tribunals, and perhaps even private national entities (for example, corporations that provide police training). In many ways, such a multiplicity of actors is desirable because the international community can draw upon specialised expertise for many of the tasks to be performed. On the other hand, the multiple tasks and the actors carrying them out raise a series of coordination problems.

The first coordination problem is one familiar to scholars and practitioners of international peacekeeping, namely coordinating between state and IGO authorities. This primarily involves the peacekeeping element of the international operation. Soldiers have usually remained under national command while serving in UN and other peacekeeping operations. The result is a confusing chain of command for operations, sometimes with indifferent, sometimes with deadly consequences. In Bosnia, the joint operational decision-making between the United Nations, NATO and various national militaries led to frequent delays and indecision, especially with respect to when and how to use retaliatory military strikes. In Somalia, Italian troops had to wait many hours for instructions from their home government before deciding whether to come to the aid of Pakistani troops under fire; such a delay proved deadly to the Pakistani forces. The intricacies of a complex emergency operation would seem to make the potential state–IGO coordination problems acute.

A second dimension is the coordination problem between IGOs and NGOs. Many of the problems in the various UN efforts in Angola can be traced back to coordination problems.[42] IGOs and NGOs operate on different schedules, answer to different constituencies and have different personnel.[43] Furthermore, to some extent they compete for the same donors during emergencies, and accordingly there may be hostility between the two groupings. Complex emergencies also present greater threats to NGO autonomy and modes of operation,[44] and therefore NGOs may be reluctant to cooperate fully with other actors. In particular, international operations have difficulties integrating the security functions carried out primarily by peacekeeping soldiers and development functions carried out by IGOs and NGOs.[45] In the long run, international financial institutions may impose fiscal constraints on the disrupted state at the same time that other international organisations are sponsoring large outlays for infrastructure, such as rebuilding roads and re-establishing a police force.[46] The UN Department of Humanitarian Affairs has taken significant steps in the direction of coordination, holding regular meetings with relevant NGOs. Yet the typical form of coordination in humanitarian emergencies is what Antonio Donini calls "coordination by default", involving only the most rudimentary exchange of information.[47]

A third element of coordination, somewhat cross-cutting the previous two dimensions, is between military and civilian officials; civilian officials here may be from the organisation sponsoring the peacekeeping operation as well as from NGOs. A number of tensions arise in the military–civilian relationship. Civilians from NGOs may have been present in the disrupted state for many years and may resent the recently arrived peacekeepers, who adopt new and different ways of attacking problems. Military personnel and those from NGOs also come from very different organisational and personal cultures, with significantly different views of militarism, gender and many other subjects.[48] Slim notes that these problems are especially manifest under conditions of low host state consent, which by definition is the situation in disrupted states. Military personnel and civilians may also be unaccustomed to working with one another, even if they are nominally part of the same organisation, for example the United Nations. Exacerbating this is the increasing lack of distinction between military and civilian roles in disrupted states; duplication, inefficiency and some conflict are likely to result. Yet, as the international community gains more experience with complex emergencies, one might expect some of these problems to diminish over time.

The final dimension involves coordination not between different actors but across different missions. Complex emergencies require different tasks and actions, but not all of these are compatible with one another. The ability to avoid contradictory actions is complicated by having those actions performed by different actors, albeit under the same operational umbrella. For example, various NGOs and the International Criminal Tribunal for the former Yugoslavia were investigating atrocities in Bosnia at the same time that UN mediators were negotiating with political officials who were leading suspects in those war crimes investigations.

There are several obvious instances where the problem of conflicting tasks might arise, and then some authoritative coordination process is necessary. The first is when some actors are pursuing "third party" roles whereas others are engaging in "primary" party actions.[49] The international community may be attempting to be impartial and not directly involved in the conflict as well as simultaneously undertaking other roles that make it a direct participant in the conflict, possibly favouring one local group over another. For example, humanitarian assistance missions may be hindered by the conduct of a pacification mission directed against a given armed group. Local actors may not be able to distinguish between the two purposes and may work to undermine the humanitarian effort.

Second, the coercive parts of the operation may contaminate the noncoercive elements. A peacekeeping force that initially serves to enforce a ceasefire and then takes on election supervision functions may have trouble retaining the acceptance of the local population. The use of force by the international community tends to engender resentment among those groups against whom such actions are directed. Thus, it is difficult to get the cooperation of those target groups in other or later aspects of the operation.

All of the coordination problems cited above need to be addressed. Some may be solved by the creation of appropriate management structures, including liaison across organisations and regular planning meetings. In other cases, there need to be changes in strategies and the acceptance of goal trade-offs in order to deal with the coordination problems.

The perils of internal conflict

Disrupted states unfortunately represent the kind of context with which international interventions have had the greatest difficulties in the past – civil conflicts. As state sovereignty has become more permeable and the barriers to intervention in internal conflicts have been lessened,[50] there has been an increase in the number of "internal" peacekeeping operations. Yet it seems clear that peacekeeping operations experience more problems in conflicts that have an internal conflict component as compared with those purely between two or more states.[51] In some ways, disrupted states are the worst manifestations of internal conflicts, primarily because of their multifaceted problems.

What accounts for the strong relationship between civil disputes and peacekeeping failure? There appear to be several explanations. First, civil conflicts often involve more than two identifiable groups. The civil component of the Lebanese conflict alone involved more than a half-dozen indigenous political factions, each with its own militia; this does not even consider the presence of terrorist groups, the Palestine Liberation Organization, Israel or Syria. By definition, an internationalised civil war involves more than two actors. Interstate disputes, in contrast, have been overwhelmingly dyadic. As the number of actors in the dispute increases, so does the likelihood that one or more of them will object to ceasefires and other aspects of the international intervention; local actors may take military action against other groups or international personnel.

Beyond the difficulty of aggregating multiple preferences in support of an international operation, the geographical constraints in a civil conflict are different from those in an interstate one. Civil instability may mean that several groups are operating in different parts of the country. This could necessitate that the international operation cover a broader territory, opening up the possibility of more violent incidents. Furthermore, unlike an identifiable international border or ceasefire line, it may be impossible to demarcate a line or area that separates the many sides in the conflict. Being from the same state and often not wearing military uniforms (indeed, most not being traditional military or para-military units at all), participants in a civil conflict are hard to identify, much less to separate when they occupy the same geographical area. Civil conflict may be quite dangerous, and the situation more difficult to control. James notes that in civil conflict "[a]rms are likely to be in the hands of groups who may be unskilled in their use, lack tight discipline, and probably engage in guerrilla tactics. Light arms are also likely to be kept in individual homes, and may be widely distributed."[52] These conditions expose peacekeeping and relief personnel to sniper fire and other problems, as well as making it virtually impossible to secure a given area fully.

The international response to civil conflicts, or at least that of UN peacekeepers, has been inappropriate and has undermined effectiveness.[53] UN planners have misread many of the situations and the traditional peacekeeping strategies have not easily translated into the civil conflict context. Conventional military doctrine is also largely unsuitable in civil conflicts.[54] Generally, one party or more in the civil conflict will be disadvantaged by the status quo, which the peacekeepers reinforce with their presence. The only method available to pursue political change is violence. This was largely the case with Unita efforts to undermine the peaceful democratisation and reconstruction of Angola.

Sustaining action versus developing an exit strategy

A final difficulty for the international community involves finding the right balance between maintaining support for the operation and being able to withdraw when the situation is stable. In other words, the challenge is to ensure that the international community does not leave too soon, while not creating a situation in which it cannot leave at all. The former problem occurs because the international community is inherently crisis driven. As noted above, this has deleterious consequences because the United Nations and other organisations are late to take action, waiting until the situation becomes severe before being compelled to act. Symmetrically, the international community has a tendency to scale back or abandon an operation once the worst of the crisis is past (and then it moves on to another crisis), but before all the work is completed. Several factors reinforce this early exit pattern. Domestic political support for the long-term deployment of peacekeeping troops is not strong in many states. When such missions involve some significant risk to those troops, there are great pressures to end the mission. The early exit from Somalia, first by US troops and then by remaining UN contingents, was a result of these pressures and the difficulties of rebuilding that state. Donor fatigue also tends to set in after a period of time and when media coverage of the situation wanes. Most international operations have experienced significant gaps between funds that are pledged at the outset of a crisis and those that are actually paid. Thus, many relief programmes need to be cut back. Overall, there are real risks that the international community will withdraw too soon from a disrupted state. The consequences are that armed conflict may recur and many of the same problems may surface again.

The flip side of the coin is ensuring that the disrupted state can survive on its own and the international community can withdraw safely. Even if the international community is willing to stay until the job is done, it needs to lay the appropriate groundwork for stability. It is clear that time-bound strategies are ineffective.[55] Most UN operations are already authorised for only limited periods. Yet peacekeeping mandates are regularly renewed or extended, so the approach of a deadline does not have the same effect as it would if the operation would really cease at that point. When decision makers in the United Nations (and in national capitals) are faced with the options of mandate renewal or operation withdrawal and a possible recurrence of warfare, they have historically opted for the risk-averse choice of continuing the international mission; stalemate without fighting is seen as preferable to possible military conflict. As long as local groups know that deadlines are essentially meaningless, however, they will have little incentive to hurry negotiations or work for a settlement. Above, I noted that one of the risks of peacekeeping operations is that they may freeze the status quo, prevent "hurting stalemates" and thereby inhibit conflict resolution.

In devising a settlement that will last, it is clear that the international community cannot impose a settlement on local parties; it must invigorate a local capacity to implement the provisions of a rebuilding plan. This is the opposite of what occurred in Somalia, where the international community left too soon, did not lay the proper groundwork, and did not work enough with local groups in devising a settlement plan.[56] It is unlikely that the local population will fully implement a series of proposals that they had little role in constructing. Such proposals may not be appropriate to the context and local actors may not feel much psychological investment in the plan. To the extent that the plan is perceived as another form of colonial imposition of values and institutions, there may be active hostility to it. Even with local support, the international community must prepare the institutions and personnel to reassume government services. The alternative is to have things fall apart when there is a withdrawal of international troops and other personnel or, almost as bad, an *inability* to withdraw and therefore the establishment of a semipermanent international receivership of the territory.

Some concluding thoughts

The problem of disrupted states that confronts the international community is a relatively new one, not so much because the component parts are unprecedented, but rather because they now occur simultaneously. It is clear that the disrupted states problem requires external assistance because such problems are not likely to be resolved and will fester without international intervention.[57] Nevertheless, in his study of international actions in complex emergencies, Weiss finds only one case of clear success (Operation Provide Comfort for the Kurds in Iraq).[58] Even there, the uniqueness of that situation may limit its applicability to the general problem of addressing disrupted states.

All in all, the international community has a moral and strategic imperative to intervene in disrupted states. Yet such interventions are fraught with potential pitfalls, and presently there are not the necessary strategies, coordination plans, international legal bases or resources to do the job properly. Nonetheless, imperfect as international community efforts may be, they still stand out as superior to the available alternatives.

Notes

1. For different phases of classical peacekeeping, see Henry Wiseman, "The United Nations and International Peacekeeping: A Comparative Analysis", in United Nations Institute for Training and Research (ed.), *The United Nations and the Maintenance of International Peace and Security* (Dordrecht: Martinus Nijhoff, 1987).
2. Gerald B. Helman and Steven R. Ratner, "Saving Failed States", *Foreign Policy*, no. 89, Winter 1992–93, pp. 3–20.
3. I. William Zartman (ed.), *Collapsed States: The Disintegration and Restoration of Legitimate Authority* (Boulder, CO: Lynne Rienner, 1995).
4. See Robert Kaplan, "The Coming Anarchy", *The Atlantic Monthly*, no. 273, February 1994, pp. 44–76; Chetan Kumar, "When Atlas Did Not Shrug: Reconstructing Failed States in an Era of Retrenchment", unpublished manuscript, 1995.
5. See below, and also John Mackinlay and Randolph Kent, "A New Approach to Complex Emergencies", *International Peacekeeping*, vol. 4, no. 4, Winter 1997, pp. 31–49.
6. Francis Mading Deng, "State Collapse: The Humanitarian Challenge to the United Nations", in I. William Zartman (ed.), *Collapsed States: The Disintegration and Restoration of Legitimate Authority* (Boulder, CO: Lynne Rienner, 1995), pp. 207–219.
7. See Gilbert Khadiagala, "State Collapse and Reconstruction in Uganda", in I. William Zartman (ed.), *Collapsed States: The Disintegration and Restoration of Legitimate Authority* (Boulder, CO: Lynne Rienner, 1995), pp. 33–47.
8. Louis Kriesberg and Stuart Thorson (eds), *Timing the De-escalation of International Conflicts* (Syracuse, NY: Syracuse University Press, 1991).
9. Jeffrey Z. Rubin, "The Timing of Ripeness and the Ripeness of Timing", in Louis Kriesberg and Stuart Thorson (eds), *Timing the De-escalation of International Conflicts* (Syracuse, NY: Syracuse University Press, 1991), pp. 237–246.
10. Similar to Edward E. Thurman, "Shaping an Army for Peace, Crisis, and War: The Continuum of Military Operations", *Military Review*, vol. 72, no. 4, April 1992, pp. 27–35; William J. Durch, "Keeping the Peace: Politics and Lessons of the 1990s", in William J. Durch (ed.) *UN Peacekeeping, American Policy, and the Uncivil Wars of the 1990s* (New York: St. Martin's Press, 1996), pp. 1–34.
11. Peter Brecke, "Conflict Early Warning and Conflict Prevention", draft manuscript.
12. Robert I. Rotberg (ed.), *Vigilance and Vengeance: NGOs Preventing Ethnic Conflict in Divided Societies* (Washington DC: Brookings Institution Press, 1996).
13. Thomas Weiss, "Military–Civilian Humanitarianism: The Age of Innocence Is Over", *International Peacekeeping*, vol. 2, no. 2, Summer 1995, pp. 157–174.

14. John Mackinlay, "Powerful Peacekeepers", *Survival*, vol. 32, no. 3, May–June 1990, pp. 241–250.
15. Paul F. Diehl, *International Peacekeeping* (Baltimore, MD: Johns Hopkins University Press, 1994).
16. See Stephen R. Ratner, *The New UN Peacekeeping: Building Peace in Lands of Conflict after the Cold War* (New York: St. Martin's Press, 1995).
17. Thomas Weiss, *Military–Civilian Interactions: Intervening in Humanitarian Crises* (Lanham, MD: Rowman & Littlefield, 1999).
18. This listing is adapted from Paul F. Diehl, Daniel Druckman and James Wall, "International Peacekeeping and Conflict Resolution: A Taxonomic Analysis with Implications", *Journal of Conflict Resolution*, vol. 42, no. 1, February 1998, pp. 33–55.
19. Diehl, *International Peacekeeping*; Brian Urquhart, "Beyond the Sheriff's Posse", *Survival*, vol. 32, no. 3, May–June 1990, pp. 196–205.
20. Larry Minear and Thomas Weiss, *Humanitarian Action in Times of War: A Handbook for Practitioners* (Boulder, CO: Lynne Rienner, 1993).
21. US Department of the Army, *Peace Operations FM 100-23* (Washington DC: Department of the Army, 1994).
22. Ibid.
23. Yves Beigbeder, *International Monitoring of Plebiscites, Referenda, and National Elections: Self-Determination and Transition to Democracy* (Dordrecht: Martinus Nijhoff, 1994).
24. Boutros Boutros-Ghali, *An Agenda for Peace* (New York: Department of Public Information, United Nations, 1992); David Cox, *An Agenda for Peace and the Future of Peacekeeping*, Report of the Mobonk Mountain House Workshop (Ottawa: Canadian Center for Global Security, 1993).
25. Michael Krepon and Jeffrey Tracey, "Open Skies and UN Peace-keeping", *Survival*, vol. 32, no. 3, May–June 1990, pp. 251–263; Sonia Jurado and Paul Diehl, "United Nations Peacekeeping and Arms Control Verification", *Contemporary Security Policy*, vol. 15, no. 1, April 1994, pp. 38–54.
26. Christopher Dandeker and James Gow, "The Future of Peace Support Operations: Strategic Peacekeeping and Success", *Armed Forces and Society*, vol. 23, no. 3, Spring 1997, pp. 327–348.
27. Diehl, *International Peacekeeping*.
28. See Durch (ed.), *UN Peacekeeping, American Policy, and the Uncivil Wars of the 1990s*.
29. Durch, "Keeping the Peace: Politics and Lessons of the 1990s".
30. James Allan, *Peacekeeping: Outspoken Observations by a Field Officer* (Westport, CT: Praeger, 1996).
31. See Thomas Weiss (ed.), *Beyond UN Subcontracting: Task-Sharing with Regional Security Arrangements and Service-Providing NGOs* (London: Macmillan, 1998).
32. Leon Gordenker and Thomas Weiss, "Devolving Responsibilities: A Framework for Analysing NGOs and Services", in Thomas Weiss (ed.), *Beyond UN Subcontracting: Task-Sharing with Regional Security Arrangements and Service-Providing NGOs* (London: Macmillan, 1998), pp. 30–45.
33. See Diehl, Druckman and Wall, "International Peacekeeping and Conflict Resolution: A Taxonomic Analysis with Implications".
34. Gordenker and Weiss, "Devolving Responsibilities: A Framework for Analysing NGOs and Services".
35. Duane Bratt, "Assessing the Success of UN Peacekeeping Operations", *International Peacekeeping*, vol. 3, no. 4, Winter 1996, pp. 64–81.
36. Amadu Sesay, "The Limits of Peacekeeping by a Regional Organization: The OAU Peacekeeping Force in Chad", *Conflict Quarterly*, vol. 11, no. 1, Winter 1991, pp. 7–26.

37. Paul F. Diehl, "Institutional Alternatives to Traditional UN Peacekeeping: An Assessment of Regional and Multinational Options", *Armed Forces and Society*, vol. 19, no. 2, Winter 1993, pp. 209–230; Carolyn M. Shaw, "Regional Peacekeeping: An Alternative to United Nations Operations", *Journal of Conflict Studies*, vol. 15, no. 2, Fall 1995, pp. 59–81; see also Paul F. Diehl and Joseph Lepgold (eds), *Regional Conflict Management* (Lanham, MD: Rowman & Littlefield, forthcoming).
38. Joseph Lepgold, "NATO's Post–Cold War Conflict Management Role", in Joseph Lepgold and Thomas Weiss (eds), *Collective Conflict Management and Changing World Politics* (Albany, NY: SUNY Press, 1998), pp. 57–81. See also Roy May and Gerry Cleaver, "African Peacekeeping: Still Dependent", *International Peacekeeping*, vol. 4, no. 2, Summer 1997, pp. 75–97.
39. Clement Adibe, "The Liberian Conflict and the ECOWAS–UN Partnership", in Thomas Weiss (ed.), *Beyond UN Subcontracting: Task-Sharing with Regional Security Arrangements and Service-Providing NGOs* (London: Macmillan, 1998), pp. 67–90.
40. Gordon Wilson, "Arm in Arm after the Cold War? The Uneasy NATO–UN Relationship", *International Peacekeeping*, vol. 2, no. 1, Spring 1995, pp. 74–92.
41. Laura Neack, "U.N. Peace-keeping: In the Interest of Community or Self?" *Journal of Peace Research*, vol. 32, no. 2, May 1995, pp. 181–196.
42. Chris Alden, "The Issue of the Military: UN Demobilization, Disarmament, and Reintegration in Southern Africa", *International Peacekeeping*, vol. 3, no. 2, Summer 1996, pp. 51–69.
43. Andrew S. Natsios, "NGOs and the UN System in Complex Emergencies: Conflict or Cooperation", in Thomas G. Weiss and Leon Gordenker (eds), *NGOs, the UN, and Global Governance* (Boulder, CO: Lynne Rienner, 1996), pp. 67–81.
44. Mackinlay and Kent, "A New Approach to Complex Emergencies".
45. Jeremy Ginifer, "Development and the UN Peace Mission: A New Interface Required?", *International Peacekeeping*, vol. 3, no. 2, Summer 1996, pp. 3–13. For some solutions, see David J. Whaley, "Improving UN Developmental Co-ordination within Peace Missions", *International Peacekeeping*, vol. 3, no. 2, Summer 1996, pp. 107–122.
46. Stephen John Stedman and Donald Rothchild, "Peace Operations: From Short-Term to Long-Term Commitment", *International Peacekeeping*, vol. 3, no. 2, Summer 1996, pp. 17–35.
47. Noted in Weiss, *Military–Civilian Interactions: Intervening in Humanitarian Crises*.
48. Hugo Slim, "The Stretcher and the Drum: Civil–Military Relations in Peace Support", *International Peacekeeping*, vol. 3, no. 2, Summer 1996, pp. 123–140.
49. Diehl, Druckman and Wall, "International Peacekeeping and Conflict Resolution: A Taxonomic Analysis with Implications".
50. Jarat Chopra and Thomas Weiss, "Sovereignty Is No Longer Sacrosanct: Codifying Humanitarian Intervention", *Ethics and International Affairs*, vol. 6, 1992, pp. 95–117.
51. Diehl, *International Peacekeeping*.
52. Alan James, "Internal Peacekeeping", in David Charters (ed.), *Peacekeeping and the Challenge of Civil Conflict Resolution* (New Brunswick, NJ: Centre for Conflict Studies, 1994), pp. 3–24, at p. 17.
53. Michael Wesley, *Casualties of the New World Order: The Causes of Failure of UN Missions to Civil Wars* (London: Macmillan, 1997).
54. Mackinlay and Kent, "A New Approach to Complex Emergencies".
55. Weiss, *Military–Civilian Interactions: Intervening in Humanitarian Crises*.
56. Omar Halim, "A Peacekeeper's Perspective on Peacebuilding in Somalia", *International Peacekeeping*, vol. 3, no. 2, Summer 1996, pp. 70–86.
57. Zartman (ed.), *Collapsed States: The Disintegration and Restoration of Legitimate Authority*.
58. Weiss, *Military–Civilian Interactions: Intervening in Humanitarian Crises*.

3

The prevention–intervention dichotomy: Two sides of the same coin?

Simon Chesterman and David M. Malone

Since NATO's intervention in Kosovo in 1999, discussion among member states on the United Nations' role in international peace and security has often been tinged with paranoia. On the one hand, a majority of member states privately (and sometimes vocally) approved of action to halt the slide of Kosovo into another Bosnia. At the same time, however, NATO's action – taken without Security Council authorisation – led to fears that more such unilateral interventions might follow.

These fears were fuelled by a speech that Secretary-General Kofi Annan gave on 20 September 1999, defending the imperative of humanitarian action in extreme situations.[1] Some viewed this speech as being more critical of those blocking effective Security Council action than of NATO for proceeding without a Council mandate. External commentators praised Annan's examination of the ethical and political dilemmas inherent in the United Nations' central role in international security relations, but he may have underestimated the degree to which the debate among member states had deteriorated.[2] He may, indeed, have exacerbated tensions by appearing to advocate military intervention.[3] This was not his intent, as he indicated in a speech delivered at an International Peace Academy seminar on humanitarian action in November 2000.[4]

Outside the corridors, meeting rooms and lounges of the United Nations, fears of a flood of unauthorised interventions proved to be greatly exaggerated. Since the death of 18 US Army Rangers in Mogadishu in

1993, the reality has been that Western powers in particular have lacked the political will to intervene meaningfully anywhere that their interests are not substantially engaged. Indeed, this has undermined properly authorised UN interventions, such as those in Sierra Leone and the Democratic Republic of the Congo. Nevertheless, reality on the ground often counts for little in the debating chambers of the United Nations; these debates have often been side-tracked by unproductive North–South bickering and a blindly legalistic approach to international relations.

In an attempt to escape these circular discussions, the Secretary-General and others have tried to shift the focus onto prevention. This approach has also been greeted with suspicion. Prevention often requires intrusive measures too, meaning that those most implacably opposed to intervention after the fact are frequently those most against prevention before it. These interlinked debates over prevention and intervention are thus reduced by some commentators to the single question of sovereignty, and to the assertion that states remain highly attached to their own sovereignty (though not always that of others).

Such recourse to the theoretical and practical bugbear of sovereignty is tantamount to an admission of failure. Instead, this chapter will explore alternative ways of advancing the debates over prevention and intervention within the United Nations. Crucially, the argument advanced here aims to shift the focus from seeing prevention as an alternative to intervention, to seeing intervention as a consequence of failed prevention.

Prevention

Prevention strategies in the United Nations

Prevention of conflict is the first promise in the Charter of the United Nations, which begins with the stated determination to "save succeeding generations from the scourge of war".[5] This promise has been consistently broken by local parties, governments and international organisations. It has also been broken, to some extent, by the scholarly community, which has only recently begun to develop policy-relevant analysis of the circumstances in which this lofty but complex goal might actually be achieved.

The ideal of UN action to forestall conflict and resolve the tensions that cause and foster it is, of course, widely shared in the abstract. Although it functioned imperfectly, the UN Security Council provided a forum that helped avoid the apocalyptic conflicts threatened by the Cold War. The General Assembly also developed some leeway to address conflict when faced with Council deadlock under the "Uniting for Peace" formula.[6] After the Cold War ended, a more activist and creative Security Council suggested that it would do more to prevent and limit conflicts, particularly those occurring primarily within state borders (and therefore outside the scope of traditional international concern). Nevertheless, the Council has proven less effective than the dramatic increase in the number of resolutions passed in the 1990s might initially suggest.[7] The Council's limitations despite increased efforts during this period are relevant to the prevention challenge.[8]

Geostrategic balancing exercises were the hallmark of the Cold War era, and conflict management (both for advantage and when matters threatened to spin out of control) the order of the day. During the Cold War, crises arose frequently between the great powers or their surrogates, and were usually the culmination of strategic ventures prepared in secret and executed with stealth. Preventive measures and action of the kind contemplated today, therefore, were rarely an option – partly because they themselves would have been thwarted by interested powers, and partly because the United Nations did not have at its disposal resources sufficient to intervene effectively in conflicts between these great powers or their clients.[9] Even so, the United Nations was able to improvise and develop some specific instruments for preventive action. The introduction of peacekeeping forces into various regional and intrastate conflicts, such as the deployment of UN peacekeeping forces in the 1956/57 Suez crisis, were a form of conflict prevention designed, in part, to prevent conflicts from escalating and drawing in the superpowers.[10]

The situation today is very different. With the collapse of the Soviet Union, the risk that disputes will escalate to the global level has greatly diminished. There are also fewer interstate disputes than before, particularly relative to the number of intrastate conflicts.[11] Occasionally a new interstate conflict will surprise the international community, for example the senseless and murderous border war between Ethiopia and Eritrea, 1998–2000. But these are relatively rare. A single superpower, or "supreme power" in the words of Egyptian jurist and diplomat Nabil Elaraby, dominates the global scene.[12] The remaining significant powers have largely refrained from jousting with each other, although certain familiar international "hot spots" (Kashmir, the Israel–Arab theatre) continue to defy successful mediation and resolution. Today, in stark contrast to the Cold War era, many conflicts are aggravated by a lack of interest and engagement by large powers in desperately impoverished pockets of the world, notably in Africa. There, local elites – often those in government – manoeuvre to corner as large a share of the inadequate national complement of power and wealth as possible, further impoverishing the poor and marginalised sectors of society. Economic factors play a much larger role in these conflicts, as has been documented in the work of Paul Collier and a number of other leading economists and political scientists.[13] These internal crises often unfold in slow motion, following familiar patterns that, given any genuine interest on the part of the outside world and a concomitant willingness to expend resources to support it, might be arrested. But this rarely happens. Many civil wars of the late twentieth century have continued to fester catastrophically in the new millennium, absorbing economic potential, social progress and many lives, and mortgaging the futures of the nations involved when the devastation might well have been prevented by international action years earlier.

Such underemphasis on prevention in the international security system is odd. Preventive action is at the centre of international health policy; it is vital to environmental policy (enshrined, for example, in the Montreal Protocol on Substances that Deplete the Ozone Layer); and it is accepted in many human rights treaties and in efforts to reduce the number and scale of natural disasters.[14] In the economic and development field, intensive scrutiny of the most intrusive sort has become the norm and preventive measures are often prescribed by the International Monetary Fund (IMF) (and accepted, however reluctantly, by governments of the affected states).[15] Yet in the security sector, prevention is practised poorly and piece-meal – if at all.

Many commentators have stressed the futility, or impossibility, of effective preventive action to forestall conflict. This is at best a partial view of the reality. Throughout most of the Cold War, preventive action was a politically fraught activity. Within the United Nations (with the noteworthy exception of peacekeeping missions), it was often argued that preventive action could take place only privately, under the good offices of the Secretary-General. This was true as far as it went, but diplomatic archives disclose few such efforts. Perhaps a better explanation is that the interstate conflicts that predominated during the Cold War typically lent themselves to preventive action only at the margins.

In the early 1990s, the nature of the conflicts attracting international attention was not well understood. Consequently, it was difficult to design strategies aimed at prevention rather than management. However, given the scope and depth of the challenge, governments, international institutions and academics took to the task early on. At the beginning of the new century, we have a much clearer idea of how and why these conflicts start, what sustains them and what kinds of intervention measures might be adopted to prevent them from escalating, occurring and recurring.[16]

There remain, nonetheless, significant obstacles to preventive action. Belligerents (states, sub-state entities, rebel forces, and so on) and potential belligerents do not welcome outside scrutiny and interference. This will often result in the underreporting of efforts to foment violence, especially in the early stages.[17] Because civil wars tend to develop slowly, and because the protagonists (particularly governments) are aware that their actions can easily be noticed, if not actively monitored, they have often argued forcefully that considerations of sovereignty should preclude outside interference of any kind.

Conditions attached to foreign development assistance relating to quality of governance, which have often targeted policies of a destabilising or potentially destabilising sort, can be seen as a kind of preventive action – provided that they are focused on the process of democratisation rather than merely the holding of elections.[18] But conditions relating to governance practices can also give rise to ill-feelings, as witnessed in countries such as Zimbabwe and Kenya. Development assistance thus needs to focus on correcting horizontal inequalities that exist in many societies and countries and may foment violent conflict, rather than simply on poverty reduction and governance per se.

The Development Assistance Committee of the Organisation for Economic Co-operation and Development (OECD) has been at the forefront of efforts to "mainstream" conflict prevention into donor development policies since 1997, and some of the first countries to adopt new practices include Sweden, Canada and the UK.[19] However, the real risk is that, unless this kind of "structural prevention" is given conceptual depth and the active backing that goes beyond rhetorical support, such efforts could easily discredit the organised international community's effort in this area. Indeed, the United Nations urgently needs to address what structural prevention actually involves, lest the call for action become more of a slogan than a policy choice and effective response. Sustainable development strategies crafted with a view to limiting the risks of conflict can be a delicate exercise for donors, since efforts to address horizontal inequalities and the host of factors that can cause violent conflict necessarily affect local political dynamics and processes. Attendant consequences include possible resistance from the "haves" (i.e. those benefiting from the status quo), or the empowerment of belligerent groups that thrive off gains derived from co-opted aid channels.[20] Systematic analysis of which actors tend to be positively influenced by aid packages and the political consequences of this is an important area of research for the future. Greatly to its credit, the World Bank has attempted to focus much more since the late 1990s than in the past on violent conflict and the development of "social capital", with case studies of Somalia, Guatemala, Rwanda and El Salvador, in an effort to give further substance to this relatively underused pillar of prevention.[21] Two projects currently being implemented in Rwanda and East Timor deliberately aim to build such capital and foster communal bonds.[22]

The UN system and its family of agencies have attempted to engage with these diverse challenges, with varying degrees of success. Through its case-by-case decisions and statements, the Security Council has chipped away at arguments in favour of absolute sovereignty and has thus managed to soften the perceptions relating to preventive action by the United Nations.[23] It has largely based its arguments on the "international peace and security" threat that flows of refugees could pose to neighbouring countries. Such arguments were advanced, notably, in the early stages of the disintegration of the former Yugoslavia, Somalia and Haiti, and in its preliminary deliberations in early 2001 regarding the overflow of refugees in Guinea from neighbouring Liberia and Sierra Leone.[24] Where action was taken (in the first three cases at the time of writing), Security Council decisions aimed at preventing even worse outcomes. The Council's decision in 1992 to authorise a preventive deployment of UN peacekeepers to the Former Yugoslav Republic of Macedonia (initially as part of the UN Protection Force (UNPROFOR), latterly as the UN Preventive Deployment Force (UNPREDEP)) was to prevent the war in Bosnia from engulfing that country.[25] Similarly, the deployment of a peacekeeping force (MINURCA) to the Central African Republic (CAR) in 1998 was explicitly preventive.[26] In fact, the initial request for international preventive action came from President Ange-Félix Patassé himself in December 1996, and was based on the potential for escalation of the internal situation, and the possibility that instability emanating from within the CAR would spread to an already unstable region.[27] As early as 1991, actions mandated by the Council in resolution 687 imposed a highly intrusive and complex regime of monitoring on Iraq in an effort to prevent it from seeking again to produce weapons of mass destruction.[28] In sum, Council decisions throughout the 1990s profoundly undermined traditional conceptions of state sovereignty, although perceptual changes have not yet been codified nor, for that matter, are they likely to be any time soon.

In general, however, prevention continues to be preached far more than it is practised at the United Nations.[29] Preventive measures are necessarily intrusive, and governments do not want UN staff poking around in their affairs (although the world media and the intelligence services of several countries do so constantly, and with considerable success). Enthusiasm for early warning may have reached a peak at the Security Council Summit of January 1992 when its members urged the Secretariat to "collect and analyse pertinent information in order to alert relevant intergovernmental organs about impending crises".[30] This invitation from the Council led to the creation, later in 1992, of the United Nations' Department of Political Affairs (DPA), with just such a mission (and also charged with supporting the Secretary-General in the exercise of his good offices). However, in spite of strong leadership by Sir Marrack

Goulding until 1997 and Sir Kieran Prendergast since then, and an increasingly professional and capable staff, the preventive drive of the United Nations has been held in check, largely by its members. This was readily apparent in the debate on the Report of the Panel on UN Peace Operations released in August 2000 (the "Brahimi Report").[31] The debate brought to light developing country concerns regarding ever more intrusive peacekeeping missions that are authorised on a highly selective basis and, according to some, deflect resources away from more urgent developmental needs throughout the "global south". The conclusions of the report called for, among other things, a radical overhaul of the UN Department of Peacekeeping Operations (DPKO) and the creation of an information and strategic analysis unit to complement and assist the Secretary-General, the DPA and the DPKO. Ultimately, the General Assembly was able to agree on additional resources for the DPKO, but punted into the future recommendations aimed at enhancing the analytical capacity of the Secretariat.[32]

Conflict trends and causes

In 1999, the International Peace Academy (IPA) launched a programme aimed at assisting the United Nations in operationalising concepts of conflict prevention. A number of findings and conclusions from the work so far on conflict trends and causes may be noteworthy. Many of the findings from current research into the causes of contemporary international conflict run contrary to conventional wisdom. For example, although experience would suggest that intrastate armed conflicts have increased in number and intensity since the end of the Cold War, there has been a rather dramatic *decrease* in the number of armed conflicts and a reduction in the impact and/or intensity of war within the same time frame, with a slight rise recorded since 1998. Ted Gurr in particular argues that these trends reflect improved efforts by the international community actively to promote mediation of disputes, to deploy force in the face of gross human rights violations and to develop post-conflict peacebuilding initiatives, but he urges caution with respect to the complacency such findings can engender, especially since, almost paradoxically, the number of "hot spots" that have the *potential* for escalation remains high.[33] Indeed, figures tentatively supporting this claim indicate that 30 per cent of all conflicts ended with peace agreements in the past 10 years, which is more than during any other decade in the past 50 years.[34]

Nonetheless, declining intrastate conflict trends could instead be due to diminishing external support for those factors that facilitate and cause conflict. In this case, the reduction in conflict probably more closely correlates to reduced support and funding for unwholesome allies and superpower proxy wars, and the (nominal at least) increase in democratic regimes across the world. This suggests two considerations. First, the role of democratic governance is important for the prevention of conflict – but that effectiveness is likely to depend at least in part on the creation of consolidated, substantive democratic processes, if not institutions themselves, around the world. Secondly, international actors need realistically and critically to assess their own foreign policies that, driven by national interest considerations, can create and facilitate the actions of belligerent regimes.

With regard to the causes of violent conflict, a survey by Anne Marie Gardner of the literature on the factors contributing to mainly intrastate conflict teases out four interrelated and prominent causes: *insecurity*, *inequality*, *private incentives*, and *perceptions*.[35] Variance among cases is explained by the host of intervening variables through which these are mediated, such as historical legacies of conflict, the pace and depth of political and economic change (including democratising regimes) and the role of external actors. Trigger events are also important in determining the unfolding of a crisis.

Arguably the most significant finding that emerges from IPA's and other research is the importance of economic factors in both contributing to and prolonging war.[36] Resource scarcity relating to high population growth, the legacies of land distribution, uneven food distribution and a lack of access to fresh water are all potential sources of conflict. Conversely, a plethora of natural resources can also increase the probability and duration of violent conflict as actors seek to enrich themselves through illicit means (such as those engaged in small arms trafficking and the mining of "conflict supporting minerals" such as diamonds). Criminal activities in civil wars, the role of the international private sector, the economic agendas of competing factions and followers in civil wars are all important areas that require further research.

In addition, research suggests that the political, social and economic disempowerment of certain groups in a society relative to others is an important cause of violent conflict.[37] Examples include unequal political access, discrimination in the education sector and inequitable treatment of certain groups within public sector employment. In each instance, conflict may occur as some groups protest against the prevailing distribution of opportunities and public goods while other groups resist attempts to redress horizontal inequalities.

Conflict prevention strategies

Most existing prevention efforts are isolated within a particular international organisation or sector of international actors. However, because the causes of conflict are interrelated and interact over what can be a prolonged time frame, effective prevention requires integrated strategy across different sectors (diplomatic, military, political, economic and social) and extended periods of engagement. A number of prevention strategies are starting to bridge traditional divisions: complex peacekeeping operations, coercive diplomacy, targeted sanctions, aid conditionality, civil society peacebuilding, and socioeconomic approaches to development. However, in order to be effective at preventing conflict, intervention strategies must be targeted at specific conflict variables or "causes", recognising that the salience of any given set of factors is likely to vary from one conflict setting to another. Coherent conflict prevention also requires ably planned, implemented and coordinated strategies in order to anticipate and avoid, to the extent possible, unintended consequences that exacerbate rather than alleviate the causes of violent conflict in a given context.[38]

It is precisely in the earlier stages of potential conflict that preventive diplomacy is likely to be most effective, because the stakes are often lower. In particular, low-profile diplomatic initiatives of the "Track 2" (i.e. unofficial or informal) variety may be most useful in the incipient stage of conflict. Focusing an international spotlight on a possible crisis could make a bad situation worse, exacerbating resentment by the ruling regime and inciting potential belligerents to manipulate the dynamics of international mediation.

However, it is late preventive diplomacy – crisis management – that tends to be the norm since earlier efforts by potential mediators are often perceived by states as an unacceptable breach of their sovereignty. In addition, states are reluctant to admit a potential failure in peacefully managing their own affairs. Although crisis management is more politically feasible than truly pre-emptive efforts, humanitarian and human rights violations may have already reached a large scale at this stage. When the stakes are high – and diplomacy becomes managing a game of chicken – coercive diplomacy, and indeed preventive defence, may be desirable.[39]

Another important diplomatic tool is the strategic authorisation of targeted sanctions, which were "dusted-off" for increased use in the 1990s by the Security Council. Recent analysis indicates that targeted sanctions can be a powerful disincentive toward violence when properly focused and enforced.[40] A potential drawback is the unintended humanitarian cost of sanctions regimes that are not sufficiently "targeted" at elites and those responsible for instigating and perpetuating war.[41] Moreover, lack of an effective monitoring regime has threatened to undermine their use – a lesson the United Nations learned on the African continent in the 1990s. Nonetheless, sanctions are likely to remain one of the most effective tools for preventive action by the Council, and serious efforts to inquire into loopholes and establish more rigorous monitoring systems were under way at the United Nations in relation to the complex Iraqi Oil-for-Food sanctions regime and those against Unita in Angola in 2000–2001.

Preventive deployment operations are an important but underutilised tool of conflict prevention. Evaluation of such operations (for example, UNPREDEP in Macedonia and MINURCA in the Central African Republic) can provide valuable insight for future operations.[42] However, the extent to which this success can be replicated depends upon a number of factors that are unlikely to be reproduced easily and relate to perceptions held among key member states regarding which situations are of strategic importance.

The barriers to preventive action are serious but not insurmountable. The most problematic obstacles relate more to effectiveness and the institutionalisation of regular mechanisms for prevention than to understanding causation or mobilising political support for action – both of which are eminently resolvable.[43] The difficulty is compounded by the rising number of actors involved in different types of conflict prevention initiatives. Despite attempts to implement and improve upon early warning mechanisms, it remains hard to identify situations that are appropriate for preventive action, and who is best placed to undertake them. This is partly due to a wealth of early warning information but a lack of accompanying strategic analysis and early response planning. It also results in part from selective reporting practices. Prevention efforts require an in-depth understanding of local context and the perspectives of potential belligerents – information and analysis that are difficult to feed effectively to the headquarters of international organisations, not least when it is processed by local NGOs.

One initiative that seeks to fill the "strategic information gap" between actors at different levels that emerged and became operational in late 2000 is a web-based joint initiative between the United Nations and Harvard University. The project seeks (particularly, though not exclusively) to provide the Department of Political Affairs with efficient online access to existing research and practice from around the world, and to provide an electronic forum that can facilitate the exchange of ideas on preventing and managing conflict.[44] A new initiative, the Conflict Prevention and Peace Forum, to place international scholarly and other expert advice at the disposal of the UN system, was launched in New York in late 2000 with UK government support. Key to this initiative's success is whether the UN Secretariat and agencies, and also Security Council members, actually wish to draw on expert knowledge and opinion. On this, the jury will be out for some time.

Mobilising resources for preventive action is another challenge, despite the fact that we know that it is cheaper to prevent wars than to fight them.[45] In the absence of actual violence, states are often unwilling to take what they see as a gamble with relatively little pay-off – because, when prevention is effective, nothing is seen to "happen". In addition, potential belligerents may not be receptive to external intervention, in part because the gains from war are often far greater than any incentives the international community can offer, and in part because preventive action is frequently "too little too late" or simply inappropriate. The strategy, local context, timing, sequencing, tools and resources brought to bear in a given situation are all appropriate in determining whether preventive action can be successful, particularly considering that a combination of both "carrots" and "sticks" is likely to be required. Even when the political will exists to "do something", there is often a significant gap between the amount of resources pledged by donors and the actual deployment of resources in the field. Furthermore, the time lag between the public commitment of funds and their disbursement can cost many lives as various types of action (military or relief) are delayed.[46] This is a continuing weakness in the UN system.

It is often difficult to see the results of successful prevention – as Sherlock Holmes observed, it is difficult to establish why a dog *didn't* bark on a given night. The consequences of failed prevention, by contrast, are known to all. The next section will examine the debate over intervention with a particular focus on its relation to the foregoing discussion of prevention and how these two debates might be more productively advanced.

Intervention

In a speech delivered on 19 July 2000, UK Foreign Secretary Robin Cook outlined what was proposed as a "framework" to guide intervention. The first of the six principles elaborated in this speech was that "any intervention, by definition, is a failure of prevention".[47] This represented a shift in the debate over humanitarian intervention. In particular, it explicitly recognised that intervention should only ever be a last resort. Implicitly, it also suggested a subtle transformation in the subject matter of this debate, as intervention came to be seen as one of many possible responses to humanitarian crises on a spectrum that included prevention.

This section will track the course of this debate, which progressed in three phases: first, by reference to shifting conceptions of sovereignty; secondly, by attempting to develop criteria for intervention; and, thirdly, by repositioning this debate as a question of failed prevention. This last phase represents the most promising line of discussion, though it leaves many questions about intervention pointedly unanswered.

Shifting concepts of sovereignty and human rights

In international law, there is both an obligation for the international community to respect state sovereignty and a duty of the state to protect and promote internationally recognised human rights. In some circumstances, these obligations may be irreconcilable. Respect for state sovereignty, with its corollary of non-interference "in matters which are essentially within the domestic jurisdiction of any state", is enshrined in articles 2(4) and 2(7) of the UN Charter. The conception of sovereignty as inviolable has been central to international law and practice since the 1648 Treaty of Westphalia. Nevertheless, it is now widely accepted that the concept of sovereignty is not absolute. For example, the prohibition against genocide and the obligation upon all states to prevent it are already firmly established in international law. Contemporary understanding of state sovereignty is steadily becoming more flexible concerning broader violations of human rights, the scope of which has also been gradually expanding.[48]

At the outset of the November 2000 IPA seminar referred to earlier, Jozias van Aartsen, Foreign Minister of the Netherlands, highlighted this shifting emphasis in international law between sovereignty and human rights.[49] Events in Rwanda, the former Yugoslavia, Sierra Leone, East Timor, Cambodia and elsewhere around the world have demonstrated that massive violations of human rights and humanitarian principles are the concern of the international community as a whole, particularly when the consequences of these violations cross international borders.[50]

It is generally the countries of the North that more openly advocate a right (or responsibility) of humanitarian intervention, whereas it is the South (and at least one permanent member of the Security Council) that gives priority to state sovereignty and non-interference. Yet, discussion of intervention often transcends the North–South division. Although several developing countries noted the preoccupation of the North with Kosovo and the precedent set by NATO's actions, and more viewed the word "intervention" with scepticism or find "humanitarian intervention" unacceptable, not all states are opposed to its intent (or, more controversially, its application) in specific cases. There have been notable interventions by southern states: Tanzania in Uganda, India in East Pakistan/Bangladesh, Vietnam in Cambodia, the Economic Community of West African States (ECOWAS) in Sierra Leone and Liberia, and, of a non-military nature, the imposition of sanctions against South Africa and

Burundi by their neighbours. Many of these target states recognise the value of (more broadly defined) "interventions" in helping to end authoritarian regimes or their practices.[51]

A related question is whether conventional notions of sovereignty are a hindrance to action by member state governments. Notably, states did not fail to intervene in Rwanda owing to concerns over state sovereignty.[52] Although legal arguments may be presented as one reason for inaction, intervention remains governed by political considerations, including international and domestic political repercussions, lack of available resources, including financial, personnel or transport, and lack of faith in the viability of success.

Criteria for intervention and the questions of codification

The debate on whether criteria for humanitarian intervention should be codified centres on two questions: first, whether and when the Security Council should intervene; secondly, and considerably more controversially, whether these guidelines should enable intervention without Security Council authorisation and in what circumstances.

The principal camps are divided into those opposed to any type of codification (predominantly developing states concerned about the erosion of their sovereignty, diminished restrictions on the use of force, or abuse of intervention for political purposes); those that favour the adoption of guidelines for use by the Security Council but oppose any codification legitimising circumvention of the Council; and those in favour of a right to unilateral intervention (the majority of which are developed states that place a high priority on human rights). The last camp is in turn divided between those who seek a "doctrine" approach and those who favour an "exception" approach.[53]

All states accept that there are circumstances in which the international community is justified in using force under Chapter VII of the UN Charter. Increasingly, however, the matters with which the Security Council is seized are essentially intrastate rather than interstate. As noted above, tension exists between the responsibility of the Council to maintain international peace and security and respect for the internal affairs of states. Those in favour of codification seek to develop a framework of criteria for considering whether the use of humanitarian intervention – that is, military action – is an appropriate and legitimate response. It is broadly accepted by the international community that discussion of whether and when the Security Council should intervene should not be unprincipled, but there is disagreement over the merits of particular cases. There has been growing debate as to whether the Council should continue determinations of intervention on an ad hoc basis or establish standing guidelines of a political or legal nature that would provide a basis for determining when such action is appropriate.

Although Security Council decisions to intervene will always be taken on a case-by-case basis (owing to feasibility, available resources and other concerns), established guidelines might help to clarify the minimum conditions necessary for intervention and could structure debate on authorising the use of force, helping the Council to reach consensus and thus ensuring its effective and timely action. These criteria might be succinctly enumerated as gravity, urgency, objectivity, acceptability, practicality, proportionality and sustainability. Some states are concerned that too strict a codification might not succeed or might result in a state of law that is more restricted than what can be deduced from article 2(7) of the Charter in combination with existing human rights instruments.[54]

Far more serious reservations, if not outright rejection, exist regarding justification without Security Council authorisation. Following the NATO action in Kosovo, some states have argued that legal considerations should not preclude military action and have advanced the idea of codifying criteria for unilateral intervention when the Council is unwilling or unable to act. As Minister van Aartsen noted, "situations will arise time and again where humanitarian intervention without a mandate will be the only way to stop large-scale human suffering".[55] Proponents of this position maintain that the international community has a responsibility to protect rather than a right to intervene.

Legal justification for unauthorised intervention is highly problematic. According to international law, the Security Council is the appropriate forum both to decide whether gross and massive violations of human rights amount to a threat to international peace and security and to take enforcement measures to deal with such violations. Although state practice in recent years suggests that humanitarian intervention without Security Council authorisation may be morally and politically justifiable in certain circumstances, the assertion that humanitarian intervention is legally justifiable as an emerging norm of customary international law cannot yet be assumed. Many states – including members of the P-5, powerful regional states, and small developing states – oppose claims to action without explicit Security Council authorisation.[56]

Developing countries in particular regard the central mission of the United Nations as limiting the discretion of states to use force in non-defensive circumstances. In particular, it is feared that codification might widen state discretion, eroding article 2(4). Intervention on "moral" grounds, particularly if codified as a legal norm, could be a step backwards, re-legitimising the use of force. Most developing states are acutely aware that they lack the power to intervene owing to disparities in economic and military development. They are concerned that intervention will occur at the whim of the great powers, rather than on the basis of consistent criteria, and that the relationship will always be non-reciprocal. Likewise, these states lack the power to oppose intervention, and therefore worry about power politics. Finally, they oppose intervention on the grounds of human rights violations when international consensus on these violations is lacking.

Although there is no consensus on guidelines for unauthorised intervention even among its proponents, it is worthwhile to consider whether such guidelines would be political or legal in nature. Because political guidelines would not provide a legal justification for intervention, many feel that legal guidelines would be preferable. Others adopt the position that codification should not formalise "an 'emergency exit' from the existing norms of international law".[57]

Adoption of legally binding criteria would likely take one of two forms: amendment of the Charter, or adoption of an international agreement. Both options would have to be ratified by the member states, and both remain problematic and unlikely, at least at the present time. The adoption of criteria for intervention might be a way to update the Charter to reflect current political realities, but many states feel that to amend the Charter would be to weaken it. Under these conditions, attempts to do so risk exacerbating differences of opinion over intervention and might ultimately do more harm than good. An alternative approach is to regard the Charter as a "living document" (comparable, for example, to the US Constitution).[58] On this basis, it is argued, the document drafted in the 1940s can be applied to the experiences of today in such a way as to provide a framework for intervention. Additional legal measures on intervention would therefore not be needed.

The second option, the adoption of an international agreement, is also difficult, but some argued that, as with the Statute of the International Criminal Court, a lack of full consensus should not be an excuse for not trying. Legally, however, such a document would be relevant only when it is least needed – that is, when the Council is in agreement on its course of action. When the Council is divided, article 103 of the UN Charter acts to prohibit any separate document being used to circumvent the Security Council and the United Nations as a whole.[59] Operationally, then, it is difficult to conceive how such a document might work unless it had universal legitimacy, especially if it was possible to invoke the right against a non-signatory state.

An alternative approach, favoured by some members of the Group of 77 (G-77), would be to undertake an exercise similar to that of the 1970 Declaration on Friendly Relations (adopted by the General Assembly as resolution 2625), which interpreted all the sub-paragraphs of article 2.[60]

A non-binding resolution of the General Assembly on the magnitude of events leading to intervention could establish norms for its use in the absence of authorisation. In the event of a humanitarian crisis during which the Security Council and/or General Assembly is deadlocked, states acting without authorisation could, under such a declaration, use force in accordance with norms of intervention laid down by the General Assembly.[61] Such a measure might be welcomed by those states that fear erosion of article 2(4).[62] However, this approach hardly seems practicable in the absence of more widespread interest in pursuing it. Indeed, most industrialised countries fear that such an exercise would boil down to an attempt by such Non-Aligned Movement (NAM) leaders as Algeria, Cuba, Egypt, India and Pakistan to produce a text precluding intervention in almost all circumstances.[63] They would not lightly engage again on this turf.

Repositioning the debate

In his 20 September 1999 speech to the General Assembly, the Secretary-General stressed that "it is important to define intervention as broadly as possible, to include actions along a wide continuum from the most pacific to the most coercive".[64] This focus beyond the specific debate on NATO's alleged "humanitarian intervention" in Kosovo was emphasised in the speech delivered at the IPA seminar on 20 November 2000, when he suggested that the term "humanitarian" be dropped or confined to non-forcible actions:

[T]he humanitarians among us are those whose work involves saving lives that are in imminent danger, and relieving suffering that is already acute. They are people who bring food to those threatened with starvation, or medical help to the injured, or shelter to those who have lost their homes, or comfort to those who have lost their loved ones.[65]

Humanitarian "action" is, therefore, not synonymous with military intervention; on the contrary, such military operations, even if undertaken for humanitarian motives, are not humanitarian in nature. Any blurring of this line risks the possibility that governments will view acceptance of humanitarian aid as "the thin edge of the wedge". Instead of seeing aid as the first step towards forcible intervention, states should be eager to allow humanitarian aid because doing so may remove the need for military intervention.

This is more than wordplay. In particular, shifting the debate away from a simple question of the legality of humanitarian intervention, *stricto sensu*, serves two distinct policy goals. First, the legal debate is sterile. It is unlikely that a clear and workable set of criteria could be adopted on a right of humanitarian intervention. Any criteria general enough to achieve agreement would be unlikely to satisfy any actual examples of allegedly humanitarian intervention. Indeed, it seems clear from the statements of NATO leaders during and after the Kosovo campaign that they would not want the air strikes to be regarded as a model for dealing with future humanitarian crises.[66] The alternative – a select group of states (such as Western liberal democracies) agreeing on criteria amongst themselves – would be seen as a vote of no confidence in the United Nations, after the decade in which, despite some obvious failures, it achieved more than in the previous half-century.

More importantly, however, the Secretary-General's position highlights the true problem at the heart of this ongoing debate. The problem is not that states are champing at the bit to intervene in support of human rights around the globe, prevented only by an intransigent Security Council and the absence of clear criteria to intervene without its authority. Rather, the problem is the absence of the will to act at all.[67] In such circumstances, the primary goal must be to encourage states to see massive and systematic human rights violations in other countries as their concern too – as part of their "national interest" – and to act, and act early, to prevent them, stop them or seek justice for them.

Conclusion

When the 19 members of NATO supported the intervention in Kosovo, each had its own public rationale for doing so: humanitarianism, regional security or upholding the principles of Security Council resolution 1199. There was no consensus on the theory, and only barely on the practice. Outside of NATO, there was agreement on neither theory nor practice. Indeed, most states continue to have deep reservations about intervention – particularly if it might legitimate circumvention of the Security Council's primary responsibility for international peace and security.

Nevertheless, circumstances will inevitably arise in which the Council is unwilling or unable to act, but where realities on the ground warrant the use of force. What, then, is the appropriate response for the United Nations?

This chapter has argued that the central problems in the respective debates over prevention and intervention are an underemphasis on action in the former, and an overemphasis on theory in the latter. Rather than contribute yet more ink to the debate on codification of intervention, the position adopted here is that incidents of humanitarian intervention, which will remain rare, exceptional and controversial, should be seen primarily as failures. Such interventions are failures both of the international security architecture (whether due to a capricious veto or not) and of the embryonic mechanisms within the United Nations and other bodies aimed at preventing the outbreak of conflict. Any intervention that takes place outside that architecture should therefore strive to obtain eventual legitimacy within it – as NATO did with its recourse to the G-8 and the adoption of Security Council resolution 1244 (1999), and as ECOWAS did following its interventions in Liberia and Sierra Leone earlier in the decade.

At the same time, all such actions should provide an impetus to develop and implement prevention mechanisms within the United Nations. In particular, greater resources should be devoted to a strategic analysis secretariat along the lines recommended in the Brahimi Report. And, if infringements of sovereignty are raised as barriers to such developments, it should be pointed out that the alternative is the increased probability of far more severe infringements in the form of intervention.

The distinction between humanitarian assistance and military intervention made by the Secretary-General in November 2000 remains valid, and perhaps necessary to protect the provision of aid and those who supply it. Yet the principles of sovereignty and human rights, humanitarianism and military force must be wedded in such a way as to do the most good for those most in need. Ultimately, the best solution to the tension between sovereignty and humanitarian principles lies in agreeing not on when to undertake humanitarian intervention but on how better to prevent the humanitarian crises that lead some to think such action is necessary.

This is, of course, an imperfect answer to the problem of humanitarian intervention. But the United Nations is an imperfect (and cash-poor) body, charged with keeping the peace in an imperfect world.

Acknowledgements

We are grateful to Jake Sherman of the International Peace Academy for his insights on humanitarian action.

Notes

1. See United Nations, *Press Release* (New York: United Nations, SG/SM/7136, 20 September 1999). This and other speeches on intervention have been collected in Kofi A. Annan, *The Question of Intervention: Statements by the Secretary-General* (New York: United Nations Department of Public Information, 1999). Lakshman Kadirgamar,

Minister of Foreign Affairs and Chairman of the Delegation of Sri Lanka, presented one of the most critical statements to the Secretary-General's proposal to the General Assembly. See also David M. Malone, "The Security Council in the 1990s: Inconsistent, Improvisational, Indispensable?" in Ramesh Thakur and Edward Newman (eds), *New Millennium, New Perspectives* (Tokyo: United Nations University Press, 2000), pp. 21–45.

2. At the UN Millennium Summit in September 2000, the Government of Canada launched a major study on this subject entitled "The International Commission on Intervention and State Sovereignty" (ICISS). The Commission was chaired by Gareth Evans, President of the International Crisis Group, and Mohamed Sahnoun, Special Envoy of the Secretary-General in Africa. Ramesh Thakur, one of the co-editors of this volume, was a member of ICISS. Its conclusions can be found in *The Responsibility to Protect: Report of the International Commission on Intervention and State Sovereignty* (Ottawa: International Development Research Centre, 2001). See also Independent International Commission on Kosovo, "The Kosovo Report" (2000).

3. On this complex issue, see Simon Chesterman, *Just War or Just Peace? Humanitarian Intervention and International Law* (Oxford: Oxford University Press, 2001); Karma Nabulsi, *Traditions of War: Occupation, Resistance and the Law* (Oxford: Oxford University Press, 1999); and Nicholas J. Wheeler, *Saving Strangers: Humanitarian Intervention in International Society* (Oxford: Oxford University Press, 2000). See also the online project by the International Committee of the Red Cross (ICRC) available at www.onwar.org.

4. Kofi A. Annan, "Opening Remarks", International Peace Academy, Humanitarian Action Symposium, New York, 20 November 2000, available at www.ipacademy.org.

5. UN Charter, Preamble. Article 1 of the UN Charter states in part and at its outset that the purposes of the United Nations are: "To maintain international peace and security, and to that end: to take effective collective measures for the prevention and removal of threats to the peace, and for the suppression of acts of aggression or other breaches of the peace, and to bring about by peaceful means, and in conformity with the principles of justice and international law, adjustment or settlement of international disputes or situations which might lead to a breach of the peace."

6. See General Assembly *Resolution* 377(v) (3 November 1950).

7. See, for a more in-depth discussion of the role of the Security Council in the post–Cold War era, David M. Malone, "The Security Council in the post–Cold War Era", in Muthiah Alagappa and Takashi Inoguchi (eds), *International Security Management and the United Nations* (Tokyo: United Nations University Press, 1999), pp. 394–408.

8. An International Peace Academy volume discusses the United Nations' role in conflict prevention: Fen Hampson and David M. Malone (eds), *From Reaction to Conflict Prevention: Opportunities for the UN System* (Boulder, CO: Lynne Rienner, 2002).

9. Lilly R. Sucharipa-Behrman and Thomas M. Franck, "Preventive Measures," *New York University Journal of International Law and Politics*, vol. 30, 1998, at p. 485.

10. The First United Nations Emergency Force (UNEF I) was authorised by the General Assembly – since the Council was paralysed on the issue – and was deployed in November 1956 "to secure and supervise the cessation of hostilities, including the withdrawal of the armed forces of France, Israel and the United Kingdom from Egyptian territory and, after the withdrawal, to serve as a buffer between the Egyptian and Israeli forces." See www.un.org/Depts/dpko/dpko/co_mission/unefi.htm, and Brian Urquhart, *Ralph Bunche: An American Life* (New York: W. W. Norton, 1993).

11. Note, however, that so-called "civil wars" are frequently fuelled by neighbours, and can spill over (as in the Great Lakes region since 1997, and in Liberia/Sierra Leone/Guinea in 1999–2001). They can also "spill in", as demonstrated by extensive external involvement in the Democratic Republic of the Congo's civil war in the early 2000s.

12. Nabil Elaraby interview with David M. Malone, New York, January 1996.
13. See, for example, Paul Collier and Anke Hoeffler, "Greed and Grievance in Civil War", World Bank Working Paper No. 2355 (May 2000); Paul Collier, "Economic Causes of Civil Conflict and Their Implications for Policy", in Chester A. Crocker, Fen Osler Hampson and Pamela Aall (eds), *Turbulent Peace: The Challenges of Managing International Conflict* (Washington DC: United States Institute of Peace Press, 2001), pp. 143–162; Mats Berdal and David M. Malone (eds), *Greed and Grievance: Economic Agendas in Civil Wars*, A Project of the International Peace Academy (Boulder, CO: Lynne Rienner, 2000); and E. Wayne Nafziger, Frances Stewart and Raimo Väyrynen (eds), *War, Hunger, and Displacement: The Origins of Humanitarian Emergencies* (Oxford: Oxford University Press, 2000).
14. See, for the Montreal Protocol and information on its implementing mechanism, the Ozone Secretariat of the UN Environment Programme, www.unep.org/ozone/mont_t.shtml.
15. For example, since the 1998 Asian financial crisis, Indonesia has submitted to intensive IMF review and has agreed to pursue policies recommended by the IMF. More broadly, see IMF, *Conditionality: Fostering Sustained Policy Implementation, IMF Survey Supplement on the Fund* (September 1997) at www.imf.org/external/pubs/ft/survey/sup0997/06condit.htm. As Lilly Sucharipa-Behrman and Thomas Franck have observed, the International Bank for Reconstruction and Development (IBRD) now imposes environmental assessments (obviously of a preventive nature) on all of its relevant projects: Sucharipa-Behrman and Franck, "Preventive Measures", pp. 516–517. In the arms control field, the Intermediate Nuclear Forces Treaty (INF), the treaties on the Reduction and Limitation of Strategic Offensive Arms (START treaties), the Nuclear Non-Proliferation Treaty and the Chemical Weapons Convention all impose on the parties to them verification and inspection procedures of a necessarily intrusive kind.
16. See chapters by Ted Gurr, Monty Marshall and Frances Stewart in Hampson and Malone (eds), *From Reaction to Conflict Prevention*.
17. Peter Wallensteen, *Understanding Conflict Resolution: War, Peace and the Global System* (London: Sage Publications, 2002).
18. Generally, popular consultation and bringing actors together at the local level can help build peace and mitigate factors that might otherwise mobilise the populace for the recurrence of conflict. However, the timing of elections is particularly important and must be determined on a case-by-case basis with close attention to local political and civil society dynamics. Poorly timed and poorly conducted elections can be destabilising and the risks during transition require close attention. Democratic transition may be easier when entrenched elites have an exit strategy and do not have a significant personal financial stake in maintaining the status quo. Some suggest that good governance should be its own reward, while others note that a "democracy dividend" from donors could provide incentives for democratisation. International IDEA, a leading international research and policy development institution headquartered in Stockholm, has consistently advanced debate on this topic. See Peter Harris and Ben Reilly (eds), *Democracy and Deep-Rooted Conflict: Options for Negotiators* (Stockholm: International IDEA, 1998).
19. See Development Assistance Committee (DAC), "Guidelines on Conflict, Peace and Development Cooperation" (Paris: OECD, 1997), and Peter Wallensteen, with contributions from Birger Heldt, Mary B. Anderson, Stephen John Stedman and Leonard Wantchekon, "Conflict Prevention through Development Cooperation", Informal OECD/DAC Task Force on Conflict, Peace and Development Cooperation, Paris, and the Department of Peace and Conflict Research, Uppsala University, Sweden, 30 November 2000.
20. For a discussion of these issues, see in particular the chapters by David Keen and David Shearer in Berdal and Malone (eds), *Greed and Grievance*.

THE PREVENTION–INTERVENTION DICHOTOMY 77

21. See Nat J. Colletta and Michelle L. Cullen, *Violent Conflict and the Transformation of Social Capital: Lessons from Cambodia, Rwanda, Guatemala and Somalia*, Conflict Prevention Series (Washington DC: World Bank Publication, 6/9/2000).
22. See www.worldbank.org for updated information.
23. See David Malone, *Decision-Making in the UN Security Council: The Case of Haiti, 1990–1997* (Oxford: Oxford University Press, 1998).
24. See Chesterman, *Just War or Just Peace?*, pp. 112–162.
25. The United Nations Preventive Deployment Force (UNPREDEP), the first of its kind, was authorised by UN Security Council Resolution 983, 31 March 1995.
26. The United Nations Mission in the Central African Republic (MINURCA) was established by Security Council Resolution 1159 of 27 March 1998.
27. See www.un.org/Depts/DPKO/Missions/car.htm.
28. See UN Security Council Resolution 687 (3 April 1991).
29. Recent stabs at the issue by the Security Council include the two Presidential Statements on the subject of conflict prevention, and the request for a follow-up report to be presented to the Council and the General Assembly in May 2000. See S/PRST/1999/34 (30 November 1999) and S/PRST/2000/25 (20 July 2000).
30. See the statements by the President of the Security Council on behalf of the Council, and especially the statement by the President of the Security Council, S/23500 (31 January 1992).
31. See Report of the Panel on United Nations Peace Operations, UN Doc A/55/305-S/2000/809 (21 August 2000), available at http://www.un.org/peace/reports/peace_operations/ ("Brahimi Report").
32. For a cogent articulation of the view, strongly held by some developing countries, that the United Nations' capacity in this area is in no need of strengthening, see statement by H.E. Mr Kamalesh Sharma, Permanent Representative of India to the United Nations on the Comprehensive Review of the Whole Question of Peacekeeping Operations in All Their Aspects (Agenda Item 86), in the Special Political and Decolonisation Committee (Fourth Committee) of the UN General Assembly, New York, 9 November 2000.
33. See the chapter by Ted Gurr in Hampson and Malone (eds), *From Reaction to Conflict Prevention*.
34. This emerged from a talk given by Peter Wallensteen at IPA's Expert Workshop (West Point, 31 January–1 February 1999). See Wallensteen, *Understanding Conflict Resolution: War, Peace and the Global System*.
35. See the chapter by Anne Marie Gardner in Hampson and Malone (eds), *From Reaction to Conflict Prevention*.
36. A recent IPA volume examines some of the economic factors at play in contemporary wars: Berdal and Malone (eds), *Greed and Grievance*. Debate in this area has been heavily influenced by the work of Paul Collier (now at the World Bank), and also by Frances Stewart, the United Nations University's World Institute of Development Economics Research (WIDER) in Helsinki and a number of other research institutions. IPA has now launched a major policy development project of its own on economic factors in civil wars, focusing on the economic activities of belligerents, on corporate motivations in theatres of conflict and on what an effective international regulatory and legal framework would need to encompass to address meaningfully white-collar crime under the cover of civil wars.
37. See Nafziger, Stewart and Väyrynen (eds), *War, Hunger, and Displacement: The Origins of Humanitarian Emergencies*.
38. For instance, several experts have argued that the programmes of some international institutions (and in particular the international financial institutions) may have indirectly contributed to the exacerbation of horizontal inequality, and hence to the probability of

violence. See in particular Susan L. Woodward, *Balkan Tragedy: Chaos and Dissolution after the Cold War* (Washington DC: Brookings Institution Press, 1995).

39. See, for a recent attempt to revive discussion on more coercive preventive instruments, Bruce W. Jentleson, "Coercive Prevention: Normative, Political and Policy Dilemmas", *Peaceworks* 35 (Washington DC: United States Institute of Peace, October 2000).
40. For a sophisticated discussion of various sanctions regimes recently mandated by the UN Security Council, see David Cortright and George Lopez, *The Sanctions Decade: Assessing UN Sanctions in the 1990s* (Boulder, CO: Lynne Rienner, 2000). The authors found a number of these sanctions regimes to have been effective, at least initially, but argue that sanctions are most useful when seen as an instrument to induce bargaining and compromise. Cortright and Lopez argue that, without diplomatic give and take, sanctions are unlikely to achieve their stated objectives.
41. See Ramesh Thakur, "Sanctions: A Triumph of Hope Eternal over Experience Unlimited", *Global Dialogue*, vol. 2, no. 3, Summer 2000, pp. 129–141.
42. See Adiodun Williams, *Preventing War: The United Nations and Macedonia* (Lanham, MD: Rowman & Littlefield, 2000).
43. See the chapter by Michael Lund in Hampson and Malone (eds), *From Reaction.to Conflict Prevention*.
44. See www.preventconflict.org. Part of the site is password protected for UN access only, but the site contains a host of other research ready to download by the regular user.
45. See, for evidence of the adage that "an ounce of prevention is worth a pound of cure", Michael E. Brown and Richard N. Rosecrance, *The Costs of Conflict: Prevention and Cure in the Global Arena* (Lanham, MD: Rowman & Littlefield, 1999).
46. See Shepard Forman and Stewart Patrick (eds), *Good Intentions: Pledges of Aid for Postconflict Recovery* (Boulder, CO: Lynne Rienner, 2000). See also Simon Chesterman (ed.), *Civilians in War*, A Project of the International Peace Academy (Boulder, CO: Lynne Rienner, 2001).
47. Robin Cook, "Guiding Humanitarian Intervention" (American Bar Association Lunch, London, 19 July 2000), available at www.fco.gov.uk.
48. Chesterman, *Just War or Just Peace?*; Wheeler, *Saving Strangers*.
49. See above note 3 and accompanying text.
50. Jozias van Aartsen, "Opening Remarks" (International Peace Academy, Humanitarian Action Symposium, New York, 20 November 2000), available at www.ipacademy.org.
51. See, generally, Chesterman, *Just War or Just Peace?*; Wheeler, *Saving Strangers*; Sean D. Murphy, *Humanitarian Intervention: The United Nations in an Evolving World Order* (Philadelphia, PA: University of Pennsylvania Press, 1996); Fernando R. Tesón, *Humanitarian Intervention: An Inquiry into Law and Morality* (Dobbs Ferry, NY: Transnational Publishers, 1997).
52. See *Report of the Independent Inquiry into the Actions of the United Nations during the 1994 Genocide in Rwanda* (New York: United Nations, S/1999/1257, 16 December 1999); Philip Gourevitch, *We Wish to Inform That Tomorrow We Will Be Killed with Our Families* (London: Picador, 1999); Gérard Prunier, *The Rwanda Crisis: History of a Genocide* (New York: Columbia University Press, 1997).
53. See, for example, Chesterman, *Just War or Just Peace?*, pp. 226–232; Wheeler, *Saving Strangers*, pp. 33–51 and sources there cited.
54. See further, Jake Sherman, "Humanitarian Action" (New York, 2000).
55. Van Aartsen, "Opening Remarks".
56. See, for example, Independent International Commission on Kosovo, "The Kosovo Report", which concluded that the intervention was "illegal but legitimate". Compare Foreign Affairs Committee, "Fourth Report: Kosovo, HC 28–I" (2000), para. 138: "we conclude that NATO's military action, if of dubious legality in the current state of international law, was justified on moral grounds."

57. See Sherman, "Humanitarian Action".
58. Tom Franck has recently developed the idea of the Charter as a "living tree".
59. Article 103 of the UN Charter reads: "In the event of a conflict between the obligations of the Members of the United Nations under the present Charter and their obligations under any other international agreement, their obligations under the present Charter shall prevail."
60. See Chesterman, *Just War or Just Peace?*, p. 51.
61. For a discussion of the Uniting for Peace procedure, see ibid., pp. 118–119.
62. Ironically, the Organization of American States, through implementation of its Santiago Declaration of 1991, has been in the vanguard of international action to protect and promote democracy (going to the heart of what sovereignty represents). The Organization of African Unity also, in 1999, decided to exclude from its work all governments that had come to power undemocratically. It is essentially most Asian and Middle Eastern countries (and Cuba) that are the "outliers" on this question, but their position dominates that of the NAM (and the G-77 where applicable).
63. An interesting phenomenon at the United Nations has been the ability of a few key developing countries with large numbers of skilled negotiators on the ground in New York and Geneva to dominate the G-77 and the Non-Aligned Movement in a UN context. Privately, many African countries disagree with G-77 and NAM positions as defined by these "lead" countries, but they have been unable to develop strategies to promote their own views within these developing country forums. Ultimately, their fear of domination by industrialised countries is even greater than their resentment over positions forced on them within the G-77 and NAM, yielding "NAM solidarity" of a geopolitically meaningless variety.
64. See above note. 1.
65. Annan, "Opening Remarks".
66. US Secretary of State Madeleine Albright, for example, stressed in a press conference after the air campaign that Kosovo was "a unique situation *sui generis* in the region of the Balkans", concluding that it is important "not to overdraw the various lessons that come out of it" (Press Conference with Russian Foreign Minister Igor Ivanov, Singapore, 26 July 1999) available at secretary.state.gov/www/statements/1999/990726b.html.
67. See, further, Edward C. Luck, "The Enforcement of Humanitarian Norms and the Politics of Ambivalence", in Chesterman (ed.), *Civilians in War*, pp. 197–218.

Part 2
Challenges for the military in disrupted states

4
Managing future chaos: The United States Marine Corps in the twenty-first century

Thomas E. Seal

The phenomenon of "disrupted states" is not new. Whether caused by war, plague, social upheavals, economic disruptions or other factors, the collapse of order in states under extreme stress has long plagued powers great and small. Variously described in terms of "small wars", "complex contingencies" or "military operations other than war", the breakdown of order in one political entity can easily infect the entire political system. During the Cold War the realities of bipolarity imposed a certain discipline on the international system, with the superpowers propping up any number of barely viable regimes in the name of order or political advantage. With the passing of that historical anomaly and the concomitant rise in the number of weak and seriously flawed national entities, managing the chaos such states generate is back on the agenda.

Managing such chaos is not strictly an American or a West European problem, nor does it necessarily require a military response. When a military response is required, however, the United States Marine Corps (USMC) is very likely to be in the forefront. Using the Marine Corps as a model, this chapter will explore the increasing importance of civil–military cooperation in responding to the challenges of disrupted states. In doing so, it will outline a vision of the future operating environment, provide insight into the Marine Corps world view, discuss the role and limitations of innovation, and suggest future cooperative endeavours in building civil–military "forces" to meet tomorrow's challenges.

Before proceeding further, it may be helpful to establish why the Marine Corps is being offered as a model for the military side of the civil–military equation. There are several reasons. First, the Marines have a long history of responding to and managing chaos. Interventions in China in 1900 and in the years bracketing the Second World War, in the Caribbean in the 1920s and 1930s, and more recently in northern Iraq, Somalia and Rwanda are a few examples. Second, Marines have led the way in thinking about such contingencies. The USMC *Small Wars Manual*, first published in 1940, distills the lessons learned in many years of limited combat and "nation-building" and still serves as a prototype document for the use of military forces in handling disrupted states. A third case for using the Marines as a model is the Corps' innovative approach to building and employing forces of special relevance. Marine operating forces are organised into extremely flexible and versatile Marine Air–Ground Task Forces, or MAGTFs. Forward deployed across the globe, MAGTFs provide the land component of naval expeditionary forces which are organised, trained and equipped to respond at short notice to a wide variety of missions, from combat operations to humanitarian assistance and disaster relief. It is this combination of forward presence, multiple capabilities and quick response that, when combined with a historical and cultural affinity for dealing with disrupted states, makes the Marines ideally suited for operations in the turbulent world of the twenty-first century.

Defining the future: Constants and trends

Given that the future is unknowable, agreement about it should be held in great disregard, especially because such agreement is often the result of the overwhelming needs and inhibitions of the present.[1]

None but the boldest futurist would categorically declare a specific vision of the future, but there is a very human tendency to fall in line with the conventional wisdom. Nowhere is this more evident than in military writing about the future operating environment. With that acknowledgement, and with Helprin's sage admonition clearly in mind, I begin my attempt to "see" what the future operating environment may entail. I will do this by looking at perceived constants in the evolution of human beings, of states and of the United States, and at trends that may serve as guideposts to future development.

The first and most important factor in determining our direction is simply stated as human nature. Based on their life-long study of history, Will and Ariel Durant have concluded that, throughout their long and bloody past, humans have been driven in large part by their very human characteristics of "acquisitiveness, pugnacity, and pride". It comes as no surprise that the institutions humans have devised to govern their actions reflect those primal urges.[2] There are of course other drivers that may be considered more noble or uplifting but, to this stage of our development, these three factors are most important.

Closely related to the nature of humans is the nature of states. The Durants were not the first to link the institutional nature of states, empires, tribes or other governing bodies to that of the people who populated them. Thucydides noted some 2,500 years ago that states went to war over matters of honour, fear and interest. More recently, David Fromkin noted a recurring pattern of politics from ancient Sumer, through the Greek city states of antiquity, to modern Europe that reflects an ongoing struggle for security, wealth and power.[3] Despite conflicting trends towards irredentism, transnational challenges and more altruistic motives for intervention (at least in rhetoric), this human dimension of international politics must still be considered generally true.

Military interventions since Vietnam have been limited in both aims and means, short in duration and mercifully cheap in blood and treasure, at least for the United States and its allies. Most notably, the recent conflict in Kosovo has blurred Western understanding of the nature of war. The emerging popular notion of "immaculate coercion", of gaining national ends through the cost-free application of high-technology, long-range, highly lethal precision weapons, is seductive. It is also at odds with reality. War is destructive and cruel and remains a risky venture for all parties. Although the West's technological lead gives it a tremendous advantage against small, poor states, the Somalia experience suggests that that advantage is not always what it seems. And it is still too early to assess fully the unintended political, military, economic, social and environmental consequences of the Kosovo intervention.

Three other constants serve as points from which to anticipate the United States' future direction. One is geography. The United States is essentially an island nation, with long coastlines serving as gateways to the Atlantic and Pacific Oceans and beyond. Open spaces, abundant natural resources and long undefended borders to the north and south also shape the US experience and national character. At the risk of oversimplification, the US national character is one of a dynamic, open society firmly grounded in the nature of its democratic institutions. A third important constant is that the United States is a status quo power. Never a pacific nation when vital interests are at stake, major shifts in world power arrangements or other perceived threats to stability will not likely escape its attention or fail to elicit a national response.

All these factors have a tremendous influence on the direction the United States will take in the future. As a leading member in a broad array of international political, economic and military arrangements, these characteristics will have a tremendous impact on the rest of the world – just as the same factors in other nations will impact on the United States and its allies.

Of the many trends shaping the future world, the amalgamation of forces rolled up into the idea of globalisation is undoubtedly the most significant. Often discussed in terms of economic interdependence and free trade, the phenomenon is actually much broader. In a recent book on the subject, Thomas Friedman describes globalisation in the context of six key areas: politics, culture, national security, financial markets, technology and the environment. He writes of the future impact of emerging "super states", "super [financial] markets" and "super individuals" such as international terrorists who will increasingly shape the future landscape.[4] These views are in line with Marine Corps thinking as the United States looks to shape its forces for maximum relevance to the emerging world.

Migration and urbanisation are closely related trends that began long ago and continue to grow in intensity. Whether for opportunity, for safety or to escape the ravages of widespread environmental degradation, the mass migration of peoples to cities is expected to continue into the future. Nowhere will this be more dramatic than in the littorals. Defined by the US Navy as those coastal regions within striking power of naval forces, the littorals will increasingly draw people, commerce and national-level organisations to those regions.[5] By 2010, 70 per cent of the world's population will live in urban areas, the majority of these in the littorals. By 2020, 80 per cent of the world's megacities, those with populations over 10 million, will lie in the littorals. This concentration will have a profound effect on the landscape and on national, regional and global economies. It will also stress the ability of emerging states to govern and provide basic services for their populations.[6] Complicating this trend is the continuing shift in population balance. In 1950, the Western industrialised democracies held one-fifth of the world's population. Today that percentage is less than one-tenth. What this may mean in terms of international relations is unclear, but it may prove to be the greatest dilemma of the new century.[7]

As the world changes, the nature of military operations will change as well. Given advances in communications, mobility, organisation and training, military forces are rapidly expanding the space that they can influence or control. Ironically, as the geographical reach of modern forces expands, the timeline for making critical decisions is contracting. Thus, lower-level commanders of widely dispersed and rapidly manoeuvring forces will have a greater need and authority to make important decisions on a decentralised basis. Although a plus for force commanders, this decentralisation of decision-making will make coordination more difficult than ever before.

This difficulty will manifest itself in two areas. The first is strictly military. As the gulf between US and allied forces expands with the growing disparities in technology investments and related force enhancements, US forces may be faced with a difficult political and military decision. Do they operate at maximum efficiency by themselves, or suboptimally with allies? Conversely, do US allies struggle to close the gap with the United States, seek alternative capabilities or drop out of the game completely? The second area is even more problematic. If coordination with other militaries is difficult, how can the US military coordinate with other non-military organisations in the area to preclude tragic consequences of miscommunication or to maximise effectiveness of coordinated military and non-military operations? This problem will be particularly acute for non-US governmental organisations, especially international organisations (IOs), non-governmental organisations (NGOs) and private voluntary organisations (PVOs). Without an organisation, a culture or a clear vision of mutual benefit from coordinated operations, the gulf between the US military and these organisations will be increasingly difficult to bridge.

Central to all of these trends is the growing realisation that existing organisational and bureaucratic structures are not always conducive to meeting the challenges of today, let alone those of tomorrow. The future will be a time of changing lanes, of breaking free of the constraints imposed by bureaucratic stove piping and jealously guarded prerogatives. Western military services are moving in this direction with varying degrees of national success. And peacetime military cooperation between nations is also expanding into coordinated concepts for future development. But the most important changes will come in increased coordination between military forces and other agencies: national, state or provincial, and local governments; the business community; academia; international organisations; and non-governmental organisations. Improved lines of coordination will be most important in responding to emerging challenges posed by humanitarian and disaster relief, asymmetric attacks and terrorism.[8]

Marine Corps world view

If the Marine Corps is to be a model of future intervention in disrupted states, it is worthwhile to explore just what makes the Marines tick. Marine Corps attitudes, methods, capabilities and even its equipment are largely determined by a rather unique view of the world. This view colours its perception of the world and, to a large degree, the world's perception of it. Undeniably steeped in the American tradition, the Marine Corps is further shaped by a number of characteristics that make it uniquely suited for service in complex contingencies in disrupted states. First are its naval character and expeditionary ethos. From the beginning Marines have been forward deployed on US Navy ships across the globe. Operating from a sea base, naval forces are well suited to operations in austere environments where "host nation" support is either unavailable or politically problematic. Through their very presence naval forces have been first to respond to overseas challenges, whether threats to US interests or opportunities to assist in humanitarian efforts. The critical importance of this capability is illustrated by the growing momentum of other US services and allied armed forces either to reshape their forces or to develop new ones to gain their own expeditionary capabilities. Such a transition requires fundamental changes in organisation, training and even equipment. Most difficult, however, will be a change in service cultures that for generations have focused on preparing for the cataclysmic conflict that characterised Cold War defence planning.

Second, the Marine Corps is a capability-based and task-organised force with a broad range of missions. Alone among US military services, the Marine Corps and the amphibious forces of the US Navy were not specifically designed to meet the Soviet challenge. Rather, they were organised, trained and equipped to respond to crises ranging from major theatre war to humanitarian assistance operations. Additionally, the Marine Corps is a general-purpose force in which every Marine is trained to function in a variety of roles. Although each Marine has a specific military occupational specialty, all are capable of performing multiple functions within existing organisational, training and equipment parameters. This fact, coupled with its flexible organisation, makes the Marine Corps perfectly suited for deployment on Navy shipping as "first responders" capable of dealing effectively with multiple challenges. For example, during the Persian Gulf crisis of 1990–1991, the same Marine and Navy force evacuated a beleaguered US Embassy in Somalia, fought a major campaign in Kuwait, and executed a major humanitarian relief operation in Bangladesh on their way home.

Finally, the Marine Corps has a proven track record of innovation that reflects its emphasis on human factors over technology. Though they make no claims of clairvoyance, Marines have pioneered a number of important capabilities, several of which are central to dealing with the problems of disrupted states. Some of the more important innovations, such as civil–military operations outlined in the *Small Wars Manual*, and its organisation into MAGTFs, have already been mentioned. These innovations and others will now be addressed in some detail.

The *Small Wars Manual* marked a significant departure in military literature. Published in 1940, after the outbreak of war in Europe, the manual looked beyond the thinking of massed armies into a different and still very relevant form of conflict. In the manual, small wars were defined as:

operations undertaken under executive authority, wherein military force is combined with diplomatic pressure in the internal or external affairs of another state whose government is unable, inadequate, or unsatisfactory for the preservation of life and of such interests as are determined by the foreign policy of our nation.[9]

Such wars are often "conceived in uncertainty" and conducted with "precarious responsibility and doubtful authority, under indeterminate orders lacking specific instructions".[10] Recognising that the source of trouble is often economic, social or political, the manual drives home the message that traditional military response is not productive. Noting that the initial problem is to restore peace, the manual specifies that peace will be illusory unless the economic welfare of the people is adequately addressed. Therefore, the role of the military was seen as creating the social, political and economic conditions for peace and prosperity, not merely searching out and destroying opposing military forces.[11] Furthermore, a chapter on the "Military–Civil Relationship" outlines the importance of military contacts with the national government (through US Department of State representatives), opposing political factions, local officials, law enforcement agencies, the judicial branch, religious factions and the press.[12] Reading this manual 60 years after its publication, it becomes apparent that, for all the many changes in the world since 1940, the essential components of defining and dealing with disrupted states are strikingly similar. Only the scale, potential lethality and entry of new actors in the drama pose significant differences.

One of the most important Marine Corps innovations is the organisation of operating forces into Marine Air–Ground Task Forces. MAGTFs come in different sizes and can be organised to accomplish specific tasks or a variety of more general missions. Regardless of size or specific mission, each MAGTF contains four elements: headquarters, ground combat, aviation and logistics. Designed primarily for combat operations, MAGTFs are extremely versatile and can respond to a full range of non-combat operations as well, without reorganising, re-equipping or retraining.

The most visible MAGTF today is the Marine Expeditionary Unit (Special Operations Capable) (MEU(SOC)). At any given time, three separate MEU(SOC)s are forward deployed on US Navy ships around the globe. Each MEU(SOC) is a MAGTF composed of the four elements mentioned above. Aside from their first-priority combat capabilities, MEUs have often been employed in a variety of stability and humanitarian assistance operations. The availability of the forward-deployed MEU, together with its offensive power, communications, transportation, engineering, medical and logistics capabilities, makes it an important asset in managing chaos in any disrupted state scenario. Add to this the ability to operate from a sea base, and the communications, surgical, supply and other support offered by the Navy, and the importance of this asset is further enhanced.

For those familiar with the United States' initial entry into Somalia, recall that the first forces were those of a MEU(SOC). Following that landing, larger forces were introduced as part of a Maritime Prepositioning Force (MPF). An MPF is a MAGTF that includes two components, a maritime prepositioned ship (or ships) and a contingent of Marines and sailors flown in to offload the ship and employ its supplies and equipment to accomplish their assigned mission. The MPF is designed to support brigade-sized or larger combat operations in a major contingency. Still, in keeping with Marine Corps traditions and culture, it is readily capable of much more, to include a variety of peace and relief operations. Because the majority of its supplies and equipment are pre-loaded on ships, the MPF has extremely robust transportation, medical, food, shelter, engineering and water purification capabilities.

The "Three Block War" suggests a vision of future challenges that are far different from those the United States has traditionally faced. In the future, Marines may provide humanitarian assistance in the morning, separate rival forces at noon and engage in open combat by day's end, all in the area of three contiguous city blocks. Through it all, Marines and the sailors who support them will maintain some level of coordination with the many agencies and organisations engaged in ongoing humanitarian operations. Given the expansion of urban areas in the littorals and attendant stresses relative to shifting population, cultural and economic centres, this scenario is increasingly one that the Marine Corps and other responders will face.

An increasingly likely and troublesome ingredient in the three block war scenario is the introduction of what are called weapons of mass destruction. Such nuclear, biological and chemical weapons, whether employed by states or by terrorist organisations, add a chilling dimension to future operations of any sort. Prompted by the 1995 sarin gas attack in Tokyo, Iraq's development of biological weapons, and the weakening controls on the former Soviet Union's weapons stockpiles, the Marine Corps activated the Chemical/Biological Incident Response Force

(CBIRF) in 1996. This organisation is manned, trained and equipped to respond to incidents involving chemical and biological weapons at home and abroad. Combining active duty military with governmental and private sector civilian advisers, CBIRF is designed to assist federal, state and local agencies train for and respond to crises. A graphic example of the "lane changes" discussed earlier, this military organisation is designed not to take over in a crisis situation but rather to support local jurisdictions in their efforts to manage the consequences of a chemical or biological accident or incident.

Operational Maneuver From the Sea (OMFTS) is the Marine Corps' overarching concept for future operations. The concept provides a blueprint for the full range of future operations, from major theatre war to humanitarian assistance and disaster relief. Although the most dramatic changes in OMFTS are seen in its war-fighting capacity, the capability enhancements attendant on the concept will have a significant impact on the Marines' ability to conduct humanitarian operations. Regardless of the type of operation, OMFTS envisions Marine forces operating from a sea base well off shore. Thus, regardless of the missions, Marines will be able to influence action ashore without need of host nation support or establishing a landward presence. Combat missions aside, the mobility of the sea-based Marine forces will allow long-distance and sustained-support operations in a variety of humanitarian missions. Whether providing security, delivering relief supplies, evacuating people threatened by natural or human-generated disasters or providing services such as medical support, potable water and rudimentary engineering work, future naval forces will be major contributors to establishing order in disrupted states. To be sure, these capabilities already exist, as evidenced by numerous combat and relief missions over the past few years. Still, by 2010 the range and speed with which Marine units can move and communicate over distance will increase substantially. This will have important implications for all other forces, agencies and organisations operating in the same area.

The concept for Other Expeditionary Operations (OEO) is the newest in a long line of Marine Corps future concepts. OEO comprises the collective, coordinated use of both traditional and non-traditional elements of national power as a cohesive foreign policy tool. Built on a tradition of non-traditional operations and an expeditionary ethos, OEO offers a framework for the integration and coordination of all elements of national power, with military forces often participating in a supporting role. Elements of power include combinations of military forces, other government agencies, non-governmental organisations, business interests and academia. Reflecting successes codified in the *Small Wars Manual*, the CBIRF and decades of expeditionary operations, OEO paves the way for coordinating not only US but international responses to the problems generated by disrupted states.[13]

Limitations on innovation

Although justifiably proud of their record of innovation, Marines recognise that there are limits. One is to confuse vision, or even a healthy imagination, with clairvoyance. Looking at the Marines' greatest achievement, the development of amphibious warfare, one can see both vision and limitations. In the 1930s the Marines not only resuscitated the concept of amphibious warfare discredited by the disastrous failure of the Dardanelles campaign, but developed the amphibious capabilities that led to victory in both the European and Pacific theatres in the Second World War. It is important to note, however, that in the 1930s Marines planned for the 1940s, not the 1960s. For all their vision in preparing for the Second World War, it is doubtful if any foresaw nuclear weapons, ballistic missiles and the space race. If one accepts that the rate of change in the twenty-first century will be greater than that of the mid-twentieth, the possibility of fixing on a specific distant vision is remote. And the dangers of doing so will be significant. As every commander knows, there is a very real danger in falling in love with one's plan and sticking with it even as changing conditions undermine its credibility. This is even truer of visions of the future, which are often strikingly similar to the headlines of the day. One thinks of the Maginot Line and the French vision of war. The line was a wonderful concept reflecting the best military thought of 1916, a horribly dismal thought in itself. Unfortunately, it was totally irrelevant long before the crucial test came in 1940.

A second limitation on innovation is that imposed by the success of previous endeavours. The West won the Cold War, but that victory gives rise to some hard questions. Does the United States rest on its laurels and enjoy a peace dividend or maintain a high level of preparedness? If it chooses the latter, does it invest in more of the same or attempt to reach new levels of capability far beyond those of potential rivals? Which choice is best? Which is good enough? Can it in fact choose, or will a decision be thrust upon it by unanticipated events?

These questions are not easily answered. But the mere fact of raising them may be more important than any specific answers – especially since any "answers" would be highly problematic at best. For the vision of the future is not a fixed point but a series of potential paths spiralling off in multiple, unpredictable directions. The alternative futures approach gives the best chance of "seeing" the future, but with two important caveats. One is that the horse you initially pick will not win. The other is that if you miss the indications and warnings of change *en route*, you will be doomed to failure.

To illustrate the point, one can postulate three distinct alternative futures. One is a linear progression of today's problems as a definition of the future: more major theatre wars (Desert Storm) and more operations other than war (Somalia). A second envisions a true revolution in military affairs and the emergence of a peer competitor, a state that could pose a credible threat to the United States. The third is a total breakdown of international order in which conflicts and wars become the order of the day. Of course, the future could just as easily include bits and pieces of all three, or something entirely new and unexpected.

Designing military forces based on such a wide-ranging and volatile target is a real challenge. Military doctrine, organisation, training and education will have to adapt to the full spread of possible missions and tasks. And equipment design raises a whole new set of problems. It typically takes 10 years or more from idea to production of military hardware. Since that hardware is so very expensive and lasts so long (30–50 years for ships and aircraft), armed forces can be hard pressed to build sufficient flexibility into their systems to ensure relevance across the spectrum of future requirements. The trick is to build a force that can handle the worst-case scenarios while remaining sufficiently flexible to cover the smaller contingencies. That has been the Marine Corps' forte for many years, and is the philosophy that drives its future development.

These are just a few of the factors that the Marine Corps sees as important indicators of the future, indicators that will have an impact on future operational capabilities. It is important to note that these same factors, and the effect they have on Marine Corps force development, are relevant to a wide array of organisations. Because of the large part the Marine Corps plays in the international response to disrupted states, a variety of IOs, NGOs and PVOs will be operating with Marine forces well into the century. It is therefore imperative that all partners in future operations understand the dynamics of change that will influence the interrelationships of all.

Obstacles to civil–military cooperation

Designing military forces is only one aspect of the larger problem of dealing with disrupted states. As the Marine Corps develops concepts to shape its future, it is increasingly important to formalise contacts with an ever-expanding range of agencies and organisations with which Marines will certainly work in the years ahead. To do so, each potential partner will have to move together to overcome some critical obstacles to cooperation.

First is a plethora of actors. If too many cooks spoil the broth, then the explosion in the number of governmental agencies, IOs, NGOs and PVOs is surely a recipe for confusion – especially when many are fiercely independent and in competition with each other for prestige and funds.

Second is mission clash. With so many players in a complex environment, the possibility of conflicting missions is real. A prime example is the tension between the requirements for security and those for providing humanitarian assistance. Determining which takes precedence and at what level of risk to whom (military or police forces, humanitarian relief agencies, the local populace) is a thorny issue that can seriously jeopardise the success of even the best-intentioned operation.

Third is communications. This issue takes several forms. The first, and most obvious, is that of language and cultural barriers between the local populace and the intervening forces, agencies and organisations. Only slightly less troublesome are the language and cultural differences among the interventionists themselves. Even within the same language group, the vocabularies and approaches to problem-solving will vary widely between military, governmental, scientific and humanitarian agency representatives. Second, in certain missions such as peacekeeping or consequence management, security classification of military operations will necessarily restrict the flow of information to those without clearances. At the same time, it will be important for the military to receive information from those organisations that it must exclude from a full and open exchange of information. Although not necessarily a "show stopper", the situation is understandably one that is antithetical to expanding trust, confidence and camaraderie. Third, the incompatibility of communications hardware and procedures can get in the way of progress, as can the access to radio bandwidth. This too is not a "show stopper", but advance cooperative planning between all participants would clearly make for smoother operations.

Fourth is institutional inertia. Institutions, regardless of mission, charter or purpose, find it difficult to effect changes from within. Trying to coordinate the efforts of dozens of independent and single-minded organisations may prove to be the most challenging aspect of any future contingency.

Conclusion

If one were inclined toward pessimism, the challenges of the twenty-first century would seem daunting indeed. But for all the potential problems of disrupted states and the impediments to coordinating the efforts of the international community to address them, there are many points of light. One is that the need for closer cooperation is becoming ever more apparent. Another is that a number of trends are under way that point us in the right direction. In the United States, the cause of inter-agency cooperation is being served by growing demands of humanitarian assistance/ disaster relief, consequence management, and homeland defence missions. In the international arena, several Western democracies are working seriously on expanding what can be called integrated operations. Such operations go far beyond what we now know as joint (all national services working together) and combined (different nations working together), with the goal of reducing barriers to efficient concerted action.

As it has throughout its history, the United States Marine Corps is playing a leading role in preparing for the challenges of the future. So long as the Navy–Marine Corps team continues to be the United States' force of choice for initial response, the obvious advantages of – in fact, the absolute requirement for – closer cooperation between all responders will inexorably drive the Marine Corps toward closer civil–military relations in meeting the many challenges of future disrupted states.

Notes

1. Mark Helprin, "Revolution or Dissolution?", *Forbes Magazine*, 23 February 1998, p. 88.
2. Will and Ariel Durant, *The Lessons of History* (New York: Simon & Schuster, 1971), p. 81.
3. David Fromkin, *The Way of the World: From the Dawn of Civilization to the Twenty-First Century* (New York: Alfred A. Knopf, 1999), p. 37.
4. Thomas L. Friedman, *The Lexus and the Olive Tree* (New York: Farrar, Straus, & Giroux, 1999), pp. 17, 18.
5. US Department of the Navy, *Naval Warfare Publication 1: Naval Warfare* (Washington DC: United States Government Printing Office, 1994), p. 73. The Royal Navy further defines littorals as the area 200 miles either side of the coastline. Ministry of Defence, Assistant Chief of Naval Staff, *The Contribution of Maritime Forces to Joint Operations and their Wider Utility* (United Kingdom: Maritime Warfare Centre, HMS Dryad, April 1999), p. 5.
6. Commandant of the Marine Corps, *United States Marine Corps Master Plan for the 21st Century* (Washington DC: Headquarters, United States Marine Corps, 8 October 1997), pp. 3–6.
7. Paul Kennedy, *Preparing for the Twenty-First Century* (New York: Random House, 1993), p. 45.
8. Lieutenant General Martin R. Steele, USMC, "Deep Coalitions and Interagency Task Forces", *Naval War College Review*, vol. 52, no. 1, Winter 1999, pp. 14–23 at p. 19.
9. United States Marine Corps, *Small Wars Manual* (Washington DC: United States Government Printing Office, 1940), p. 1.
10. Ibid., p. 9.
11. Ibid., pp. 15, and 16.
12. Ibid., pp. 41–47.
13. United States Marine Corps, *Other Expeditionary Operations (DRAFT)* (Washington DC: Headquarters, United States Marine Corps, July 1999).

5

Complex emergencies and military capabilities

Frederick M. Burkle, Jr

Where civil blood makes civil hands unclean – *Romeo and Juliet*

Complex emergencies today represent the ultimate pathway of state disruption. Zwi and Uglade argue that recent conflicts such as those in northern Iraq, Somalia, Rwanda, Angola, the former Yugoslavia and the province of Kosovo should be interpreted as complex political disasters where "the capacity to sustain livelihood and life is threatened primarily by political factors, and in particular, by high levels of violence".[1] Although each of the over 38 major conflicts that occurred in the decade since the end of the Cold War is unique, all share similar characteristics:
- administrative, economic, political and social decay and collapse;
- high levels of violence;
- cultures, ethnic groups and religious groups at risk of extinction;
- catastrophic public health emergencies, in which over 70 per cent of the victims are civilians, primarily children and adolescents;
- conflict is primarily internal, with major violations of the Geneva Conventions and the Universal Declaration of Human Rights;
- increased competition for resources between groups in conflict;
- increased migration of refugees or internally displaced populations;
- such emergencies are long-lasting and widespread.

The "complexity" of these emergencies refers to the multifaceted responses initiated by the international community and further complicated by the lack of protection normally afforded by international treaties, covenants and the United Nations Charter during conventional wars. It tends to be the case in such situations that, once disasters catalyse a complex emergency and expose major public health deficiencies, there is a lack of proper resources to respond, a lack of a security capacity and a lack of a management capacity – as a result of which politically favoured populations do better, with ongoing negative consequences.

Health resources, both civilian (those provided by United Nations agencies, the International Committee of the Red Cross (ICRC), the International Federation of Red Cross and Red Crescent Societies, and many non-governmental organisations) and military, have played a major part in the emergency response, recovery and rehabilitation phases of complex emergencies. In the process, health providers have made major advances in assessment, management, education, training and research,[2] and they remain among the few existing political consciences still available for vulnerable populations worldwide. To be both successful and safe in complex emergencies, health providers need to expand their knowledge base to include issues of integrated management, transportation, logistics, communication, negotiation and mediation, security and international humanitarian law.

Complex emergencies will continue to threaten the health of nations. In this chapter I describe the various contributing factors, deficiencies and needs most likely to precipitate future complex emergencies and outline the sorts of responses that will be needed to deal with them. This chapter draws not only on research but also on analysis of the experience of international and non-governmental organisations (NGOs) in dealing with many of the complex emergencies of the 1990s.

Factors influencing future complex emergencies

Complex emergencies existed during the Cold War era but responses were limited or non-existent, primarily because of vetoes on action in the UN Security Council.[3] They will probably continue as post–Cold War phenomena through the early part of the next decade, predominantly in Africa, Asia and South and Central America. As existing governments collapse, militaries become increasingly supported by undisciplined paramilitaries, while insurgents and organised gangs and warlords gain power; the collapse is usually preceded by worsening corruption, criminalisation of government and suspension of the rule of law, such as in Russia and the Congo. In disrupted states, hospitals and clinics are the first to be destroyed and the last to be rehabilitated.[4] Indigenous healthcare providers become refugees early, and those who remain, as in Rwanda and Kosovo, are often targeted or intimidated if they defend the rights of patients.

Small-scale conflicts average 25–35 each year[5] and will require cohesive sociopolitical and economic efforts to prevent them from developing into complex emergencies. By monitoring small-scale disasters we can define the "public health" capacity and capability in many countries by exposing the vulnerabilities and inequities that typically lead to conflict situations. Major humanitarian emergencies caused by natural or technological disasters (35–60 per year and 15–25 per year, respectively)[6] used to be considered conceptually separate from complex emergencies. But in weakened and disrupted states a natural disaster such as flood, famine or deforestation or a major episode of industrial poisoning can expose the same vulnerabilities.

Political and legal factors

Political and legal factors play a significant role in the generation of complex emergencies. An emerging view is that conflict related to ethnic issues is catalysed in disrupted states by the need of ethnic groups to fall back on what is considered safe and familiar.[7] Territorial buffer zones that once separated ethnic groups disappear, causing increased competition for resources and migration of large populations, either as refugees who cross national boundaries or as internally displaced populations. With the onset of complex emergencies, ethnic-based "ancient animosities" have been savage.[8] Of the more than 6,000 cultures that entered the 1990s some have disappeared through natural assimilation alone. State disruption, however, has placed many minority cultures at risk of extinction. The rate of extinction is so alarming that, if it continues, fewer than 600 cultures will remain by the year 2005.[9] Also, the more removed the culture is from the developed world, the less interest and protection it generates.

Culturally defined customs, skills and arts passed along to succeeding generations include the foundations of health and public health refinements that allow a people to survive. When a culture is lost, so too is the inextricably connected professional and institutional memory of public health measures. Mitigation of public infrastructure and rehabilitation projects alone are not enough. This raises the question of whether the loss of a culture, as a consequence of a complex emergency, should be addressed as a critical strategic, political and security issue.

Membership of the UN General Assembly broadly requires states to adhere to the Universal Declaration of Human Rights. Once the declaration is violated, several UN chapters allow the Security Council to bypass the sovereignty of the state where rights are being violated, in favour of non-permissive humanitarian intervention. Legally defining select complex emergencies such as genocide requires, under international treaty, a sanctioned external force to enter the conflict and stop the slaughter. Political failure to do so (as in Rwanda and Cambodia) has caused a widening gap between claims of protection and actual outcome. Solutions to the problems of disrupted states will require greater international political decisiveness to overcome legal constraints. A first step is to give internally displaced populations the same legal protection as refugees. Success will then be judged by a reduction in the exceedingly high mortality rates of internally displaced people and their vulnerable populations – for example, unaccompanied minors.

Socioeconomic factors

Population increases have always been a threat to social stability. It is not the increase itself but the changing patterns of population that have the greatest potential for contributing to conflict. Both have major health implications. Urban slums currently contain over half the poor people in the developing world, mostly women with children and inadequate support systems. The numbers of major cities with populations over 1 million are increasing, without a comparable growth in public health infrastructure such as sanitation, water supplies and clinic services. Migration of populations for both environmental and economic reasons will dominate the next decade, especially in Asia, where resources per head are the least. Early in the 2010s, urban populations in the developing world will exceed rural ones for the first time in history. The need for humanitarian assistance is already moving from rural to urban areas. However, critical issues such as the defence of urban public health infrastructure, sanitation and access to water are not being addressed in existing education, training, and research and management forums.

Unfortunately, political and economic realities make some victims more deserving than others, suggesting that some weakened or disrupted states – those that are considered economically interdependent and geopolitically critical by developed governments – will be favoured as recipients for humanitarian assistance and disaster relief. The future requires a transparent humanitarian architecture and a balance sheet of budgeted priorities and coordination of donor agencies that is internationally mandated and monitored. Health providers are uniquely qualified as lobbyists and advocates to diminish international fears of governmental self-interest, hypocrisy and racism in determining humanitarian priorities.

Environmental security factors

Major environmental and ecological abuses occur from deforestation, the damming of waterways, human-generated flooding and loss of topsoil, pollution and the consequences of nuclear, biological and chemical (NBC) hazards. Environmental security is aimed at preventing "serious political and social instability stemming from human activities which reduce the environment's capacity to sustain life".[10] The term encompasses many of the public health issues inherent in complex emergencies, but on a larger scale and with both national and regional ramifications. One can argue that there is a causal relation between the severe deforestation of the North Korean peninsula and environmental degradation, food and fuel scarcity and smouldering conflict. Security, in general, is being redefined. It is no longer solely thought of in terms of defence and military resources. The past decade was one of multiple failures confronting vulnerable civilian populations, forcing more attention to be placed on human, food and environmental security and demanding that governments take responsibility. Public identification of such factors will demand that governments take action even though such action might lead to military involvement.

Research issues

Initial responses in the field to complex emergencies were understandably ad hoc. No foundation of applied health research exists for complex emergencies as it does for natural and technological disasters or for conventional cross-border wars. Major challenges were quickly identified in organisational management, refugee care, triage of victims, water and sanitation, nutrition, communicable diseases, and psychosocial, gender and reproductive issues. Victims in developing countries have high mortality and morbidity from violent trauma, epidemics, starvation and severe psychosocial disabilities. These public health consequences of refugee displacement and overcrowding affect all age groups, particularly infants and children under 5.[11] Similar consequences are evident in the developed countries of Iraq, Yugoslavia and Chechnya, where heightened trauma and the complications of undernourishment, dehydration and untreated chronic diseases in infants and elderly people often dominate the clinical picture.[12]

The World Health Organization and the Macfarlane Burnet Centre for Medical Research in Melbourne have begun to document studies that will build the foundation of research.[13] One effect is that reports which first raised awareness of human rights and gender and reproductive issues are being transformed into operational programmes. Human rights abuses are now documented and a response coordinated, with early psychosocial and legal counselling offered by advocacy organisations. Gender-specific health programmes have benefited from early assessment tools and standardised management protocols.[14] Health providers must come to recognise that they often serve a wider humanitarian mitigation and prevention package that requires specialised education and training to support protection, standardised documentation and accountability for abuses.

Lack of information-sharing among major players in complex emergencies, and failed or incompatible communications systems, are important paralysing factors. Information technologies in Bosnia required high maintenance and overburdened staff resources but did not contribute to the overall efficiency of field operations. There is promise in field-tested satellite telecommunications and image-gathering, event-monitoring and early warning database systems, and handheld computer links to organisational and research centres.[15] A major challenge for information technologies is not only to aid efficiency but to serve as a tool for fostering collaboration between otherwise constrained vertical organisations.

Public health responses

Since the 1991 crisis in northern Iraq, all decision makers (civilian and military) have been required to manage the "public health". Failure to do so has been attributed partly to the inability of decision makers to consult and use public health consultants and advisers.[16] The events of the 1990s show that public health no longer refers only to health and medical care but also encompasses transportation, communication, the judiciary, public safety and all those disruptions in complex emergencies that must be corrected before a village, town, city or nation can function. This will further encourage the crossing of professional boundaries required for integrated assessments and information-sharing and ensure the place of health professionals in the planning process. In current political–military implementation plans (for example, United States Presidential Decision Directive 56), normalisation of health indicators is considered the major measure of effectiveness, yet health professionals, other than those used to serve the forces themselves, are rarely considered in planning.

Lack of education and female illiteracy have traditionally topped the list of major factors contributing to overall child mortality and morbidity in the developing world. In the 1990s, the moral integrity of governments and the presence of public health infrastructure (both absent in complex emergencies) replaced these traditional public health indicators. This is especially true in some refugee camps, where no education occurs, girls and women have no rights and receive less than their fair share of food and commodities, and male children are recruited into the military. Refugee camps are anomalies of society. Steps must be taken to prevent their growth, except in support of emergency and short-term humanitarian missions. The ability to prevent the establishment of long-term camps will be a major measure of effectiveness.[17]

Communicable diseases thrive in the overcrowded environment of camps, with unsanitary and disrupted infrastructures and promiscuous defecation by children. Initially, health programmes in complex emergencies did not deal with tuberculosis in refugee camps. However, the prevalence in camps was found to be 4–6 per cent, often with resistant forms far beyond the alert rates for conventional communities. Dengue fever has emerged as a unique economic indicator of decaying urban infrastructure, prompting closer scrutiny by economists and public health authorities alike.[18] Fears of the transnational spread of communicable diseases from camps and countries with poor public health are among the leading concerns of the developed world. The public in the developed world expects that relief programmes will not increase the risk to their lifestyles, so donors will in future demand attention to the prevention, containment and eradication of infectious agents.

The need for civil–military responses

Wanton violations of the Geneva Conventions have included unprecedented and widespread rape; massacres; sniper targeting of children, adolescents and pregnant women; attacks on feeding centre hospitals; diversion of food by warring factions; and attacks on relief workers (for example, at least 40 Red Cross workers were killed in the second half of the 1990s). Peacekeeping forces have also experienced casualty rates statistically higher than if a decisive force had been used.[19] These violations are too often relegated to minor news stories and have failed to achieve the level of international concern and debate they deserve. The success of humanitarian assistance will depend on the ability of international organisations to reinstate and enforce these basic protections.

Peacekeeping forces have been restricted by ambivalent mission statements and weak rules of engagement, making them ineffective in past complex emergencies – for example, the UN Protection Force (UNPROFOR) in former Yugoslavia. Under Chapter VII of the UN Charter, peace enforcement operations, such as those in Haiti and Kosovo, separate warring factions or quell a conflict before a peace agreement is in place. The requirements for humanitarian assistance may be at their peak during this phase. Future expectations are that the military and humanitarian relief organisations will plan and exercise together to ensure relief and security to populations during times of active conflict and heightened risk.[20] Chapter VII requires the coordination, monitoring and enforcement of international humanitarian and human rights law, so health providers must understand that the role they play in documenting abuses under the law requires a degree of civil–military collaboration without compromise of agencies' autonomy.

The future will probably provide more political clout to regional organisations, and regional peacekeeping battalions will develop under a more robust UN Standby Arrangements programme. Unfortunately, previous work to optimise civil–military coordination was compromised in the initial intervention over Kosovo, which was run by NATO. NATO political decisions had the secondary effect of bypassing the humanitarian architecture already in place, specifically the UN Office for the Coordination of Humanitarian Affairs and the early implementation of the UN High Commissioner for Refugees (UNHCR) as the lead agency for humanitarian organisations.

Managing the consequences of nuclear, chemical and biological events, whether accidental or caused by terrorists, is beyond the capabilities of most countries. Coordination of the management of consequences requires a joint process that marries governmental decision makers, tactical-level scientists, trained relief workers and the military with self-sufficient and tailored operational-level task forces. To date, only a few non-governmental organisations have shown interest in integrated education and training, and the international organisations' capabilities are lacking, especially in chemical and biological support.

A slow and somewhat unsure evolution of civil–military relations occurred in the 1990s. There was an understanding that collaboration is essential, but problematic, with both sides ambivalent about coordination and information-sharing. Describing the evolution process is difficult in itself, in that the events that drove the process were as complex as the emergencies themselves. Michael Pugh suggests that a phase-related process occurred, beginning in the early 1990s with what he refers to as the classical humanitarianism phase.[21] Here the disrupted states and the complex emergencies that they produced were considered to be short-lived events, the response to which was based primarily on humanitarian need. This phase was dominated by humanitarian relief organisations, and military involvement was considered competitive and obstructive to the impartiality and neutrality sought by the relief agencies. Pugh's second phase, referred to as political humanitarianism, evolved from awareness that assistance without a political solution achieves nothing. This mid-1990s phase favoured assistance geared toward conflict resolution, peace building and development, and policies that would achieve desirable political, social and economic outcomes. Increasingly, UN Security Council resolutions favoured human rights over sovereignty as intervention criteria, but the UN member states became more and more concerned, recognising that these complex emergencies had become more dangerous, longer lasting and more frequent.

In the late 1990s, Pugh suggests that a convergence of the first two phases occurred with recognition that these complex emergencies were indeed wars, although internal in nature, and required a military security and protection tool. Characteristic of this military humanitarianism phase is the assumption that nations have a duty to provide assistance to those with the right to receive it. What began in the early 1990s as peacekeeping operations, under Chapter VI of the UN Charter, were operational failures. Three years after UNPROFOR forces entered the former Yugoslavia, 30 new UN resolutions moved the forces under Chapter VII peace enforcement protection (non-UN and UN coalition military forces) to quell further violence, to provide protection to the humanitarian relief process and to prevent human rights abuses. Only when an accord or agreement was signed would Chapter VI forces enter as peacekeepers. As such, Chapter VII resolutions were mandated in UN Security Council decisions for Haiti, Kosovo and East Timor. These decisions also demanded improved coordination between civilian and military organisations, in security and information coordination but also in the delicate transition from peace enforcement to peacekeeping. At the same time, the UN reform movement developed a humanitarian coordination focus under the Office for the Coordination of Humanitarian Affairs (OCHA), which would supply a Humanitarian Coordinator in the field, representing the UN Secretary-General, and means to optimise civil–military coordination at every level.

The first real test of coordination under Chapter VII forces with OCHA, UNHCR and ICRC occurred in East Timor in September 1999. The International Force for East Timor (INTERFET) forces (Australia, the United Kingdom, France, New Zealand and the Philippines) prepared for deployment in northern Australia, with the UN agencies and NGOs. Initially the Humanitarian Coordinator set up a UN Civil–Military Cooperation (CIMIC) team in Darwin to optimise close cooperation with the military forces and, upon deployment to Dili, the coordination centre in Darwin became a logistical support centre. OCHA coordination functions occurred simultaneously in Geneva and in the Office of the UN Resident Coordinator in Jakarta; a UN Humanitarian Operations Centre (UNHOC) and eventually a UN CIMIC team operated in Dili, with the aim of establishing a Joint Civil–Military Logistics Centre in-country. The CIMIC team also developed a civil–military cooperation document designed to defuse civil–military competition over resources and to coordinate the use of military resources in direct support of humanitarian assistance operations. In time, CIMIC had representation from civilians and military personnel from indigenous, UN and non-UN organisations. At daily meetings, INTERFET-provided security updates, requests for facility protection and security escorts for relief convoys were the focus of discussions. The UN CIMIC staff pressed INTERFET not to replace civilian resources but to complement them. It became clear that, under a Chapter VII situation, a different order of priorities would need to be established with both military and civilian planners. Under the old military model, INTERFET also established its own Civil–Military Operations Centre (CMOC). This functioned as an information and logistics centre for the UN agencies and NGOs but was felt to be less instrumental and effective than the INTERFET CIMIC representation at the UN CIMIC meetings.

As regards lessons learned, Elmquist, Chief of the Military and Civil Defence Unit for OCHA, suggests that the "civil–military relationship consists of three parts: 1) joint planning, 2) coordination of military support to humanitarian operations performed by civilian agencies/organizations, and 3) coordination ... of humanitarian operations performed by the military at their own initiative".[22] If we embrace Pugh's concept of phase-related evolution in civil–military operations, Chapter VII operations will remain dominant, forcing the international community to refine the coordination process and to define the specific roles of the coordination bodies. These must be adopted, by both civilians and military, as inherent and instinctive to operational responsibilities and not be left to ad hoc decisions of commanders in the field. In addition, the traditional crisis action planning cycle inherent in most militaries leaves little room for coordination of civilian organisations until the execution phase of deployment. In the East Timor operation, the Task Force Commander and OCHA's Humanitarian Coordinator did not meet to discuss their future cooperation prior to deployment from Darwin. Civilian organisations need to be an integral part of the early planning cycle along with development of integrated measures of effectiveness. This concept, although offered as a solution and as a lesson learned, has been resisted, primarily by the military, for too long. Similar entrenchment of territory denies planners reasonable options, not only for complex emergencies but also for consequence management of NBC events and other large-scale disasters, where the public demands responsible civil–military coordination and cooperation.

Much of the success in East Timor has been attributed to the leadership and experience of the OCHA Humanitarian Coordinator. This underscores the need to ensure professionalism and operational respect in the decision-making ranks, both civilian and military. As of this writing, the Chapter VII force, led by the Australian Defence Force, has been redeployed, shifting leadership to a multinational Chapter VI peacekeeping force led by the Philippines. A continuing dilemma is to determine when a definable end-state exists, what measures success, and who decides.

Lastly, when the international relief community entered East Timor they encountered endemic diseases such as dengue fever, malaria, Japanese B encephalitis and skin disorders. Individual Australian Defence Force units suffered compromise from both dengue and malaria outbreaks. Preventive medical measures, whether civilian or military, are the only way to control, prevent and mitigate such diseases. Poisonous snakes, scorpions and plants are common dangers to which many relief workers were unaccustomed. Non-medical factors in water, sanitation and shelter contributed to the mortality of infants and children under the age of 5 in West Timor refugee camps. Within East Timor, the majority of internally displaced persons sought refuge with relatives, making it difficult to determine the number of displaced persons in need.

Conclusion

The 1990s will be viewed as the decade of the emergence of complex political disasters, but we are unlikely to see the end of them. Many people argue that the role of the international community and the effectiveness of humanitarian assistance have been seriously flawed. Even though health programmes have matured greatly, with the professionalisation of providers, codes of conduct,[23] and research and field-based education programmes, health providers have been frustrated at meeting the challenge to save lives, only to find themselves sliding back into crisis again. The lessons gained from experience in recent complex emergencies will have ready application to future political trials and conflicts.

Acknowledgements

An earlier version of this chapter appeared in the *British Medical Journal*, vol. 319, 14 August 1999, pp. 422–426.

Notes

1. A. Zwi and A. Uglade, "Political Violence in the Third World: A Public Health Issue", *Health Policy and Planning*, vol. 6, 1991, pp. 203–217.
2. See Médecins sans Frontières, *Refugee Health: An Approach to Emergency Situations* (London: Macmillan, 1997); Michael J. Toole and Ronald J. Waldman, "Refugees and Displaced Persons: War, Hunger and Public Health", *Journal of the American Medical*

Association, vol. 270, 1993, pp. 600–605; M. Toole, S. Galson and W. Brady, "Are War and Public Health Compatible?", *The Lancet*, vol. 341, 1993, pp. 1193–1196; Pierre Perrin (ed.), *Handbook on War and Public Health* (Geneva: International Committee of the Red Cross, 1996).
3. John Borton, "An Account of Coordination Mechanisms for Humanitarian Assistance during the International Response to the 1994 Crisis in Rwanda", *Disasters*, vol. 20, 1996, pp. 305–323.
4. Robin M. Coupland, "Epidemiological Approach to Surgical Management of the Casualties of War", *British Medical Journal*, vol. 308, 1994, pp. 1693–1697.
5. *World Conflict List* (Alexandria: National Defense Council Foundation, 1 June 1998).
6. Ibid.
7. See H. Kane, "The Hour of Departure: Forces that Create Refugees and Migrants", *Worldwatch*, June 1995, pp. 18–25; United Nations High Commissioner for Refugees, *The State of the World's Refugees: A Humanitarian Agenda 1998–1999* (New York: United Nations, 1999); International Federation of Red Cross and Red Crescent Societies, *World Disasters Report 1997* (Oxford: Oxford University Press, 1997).
8. Shashi Tharoor, "Confronting Ancient Animosities", *Washington Post* (National Weekly Edition), 16 February 1998, p. 34.
9. Public Broadcasting System, *All Things Considered: Cultures* (Washington DC: National Public Radio, 1997).
10. A. L. Bradshaw, *International Environmental Security: The Regional Dimensions* (Carlisle Barracks, PA: Center for Strategic Leadership, 1998).
11. See B. T. Burkholder and M. J. Toole, "Evolution of Complex Emergencies", *The Lancet*, vol. 346, pp. 1012–1014; Division of Emergency and Humanitarian Action, *Applied Health Research in Emergency Settings* (Geneva: World Health Organization; Melbourne: Macfarlane Burnet Centre for Medical Research, 1999).
12. R. Brennan and B. T. Burkholder, unpublished data.
13. Division of Emergency and Humanitarian Action, *Applied Health Research in Emergency Settings*.
14. Reproductive Health of Refugees Consortium, *Refugees and Reproduction Health Care: The Next Step* (New York: International Rescue Committee, 1998); Celia Palmer, Louisiana Lush and Anthony Zwi, "The Emergency Policy Agenda for Reproductive Health Services among Populations Affected by Conflict", *Disasters*, vol. 22, 1998, pp. 236–249.
15. V. Garshnek, K. Shinchi and F. M. Burkle, "Disaster Assessment and Satellite Communications on the Threshold of a New Era", *Space Policy*, vol. 14, 1998, pp. 223–227.
16. Larry Minear, Thomas G. Weiss and Kurt Campbell, *Humanitarianism and War: Learning the Lessons from Recent Armed Conflicts* (Providence, RI: Thomas J. Watson Jr Institute for International Studies, Brown University, 1991).
17. F. M. Burkle, Jr, K. A. W. McGrady, S. L. Newett, J. J. Nelson, J. T. Dworken, W. H. Lyerly, Jr, A. S. Natsios and S. R. Lillibridge, "Complex, Humanitarian Emergencies: III. Measures of Effectiveness", *Prehospital Disaster Medicine*, vol. 10, 1995, pp. 48–56.
18. "Dengue Fever, a Man-made Disease", *The Economist*, 2 May 1998, p. 21.
19. Barry M. Blechman and J. Matthew Vaccaro, *Training for Peacekeeping: The United Nations' Role* (Washington, DC: Henry L. Stimson Center, 1994), pp. 1–36.
20. Frederick M. Burkle, Jr, "Military Security: Lessons for Relief", in Jennifer Leaning, Susan M. Briggs and Lincoln C. Chen (eds), *Humanitarian Crises: The Medical and Public Health Response* (Cambridge, MA: Harvard University Press, 1999), pp. 293–307.
21. Michael Pugh, "Intervention and Humanitarian Actions: Trends and Issues", *Disasters*, vol. 22, no. 4, 1998, pp. 339–351.

22. M. Elmquist, *CIMIC in East Timor* (Geneva: Disaster Response Branch, UN Office for the Coordination of Humanitarian Affairs, 1999).
23. *Humanitarian Charter and Minimum Standards in Disaster Response* (Geneva: Sphere Project, 1998), pp. 2–56.

Part 3
Ending violence

6
Violence, sovereignty and conflict resolution

Raimo Väyrynen

The nature of contemporary conflict

Civil war has been a constant feature of international relations; it was not invented in the 1990s. During some historical periods, the state has been able to monopolise violence in society but, as a rule, the centralised control of violence has not been enduring. Domestic order has been broken down by civil wars, revolts and famines and by other humanitarian disasters. Alternatively, the coercive power has been centralised so strongly in the hands of the autocratic state that people have had only very limited opportunities to exercise their rights. Predatory rulers have never disappeared, and this very fact has also helped to catalyse popular responses.[1]

Only in the second half of the twentieth century did developed societies seem to move to a stable internal peace in which the risk of civil war had all but disappeared. The exceptions are those countries, such as the United Kingdom and Spain, where ethnic or religious tensions continue to engender violence. However, compared with most civil wars, the number of casualties in these conflicts has remained quite small and is now, moreover, in decline. In developed countries, traffic accidents are the biggest risk for most people.

Domestic terrorism does not usually serve any integral political function but, as Michel Wieviorka says, it "betrays the disintegration of some collective action".[2] In that sense, terrorism is a failed form of transformative political action. Domestic terrorism purports to challenge, through assassinations and kidnappings, the state monopoly of violence, but usually the result is the opposite – the surveillance and repression of the opposition by the state is strengthened further. In reality, domestic terrorism in industrialised countries is increasingly a reflection of international terrorism because the purely domestic sources of terrorist violence have been drying up. Terrorist acts may still be carried out by secessionist groups, as Chechens have done in different parts of Russia, but intrastate terrorism has lost its power and justification.

In contrast, international terrorism continues to be active and it has become, moreover, increasingly professional and technically savvy. Such terrorism grows, in part, out of the economic and political dislocations in the world's peripheral areas where there are pools of unemployed young men waiting for recruitment. Their employers, however, tend to be educated and experienced men who run the terrorist networks like a transnational corporation, which has its own sources of income, employees, training facilities and insurance systems for the families. The difference is in the goals: terrorist organisations aim to spread uncertainty and fear, using them to pursue a variety of political goals (although some groups are in the terrorism business mostly for money).

Some terrorist organisations aim at a revolution that would alter the political structure and ideological principles of the target society. Terrorism is, however, too weak and counterproductive an instrument to kindle social or religious revolutions, whose outbreak requires bigger socioeconomic grievances and political discontentment. In other words, revolutions can seldom be started from the top or from outside.

Historical evidence makes it clear that major interstate wars have often been precipitants of revolutions. On the other hand, revolutionary societies are often eager either to spread the revolution or to defend its results. This tends to lead to wars by revolutionary states against status quo powers. Recently, however, the revolutionary tide seems to have subsided, even though it is probably too early to suggest that revolutions belong to history. They are a possibility as long as the global economic realities and cultural conceptions of modernity continue to displace and clash with the traditional social structures and cultural values.[3]

Against this backdrop, it can be suggested that the almost non-existent threat of civil war in industrialised countries is associated with the waning risk of interstate wars among the leading powers. Here the causality seems to be going in both directions: internal stability and democracy contribute to peaceful external relations, but international peace also helps to maintain domestic tranquillity. In the end, neither lasting domestic stability nor interstate peace may be possible without the other.

This statement can be critically tested by the experiences of the countries in transition from a centralised economic and political system to a market economy and democratic polity. In some cases, such as the Czech Republic and Slovakia, the secession or division of political units has taken place peacefully, but in many others the result has been violent. In the former Soviet Union, one need only mention Chechnya, Abkhazia and South Ossetia in Georgia, and Transdniestria in Moldova. In all these cases, separatist movements, often with external support, have resorted to arms against a sovereign state. This support has typically come from within Russia.[4]

The important thing is that, in all these cases, warfare has remained geographically limited; it has not escalated horizontally to encompass relations between sovereign state actors (although some might consider the war in Chechnya to be an interstate war, not to speak of wars in the former Yugoslavia). The only clear-cut exception in the former Soviet Union is the war between Armenia and Azerbaijan over Nagorno Karabakh. This has clearly been an interstate conflict over the control of a contested territory and its ethnic character.

Today, we have reached a situation in which major intra- and interstate wars in Europe have been declining for several decades, thus realising the hope of peaceful change and giving rise to a security community among industrialised countries. One has to be a diehard realist to dare to predict that there is a real risk of war between states in the transatlantic or the European system. This is a result of the maturing of an international system in which internally stable and mutually interdependent sovereign states manage their relations in a peaceful manner.

In interstate relations, a similar positive development can be discerned in selected regions of the South, including Latin America, South-East Asia and possibly East Asia. In these regions, various security regimes and limited security communities have been growing more robust. On the other hand, in most regions there are still major risks of internal instability, owing either to domestic conflicts or external pressures, which might escalate into interstate confrontations. This risk is very obvious in the Middle East, whereas in South Asia, despite the precarious situation in Pakistan, the risk seems to be different; if a war starts there, it will be the result of tensions between states.

Regional cases

The situation in South America is intriguing; since the 1940s, countries in the region have been able to avoid major interstate wars (the limited border war between Ecuador and Peru or the past tensions between Argentina and Chile notwithstanding). The history of the political and military relations of South American countries is complex and punctuated by military rivalries and even wars. However, interstate war has been withering away in the post-war period and, according to some views, in irreversible manner since 1975–1980. This shift means that a major military confrontation in the region has become increasingly unlikely.[5]

This has been the case in spite of domestic economic turmoil, political instability and military intervention in most countries of the region. Some argue that, in South America, a firewall has been successfully set up between intra- and interstate conflicts. A recent counterexample to this conclusion is obviously Colombia, whose civil war is spilling over to neighbouring countries, especially Ecuador and Venezuela. Yet even in this case the risk that governments will start a war with each other seems to be small (especially now that Peru has settled its border disputes with Chile and Ecuador and Argentina and Chile have made similar progress).

Even if the focus is shifted to Central America, the conclusion on the existence of a firewall seems to hold. True, in the 1980s and the early 1990s, Central America was in turmoil, and civil wars and humanitarian emergencies were plaguing the area. The ideological character of the conflicts converted them into a regional confrontation in which intrastate fighting became associated with political coalitions and military confrontations across the borders. However, after peace in Central America was gradually achieved in the 1990s, it has taken hold and the return to large-scale civil wars, not to speak of the risk of interstate wars, is unlikely.

Thus in South America, and less firmly in Central America, internal stability and external peace have become mutually reinforcing. As a result, state failures, for either internal or external reasons, are unlikely. This makes it justified to speak, as Kacowicz does, of a zone of peace in the region. Latin America has become a rather rare case in the South where major international interventions are not needed to extinguish civil wars and to provide relief in the humanitarian crises associated with them. This does not mean, of course, that all is well in the region; social dislocations and economic crises have fuelled violent protests, as has happened, for instance, in Argentina and Bolivia. Moreover, political stability continues to be precarious in Ecuador and Venezuela too.

In South-East Asia, the region has been plagued by political, financial and environmental crises in which the Association of South East Asian Nations (ASEAN) has been relatively powerless to intervene. Political problems have been manifested by autocratic regimes, irregular power transfers and the resort to violence in the struggle for resources and ethno-religious dominance. The after-effects of the 1997 economic crisis are still felt owing to its negative social consequences and the continued fragility of the financial systems. The problems have been particularly pronounced in the most populous country of the region, Indonesia, where violence has been widespread and the social crisis serious.[6]

Yet, interstate relations, even within the expanded ASEAN, have been relatively peaceful; many scholars argue that a stable peace zone of sorts has been created in the region. Compared with the instability in the region in the 1960s, and even in the 1970s, this is undoubtedly a remarkable development. This "long peace" since 1968 has been often interpreted as resulting from the special "ASEAN Way" of consultation and consensus among the member states. Despite adverse historical and geographical factors and cultural differences, an authoritarian social construction of peace seems to be possible.[7]

A more critical interpretation suggests, though, that the primary purpose of the ASEAN Way has been to avoid interventions that could have undermined the position of a "fellow" authoritarian government.[8] If this interpretation is accepted, then the authoritarian peace in ASEAN could be jeopardized by the gradual democratisation of the region. So far, the internal turmoil – primarily in Burma, Indonesia and the Philippines – has not spilled across international borders, causing violent conflicts between member states.

An interstate war in South-East Asia is unlikely, but there are fears that, owing to the potential internal instabilities, ASEAN will turn out to be an incomplete, "imitation community". This observation leads to a rather pessimistic conclusion: "ASEAN, to put it bluntly, has floundered in its attempts to manage both the regional economic crisis and its legacy of intercommunal violence. Its doctrine of non-interference in the internal affairs of member states has only intensified the failure."[9] It is seems that the process of nation- and state-building in South-East Asia has not progressed as far as it has in Latin America, where it has had more time to mature.

In Africa, the distinction between civil and international wars is not, in most cases, very meaningful. In the Democratic Republic of the Congo, for instance, the internal and external dimensions of war are rolled into one regional conflict formation, which has proved to be almost intractable. Its individual political elements can be separated only with difficulty from the whole in which the struggle for the control of natural resources is an important factor. In general, the Great Lakes region is divided not so much by international boundaries as by the ethnic divisions and economic spheres of influence cutting across borders.

Similarly, in the West African conflict formation comprising Liberia, Sierra Leone and Guinea, internal and external aspects of the crisis are inextricably interlinked. As is well known, in both Liberia and Sierra Leone the humanitarian emergency has resulted from the military operations and atrocities that the various factions have used to maintain their control of lucrative deposits of and trade in natural resources, especially diamonds and tropical wood. Subregional links are reflected, for instance, in the support of Charles Taylor's Liberia for the Revolutionary United Front opposition in Sierra Leone, whose refugee crisis has, in turn, spilled over into Guinea, destabilising that country. Fortunately peace seems to be dawning in Sierra Leone, but unfortunately not in the entire region. Most recently, Taylor's government has expanded its military operations to Guinea in order to stem the spread of rebellion against his government.[10]

The informal political and economic map of Africa is very different from the formal boundaries of the region. Ethnic ties and transnational trading networks cut across the national borders drawn by the colonial powers. Efforts at democratisation and economic reforms interact in a complex manner with patron–client relations and are a potential source of political and military instability within countries. At the same time, internal changes are contagious and affect developments in other countries. The divide between the internal and external spheres of states is more often than not blurred and ambiguous. Therefore, the sovereignty of African states is frequently more imagined than real and exists only because of its recognition by and the support of the former colonial power and international institutions.[11]

The problem of civil and cross-border wars is not as pervasive in Europe, the Middle East and most parts of Asia as it is in Africa. Yet there are several regions in which either such wars are raging or the hold of peace is tenuous. Military stability has been gradually restored in most of the Balkans, but the situation continues to be precarious, especially in the subregion composed of Kosovo, Macedonia, Montenegro and Serbia. The South Caucasus is not as volatile as it used to be in the early 1990s, but Georgia remains badly divided, no real end is in sight of the fighting in Chechnya, and the conflict over Nagorno Karabakh continues despite some rapprochement. In addition, the war in Afghanistan is spilling over to the region, especially Georgia.

The threat of instability and violence continues to be pervasive in Central Asia, where Tajikistan is the most volatile and destitute of the countries in the region, but the risk of instability exists in Kyrgyzstan and possibly also Uzbekistan. The mixture of elements of autocratic governments and religious fundamentalism, oil and great power interests does not bode well for a stable future. The war in Afghanistan has stimulated great power interest in Central Asia, manifested in new military deployments and political presence. An interstate war in the region is unlikely and, over the short term, the external presence may even have stabilising effects. However, internal problems in the countries of the region are serious and may well continue to spill across borders.[12]

In South Asia there are several military hotspots, including Kashmir, civil war in Sri Lanka and escalating violence in Nepal. In Sri Lanka,

Norwegian mediation has brought some prospects for peace in the war-torn country, whereas in Nepal violence between the government and rebels has been escalating. The pressures to find a peaceful solution to the Kashmiri conflict have increased, but it seems to be as intractable as ever. Even the failure of the Pakistani state, suffering from internal instability and economic predicament, cannot be entirely excluded from the realm of possibilities. Such a risk is minimal in India, although it too is dotted with several local conflicts in which communal violence is a dominant mode.

East Asia has escaped both internal and interstate war for almost half a century now. Despite some predictions to the contrary, the internal stability of China is hardly threatened in the short- or even medium-term future. The only country in the region where there is a real threat of an internal meltdown is North Korea, which suffers from a combination of political autocracy, economic backwardness and humanitarian crises. In interstate relations, the biggest risk of conflict is in relations between China and Taiwan.[13] The future of these relations hinges on their competing claims of sovereignty over the island, and obviously also on US policy in the region.

If, in a somewhat Eurocentric fashion, Europe is regarded as a benchmark of stable peace, in which both internal and external stability coincide, what does the rest of the world look like? It seems that South America comes closest to that benchmark because respect for national sovereignty and internal democratisation seem to be mutually supportive, although economic crises are wreaking social and political havoc. One finds similar features in the sovereignty–stability nexus in the ASEAN and East Asian cases, although in both of these regions there are some rather serious threats of domestic instability (especially in Burma, Indonesia, possibly the Philippines, and North Korea).

One can nevertheless argue that all these regions have been moving in the direction of stable peace zones. Save for the Palestinian issue, this development is not entirely inconceivable in the Middle East and Maghreb either, although for many this conclusion may seem overly optimistic. South Asia remains a question mark and could either slide into instability and war or gradually institutionalise peaceful relations both internally and between states. However, most countries are quite deeply divided along regional, ethnic or religious lines, and this fosters instability and creates problems for the territorial definition of their sovereignty.

The political, economic and ethnic borders between the internal and the external have largely collapsed in most parts of Africa, and military clashes have become involved in the transnational and regional conflict formations. A similar development can be discerned in Central Asia and, to a lesser degree, in the Caucasus. In Central Asia, cross-cutting ethnic and economic ties, especially in the Ferghana Valley, pose challenges to the national definition of sovereignty of the states in the region. In the Caucasus, this problem is posed by the interstate contestation over various enclaves and their conflict-ridden relations with the central governments.

In the 1980s and the 1990s a similar regional combination of internal and external conflicts appeared in Central America and the Balkans. However, in both of them a certain process of restructuring and consolidation of the nation-states is now taking place. In fact, Central America may be becoming a fairly durable peace zone. In the subregional system composed of Serbia, Macedonia, Montenegro and Kosovo (and even Bosnia), on the other hand, this process continues to be quite tenuous. Much depends on the future status of Kosovo, the resolution of the ethno-political conflict in Macedonia and the constitutional settlement of relations between Serbia and Montenegro. The combination of internal stability and external sovereignty in Slovenia and Croatia is showing the way to the rest of former Yugoslavia and its neighbours.

Sovereignty

The global tour in the previous section lends support to one, admittedly hypothetical, conclusion: the institutionalisation of national sovereignty contributes to the internal and external stability of a region. In other words, sovereignty matters and it seems to matter a lot.[14] As a rule, the neighbours respect each other's territories and borders, and do not make military efforts to alter them. Not only has the norm of territorial integrity rooted deeper than ever before in international relations, but sovereignty has become a sort of semi-public good. It is divided, by definition, among the state actors and it seems to have beneficial contextual effects that all state actors can enjoy. If this is the case, we can speak of the gradual emergence of a global political culture centred on the respect for national sovereignty that even prompts efforts to rebuild states that have failed.

This view can be contrasted with the argument that national self-determination, which often directly contradicts the principle of sovereignty, is becoming an international norm. This argument is based on a selective reading of history: national sovereignty and self-determination have not necessarily been opposed to each other; they may both have been subjected to the imperial overlay or they have been fused into a synthesis of the "nation-state".[15] However, during the past couple of hundred years, the state seems to have been the winner and self-determination the loser, but is the tide turning now?

If it is, will the norm of national self-determination seriously challenge that of territorial sovereignty to solve the contradiction, which has been characterised as a "glaring logical and ethical inconsistency". Those who believe in the growing confrontation between statist and communal forms of political organisations have made efforts to reconcile, in various practical ways, these two competing norms and their implications for the political order.[16] There are, indeed, examples of national self-determination making progress – including East Timor and Kosovo – but these have invariably been assisted by the international community. As a result of the ceasefire concluded in February 2002, the Tamil nation in Sri Lanka may gain more autonomy – one of the few cases in which the United Nations has not been involved.

In most other cases, the norm of national self-determination seems to apply much more strongly to external than to internal colonies. In the case of external colonies, the recognition and enforcement of the self-determination norm do not violate the core elements of the sovereignty doctrine, whereas realisation of the self-determination norm would do so.[17] The harsh treatment of internal colonies by the capitals – for instance Moscow's policy in Chechnya or Beijing's in Xinjiang – is testimony to the importance attached to the principle of sovereignty and control of internal peripheries.[18] In sum, in the contest between sovereignty and self-determination, sovereignty seems to be winning hands down, both historically and today.

This suggests that the institution and norm of national sovereignty can be an important element in efforts to prevent and resolve violent conflicts. One reason for this is that sovereignty is conducive to identity-building, which in turn supports domestic political authority and legitimacy. Although economic globalisation has been seen, often in an exaggerated way, as undermining the state and its authority, it has also been noted that, "as a dimension of state sovereignty, identity is the least affected by globalization".[19] It can thus be assumed that, if the identity, diversity and legitimacy of the state can be consolidated, the sovereignty principle will be recognised and the ensuing contentment will be able to tame any aggressive tendencies in foreign policy.

Of course, this assertion runs counter to much of the literature that suggests that sovereignty and nationalism are major causes of wars because they divide political units into mutually antagonistic containers of power. In addition, one has to admit that this generalisation is based on the European, North American, Latin American and, to some extent, South-East Asian and East Asian experiences. In all these regions, the predominant principle of regional politics is the non-intervention of states in each other's internal affairs and mutual respect for territorial integrity. Mark W. Zacher has even argued that the decline of "coercive territorial revisionism" has ushered in a new international norm of territorial integrity, especially since the Second World War. An important reason for this change, in addition to ideational factors, is that regional and global economic integration has significantly reduced the gains to be derived from territorial conquest.[20]

This means that, in addition to legal sovereignty, a Westphalian sovereignty prevails in these regions; states do not try forcibly to infiltrate the domestic authority structures of other states. Relations between states are based on mutual conventions and contracts instead of coercion or imposition.[21] By avoiding interference in the internal affairs of neighbours, and thus respecting the norm of sovereignty, states at the same time protect their own internal sovereignty.

This interpretation approaches the traditional idea that sovereignty is the central constitutive feature of both the territorial state and the contemporary international system, and possibly a main cause of peace. It is also opposed to interventionist policies conducted in the name of humanitarianism. As Friedrich Kratochwil argues, an approach stressing the principle of sovereignty leads to a rather restrictive view of the permissibility of external intervention without the consent of the target country. According to this view, intervention is acceptable only if it is undertaken in accordance with Chapter VII of the UN Charter.[22]

The conclusion emerging from this analysis is that the institutionalisation and the strengthening of comprehensive sovereignty seem to contribute to stable internal and external relations between states. This presupposes, of course, that they do not use their sovereign status contrary to international law; in other words, as a platform for the accumulation of offensive military capabilities and territorial expansion. In fact, we are speaking here of a kind of benign sovereignty that establishes a contract for the proper rules of territorial behaviour between states and permits them to expand non-territorial economic and cultural exchanges, usually between non-state actors. In fact, these exchanges may promote cooperative security and peace more effectively than sovereignty, whose impact is more indirect than direct.

To be able to promote peace, states should adopt the principle of sovereignty in its entirety and not use some of its components selectively. Another way to tackle this issue is to say that "dynastic" sovereignty is bad, whereas "civic" sovereignty and nationalism are good. In other words, sovereignty is conducive to peace if it grows out of relatively decentralised political and economic systems within states. This comes close to stating that democratic and capitalist sovereignty is better than autocratic and planned sovereignty. Sovereignty thus becomes an intermediary mechanism by which the internal system of the state is projected outside and related to other states.

What does this mean in practice today? In regions that have been ravaged and disrupted by wars, the only viable route to peace is the reestablishment of sovereign states whose mutual relations are regulated by international laws and other rules. It is difficult to think that there is any other way for a failed state, or region for that matter, to reach a stable political arrangement. The reason for this is that compliance with the norms of sovereignty creates an equilibrium that is easy to understand and follow if all the states in the region are status quo powers. In such an equilibrium, external powers are also inhibited from intervening in a malign manner in intraregional affairs and thus wrecking the peace.[23]

With the new millennium, the process of sovereign consolidation has started in the Balkans, where Slovenia has already crossed the finishing line and Croatia is approaching it. The power transition in Serbia opened up new possibilities for moving in this direction, but the process has only just started and the issue of sovereignty remains unresolved in relation to Montenegro, Kosovo and perhaps even Bosnia. In Macedonia, the establishment of stable sovereign statehood continues to be an open issue; consolidation of its external sovereignty requires the finalisation of arrangements that will assure internal peace. Final peace will not return to the Balkans until the states in the region establish a full internal and external sovereignty that is reasonably democratic in nature.

In the Caucasus, there are some encouraging signs, especially in relations between Armenia and Azerbaijan, but the sovereignty of Georgia, without even mentioning Chechnya, remains badly compromised. Central Asia is frozen in a time warp: its relative stability is maintained by dynastic internal rule that has so far helped to contain conflicts that are festering in the region. These conflicts are a volatile combination of the suppression of opposition, economic decline, environmental deterioration, ethnic competition and religious fundamentalism. War in Afghanistan and the presence of foreign forces in some of the Central Asian countries have postponed the time of reckoning, but they cannot ensure their internal stability over the long term.

The consolidation of pre-existing national sovereignties is, of course, a conservative strategy that contradicts the principle of national self-determination, which continues to have supporters among both the subordinated populations and international academic experts. The advocacy of self-determination is manifested in calls to partition existing political units and in that way to provide critical national groups with their own national state.

What if this goal requires the division of existing, legally independent, states? Does the control of violence in the Balkans require Bosnia's partitioning and Kosovo's and Montenegro's independence? Will the situation in South Caucasus continue to produce casualties until Georgia is divided and Chechnya becomes independent? In particular, Mearsheimer,

Van Evera and Kaufmann have consistently advocated such solutions, although with some reservations and qualifications.[24]

In some cases – for example, where the prevailing division has become so artificial that no one is seriously committed to it any more – the consolidation of sovereignty by dividing an existing political unit may be a necessary step to peace. In Africa in particular, where current political divisions may cut seriously across existing lines of identity, such as the Hutu–Tutsi divide in the Great Lakes region, it has been suggested that only the reorganisation of the entire political map of the region would be able to bring about stability.[25] Africa can also be used as an example where the public nature of statehood has been privatised and a plethora of non-state actors, from mercenaries to diamond dealers, have emerged to complement and even displace the state.[26]

In such a fragmented continent, it would be an onerous and perhaps impossible task to create robust sovereign states. This effort would be hindered not so much by ethnic divisions as by the prominence of kinship-based dynasties and even tyrannies.[27] Partly for this reason, it would be difficult to establish any alternative political organisation that would give a new lease of life to territorial states, however weak and artificial. It is always more costly to set up new political institutions than to let the old ones linger on and try to strengthen them.

In sum, one should not underestimate the practical difficulties of establishing new sovereign territorial units. One needs to ask who would do it and with what resources and goals in mind. Moreover, one should not underestimate the human costs of territorial separation. In multi-ethnic regions, such a strategy might well require extensive population transfers that would uproot people from their homes and create new sources of conflict. The basic objection to the partitioning approach is that the consolidation of sovereignty is a long-term process that necessarily takes time. Therefore, the establishment of a new sovereign entity first of all does not help to solve most of the problems, and it often creates new troubles, such as confrontations between those who stayed and those who left and are now returning.

There is also evidence to counter the emphasis on sovereignty as a benign conflict resolution method. In the Middle East, one could argue, both territorial division and national sovereignty are quite well established (with the exception, of course, of the Palestinian issue). Yet, the prospects of either internal turmoil or external aggression cannot be ruled out in the region. There are almost daily forecasts of imminent unrest in countries such as Egypt and Saudi Arabia. An important reason for the failure of the Arab countries to consolidate their national existence is the economic stalemate and perhaps the appeal of pan-Arab identities (in the plural rather than in the singular).

The same conclusion may apply to South Asia, where India remains at loggerheads with Pakistan over Kashmir and has a porous and uncontrollable border with Bangladesh. In North-East Asia, despite the strict territorial division and formal sovereignty of both South and North Korea, their relations can hardly be characterised as stable, despite rays of sunshine in recent years. On the other hand, the consolidation of China's sovereignty on the mainland seems successfully to have served its own coherence and the stability of the entire region.

These examples suggest that either the benevolent effects of sovereignty can be overwhelmed by ideological tensions and the competition for power (South Asia and Israel–Palestine relations) or sovereignty can be converted into an asset serving hostile purposes (the Korean Peninsula). In addition, the risk of a military confrontation between China and Taiwan is all about sovereignty: Taiwan's international status continues to be controversial and China will in no circumstances accept Taiwan's formal independence. Thus, respect for the principle of sovereignty and its consolidation is not a panacea in mitigating and solving violent conflicts, but it seems to be the best general approach.

Does external intervention work?

A corollary of the emphasis on the virtues of sovereignty is that external intervention in the internal affairs of other states should be avoided for both legal and practical reasons. A conviction has been growing that very little good will follow from the intervention, even if the intention is to mitigate the consequences of a violent conflict and humanitarian emergency in the target country. This advice has gained support from experiences in places such as Somalia and Angola and historical evidence that external interventions in general have failed to produce any lasting and tangible results.[28]

The non-intervention prescription is, however, controversial and runs counter to recent international efforts to develop more effective and just methods of conflict management in which international engagement and assistance have been considered to be key elements. In effect, these are efforts to develop a new doctrine of humanitarian intervention that is both effective and legitimate and, therefore, is bound to be limited. In addition, the horrendous consequences of non-intervention, especially in Rwanda in 1994, are a constant reminder that non-action should not be accepted as an option in some circumstances.

The question is, in other words, to what extent is the international community able and willing to stave off or resolve violence. The hardest cases are areas where intra- and interstate wars are waged and may even have crystallised into a semi-permanent and intractable condition of regional conflict formation. A reasonable answer to this dilemma seems to be that, although the chances of successful international intervention are almost always limited, it should be tried anyway, at least in some form, because of the high costs of inaction. However, owing to various constraints on intervention and its results, there is no single and simple formula for its planning and conduct.

Leaving aside interventions made in the name of collective security, the primary argument for intervention is the humanitarian one; i.e. the costs of inaction are too high to be tolerated. Of course, intervention may also aim to prevent the horizontal spread of violence to other countries in the region. In recent times, some efforts have been made to estimate the opportunity costs of international (in)action in humanitarian and other crises. A standard conclusion has been that the economic and human costs of inaction are almost always higher than those of a preventive engagement.[29]

Therefore, it seems to make sense to launch preventive diplomatic and even military operations even if they are considered to have only limited effectiveness. As mentioned above, the Rwandan example is repeatedly quoted as evidence of how the reluctance of international actors, including the United States and the United Nations, to become engaged in the crisis permitted an unbearable human toll. Even the dispatch of a few thousand peacekeepers would have significantly limited the number of victims.[30] Similarly, the delay in international action in Bosnia in 1992–1995 obviously significantly increased the human costs of the conflict compared with early engagement.

According to another argument for international engagement, it is better to launch it early on because intervention cannot be avoided in any case; in the end, learning about atrocities, the mass media and international public opinion will pressure governments to act. Obviously, early action to shape the situation on the ground has more influence than late intervention when the conflict has already deteriorated. Despite sceptical counterarguments, one should not underestimate the role of the media and public opinion in galvanising governments and international organisations into humanitarian and political action. After all, there seems to be an emerging humanitarian norm to mobilise international action in crises that threaten to cost a lot of lives.

One should not exaggerate, though, the impact of the norm of humanitarian engagement – it is often pushed to the background. Major powers appear to have a declining motivation to participate in multilateral peace operations to stem violence in local crises. This trend is most visible in the US case; the Bush administration has been developing a non-intervention doctrine to be cancelled only if there are major national interests at stake.

The aftermath of September 11 corroborates this assumption; the United States would not necessarily have struck against Afghanistan if it had not itself been the target of terrorist attacks, and even then Washington shows little interest in participating in the UN peacekeeping operation after its unilateral strikes.

Neither can one expect that the new crisis management capability of the European Union will be readily available to prevent or resolve local humanitarian crises. This is obviously a controversial argument because the European Union is expected to have, by 2003, a total of 60,000 troops and their military assets available to implement the Petersberg tasks of rescue, peacekeeping and peacemaking. The European Union has invested significant political capital in this project, but it is unclear how, in a crisis, the European Union will be able to take the necessary political decisions to use these forces and coordinate its actions with NATO. In particular there are reasons to be cautious about the European Union's willingness to endanger its troops if the operation were to take place in a severe military crisis.

Even if the major powers are prepared to act, the success of a peace operation is by no means assured; it is very difficult to import external solutions to a protracted civil war. In some wars, the parties pursue military victory, or the spoils of war, almost single-mindedly; no other outcome is acceptable. Looking back over a few decades, Angola, Colombia, the Democratic Republic of the Congo (DRC) and Sudan come immediately to mind as examples of this determination to fight. In the past, Sri Lanka was not much different in that regard, although there now seems to be a glimmer of a compromise between the parties on substantive Tamil autonomy as a condition for ending the violence.

A different kind of obstacle is the availability of divisible and marketable resources that can be sold to foreign markets to finance the war and enrich the warlords. In such a situation, the leaders of the warring parties have only limited interest in ending the war from which they are benefiting financially. The hoarding of assets in a war economy becomes an enduring reason to continue to fight. All the countries mentioned above provide evidence of the self-sustaining economic nature of many civil wars.[31]

The United Nations has recently documented in great detail how the military and political leaders of countries intervening in the war in the Congo have used the war situation for personal enrichment by looting the country's natural resources. The key military and civilian officials in Rwanda and Uganda – and also in the Ivory Coast and Togo – are singled out in the report for special mention as beneficiaries of intervention in the Congo. In addition, one should remember that politicians and the military from Namibia and Zimbabwe have also been involved in and benefited from the war in the DRC.[32]

In summary, the international community is facing a dilemma: external intervention is needed to reduce the casualties of civil wars and humanitarian emergencies, but such engagement usually happens in an unforgiving environment and may be counterproductive both for the subject and for the object of intervention. Peacekeeping is a safer alternative than direct intervention, but its results depend critically on political factors, which in protracted civil wars often work against the interests of peace.[33] The causality from intervention to its results is anything but clear, partly because of the delayed, indirect and mediated effects of action. Is it still justified to urge international engagement, especially if only marginal results can be expected?

The answer to the initial question should perhaps be qualified. If violence and human suffering are primarily due to the state failure that is fuelling political instability and public disorder, intervention followed by a nation-building effort could be justified. The engagement would probably be costly and moderately risky but, if it promises to restore the internal coherence and external sovereignty of the target country, intervention would seem to be worthwhile. In this regard, interventions in Kampuchea and Mozambique were positive accomplishments, though not at all unproblematic. In the case of success, the target country would also produce positive externalities by radiating stability to neighbouring countries.

If, however, the conflict is primarily the result of protracted fighting between warlords for local control and the spoils of war, external intervention is unlikely to bring an end to the war. If intervention is contemplated, the warlords must first be weakened by isolating them from the world as completely as possible and cutting off their financial lifelines. Targeted "smart" sanctions and measures such as the international certification of "conflict diamonds" seem to be effective means in this regard. Once the warlords start losing their power and money, a determined international intervention might produce the desired results, as happened recently in Sierra Leone. In some cases, even the use of private military enterprises, such as the Executive Outcomes in Sierra Leone, could be a better solution than inaction.

Negotiations

The successful negotiation and mediation of violent crises depend on the parties being organised and the leaders being able and willing to control their troops and deliver the promises given at the negotiating table. This presupposes, of course, that faction leaders will negotiate in good faith with each other and with the mediators. This may, however, be a doubtful proposition derived from conflict resolution theory rather than harsh reality. Negotiations are not a laboratory, but politics by other means; they aim either to consolidate the gains of the war or to obtain rewards that remained beyond reach in the field.

There is enough evidence from Angola, the DRC, Sierra Leone and other violent conflicts that negotiations are often used as a diversion to help to reinforce troops and obtain other necessities of war. In such a situation, peace talks are just an expedient that the faction leaders use to play the game of war. Even if there is some serious effort to end the war, the partial nature of proposals, which fall short of restructuring the entire political situation, often means that a peace agreement does not hold, as witnessed by the failure of the Lusaka peace process in Angola.[34]

The lack of loyalty among the parties to a war has become a genuine problem in peace talks. In many a case, the members of military factions are not necessarily linked by any ideological or even ethnic bonds. They band together because war gives them the opportunity to reap some economic gains, either by plundering or by belief in promises that, after victory, their needs will be met. Because this seldom happens and soldiers remain as poor as they have always been, the result is resentment expressed in protests and violence. This resentment can even be used politically to further the ends of the leaders (as has happened in Zimbabwe).

A related development is the proliferation of the number of parties to a civil war – the DRC, Congo-Brazzaville and Somalia are perhaps the best examples. These parties become political, ethnic or religious clubs whose task is to provide their members with physical protection and some basic services that the state is unwilling or unable to deliver. The formation of clubs reinforces the conflict and prolongs negotiations. It is difficult to achieve a positive outcome, and even if this happens the results are unlikely to hold.[35]

The military factions in today's civil wars are often composed of people who have few alternatives or places to go. This is especially the case with child soldiers; for them the military band becomes a new home in which their basic needs may be met, though at the risk of losing their personal identity or even life and limb. Against this backdrop, it is unrealistic to expect the military factions to behave like traditional armies and operate as rational actors. The increasingly irregular nature of warfare is creating new political and legal problems, which the sovereign states have been unable to regulate by the laws of war.[36]

According to William Zartman's dictum, success in mediation requires that the conflict is ripe for resolution. This statement is, of course, tautological, yet it rings true in many ways. The parties must be ready, owing to war fatigue or for some other real reason, to seek peace and give up the role of a spoiler or an opportunist in the peace process. Ripeness is supposed to bring with it moderation and reason, which will help to pave the way for a negotiated solution. More generally, Zartman suggests that the movement from one phase of the conflict cycle to another requires a stalemate, a kind of crisis, that kindles new initiatives.[37]

However, even ripeness and stalemate may be difficult to convert into a successful peace agreement. The case of Burundi shows how deep-seated fears and the problems of power distribution create obstacles to a solution even when a master mediator, Nelson Mandela in this case, is trying to nudge the parties towards a solution (for which they may, in principle, be ready). To use the language of institutional economics, the transaction costs of negotiations and peace are too high to overcome the habits and spoils of war.

The problem is simply that contemporary local crises are so complex, and the variety of actors, levels and interests is so great, that even the best methods of negotiation and mediation are inadequate to the task. Therefore, in many crises, it is almost impossible to "get to yes" by any standard styles of negotiation. In this situation one has to seek alternative approaches that stress the transformation rather than the settlement of conflicts.[38]

Conclusion

I have been sceptical in this paper about the chances of reaching negotiated solutions through international mediation or intervention and thus putting an end to violence and suffering in local wars and humanitarian emergencies. Yet I do not underestimate the importance of negotiated and other peaceful solutions. Clearly, in many situations there is no alternative but to support local efforts at peacebuilding and to try, by external means, to alter the balance of incentives in the direction of a ceasefire and peace agreement. Success in such efforts may require innovative and even unconventional means that are not found in the handbooks of diplomacy.

What I wanted to point out was that there are no easy solutions to civil wars and humanitarian disasters. For instance, power-sharing is a good idea, but it is, in many cases, very difficult to agree on and even more difficult to implement. One party's power-sharing is often another's grab for power. Peace agreements and power-sharing arrangements often break down and war starts again. Therefore, structural solutions, such as consistent support for the principle of national sovereignty and territorial integrity, may, in the end, offer the most promising way out of the current dilemma. Obviously, such structural remedies are not enough by themselves – they may be construed as necessary, though not sufficient, conditions for a more stable peace.

Notes

1. Charles Tilly, *European Revolutions 1492–1992* (Oxford: Blackwell, 1993), documents in detail the recurrence of revolutions and revolts in major European countries. In a similar vein, Fred Halliday, *Revolution and World Politics: The Rise and Fall of the Sixth Great Power* (London: Polity Press, 1999) notes at pp. 3–7 the "centrality of revolution ... along with war, in the formation of world politics".
2. Michel Wieviorka, *The Making of Terrorism* (Chicago: University of Chicago Press, 1993).
3. Halliday, *Revolution and World Politics*, pp. 237–243, 323–338. See also Theda Skocpol, *Social Revolutions in the Modern World. A Comparative Analysis of France, Russia, and China* (Cambridge: Cambridge University Press, 1979).
4. See Raimo Väyrynen and Leila Aliyeva, "The South Caucasus: The Breakdown of the Soviet Empire", in Wayne Nafziger, Frances Stewart and Raimo Väyrynen (eds), *War, Hunger, and Displacement: The Origins of Humanitarian Emergencies* (Oxford: Oxford University Press, 2000), vol. II, pp. 401–436; Terrence K. Hopmann, "Disintegrating States: Separating without Violence", in I. William Zartman (ed.), *Preventive Negotiation: Avoiding Conflict Escalation* (Lanham, MD: Rowman & Littlefield, 2001), pp. 113–164.
5. See Andrew Hurrell, "An Emerging Security Community in South America?", in Emanuel Adler and Michael Barnett (eds), *Security Communities* (Cambridge: Cambridge University Press, 1998), pp. 228–264; Arie Kacowicz, *Zones of Peace in the Third World: South America and West Africa in Comparative Perspective* (Albany: State University of New York Press, 1998).
6. Chris Manning and Peter Van Diermen (eds), *Indonesia in Transition. Social Aspects of Reformasi and Crisis* (London: Zed Books, 2000).
7. Amitav Acharya, "Collective Identity and Conflict Management in Southeast Asia", in Adler and Barnett (eds), *Security Communities*, pp. 198–227; Alan Collins, "Mitigating the Security Dilemma the ASEAN Way", *Pacifica Review*, vol. 11, no. 2, 1999, pp. 95–114; and Timo Kivimäki, "The Long Peace of ASEAN", *Journal of Peace Research*, vol. 38, no. 1, 2001, pp. 5–25.
8. Raimo Väyrynen, "Stable Peace through Security Communities? Steps towards Theory-building", in Arie Kacowicz et al. (eds), *Stable Peace among Nations* (Lanham, MD: Rowman & Littlefield, 2000), pp. 108–129 at pp. 121–124.
9. David Martin Jones and Michael L. R. Smith, "ASEAN's Imitation Community", *Orbis*, vol. 46, no. 1, 2002, pp. 93–109 at p. 107. A balanced yet critical assessment of ASEAN is provided by Jeannie Henderson, *Reassessing ASEAN*, Adelphi Paper 328 (London: International Institute of Strategic Studies, 1999).
10. See William Reno, *Warlord Politics and African States* (Boulder, CO: Lynne Rienner, 1998). On most recent developments in the region, see John L. Hirsch, "War in Sierra Leone", *Survival*, vol. 43, no. 3, 2001, pp. 145–62, and Lansana Gberie, *Destabilizing Guinea: Diamonds, Charles Taylor and the Potential for Wider Catastrophe* (Ottawa: Partnership Africa Canada, 2001).
11. Christopher Clapham, *Africa and the International System: The Politics of State Survival* (Cambridge: Cambridge University Press, 1996). On the porousness of African borders, see Paul Nugent and A. I. Asiwaju (eds), *African Boundaries: Barriers, Conduits and Opportunities* (London: Pinter, 1996).
12. Ahmed Rashid, "The New Struggle in Central Asia.", *World Policy Journal*, vol. 17, no. 4, 2001, pp. 33–45; and Alexei Vassiliev (ed.), *Central Asia: Political and Economic Challenges in the Post-Soviet Era* (London: Saqi Books, 2001). See also Roy Allison and Lena Jonson (eds), *Central Asian Security: The New International Context* (London: Royal Institute of International Affairs, 2001).

13. For a historical and structural analysis of the power configurations and stability in East Asia, see Suisheng Zhao, *Power Competition in East Asia. From the Old Chinese World Order to the Post–Cold War Regional Multipolarity* (New York: St Martin's Press, 1997).
14. For an opposite view, see Christopher Morris, *An Essay on the Modern State* (Cambridge: Cambridge University Press, 1998), pp. 217–227.
15. Hagen Schulze, *States, Nations and Nationalism: From the Middle Ages to the Present* (Oxford: Blackwell, 1994).
16. Gidon Gottlieb, *Nation against State. New Approach to Ethnic Conflicts and the Decline of Sovereignty* (New York: Council on Foreign Relations Press, 1993).
17. Michael Hechter and Elizabeth Borland, "National Self-Determination: The Emergence of an International Norm", in Michael Hechter and Karl-Dieter Opp (eds), *Social Norms* (New York: Russell Sage Foundation, 2001), pp. 186–233 at pp. 203–206.
18. The distinction between external and internal colonies is not, of course, always clear. For instance, how long must the conquered national community, for example Tibet, be a part of the larger unit before it changes from being an external to an internal colony? On the other hand, the liberation of the internal colony can take place very swiftly, as happened in Kosovo.
19. Paul Haslam, "Globalization and Effective Sovereignty: A Theoretical Approach to the State in International Relations", *Studies in Political Economy*, vol. 58, no. 1, 1999, pp. 41–68 at pp. 60–63.
20. Mark W. Zacher, "The Territorial Integrity Norm: International Boundaries and the Use of Force", *International Organization*, vol. 55, no. 2, 2001, pp. 215–250.
21. Stephen Krasner, *Sovereignty: Organized Hypocrisy* (Princeton, NJ: Princeton University Press, 1999).
22. See Friedrich Kratochwil, "Sovereignty as Dominium: Is There a Right of Humanitarian Intervention?", in Gene Lyons and Michael Mastanduno (eds), *Beyond Westphalia? State Sovereignty and International Intervention* (Baltimore, MD: Johns Hopkins University Press, 1995), pp. 21–42.
23. For a related theoretical argument and empirical support for it, see Benjamin Miller, "The Global Sources of Regional Transitions from War to Peace", *Journal of Peace Research*, vol. 38, no. 2, 2001, pp. 199–226, and Benjamin Miller, "Hot Wars, Cold Peace: An International Regional Synthesis", in Zeev Maoz and Azar Gat (eds), *War in a Changing World* (Ann Arbor: University of Michigan Press, 2001), pp. 93–142.
24. Chaim D. Kaufmann, "When All Else Fails: Ethnic Population Transfers and Partitions in the Twentieth Century", *International Security*, vol. 23, no. 2, Fall 1998, pp. 120–156.
25. Jeffrey Herbst, *States and Power in Africa: Comparative Lessons in Authority and Control* (Princeton, NJ: Princeton University Press, 2000).
26. Christopher Clapham, "Degrees of Statehood", in Sarah Owen Vandersluis (ed.), *The State and Identity in International Relations* (London: Macmillan, 2000), pp. 31–48.
27. Bill Berkeley, *The Graves Are Not Yet Full: Race, Tribe and Power in the Heart of Africa* (New York: Basic Books, 2001).
28. Evan Luard, *The Blunted Sword: The Erosion of Military Power in Modern World Politics* (New York: New Amsterdam, 1988), pp. 81–106.
29. Michael Brown and Richard Rosecrance (eds), *The Costs of Conflict: Prevention and Cure in the Global Arena* (Lanham, MD: Rowman & Littlefield, 1999).
30. Scott Peterson, *Me against My Brother: At War in Somalia, Sudan, and Rwanda* (London: Routledge, 2000), pp. 289–302. For a devastating report on the US inaction in Rwanda, see Samantha Power, "Bystanders to Genocide: Why the United States Let the Rwandan Tragedy Happen", *The Atlantic Monthly*, vol. 288, no. 2, 2001, pp. 84–108.
31. David Keen, *The Economic Functions of Violence in Civil Wars*, Adelphi Paper 320 (London: International Institute for Strategic Studies, 1998); and Mats Berdal and

David Malone (eds), *Greed and Grievance: Economic Agendas in Civil Wars* (Boulder, CO: Lynne Rienner, 2000).
32. *Report of the Panel of Experts on the Illegal Exploitation of Natural Resources and Other Forms of Wealth of the Democratic Republic of the Congo* (New York: United Nations, 12 April 2001) and *Addendum to the Report of the Panel of Experts on the Illegal Exploitation of Natural Resources and Other Forms of Wealth of the Democratic Republic of the Congo* (New York: United Nations, 13 November 2001).
33. Raimo Väyrynen, "Peacekeeping or Intervention: A Global Dilemma", in Young Seek Choue (ed.), *Will World Peace Be Achievable in the 21st Century?* (Seoul: Kyung Hee University Press, 2000), pp. 315–345.
34. Paul J. Hare, "Angola: The Lusaka Peace Process", in Chester A. Crocker, Fen Osler Hampson and Pamela Aall (eds), *Herding Cats: Multiparty Mediation in a Complex World* (Washington DC: United States Institute of Peace Press, 1999), pp. 645–661.
35. Robert D. Congleton, "Ethnic Clubs, Ethnic Conflict, and the Rise of Ethnic Nationalism", in Albert Breton, Gianluigi Galeotti, Pierre Salmon and Ronald Wintrobe (eds), *Nationalism and Rationality* (Cambridge: Cambridge University Press, 1995), pp. 71–97; and Marie-Joëlle Zahar, "Protégés, Clients, Cannon Fodder: Civil–Militia Relations in Internal Conflicts", in Simon Chesterman (ed.), *Civilians in War* (Boulder, CO: Lynne Rienner, 2001), pp. 43–65.
36. Ian Clark, *Waging War. A Philosophical Introduction* (Oxford: Oxford University Press, 1988), pp. 73–97.
37. I. William Zartman, "Negotiations and Prenegotiations in Ethnic Conflict: The Beginning, the Middle, and the Ends", in Joseph V. Montville (ed.), *Conflict and Peacemaking in Multiethnic Societies* (New York: Lexington Books, 1991), pp. 511–534.
38. This idea is further developed in Raimo Väyrynen, "From Conflict Resolution to Conflict Transformation: A Critical Review", in Ho-Won Jeong (ed.), *The New Agenda of Peace Research* (Aldershot: Ashgate, 1999), pp. 135–160.

7
Waging peace and ending violence in the twenty-first century

Cees de Rover

This chapter sets out to identify the causes of violence within society. It then attempts to locate the consequences of and reactions to eruptions of violence in the framework of the current collective international security system. I argue that the nature of modern conflict and the structure of that collective security system conspire to render it virtually ineffective as a tool for preventing or ending violence. Proposals to ameliorate some of the worst excesses and anomalies of that system are then introduced.

In the third section of this chapter an attempt is made to address in more detail one particular response to the occurrence of violence, namely armed response and intervention, with special reference to operations led or sponsored by the United Nations. Particular emphasis is put on the changing nature of those interventions and the issues that have arisen as a direct result of that evolution, including the question of rules of engagement, the issue of troop accountability and the possibility of a conflict of laws. This part also looks at the implications of UN forces acting as a substitute for or complement to national law enforcement authorities upon the territory of a single state. The example of Kosovo is used to illustrate some of these problems and their potential solutions.

The final section of this chapter aligns the findings of the previous sections in order to build and sustain the thesis that current responses to violence in society are too much geared towards repression and do little or nothing to acknowledge and use the distinct possibilities for prevention and de-escalation. Taking as my point of departure the observation that the objectives of the international community are peace and security based on the principles of democracy, human rights and the rule of law, I maintain that the appropriate strategy to achieve that objective is based on waging peace rather than on waging war.

Causes of violence

Much has been and is being written on the root causes of armed conflict, or of violence more generally. Ethnic tension, poverty, illiteracy, an uneven distribution of income, discrimination, religious intolerance and cultural differences as exigencies of a given society have all been pointed to as valid causes for violence to erupt.[1]

It is my view that the identification of the causes of violence as presented above has the inherent risk of oversimplifying the true dimensions of the problem. Why do certain societies explode into violence, whereas others do not? For every instance of one or a combination of the above features leading to acts of violence or war, one could point to a society of similar constitution with similar features, which have never led to an outburst of violence. Several authors have pointed this out.[2] In their explorations they inadvertently identify one factor that could well represent a potential cause for violence and conflict, namely the attitudes and practices of national governing bodies in relation to individual and collective human rights and freedoms. The essence of the argument in fact reflects Maslow's famous pyramid of human needs. Human beings seek food, shelter and security, and in that order. Only after their initial and basic needs have been fulfilled will individuals seek opportunities for development in terms of career, self-establishment and personal development. The world today provides ample examples of the fact that the satisfaction of basic needs is not an issue of equitable distribution. Hence there exist at times huge discrepancies within countries between those who have and those who have not. Individuals with grievances arising from the deprivation of basic needs naturally tend to express those grievances collectively. In most countries, ultimate responsibility for the allocation or exchange of the means to satisfy basic needs lies with entities of the state and the government. Therefore, the ultimate test of government accountability is the level of accessibility of its institutions in terms of active and effective participation by the people in the determination of government policy and practice. Especially for those groups in a society who are struggling to fulfil their most basic needs, such participation will be much more a vital issue of development than a political interest that may or may not be granted.

When, as in Burundi and Rwanda, effective control over resources as well as political power are mainly in the hands of one ethnic group, we can of course see the events of 1994 onwards as a problem of ethnicity. However, identifying the demon of ethnic hatred as the root cause of the 1994 genocide is probably more about soothing our guilty consciences than about identifying a root cause. It is tempting to look back on history and to ask whether the successive colonising powers in both Rwanda and Burundi demonstrated much foresight in entrusting only one social group with all the tasks related to administration and governance. Much later, the introduction of democratic, free and fair elections in both countries created an untenable situation. On the one hand there was a social group who had for generations been deprived of political power and equitable access to resources, and were hungering to take an active part in the conduct of public affairs. On the other hand there was a social group who had been ruling the country for generations, and were unwilling to give up or even share their position of power and control and were afraid of the immediate consequences of free and fair elections. Some West European countries even went so far as actively to support attempts to stop the process of democratisation. To brand the ensuing conflict as essentially ethnic in its origin is a thinly veiled attempt to detach it from international involvement or responsibility, and to consider it first and foremost a matter of domestic jurisdiction. The attempt was of sufficient consequence to make the entire international community decide to withdraw physically from Rwanda and abdicate responsibility for what subsequently happened.[3]

In connection with the above reasoning there are two particular points of interest. The first is that all governing authorities, including democratically elected governments, have a proven difficulty in recognising and respecting the rights and needs of minority groups in their society. In spite of democratic, free and fair elections, the governing majority can be seen to show tendencies towards a "winner takes all" mentality and to use their position of power to enforce their own position. Often the development of a meaningful dialogue with minority groups is not considered an issue because it is perceived as a sign of defeat. The ensuing lack of constructive dialogue and of adequate representation of minority views and needs at government level results in polarisation between the government and minority groups, with the first signs of a protracted social conflict emerging. The absence of governmental support and the perceived connection with unfulfilled social needs can easily result in discord over the distribution of economic and political power. If it is not countered and de-escalated at that stage, such discord eventually provides the seed-bed for a violent uprising.[4]

The second point of interest is the link between actual and potential violence and the extent to which economic, social and cultural rights are protected. The international political system has traditionally given priority to civil and political rights. Economic and social issues in particular have almost invariably been treated on a different level.[5]

The fundamental question is whether in fact the relationship between both sets of rights and their implementation at the national level must be seen as a determinant of prevailing national realities. This means that, in a context of unfulfilled social needs, the first priority is to establish just conditions of life and living. As the German author Berthold Brecht wrote: "Zuerst kommt das Fressen, und dann kommt die Moral" ("Food comes first, then morals"). The insistence of the West on the importance of civil and political rights must make little sense to the homeless, jobless, poverty-stricken and starving populations of too many countries in our world today. Their situation and immediate needs leave little room for interests that are not linked to immediate survival. However, their plight may easily lead to discontent, turning militant once the perception takes hold that their governments are unwilling or unable to address their needs effectively.

International law and international security

The nature of armed conflict is changing. The occurrence of armed conflict and violence is less and less the consequence of a dispute between two or more states, and increasingly the consequence of disputes within states. At the same time, these non-international conflicts are of great complexity. Along with the involvement of state actors, they entail the active involvement of various groups within a society. At times there are also a number of "hidden" parties, such as large multinational corporations, foreign governments and foreign private organisations. In addition to this we must consider the involvement of the United Nations or of regional security alliances, which through their actions may well become parties to ongoing conflicts.

Under current rules of public international law, conflicts within the borders of a state in principle fall within the domestic jurisdiction of that state, and there is no legal entitlement for the international community to intervene. The only exceptions to this rule are internal conflicts that pose a threat to international peace and security. In such conflicts international intervention is, at least in theory, a possibility.[6]

The main features of the current collective security system are a prohibition on the use of force between states, except in the case of legitimate self-defence, combined with a prohibition on the United Nations' intervening in matters that are essentially within the domestic jurisdiction of a member state. This system for the protection of international peace and security, as established with the entry into force of the UN Charter, had serious shortcomings right from its inception. The Charter did little or nothing to recognise the already decentralised world order, the existing differences in political systems and interests, or the economic and social realities of individual UN member states and their cultural differences. In fact, from day one, that very world order has made it in effect impossible for the collective security system to function as it was envisaged.

Immediately after the ending of the Second World War, the main concern was obviously with the prevention of further interstate wars. The allocation of veto power to each of the five permanent members of the Security Council was without doubt an attempt to introduce checks and balances as well as to disable unilateral military action. Today, the Security Council has still to prove its worth in relation to the purposes for which it was created. To date, not one example can be given of the United Nations actually having put an effective stop to interstate violence.[7] This is largely owing to the fact that the veto system, being used more for the political motives of the five permanent members than for the sake of international peace and security, has repeatedly served to paralyse and incapacitate the organisation. What has been lacking is the political will to change the system as regards the obstacle posed by veto power. This lack of political will is founded on the reluctance of the most powerful states possibly to compromise their own sovereignty.[8]

The collective security system as it currently stands is thus completely unable to deal effectively with situations of armed conflict. This is true not only for international armed conflict, but even more so for situations of armed conflict or violence within the borders of a single state. The only possibility for UN intervention in the territory of a state is if the situation in that state poses a threat to international peace and security. Although there have been a few occasions when the UN Security Council has deemed such a situation to exist (for example, Somalia in 1992, Rwanda, and the former Republic of Yugoslavia), in an even larger number of situations similar circumstances did not trigger that response (for example, Sudan, Algeria, Burundi, Colombia, and Somalia in 1999). What these examples serve to underline is the fact that UN intervention in the territory of a state is currently not predictable. There are no clearly defined criteria for such interventions, nor can such criteria be derived from cases where such intervention did or did not take place. What remains is an image of randomness, which takes on shape only when viewed through the looking glass of the political or economic interests of the permanent members of the Security Council.

The NATO intervention in Kosovo and the former Republic of Yugoslavia provides a good example of the current state of unpredictability, as well as of the way in which economic and political interests are given primacy over law. No matter how understandable NATO's decision may appear in the light of our failing collective security system, it does raise very serious questions.

First, in terms of public international law, the NATO actions are unlawful.[9] In addition, it is important to understand that the NATO actions do not derive any legitimacy from the unanimity of NATO member states. Ultimately, legitimacy for such interventions can be obtained only through consultation with all UN member states to achieve their acceptance of the intervention as the last remaining option. This acceptance should be sought before the actual intervention takes place, and is definitely not to be construed after the fact.

Secondly, it is not correct to leave the decision on the use of power, and the definition of what constitutes justice in particular cases, in the hands of those who ultimately exercise that power. If that happens, intervention will definitely become an option open only to those able to wield the sword, putting the destiny of world order under the immediate control of the most powerful states.

Finally, in terms of accountability it cannot be left up to NATO to be judge and jury where its own actions, choices and omissions are concerned. As far as the NATO intervention in Kosovo is concerned, arguments of ethics and morality have found wide-ranging support. However, it is shameful to have to conclude also that NATO, in its initial resolve, failed to put a stop effectively to the deeds for which it went into action. Although NATO aimed to end the ethnic cleansing in Kosovo, it was too preoccupied with political responses and public opinion at home and too much governed by a zero tolerance of casualties. Consequently, the NATO actions were spun out over a period of nearly three months – during which time a further 700,000 Kosovo Albanians were forcibly evicted from their homes, becoming refugees in neighbouring countries or displaced within their own. Seen in that light the NATO actions also raise an issue of proportionality related to the use of force. Force was used because it was deemed to be the sole remaining option, but it was used in such a manner that it was insufficient effectively to end the violence against which it was being employed. The NATO resolve and actions in Kosovo are in stark contrast to events in Krajina in 1995. The forcible eviction of 600,000 Serbs by the Croat armed forces went largely unremarked by the international community, including NATO, and no sanctions at all were imposed. In fact, allegations have been made that these evictions were effected with the active support of the US and German governments.

It is true that the collective security system needs an overhaul. Its proven unsuitability to ending international armed conflicts, as well as its limitations concerning situations of conflict and/or violence in the territory of a single state, serve to underline this need. In addition, the system is increasingly politicised, and decisions regarding international peace and security are principally governed by the economic motives and political interests of the most powerful states within the UN system.

It is beyond the scope of this chapter to propose even the most rudimentary structure of a future world order. However, recent experience has taught us that any system will fail if it does not meet certain basic requirements:
- A credible collective security system must be built on the positive engagement and support of UN member states.
- This system must be anchored in public international law.
- The system must set out to safeguard peace and security at both the national and the international level.
- States must acknowledge that the prohibition of interference in matters essentially within domestic jurisdiction does not apply to situations and/or circumstances where systematic and gross violations of human rights pose a threat to peace and security within a single state.

Other, more detailed proposals could be made with a view to democratising and enhancing the effectiveness of the international security system. Assuming that the United Nations and its Security Council remain the lynch pin of that system, certain minimum reforms will be necessary. First, given that the rationale behind establishing the veto power for the permanent members of the Security Council is no longer valid, that veto power should be annulled.[10] In fact, the question may be asked whether the idea of permanent membership should not be abolished in favour of a more democratic system. The Security Council as a whole could decide on issues relating to peace and security. The voting procedures on matters relating to peace and security should require a total of nine affirmative votes, including the affirmative vote of at least three out of five permanent members of the Council. Only multilateral interventions under the auspices of the United Nations should be allowed. The implementation of Security Council resolutions through regional security alliances should remain an option.

Finally, experience has clearly demonstrated the dangers of relying too heavily on one state or group of states for "peace enforcement". Attention should be given to a more equitable distribution of the burden where UN intervention missions are concerned. The current levels of control exercised by the United States over such missions in terms of their actual establishment, as well as on issues relating to force composition and command, do not reflect a collective and democratically functioning security system. Many countries in Africa, Europe, Latin America and Asia have effective and efficiently functioning armed forces at their disposal. It should always be possible to implement UN operations in the absence of, or at least without total reliance on, the usual actors.

UN intervention with armed force

The United Nations has the possibility under its Charter to use air, sea or land forces as may be necessary to maintain or restore international peace and security. On a number of occasions the United Nations has resorted to the use of these powers. In more recent times these powers have also been brought to bear in situations where a conflict within the borders of a state was held to pose a threat to international peace and security (northern Iraq in 1992; Somalia in 1992 and 1993; Bosnia-Herzegovina in 1995).

An analysis of the UN potential to intervene with armed force in order to end or prevent violent conflict requires an understanding of how the organisation has functioned in the past. At the outset, the interventions were classical peacekeeping missions, with UN forces deploying to monitor a negotiated ceasefire between warring parties. Gradually the mission typology has changed to include what have come to be known as "peace enforcement" and "peace-restoring" missions. With the change in typology there have been changes in the armament, appearance and operations of UN forces.

However, the most fundamental consequence of the changing nature of UN intervention is the way these changes have affected the position of the United Nations itself as a neutral, independent intermediary. In the classical peacekeeping missions, the actions and responsibilities of the United Nations were limited to monitoring and moderating the ongoing negotiations between parties. The United Nations did not engage in discussions as to what was right and wrong between parties. With the introduction of peace enforcement and peace-restoring missions, the United Nations has lost much of its neutral intermediary position. Through intervention with armed force the United Nations becomes a party to an ongoing conflict, irrespective of the intervention's objective. For example, the UN intervention in Somalia, to save 300,000 civilians from death through starvation, was largely driven by humanitarian motives. However, the mass starvation of these civilians was in fact a method of warfare of one of the major faction leaders at the time. The UN actions to avert the threat of mass starvation were not considered an act of humanity by them, but rather seen as a declaration of war. This reality does not alter the reason for the UN intervention, nor does it make that particular intervention less valid. However, it does change the role and position of the United Nations itself. In such contexts, the issue of international peace and security is no longer the object of a dialogue between warring parties under UN supervision, but is forced upon those parties by the United Nations in the name of the interests of the international community.

It is debatable whether the United Nations itself is sufficiently aware of, and acting upon, its changing position. In peace enforcement as well as in peace-restoring missions it will be virtually impossible for the United Nations to avoid becoming a party to the conflict, if not in fact then at least in terms of perception. In such cases the UN involvement creates an additional complication, which must be taken into consideration if a conflict is to be successfully resolved. Outrages committed against the civilian population by UN troops, as happened in Somalia by Canadians and in Rwanda by Belgian soldiers, will inevitably exacerbate the conflict and further compromise the so-called neutrality and impartiality of the intervention.

At the same time these examples shed light on another problem in relation to UN intervention, that of the mandate of UN forces and the accompanying rules of engagement. The mandate for any UN intervention is drawn up by the Security Council. However, it is not the Security Council that subsequently defines the rules of engagement for intervening forces. This exercise is normally left to the UN Force Commander.

Much has been written about whether UN troops can be considered to be bound by multilateral treaties in the field of human rights and/or international humanitarian law.[11] In law there seems little basis to argue that UN troops are bound by these provisions, for the simple reason that the United Nations as an organisation is not a state and therefore cannot, for instance, become a high contracting party to the Geneva Conventions of 1949. In practice, UN troops come from countries that invariably have ratified the very same conventions, with clear consequences for the constituency and practices of their national armed forces. In situations of armed conflict, serious and systematic violations of human rights are as much a cause as they are a consequence of those conflicts. When the United Nations engages force to end such conflicts and violations, it is hard to understand – or even to defend – its troops not being bound by the very provisions of public international law they seek to protect.

The United Nations has come to embrace this point of view, which has found its way for instance into the Status of Armed Forces Agreement, which accompanies a mandate as formulated by the Security Council. In this document it is clearly stipulated that UN forces are bound to respect the principles and rules of international humanitarian law. The reality remains that it is still the Force Commander who has to ensure that the implications of this statement are clearly introduced into rules of engagement and more particularly reflected in orders for opening fire. This raises questions about the uniformity, consistency and transparency of actual mission implementation by UN troops and its control. For example, in the case of the UN mission in Somalia irreconcilable differences in views between UN contingents from different nationalities resulted in distinct practical differences in mission implementation between those contingents, and equally distinct differences in terms of outcome.[12]

Another important issue relating to UN operations is that of judicial control over UN troops and their accountability. At present no structure offers a satisfactory solution for this problem. Within the United Nations there is no system for independent judicial control or other control over the implementation of a UN mission. As the United Nations increasingly is being challenged over its interventions and the ways in which they are executed, as well as over those it fails to make, this issue urgently requires redress. No doubt the establishment of the International Criminal Court will go some way to ensuring the judicial control described above. However, it is already clear that the mandate of the Court does not provide comprehensive cover for all actions undertaken by armed forces under UN auspices. This may serve to underline the reluctance of the most powerful states to subject their troops to international control when acting under the auspices of the United Nations.

The youngest branches on the tree of interventions under the auspices of the United Nations are interventions executed upon the territory of a single state. Increasingly, these missions are of the peace enforcement and/or peace-restoring variety, which raises fundamental issues of law. There are two distinct working possibilities for such interventions: the UN forces act either as a substitute for, or as a complement to, national authorities. In both cases the interesting question is which set of laws governs the UN operation – domestic law or international law? In Kosovo, while a Status of Armed Forces Agreement was still to be concluded, KFOR soldiers effected the arrest of civilians, and in two instances used intentional lethal force. This does give rise to the question of on what legal basis they could possibly justify their actions. More specifically it gives rise to the question of which legal and judicial system subsequently exercises the required independent control over such arrests or use of force.[13]

More and more UN troops in peace enforcement missions take on responsibilities and assume functions that in normal circumstances would have been carried out by national law enforcement organisations. Generally, UN military troops are poorly prepared to carry out such missions and functions (sometimes also referred to as situations other than war). Their knowledge and skills in policing techniques and tactics are at best uneven, while their knowledge and understanding of legal requirements in relation to police performance are generally insufficient.[14] The latter fact may be demonstrated by the distribution to troops of pocket cards with printed rules of engagement for such situations. In short, current levels of training of members of armed forces fail to acknowledge sufficiently the fundamental differences between police and military operations.

The substitution of national law enforcement authorities by UN forces, or the incorporation of UN forces into national law enforcement structures, raise other important issues, which are yet to be adequately addressed. The assumption of such authority would, presumably, have to be justified with reference to public international law and based upon existing international legal principles. Any other possibility (for example, placing the mission under the scrutiny and control of a national judicial system) would be untenable because it would undermine the very notion of the collective security system. In addition, it is highly unlikely that troop-contributing nations would agree to their forces acting under the jurisdiction or legal control of the host state against which it has been moving with force.

Naturally, UN intervention in armed conflict must not be limited to the achievement of basic military objectives. Ensuring a lasting peace is more about restoring the basic functions of societies than it is about effectively ending hostilities. Peace is more than the mere absence of war. It is heartening to note that the international community – or at least the United Nations – is beginning to recognise and act upon this reality. A report by the UN Secretary-General to the Security Council, pursuant to paragraph 10 of Security Council resolution 1244 (1999), outlined the main concept for the international civilian presence to be established in Kosovo. The report delineated coverage for issues relating to: (a) the interim civil administration; (b) humanitarian affairs; (c) institution-building; and (d) reconstruction.[15] This report, which drew the outlines of the UN Mission in Kosovo, touched on all aspects and functions of society and set out to rebuild and reconstruct a democratically functioning society, with clear guarantees for the promotion and protection of human rights.

Waging peace

As demonstrated above, for the United Nations or the international community to declare war on violence within the state is not a solution. At best it complicates a conflict through the introduction of further parties, while at the same time serving further to entrench the actual conflict. The immediate outcomes of war in terms of destruction and irrevocable human suffering can hardly be deemed desirable by exponents of a collective security system, which is essentially based upon the promotion and protection of fundamental human rights and freedoms. At the very beginning as well as at the very end of armed conflict stand human beings. Not only must actions undertaken to safeguard peace and security focus on civil administration, social institutions and governmental authorities. They must also and primarily concentrate on the well-being of people. Peace talks, round tables, conferences, negotiations, media drives and campaigns must include all parties to a conflict. All too often this is not the case. Whatever was part of the problem must be taken into account as part of the solution to be established. If not, the solution will not truly reflect the underlying problem and the conflict will not really be resolved.

It has been said before that the international community is better at cleaning up after conflicts than at preventing them in the first place. Once again, Kosovo provides an instructive example. The massive operation to be undertaken in the Balkans was praised in the previous section for its attention to and focus on civil and social structures. However, it is ironic to note that many of the measures now proposed are in fact the very ones that could have served to prevent the conflict from escalating in the first place. It is time for the international community finally to learn from the lessons of the past and finally to end the war. It is time to wage peace.

Notes

1. See, for example, Pierre Hassner, "From War and Peace to Violence and Intervention: Permanent Dilemmas under Changing Political and Technological Conditions", in Jonathan Moore (ed.), *Hard Choices: Moral Dilemmas in Humanitarian Intervention* (Lanham, MD: Rowman & Littlefield, 1998), pp. 9–28; Charles W. Kegley and Margaret G. Hermann, "A Peace Dividend? Democracies' Military Interventions and Their External Political Consequences", *Cooperation and Conflict*, vol. 32, no. 4, December 1997; Alberto R. Coll, *The Problems of Doing Good: Somalia as a Case Study in Humanitarian Intervention* (New York: Carnegie Council Case Study Series on Ethics and International Affairs no. 18, 1997); Juan Somavia, "The Humanitarian Responsibilities of the United Nations Security Council: Ensuring the Security of the People", *Development in Practice*, vol. 7, no. 4, 1997.
2. See Helmut Willems, "Development, Patterns and Causes of Violence against Foreigners in Germany: Social and Biographical Characteristics of Perpetrators and the Process of Escalation", *Terrorism and Political Violence*, vol. 7, no. 1, Spring 1995, pp. 162–181; Edward E. Azar, *The Management of Social Conflict: Theory and Cases* (Aldershot: Dartmouth, 1990), pp. 5–17; David A. Lake and Donald Rothchild, "Containing Fear: The Origins and Management of Ethnic Conflict", *International Security*, vol. 21, no. 2, Fall 1996, pp. 41–75.
3. See Romeo A. Dallaire, "The End of Innocence: Rwanda 1994", in Moore (ed.), *Hard Choices: Moral Dilemmas in Humanitarian Intervention*, pp. 71–86; Ian Martin, "Hard Choices after Genocide: Human Rights and Political Failures in Rwanda", in Moore (ed.), *Hard Choices: Moral Dilemmas in Humanitarian Intervention*, pp. 157–175.
4. Christina M. Cerna, "Universal Democracy: An International Legal Right or the Pipe Dream of the West?", *New York University Journal of International Law and Politics*, vol. 27, no. 2, Winter 1995, pp. 289–329.
5. Fundamentally differing and irreconcilable views on the ranking of civil and political rights, on the one hand, and economic, social and cultural rights, on the other, led to the establishment of two separate Covenants in the period between 1954 and 1966. In law we content ourselves with the affirmation that both sets of rights are indivisible, interrelated as well as interdependent – meaning that one set of rights cannot be seen as separate from the other or as having priority over the other. In reality, it is a lawful

possibility for states to ratify only one or the other Covenant, or neither. Based on what I said earlier, the fundamental question is whether the viewpoint that both sets of rights have equal importance can in fact be maintained. It is hardly a coincidence that the proponents of the argument that precedence should be given to economic, social and cultural rights were representatives of states that in their national context were experiencing difficulties in meeting the basic social needs of their people. Likewise it is not surprising that the strongest arguments for the precedence of civil and political rights were made by representatives of states where issues of democratic governance and popular participation in the conduct of public affairs were already on their way to becoming a reality. In addition, it must not be forgotten that these discussions about the different sets of rights and the attempts at their codification were conducted against the backdrop of the emerging Cold War. Although arguments in part reflected ideology as well as national reality, both camps used their reasoning with equal vehemence and determination as an instrument of Cold War politics against the other camp.

6. Kofi A. Annan, "Peacekeeping, Military Intervention, and National Sovereignty in Internal Armed Conflict", in Moore (ed.), *Hard Choices: Moral Dilemmas in Humanitarian Intervention*, pp. 55–69; Kegley and Hermann, "A Peace Dividend? Democracies' Military Interventions and Their External Political Consequences".
7. See also Michael J. Glennon, "The New Interventionism: The Search for a Just International Law", *Foreign Affairs*, vol. 78, no. 3, May–June 1999, pp. 2–7.
8. Samuel M. Makinda, "Sovereignty and International Security: Challenges for the United Nations", *Global Governance*, vol. 2, no. 2, May–August 1996, pp. 149–168.
9. See also Bruno Simma, "NATO, the UN and the Use of Force: Legal Aspects", *European Journal of International Law*, vol. 10, no. 1, 1999, pp. 1–22; and Antonio Cassese, "*Ex iniuria ius oritur*. Are We Moving towards International Legitimation of Forcible Humanitarian Countermeasures in the World Community?", *European Journal of International Law*, vol. 10, no. 1, 1999, pp. 23–30.
10. The abolition of the veto may seem to be an unrealistic goal, in view of the fact that it can only be given up by its holders. However, history provides encouraging examples, including the English House of Lords, which unexpectedly gave up its veto powers earlier in the twentieth century.
11. See, for example, Hilaire McCoubrey and Nigel D. White, *The Blue Helmets: Legal Regulation of United Nations Military Operations* (Aldershot: Dartmouth, 1996); Brian D. Tittemore, "Belligerents in Blue Helmets: Applying International Humanitarian Law to United Nations Peace Operations", *Stanford Journal of International Law*, vol. 33, no. 1, 1997, p. 61.
12. See Robert G. Patman, "Disarming Somalia: The Contrasting Fortunes of United States and Australian Peacekeepers during United Nations Intervention, 1992–1993", *African Affairs*, vol. 96, 1997, pp. 509–533.
13. My views on this point were solicited by Amnesty International in London and are reflected in the letter by Amnesty International's Secretary General Mr Sané (Ref: IOR 23/6/99/YT) to the UN Secretary-General (in response to his report to the Security Council of 12 June 1999, pursuant to UN Security Council resolution 1244) under the heading "clarify legal basis for exercising of public safety and order responsibilities".
14. See Cees de Rover, "Trading Places? The Compatibility of Police and Military Roles", *Kernvraag*, 1999/2, No. 120, The Hague, the Netherlands.
15. *Report of the UN Secretary General to the Security Council, Pursuant to Paragraph 10 of Security Council Resolution 1244* (New York: United Nations, S/1999/672, 12 June 1999).

8

Mercy and justice in the transition period

Helen Durham

The quality of mercy is not strain'd,
It droppeth as the gentle rain from heaven
Upon the place beneath: it is twice bless'd;
It blesseth him that gives and him that takes – *Shakespeare*

Mercy, as Shakespeare so eloquently reminds us, is intrinsically a romantic and ideal notion. In technical terms, mercy can be administered only by "victors" and implies discretionary application to a defeated group. Philosophically it involves recognising that "people do wrong", and could be seen as the gentle art of knowing what to overlook. It is steeped in morality: ethics with hints of religion. It is an ideal for which to strive. When dealing with states in a transition period – movement from armed conflict or civil strife to civil society – mercy is not appropriate to locate the paradigm of rebuilding within. Mercy will and must have a role to play in reconstituting society after massive trauma; it should not, however, play a foundational part in this process.

Justice, on the other hand, is a system of bringing individuals to trial before a court of law. It involves the judiciary, in a full process that must be accorded respect and can be seen to be less reliant upon discretion. Justice is designed to be impartial in its dealings. It can be tempered by mercy, but philosophically justice strives for equity, not kindness.

Following the cessation of hostilities and civil strife, the bringing to account and punishment of perpetrators of violations of human rights and international humanitarian law (that is, the law of armed conflict) have been acknowledged to be a necessary precursor to the restoration of legal, political and social order. As the conclusion of the thirty-eighth report from the US Foreign Policy for Peace Conference argues:

> Failure to hold war criminals and human rights offenders fully accountable for their deeds may be politically (and militarily) expedient in the immediate post-conflict environment, but in the long term such failures significantly undermine the chances for genuine national reconciliation and peace. Recent experience has shown that a society's failure or inability to assign accountability for past wrongs breeds cynicism and prevents healing.[1]

Writers in this area also highlight the role post-conflict prosecutions play in publicly acknowledging the suffering of survivors and victims,[2] as well as fostering a collective understanding of what has occurred during a horrific period. These factors are critical in the quest for national reconciliation and the recording of an accurate history. Furthermore, prosecution has broader value than merely punishing those who are found guilty and attempting to deter those who consider acting illegally. For example, Zuroff has argued that "[t]he public trials of [Nazi] criminals have played an important role in educating the public regarding the Holocaust and undermining the propaganda of Holocaust deniers".[3]

There is also direct evidence that citizens in a number of countries moving away from civil strife and towards civil society see the need for justice. To mark the fiftieth anniversary of the Geneva Conventions in August 1999, the International Committee of the Red Cross (ICRC) launched a "People of War" project with the aim of giving the general public a chance to air their views on a range of issues relating to war. A number of countries were identified and over 1,000 individuals from each country were surveyed. Focus groups and in-depth, face-to-face interviews were also held. Civilians and combatants alike shared their experiences and opinions on what basic rules should apply in war.

In responding to the question "Are there rules or laws that are so important that, if broken during war, the person who broke them should be punished?" time and time again people from all walks of life around the world expressed their desire for war crimes prosecutions. In Colombia, 71 per cent answered yes to this question, in Bosnia–Herzegovina 82 per cent, and in Somalia 63 per cent. In the Russian Federation, the United Kingdom, the United States and France, three-quarters of the public said that violators should be punished. Answers to the question of who should be responsible for punishing the wrongdoers were also sought. In Somalia, 51 per cent believed that Somalis – be they in the courts, members of the government, military or civilians – should be in charge of such cases and expressed concern about the lack of central government. In Bosnia–Herzegovina, on the other hand,

Over 60 per cent – rising to two-thirds of Bosnians and Croats – believe an international criminal court should be responsible for punishing wrongdoers. Just 2 per cent think the military should judge and punish war criminals. In fact, only a minority would turn to any of the national institutions. The Serbs have much less confidence in an international criminal court, though half believe it should assume responsibility for punishing war criminals.[4]

Domestic prosecutions

Although a vast majority of states have ratified the Geneva Conventions and thus are required to prosecute those accused of war crimes, this does not occur regularly or consistently.[5] States in transition periods are likely to experience technical difficulties within their legal systems. Even if the judiciary of a country is still intact, domestic prosecutions are often lengthy and sentencing may appear inadequately to reflect the severity of the crimes. Parties may be tempted to inflict swift and what they perceive to be "appropriate" punishment by extrajudicial means. Alternatively, the party with the greatest political and military power may hold mock trials in an attempt to placate both the masses and the international community, vindicating their own and condemning their opposition. In either case the process lacks impartiality and legality and does not assist in the restoration of civil society.

For the administration of justice to be legitimate, it must be applied by an independent and competent court with the requisite jurisdiction. It is also not enough for justice to be done; justice must also be *seen* to be done. The local as well as international community must feel confident that perpetrators have been brought to appropriate justice in an objective and impartial manner. In certain instances the perception of justice may therefore be advanced if the arbiter is an international legal institution rather than a party with vested interests – whether they be allies or victims of the accused. Current debates on the need for international rather than domestic investigations and prosecutions for the atrocities committed in East Timor highlight this point.[6] It is this issue – international criminal prosecutions – that constitutes the chief focus of this chapter.

Alternatives to prosecution

It is important to acknowledge that prosecution is not the only model for dealing with the past by states in transition. There are challenges to the assertion that rebuilding a society necessitates the hosting of trials; in fact a range of alternatives for encouraging post-conflict accountability have been implemented throughout the world.[7] Such mechanisms include the granting of complete amnesties and a range of official commissions of investigation in countries such as Israel, Guinea, Uganda, Argentina and Chile.[8] The South African Commission on Truth and Reconciliation is perhaps the best known. The South African Minister of Justice in 1995 stated that a "commission is a necessary exercise to enable South Africans to come to terms with their past on a morally acceptable basis and to advance the cause of reconciliation".[9] Although I will not deal with this Commission in detail, this process designed to aid forgiveness (while not forgetting past wrongs) is of some note. The Commission has the discretion to be less adversarial and punitive than other modes and is empowered to grant wide amnesties. However, amnesties can be granted only for acts deemed political, not those committed for personal gain or malice. The Commission also affords victims the opportunity to relate the violations they have suffered and receive reparation. It is a system that combines mercy and justice with a commitment to national unity, long-term peace and stability.[10]

Ad hoc international criminal tribunals

In the early 1990s, news of the atrocities occurring in the conflict in the Balkans resulted in a reassessment of the need for national security matters to be tempered by the international legal system. As Professor Bassiouni noted, the "events in Yugoslavia and Rwanda shocked the world out of its complacency and the idea of prosecuting those who committed international crimes acquired a broad base of support in world public opinion and in many countries".[11]

In response, the UN Security Council established the International Criminal Tribunal for the former Yugoslavia pursuant to unanimous resolutions 808 of February 1993 and 827 of May 1993. The International Criminal Tribunal for the former Yugoslavia has the capacity to try individuals for international crimes including genocide, crimes against humanity, grave breaches of the Geneva Conventions and war crimes. A year later, a similar international criminal tribunal was created by the Security Council pursuant to resolution 955 to try breaches of international criminal law in Rwanda. The International Criminal Tribunal for Rwanda can also try individuals for genocide, crimes against humanity and war crimes. Because the conflict in Rwanda was internal rather than international, "grave breaches" of the Geneva Conventions are not relevant. Rather it has jurisdiction over violations of article 3 common to the Geneva Conventions and of Additional Protocol II.

The creation of these tribunals was an unprecedented and significant step in international criminal law. Although the world had witnessed a range of international trials after the Second World War, including those held at Nuremberg[12] and Tokyo,[13] the International Criminal Tribunal for the former Yugoslavia and the International Criminal Tribunal for Rwanda are the first international penal mechanisms established neither by victors nor after the conflict. Furthermore, because they were established by the Security Council pursuant to Chapter VII of the United Nations Charter, they create a binding obligation on all member states to assist and cooperate fully with the Tribunal if requested.

As of November 2001, the International Criminal Tribunal for the former Yugoslavia had publicly indicted 79 individuals and had 50 in custody.[14] The International Criminal Tribunal for Rwanda had indicted 55 persons and had 53 in custody.[15] Indictments and prosecutions from both Tribunals include a range of actors, from "small fish" to extremely powerful individuals such as President Milosevic of Yugoslavia and Jean Kambanda, the former prime minister of Rwanda. The International Criminal Tribunal for the former Yugoslavia does have jurisdiction over Kosovo and has indicated that it will not treat the recent activities of NATO in any manner different from other military offensives.[16] However, Chief Prosecutor Carla del Ponte announced in an address to the UN Security Council on 2 June 2000 that a criminal investigation into the 1999 NATO air campaign would not be opened.[17]

The handful of judgments from these tribunals to date have made significant advances in international criminal jurisprudence on topics such as the Security Council's authority to create such bodies; their relationship with national courts; jurisdiction; trials in absentia; evidentiary matters; challenges to judges; and elements of the crimes – to name a few.[18] Decisions from these Tribunals have also had a crucial impact on the way the international community views and prosecutes sexual violence.[19]

The proposed Cambodian tribunal

In July 1998, the UN General Assembly passed resolution 52/135 to establish a Group of Experts to undertake three tasks: (1) to evaluate the existing evidence to determine the nature of the crimes committed by Khmer Rouge leaders in the years 1975–1979; (2) to assess the feasibility of bringing Khmer Rouge leaders to justice; and (3) to explore options of bringing such leaders before international or national jurisdiction. The Group, chaired by Sir Ninian Stephen, reported that the patterns of abuse fell into four categories: forced population movements; forced labour and inhumane living conditions; attacks on enemies of the revolution; and purges within the party.

Apart from the "show trials" of Pol Pot, *in absentia* trials of Ieng Sary and the recent trials of those accused of the murder of foreign nationals, the Khmer Rouge have not been held accountable for their actions during the 1975–1979 period when an estimated 1.7 million (or 20 per cent of the population) were killed. The Group's report notes that, owing to the time delay, difficulties will arise with the gathering of evidence. There is no doubt that some witnesses will have died and other physical evidence will have decayed. Nevertheless, it should be acknowledged that the Documentation Center of Cambodia, originally set up by Yale University, has compiled substantial records relating to this period. Moreover, some physical evidence is still locatable.

The Group of Experts proposed two options for bringing individuals to justice in this instance. One option involved a tribunal established under Cambodian law and the other a tribunal established by the United Nations. Because of a range of factors, including the level of corruption within the Cambodian legal system and a lack of public confidence in the judiciary, the Group recommended the latter option. A number of innovative suggestions can be found in the report relating to the method of establishing such a UN tribunal.

The report argued that, unlike the situation in the former Yugoslavia and Rwanda, Cambodia is a country where for the most part peace prevails. Thus a resolution under Chapter VII of the UN Charter, as was used to create the previous two ad hoc tribunals, may not be appropriate. The Group examined the potential of creating a tribunal under Chapter VI of the Charter, although it cautioned that in this case the Court might lack the power to issue binding orders to other states. However, the Group advised that in the reality of international life there may be little difference between a tribunal established under Chapter VI or VII. The experiences of the ad hoc tribunals indicate the necessity of voluntary cooperation:

not even a Chapter VII mandate has prevented the existing tribunals from encountering non-compliance with their orders ... This strategy of moving from Chapter VI to Chapter VII has been used by the Council in the past. And, as noted, it is possible for the Council to make binding decisions under other parts of the Charter.[20]

Another suggestion included the creation of a tribunal by the General Assembly under its recommendatory powers found in Chapter VI of the Charter, in particular articles 11(2) and 13. Once again the report commented that an Assembly-created tribunal would also rely on the voluntary compliance of states. The report left open the creation of a tribunal by other organs of the United Nations, including the Economic and Social Council or the Secretary-General. After exploring these options, the Group expressed its preference for a tribunal established by the Security Council under Chapter VII or VI or any other relevant part of the Charter.

The United Nations considered this report and made a number of recommendations for the creation of an international criminal tribunal. However, the Cambodian government rejected the formulas proposed by the United Nations, preferring to create its own tribunal. In August 2001 legislation was enacted in Cambodia establishing the framework for a UN-assisted tribunal to try leaders of the Khmer Rouge. However, the form of this tribunal remains uncertain. Only if a memorandum of understanding (MoU) with the United Nations is established will it become clear whether the tribunal will be dominated by the UN or the Cambodian legal system.[21] Whatever the outcome of negotiations, the range of options expressed by the Group of Experts for the creation of new international criminal tribunals may set an interesting precedent for future tribunals.

The International Criminal Court Statute

The creation of an international criminal court was mooted for over a century.[22] In the past 50 years a number of attempts were made to draft a statute for such an institution; however, the Cold War stifled prospects of serious discussions. Only in November 1992, in the wake of the collapse of the Soviet Union, did the UN General Assembly request that the International Law Commission draft a Statute for an international criminal court.[23] This action was largely motivated by a coalition of Caribbean states, which believed that an international criminal court would assist them in confronting and combating the transnational problem of drug cartels.[24] This initiative culminated in 1994 with the submission to the General Assembly of a Draft Statute establishing an international criminal court.[25]

In submitting the Draft Statute, the International Law Commission recommended that the General Assembly call a conference to finalise the process. However, owing to a lack of agreement on various issues among states, an ad hoc Committee was created to continue discussions.[26] The Committee's failure to arrive at a consensus on the international criminal court resulted in the General Assembly's establishing a Preparatory Committee to rework the Draft Statute so as to develop a widely accepted text. Six Preparatory Committee sessions were held at the United Nations in New York between March 1996 and April 1998. Subsequently, a United Nations Conference of Plenipotentiaries on the establishment of an international criminal court was held in Rome from 15 June to 17 July 1998. Over this five-week period a Statute for the International Criminal Court was created.

The International Criminal Court entered into force on 1 July 2002, after 60 states had ratified the Statute.[27] It is located in The Hague with links to the United Nations. The International Criminal Court is not retrospective and will be able to try individuals accused of committing crimes only from the date on which it entered into force. Thus there will still be a need for the tribunals for Rwanda and the former Yugoslavia as well as others such as the proposed Cambodian tribunal. The International Criminal Court will not replace national prosecution, but will complement national courts. Except in situations of referral from the Security Council, the International Criminal Court (ICC) has jurisdiction only when a state is "unwilling or unable genuinely to carry out the investigation or prosecution" (article 17). The permission of either the state on whose territory the crime occurred or the state of which the person accused is a national is required before the ICC can exercise jurisdiction (article 12).

The Rome Statute is divided into 13 parts,[28] consisting of 128 articles fronted by a preamble. Major principles underlying the creation of the International Criminal Court are mentioned in the preamble as well as articulated in specific articles. A central principle is that it does not seek to replace domestic courts. Rather, several references are made to the fact that the International Criminal Court is complementary to national criminal jurisdictions. The preamble emphasises that it remains "the duty of every State to exercise its criminal jurisdiction over those responsible for international crimes".

The International Criminal Court has jurisdiction over the crimes of genocide, crimes against humanity and war crimes. The crime of aggression will also be included in the International Criminal Court Statute after further work has been done to create a clear and widely accepted definition of this crime. The definition of genocide reflects that given in the Genocide Convention (article 6). The definition of crimes against humanity does not demand a nexus to armed conflict and requires "widespread or systematic attack directed at any civilian population" (article 7). The list of such crimes includes murder; extermination; forcible transfer of population; torture; persecution; enforced disappearance; apartheid; and "other inhumane acts of a similar nature". There is a specific and detailed list of crimes concerning sexual violence, including rape, sexual slavery and enforced pregnancy (article 7(1)(g)).

The war crimes provision states that the International Criminal Court shall have jurisdiction in respect of "war crimes in particular when committed as part of a plan or policy or as part of a large-scale commission of such crimes", thus not creating a strict threshold (article 8(1)). Grave breaches of the Geneva Conventions are included (article 8(2)(a)) as well as other serious violations of the laws and customs applicable in international armed conflict (article 8(2)(b)). The provisions of article 3 common to the four Geneva Conventions are listed (article 8(2)(c)), as well as a range of crimes committed in non-international armed conflict, such as attacking civilians not taking part in hostilities (article 8(2)(i)); attacking humanitarian workers (article 8(2)(ii)); sexual violence (article 8(2)(vi)); and actively using children under the age of 15 in hostilities (article 8(2)(vii)). There are three methods for a case to be referred to the International Criminal Court. Article 13 allows a case to be referred to the International Criminal Court by the Security Council acting under Chapter VII of the UN Charter. Additionally, referrals can be made by states parties and by the International Criminal Court Prosecutor.

The Statute for an International Criminal Court was and is a significant achievement, which received the support of 120 countries at the Rome Conference. It was opposed by only 8 states, while 21 states abstained from voting. The exact role it will play in assisting states in their transition from civil strife to civil society is yet to be seen. Most significantly, its creation demonstrates a tangible desire to implement international enforcement mechanisms of international human rights and humanitarian law.

Gathering evidence for international prosecutions

A crucial factor in any attempt to implement international justice is the need for the identification and creation of mechanisms to gather evidence. Even states with legal infrastructures intact can experience difficulties in finding witnesses prepared to come forward and in ensuring that physical evidence is not destroyed or hidden. For states in a period of transition wishing to utilise international tribunals or courts, there will often be an inherent lack of traditional investigative bodies such as the police. In recent times, UN investigators have played a significant role in exhuming bodies in places such as the Balkans and East Timor.[29] In the future, particularly now the International Criminal Court has entered into force, this role will increase and adequate resources will need to be allocated for these tasks. There are also a number of international "freelance investigators" of atrocities, the most famous being "Nazi Hunters" such as Simon Wiesenthal. However, such individuals can be seen as more useful in creating public awareness and mobilising political will to prosecute rather than actually becoming a substantial part of the judicial process.[30]

States emerging from civil strife are very likely to have a large number of non-governmental organisations (NGOs) and non-state actors present. The International Criminal Tribunal for the former Yugoslavia, the International Criminal Tribunal for Rwanda and the International Criminal Court allow the submission of evidence from a broad range of sources, including NGOs.[31] Experiences from the ad hoc tribunals indicate that NGOs are essential in providing relevant evidence and in many instances are the only institutions to witness atrocities. However, the issue of NGOs and non-state actors providing evidence is a controversial one. In particular, humanitarian non-state actors, such as the ICRC, do not wish to be involved in the judicial process.

NGOs and non-state actors can be roughly divided into two groups: humanitarian actors and human rights actors. Obviously these two categories do not fit every organisation, and a number of actors will fall into both groups at different times during their various activities. There is also a practical need to acknowledge the integral interrelationship between human rights activities and humanitarian relief.[32] However, for the purposes of this chapter the two categories are useful tools for exploring the attitudes within the NGO community towards gathering evidence for international criminal prosecutions.

Humanitarian actors

International humanitarian organisations, such as the ICRC, Médecins sans Frontières (MSF) and the United Nations High Commissioner for Refugees (UNHCR), work on the ground and in the field during armed conflict or times of crisis. Hence, to undertake their tasks they require access to victims of conflict and often the cooperation of the authorities in control, whether these be the warring parties or the government. For access and cooperation it is necessary for humanitarian organisations to have a degree of trust and relatively good relations with those in power. Moving beyond their traditional role of assisting victims and into the role of denouncing offenders could create problems with their operations in these countries. Furthermore, in providing evidence, the personal security of staff members in the field may be compromised. If members of humanitarian organisations testify at the International Criminal Court or other judicial bodies, this is likely to have a serious impact upon their negotiations, various relationships and capacity to deliver assistance to the needy.

Rather than wanting to provide input to the prosecutor's investigation, some humanitarian organisations wish for protection against giving evidence, or at least the discretion to decide whether or not they are involved in the process. This is so they can continue to fulfil their mandate of relieving the suffering of victims on the ground and delivering services during periods of crisis. This mandate often relies upon humanitarian actors remaining separate from the penal system. As Jacques Stroun, Deputy Director of Operations of the ICRC states, "public denunciation, for instance, may sometimes compromise the dialogue with the authorities concerned and jeopardize work for victims in the field".[33]

If such organisations are seen to provide evidence of what they have witnessed, they may be accused of taking a partial approach, which could result in the denial of access. Even if access is not denied in the particular conflict from which they provide evidence, it is certainly possible the organisation's activities could be limited in the context of other conflicts. It is not just the issue of access and trust with the authorities that is a consideration; a number of humanitarian actors use the principle of neutrality as an ideological position as well as a pragmatic tool.[34] The fear of allegations of a lack of independence in providing evidence at prosecutions is a genuine concern for many of these organisations.

Not all humanitarian organisations require access to the same degree, and often it is a philosophical dilemma as much as a practical issue whether to remain quiet after witnessing atrocities. Unlike many other humanitarian organisations working in the field, MSF bears witness to violations of basic humanitarian principles and denounces them publicly. MSF believes this is a vital part of its humanitarian mandate and commitment. As Fabien Dubuet from MSF in Paris writes:

To denounce publicly violations of our medical duties and serious breaches of humanitarian law is at the heart of the MSF identity since 1971. But we are not a human rights organization. The priority is to protect people: it means that we have to make noises at the right time, to alert rather than prove. Our main task is not to investigate and prove situations. We speak of violations we have witnessed through our medical activities ... Our message is the one of a medical and humanitarian organization that witnesses on-going war crimes and crimes against humanity on the field and that thinks for those crimes there is an absolute need for justice, beyond medical care.[35]

On the other hand, the ICRC will not give evidence.[36] In negotiations to develop rules of procedure and evidence for the International Criminal Court, the ICRC advanced its unique position and advocated a confidentiality rule. The ICRC stated four reasons for this distinct treatment: (1) in discharging its mandate, the ICRC obtains information on the basis of a relationship of confidence; (2) the element of confidentiality is essential to the full and satisfactory maintenance of the relationship between the ICRC and warring parties; (3) it is universally accepted (for example in the Geneva Conventions and Protocols) that it is in the international interest to foster this relationship; (4) the disclosure of information in breach of the ICRC's confidentiality rule would cause irreparable damage to the ability of the ICRC to perform the functions allotted to it and thus to the international public interest.[37]

These arguments were confirmed in a decision of the International Criminal Tribunal for the former Yugoslavia Trial Chamber III in July 1999. The issue related to a motion filed by the prosecution in the "Simic and Others" case regarding a former ICRC employee giving evidence on facts coming to his knowledge by virtue of his employment. The Tribunal ruled that customary law provided the ICRC with "an absolute right to non-disclosure of information relating to the work of the ICRC in the possession of an ICRC employee. Consequently no issue arises as to the balancing of the ICRC's confidentiality interest against the interest of justice."[38]

The dilemma faced by humanitarian organisations in the prosecution of those who perpetrate atrocities is ironic in the sense that, of all non-state actors, these organisations have access to the most valuable evidence. Being in the field, often in the middle of breaches of international humanitarian and human rights law, and regularly in contact with the perpetrators, humanitarian actors could provide the richest and most credible details to the prosecutor. However, owing to the practical considerations of their work they are unable to assist in this manner, choosing to focus upon immediate assistance and access to victims. The tension experienced by humanitarian actors between access and justice and between short-term security and long-term development will continue to grow as international criminal law expands.

Human rights actors

NGOs, which focus on human rights, by their very nature, are well equipped to assist the Tribunals in their investigation work. I say this because human rights organizations focus on the monitoring and reporting of human rights violations and seek to prevent future violations. This function is not inconsistent with that of the Tribunal.[39]

Human rights actors tend to be less visible in the field undertaking practical operations and more focused upon advocacy issues. For example, although organisations such as Amnesty International and Human Rights Watch need to gather their data in countries with human rights abuses, the vast bulk of work is done in cities such as London and New York. It is at these sites that campaigns are developed and distributed throughout the world. In many circumstances such campaigns involve education, monitoring states' human rights situations and denunciation.

Thus, the giving of evidence at international trials involves less threat to the daily work of human rights organisations. This is because, in general, human rights actors are less reliant upon trust and detailed negotiations with potential perpetrators. Those gathering evidence for human rights advocacy campaigns tend to undertake very short research trips, develop relationships with local NGOs and often utilise detailed statements from individuals no longer in the country – for example, refugees who are sheltering in another state. Often human rights organisations have to be extremely discreet about the initial source of their information and have strict verification processes. Owing to these factors, human rights actors may occasionally have difficulties in obtaining evidence, compared with humanitarian actors. However, there are fewer restrictions on the use of this information once it is in the possession of human rights organisations.[40]

A number of large human rights actors have substantial technical expertise in international criminal law. As a group, respected human rights organisations also have the support of the academic community and the media. Combined with the willingness and the commitment to give evidence, this can result in human rights actors playing a crucial role in international criminal prosecutions.

There is a great need for humanitarian and human rights organisations to consider deeply what role they wish to play in the prosecution of those accused of atrocities. Questions to be asked at an institutional level include how the gathering and supplying of evidence will affect an NGO's mandate, and philosophically what stance an organisation will take in relation to prosecutions in a disrupted state. The case of the ICRC is unusual owing to the organisation's strict principles and limited mandate. It also must not be forgotten that the ICRC is necessary in an environment where other humanitarian and human rights actors exist who are prepared to focus upon justice and advocacy. All actors in the field need to develop ideologies that move beyond mere rhetoric to deal with increasingly complex environments and the pressure that will inevitably arise to assist in the quest for justice. As Nicholas Leader states: "In order to promote the primacy of the humanitarian imperative, agencies need to be sure of their principles, and ensure that they live by them."[41]

Conclusion

The qualities of mercy and justice must not be forgotten in any attempt to reconstitute civil society after civil strife. How a community chooses to deal with the "history of horrors" it has endured must be carefully thought through, with long-term vision as well as a focus upon short-term necessities. In many instances, the prosecution of those accused of the commission of atrocities may not be appropriate, yet in many other instances it may be the best way to ensure that a society moves forward. Irrespective of the final decision, the increasing development and interest in international criminal law require all those with the task of rebuilding a state to have a good understanding of the relevant legal mechanisms.

Acknowledgements

I would like to thank Zoe Darmos for her assistance in preparing this chapter.

Notes

1. *Report of the Thirty-Eighth Strategy for Peace, US Foreign Policy Conference: "Accountability and Judicial Response – Building Mechanisms for Post-Conflict Justice"* (Muscatine, IA: The Stanley Foundation, 1997), p. 9. Copies of this report are available on the Internet at http://www.stanleyfdn.org/confrpts/USFP/SPC97/AJR97.html.
2. See, for example, Dann Bronkhorst, *Truth and Reconciliation: Obstacles and Opportunities for Human Rights* (Amsterdam: Amnesty International, Dutch Section, 1995).
3. Efraim Zuroff, *Occupation: Nazi-Hunter – the Continuing Search for the Perpetrators of the Holocaust* (New Jersey: Simon Wiesenthal Center, 1994), p. 224.
4. Greenberg Research, Inc., *People on War Country Report – Bosnia–Herzegovina: ICRC Worldwide Consultation on the Rules of War* (Geneva: International Committee of the Red Cross, 1999), p. 24.
5. Article 49 of the first Geneva Convention states: "Each High Contracting Party shall be under the obligation to search for persons alleged to have committed, or to have ordered to be committed, such grave breaches, and shall bring such persons, regardless of their nationality, before its own courts."
6. Concerns have been raised over the commitment of Indonesia to investigate and prosecute individuals accused of a range of crimes relating to East Timor. See, further, Anthony Goodman, "UN Urged to Act on Timor", *The Age*, 23 December 1999, p. 8; Lindsay Murdoch, "Generals Get Set to Fight Allegations of Atrocities", *The Age*, 17 December 1999, p. 11; Lindsay Murdoch, "Atrocities Panel to Question Wiranto", *The Age*, 10 December 1999, p. 12.
7. See Neil Kritz (ed.), *Transitional Justice: How Emerging Democracies Reckon with Former Regimes* (Washington DC: United States Institute of Peace Press, 1993).
8. Daan Bronkhorst, "Official Commissions of Investigation", in Bronkhorst, *Truth and Reconciliation: Obstacles and Opportunities for Human Rights*, pp. 69–90.
9. Mr Dullah Omar, Minister of Justice, South Africa. See Truth and Reconciliation homepage: http://www.truth.org.za/legal/index.htm.
10. For details on the South African Truth and Reconciliation Commission, see http://www.truth.org.za/legal/index.htm.
11. A. Hays Butler, *The Establishment of a Permanent International Criminal Court: A Selective and Annotated Bibliography* (New Brunswick, NJ: Rutgers University, 1998), p. 6.

12. For details, see Telford Taylor, *The Anatomy of the Nuremberg Trials* (New York: Alfred A. Knopf, 1993).
13. *Charter of the International Military Tribunal for the Far East*, TIAS no. 1589.
14. International Criminal Tribunal for the former Yugoslavia, http://www.un.org/icty/glance/index.htm.
15. International Criminal Tribunal for Rwanda, http://www.ictr.org/english/cases/index.htm and http://www.ictr.org/english/factsheets/detainee.htm.
16. The Tribunal is obliged to scrutinise all relevant submissions. According to Paul Risley, spokesperson for the Chief War Crimes Prosecutor Carla del Ponte, it "is incumbent on the tribunal to continue its mandate, which covers all the participants in armed conflict in the former Yugoslavia"; see Richard Norton-Taylor, "Nato Accused of Breaching Law in Kosovo Air Campaign", *Guardian Weekly*, 13–19 January 2000, p. 4.
17. Office of the Prosecutor, "Prosecutor's Report on the NATO Bombing Campaign", http://www.un.org/icty/pressreal/p510-e.htm, 13 June 2000.
18. For a detailed examination of recent legal developments in the International Criminal Tribunal for the former Yugoslavia, see Sean Murphy, "Progress and Jurisprudence of the International Criminal Tribunal for the Former Yugoslavia", *American Journal of International Law*, vol. 93, no. 1, January 1999, pp. 57–97.
19. Much has been written on this topic. See, for example, Kelly Askin, "Sexual Violence in Decisions and Indictments of the Yugoslav and Rwandan Tribunals: Current Status", *American Journal of International Law*, vol. 93, no. 1, January 1999, pp. 97–123.
20. *Report of the Group of Experts for Cambodia Pursuant to General Assembly Resolution 52/135*, 18 February 1999, p. 40.
21. Luke Hunt, "Australian Judge Tipped for Role in Khmer Rouge Trial", *Canberra Times*, 23 August 2001, p. 10.
22. Christopher Hall, "The First Proposal for a Permanent International Criminal Court", *International Review of the Red Cross*, no. 322, March 1998, pp. 57–74.
23. GA Res 47/33, UN GAOR (73rd mtg), UN Doc A/RES/47/33 (1992) 3.
24. Benjamin Ferencz, "An International Criminal Code and Court: Where They Stand and Where They're Going", *Columbia Journal of Transnational Law*, vol. 30, no. 1, 1992, pp. 375–399.
25. *Report of the International Law Commission on the Work of Its 49th Session* (United Nations, 49 UN GAOR (Supp 10/90), UN Doc A/49/10, 1994).
26. GA Res 49/53, 49 UN GAOR (Supp 49), UN Doc A/49/49 (1994).
27. As of October 2002, 81 countries had ratified or acceded to the Rome Treaty. These are Andorra, Antigua and Barbuda, Argentina, Australia, Austria, Belgium, Belize, Benin, Bolivia, Bosnia and Herzegovina, Botswana, Brazil, Bulgaria, Cambodia, Canada, Central African Republic, Colombia, Costa Rica, Croatia, Cyprus, Democratic Republic of the Congo, Denmark, Dominica, Ecuador, Estonia, Fiji, Finland, France, Gabon, Gambia, Germany, Ghana, Greece, Honduras, Hungary, Iceland, Ireland, Italy, Jordan, Latvia, Lesotho, Liechtenstein, Luxembourg, Malawi, Mali, Marshall Islands, Mauritius, Mongolia, Namibia, Nauru, the Netherlands, New Zealand, Niger, Nigeria, Norway, Panama, Paraguay, Peru, Poland, Portugal, Romania, Samoa, San Marino, Senegal, Sierra Leone, Slovakia, Slovenia, South Africa, Spain, Sweden, Switzerland, Tajikistan, the Former Yugoslav Republic of Macedonia, Timor-Leste, Trinidad and Tobago, Uganda, United Kingdom, United Republic of Tanzania, Uruguay, Venezuela and Yugoslavia.
28. The 13 parts are: (1) Establishment of the Court; (2) Jurisdiction, Admissibility and Applicable Laws; (3) General Principles of Criminal Law; (4) Composition and Administration of the Court; (5) Investigation and Prosecution; (6) The Trial; (7) Penalties; (8) Appeal and Revision; (9) International Cooperation and Judicial Assistance;

(10) Enforcement; (11) Assembly of States Parties; (12) Financing; and (13) Final Clauses.
29. Carmel Egan, "Investigators to Dig up Massacre Victims", *The Australian*, 11 January 2000, p. 6.
30. There is little doubt that Dr Efraim Zuroff, the Director of the Simon Wiesenthal Center, has played a large part in the calls on the Australian government to investigate and prosecute Mr Konrad Kalejs. In a statement to the media he noted that if "the authorities in Australia had invested one hundredth of the resources and energy that Mr Kalejs and his cohorts invested in murdering Jews in the Holocaust he would be sitting in prison now"; see Martin Daly, Simon Mann, Janine McDonald, "Konrad Kalejs Flies in to a Storm of Protests", *The Australian*, 8 January 2000, p. 1.
31. For example, article 15(2) of the International Criminal Court Statute states: "The Prosecutor shall analyse the seriousness of the information received. For this purpose, he or she may seek additional information from States, organs of the United Nations, inter-Governmental or non-Governmental organisations, or other reliable sources that he or she deems appropriate, and may receive written or oral testimony at the seat of the Court."
32. Philip Alston, "Introductory Speech", in *Final Report of the Conference on the Cooperation between Humanitarian Organizations and Human Rights Organizations* (Amsterdam: Médecins Sans Frontières, 1996), p. 8. Alston states that cooperation between humanitarian and human rights organisations "is no longer an optional proposition but a necessity ... The reality is there is no option but to explore the interlinkages between these different concerns and to seek to develop some different forms of cooperation, albeit carefully tailored to the needs of the situation".
33. Jacques Stroun, "International Criminal Jurisdiction, International Humanitarian Law and Humanitarian Action", *International Review of the Red Cross*, no. 321, November–December 1997, pp. 623–634 at p. 625.
34. For further discussion of the principle of neutrality and humanitarian actors, see Hugo Slim, "Relief Agencies and Moral Standing in War: Principles of Humanity, Neutrality, Impartiality and Solidarity", *Development in Practice*, vol. 7, no. 4, November 1997, pp. 342–352.
35. Fax from Fabien Dubuet, MSF, Paris, 14 January 1999.
36. For a detailed examination of the approach of various humanitarian organisations, see Paul Bonard, *Modes of Action Used by Humanitarian Players: Criteria for Operational Complementarity* (Geneva: International Committee of the Red Cross, 1999).
37. International Committee of the Red Cross, *The ICRC's Confidentiality Rule and the International Criminal Court: Complementarity of Action in Implementing International Humanitarian Law* (Geneva: International Committee of the Red Cross, July 1999), p. 20. This paper was presented by the International Committee of the Red Cross at the Second Session of the Preparatory Commission for the Establishment of an International Criminal Court in New York, 26 July–13 August 1999.
38. "Trial Chamber III Rules That ICRC Need Not Testify before the Tribunal", Press Release JL/P.I.S./439-E, The Hague, 8 October 1999.
39. Graeme Blewitt, "The Relationship between NGOs and the International Criminal Tribunals", in *Final Report of the Conference on the Cooperation between Humanitarian Organizations and Human Rights Organizations* (Amsterdam: Médecins San Frontières, 1996), p. 21.
40. Interview with Donato Kiniger-Passigli, External Relations Officer, International Criminal Tribunal for the former Yugoslavia, The Hague, 5 November 1996.
41. Nicholas Leader, "Humanitarian Principles in Practice: A Critical Review", *RRN Discussion Paper*, no. 16, December 1999, p. 5.

Part 4
Reconstituting political order

9

Institutional design and the rebuilding of trust

William Maley

Without trust, a "society" hardly merits the name. This may seem a terse summation of an exceedingly complex set of problems, but at least it serves to alert us to a challenge that all too often confronts those who happen to be residents of disrupted states. Hobbes's nightmare of a war of all against all is rarely, if ever, realised in the real world,[1] but it retains its relevance as a warning of the dangers that attend a breakdown of the mechanisms sustaining social order. In circumstances where such mechanisms have been substantially compromised, complex remedies are likely to be required in order to facilitate the delicate process of reconstituting political order.

The aim of this chapter is to explore in more detail the problems that arise from an erosion of trust within disrupted states, and the approaches to the design of institutions that can help to alleviate or overcome these problems. The chapter is divided into three sections. The first examines the dimensions of trust, the problems for social order that can spring from a decline in trust, and remedies that might be adopted in response. The second section focuses specifically on institutional remedies, addressing in turn the questions of what marks an effective process of institutional design, what substantive issues need to be considered in designing institutions to restore stability in disrupted states, and how such institutions might be legitimated. The third section deals with the strengths and weaknesses of various concrete institutional options.

Trust and politics

The idea of "trust" has recently figured quite prominently in the work of political theorists, especially in the context of debates about the requirements for the efficient operation of democratic political systems. In a number of Western democracies, opinion poll evidence has pointed to declining levels of "trust" in government, and some observers have interpreted low voter turnout at elections as exposing a wider problem of declining governmental legitimacy. However, running through these debates are subtly varying understandings of "trust", as well as distinct perspectives on the relationship of "trust" to other factors that impinge upon democratic functioning. Broadly, trust can be defined in terms of expectations: "to trust means to hold some expectations about something future or contingent or to have some belief as to how another person will perform on some future occasion. To trust is to believe that the results of somebody's intended action will be appropriate from our point of view."[2] In the following discussion, which is concerned more with senses of "trust" pertinent to disrupted states, I want first to draw a broad distinction between anonymous trust and face-to-face trust. Neither of these directly involves trust in organisations, such as militias, armies or even governments. As Russell Hardin has plausibly argued, trusting institutions "makes little sense for most people most of the time",[3] and this warning is especially pertinent in disrupted states.

Anonymous trust arises where the trust that one grants to one's fellows is grounded not in specific knowledge about their individual interests or dispositions, but simply in the knowledge that they too are members of some collective of which one can claim membership. This may be a collective of citizenship within a state, or of membership of some other type of ethnic, religious or social community or group. The phenomenon of anonymous trust is not an undiluted good: it can form the basis for the acceptance of pernicious incitements directed against those who are not members of the group. Nor should one expect it to be a ubiquitous feature of any normal person's dispositions; anonymous trust may be much more readily granted when the risk of granting trust is low than when the risk is high. However, it is at the same time an important foundation for cooperative behaviour: anonymous trust can be a significant component of social capital.[4] The challenge in a disrupted state is to reconstitute the boundaries of anonymous trust so that they embrace the entire citizenry. Unless this challenge is met, there will be no "mass politics", but only "intercommunal politics", of a kind that has scarred lands as otherwise remote as Ulster and Rwanda.

By contrast, face-to-face (or interpersonal) trust is grounded in specific knowledge about the interests or dispositions of those whom one trusts.

It is also a significant element of social capital. If individuals cannot trust those whom they encounter on a regular basis, and about whom they can form clear expectations, local cooperation and the benefits that flow from it will be difficult to sustain.

What problems flow from the breakdown of trust? There are many, but two deserve particular attention. The first problem is that of unworkable political communities, and Kosovo before (and arguably after) NATO's 1999 intervention provides a good example. There, one found anonymous trust at relatively high levels within the major communities – Serb and Albanian – but a catastrophic dearth of anonymous trust between the two. The net result was that politics in the territory assumed a zero-sum character, and respect for the rights of individuals declined disastrously, ultimately prompting pressure for international intervention. Such a slide in anonymous trust does not simply "happen", but reflected the role of political incentives in structuring the behaviour of individuals.[5] And, as Brian Barry has warned, once ethnic feeling "has been whipped up, it has a terrifying life of its own",[6] and this makes the reconstitution of anonymous trust peculiarly difficult.

The second problem is that of disunified political elites. Political stability in the modern state has historically owed a great deal to elite unity,[7] either consensual (as found in established democracies where there is agreement as to the fundamental rules of the "game" of politics) or ideological (as found in durable dictatorships where dissent at elite level is ruthlessly suppressed in the name of some overarching value system). In the absence of such elite unity – in other words, if face-to-face trust breaks down within a ruling elite – political order is difficult to sustain. Here, the cases of Afghanistan and East Timor are instructive. In Afghanistan, the emergence of severe divisions within the national political elite played a key role in the breakdown of political order which culminated in the communist coup of April 1978.[8] In East Timor, a high level of elite fragmentation supplied the Indonesian military with ready surrogates to conduct rampages against those who voted for independence in the August 1999 popular consultation.[9] In each case, the consequences for ordinary people were catastrophic. The foreign occupation that these countries endured has created an additional problem: how to cope with collaborators. France is still struggling with the legacies of collaboration more than half a century after its liberation from German occupation, as the appearances before French courts of René Bousquet, Paul Touvier and Maurice Papon illustrate;[10] it would be a brave person who expected the Afghans or the East Timorese to shrug off this burden any more quickly, although statesmanlike leaders can help change the climate.

Once trust has broken down, steps to restore it can be taken in at least three different ways. The first is through the immediate deployment of an adequate neutral force to provide security. The second is through long-run attempts to resocialise the population. The third is through the redesign of institutions.

The aim of an adequate neutral security force is to provide a sufficient degree of security that political actors need not strike pre-emptively against their opponents for fear that they will otherwise fall victim to a pre-emptive strike themselves. As Barbara F. Walter has argued, the greatest challenge facing civil war opponents "is to design a treaty that convinces the combatants to shed their partisan armies and surrender conquered territory even though such steps will increase their vulnerability and limit their ability to enforce the treaty's other terms".[11] A somewhat similar point has been made by Charles King:

> In civil wars, external powers are often the only available generator of trust between the contesting parties ... Trust among the belligerent parties thus depends on each side feeling sufficiently secure in its own position to accept the legitimacy of contending interests and to discuss ways in which those interests might be accommodated in a final settlement.[12]

One only need look at cases where such an adequate force was *not* available to appreciate the force of these observations. In Angola, the efforts of the United Nations Angola Verification Mission II (UNAVEM II) were thwarted when, following the September 1992 elections, a key party, Unita, declined to accept the results, as a result of which armed conflict resumed.[13] In Rwanda, the Arusha Peace Agreement of 4 August 1993 was followed by the deployment of the United Nations Assistance Mission for Rwanda (UNAMIR), of which General Roméo Dallaire was the Force Commander. However, the force at his disposal was entirely unequal to the task of creating a proper security environment, and was unable to arrest the slide towards genocide of ethnic Tutsis and moderate Hutus, which broke out in April 1994.[14] In East Timor in 1999, there was no security force at all; astonishingly, the 5 May 1999 Accords on East Timor left the maintenance of security in the hands of Indonesia, which, as subsequent events showed, was the very party that could not be trusted with such a task.[15] The difficulty, of course, in securing the deployment of adequate neutral security forces is one of *will*: unless interests of states are sufficiently engaged, they may prove quite resistant to suggestions that they have a duty of any kind to contribute to what are likely to be complex and challenging missions.

Resocialisation of a population involves addressing not immediate fears for security, but more entrenched cognitive and cultural dispositions that militate against the restoration of trust. It is not in any sense a short-term palliative, but rather a long-term prerequisite for the restoration of political stability. Harry Eckstein has famously argued that "a government will tend to be stable if its authority pattern is congruent with the other authority patterns of the society of which it is a part".[16] In disrupted states, social authority is typically fragmented, with little evidence of a residual civic culture. The reconstitution of such a culture, embodying certain minimal norms of tolerance and compromise, is vital if the problems of disruption are to be overcome. A well-constructed foreign occupation can sometimes assist this process: those German *Länder* that were occupied by the Americans, British and French and subsequently formed the Federal Republic of Germany provided a good example of a new, democratic politics being fostered by effective resocialisation. A similar challenge faced the NATO forces that occupied Kosovo as a result of the March–May 1999 conflict. However, many disrupted states do not have the benefit of such a presence. This places a heavy burden on the third step that can be taken to restore trust, namely the redesign of institutions.

All societies are marked by a complex array of institutions, in the sense of "a set of rules that structure social interactions in particular ways", where "knowledge of these rules [is] shared by the members of the relevant community or society".[17] Institutions in this sense help make up what Jon Elster has called "The Cement of Society".[18] My focus, however, is on institutions in a more formally political sense, namely on those instrumentalities of the state within which competition for the right to exercise political power takes place. Different institutions can offer incentives for people to behave in different ways, for example cooperatively rather than antagonistically. In this way, they feed into culture: "Institutions generate distinctive sets of preferences, and adherence to certain values legitimizes corresponding institutional arrangement."[19] It is for this reason also that institutional design can play a useful role in promoting the rebuilding of trust.

Some principles of institutional design

The process of institutional design in disrupted states can take many forms. It may be carried out under the auspices of an occupying power (as in the case of the 1947 Japanese constitution), or as part of an internationally organised process of political transition (as in Cambodia in 1993), or as a result of bargaining between domestic political forces (as in South Africa during the transition from white minority rule). Whichever approach is adopted, certain basic nostrums are of value in determining how institutional design in disrupted states should proceed.

First, institutional design should not be overlooked. Too often, institutional design, although formally recognised as an important part of a process, receives little or no attention. In Afghanistan in 1991–1992, the United Nations sought to promote a peace process based on a statement issued by the Secretary-General on 21 May 1991, which envisaged "free and fair elections, taking into account Afghan traditions, for the establishment of a broad-based government", but at no time did it give any attention to the questions that would need to resolved for electoral institutions to be put in place.[20] The process ultimately collapsed under the weight of its own contradictions,[21] but it was in any case headed for disaster because of the neglect of key institutional dimensions.

Second, institutional design should not be rushed. Although there is always a risk that undue delay may give spoilers the opportunity to mobilise, time is needed both for designers to come to terms with their tasks and for the full implications of different proposals to be absorbed by those most likely to be directly affected. In Cambodia, the Paris Accords of 1991 provided for the United Nations to preside over an election to a constituent assembly that would be responsible for drafting a new constitution. However, the United Nations was so preoccupied with the responsibility of running the elections for the assembly that very little thought was given to what type of institutions might be recommended to the assembly once it met. Although the United Nations' Chief Electoral Officer, Professor Reginald Austin, took the time to prepare a basic memorandum on the tasks the constituent assembly would need to perform, he was almost alone in paying attention to the issue. As a result, the constitution of September 1993, drafted largely in secret by a small committee, contained critical flaws such as the one that in 1995 permitted the expulsion of former Finance Minister Sam Rainsy from the National Assembly on the grounds that he had been expelled from the party of which he had originally been a candidate.[22] This was in turn a crucial event along the path to the coup of July 1997, which fundamentally compromised the outcome of the United Nations Transitional Authority in Cambodia (UNTAC) operation. By contrast, the South African transition of 1994 came as the culmination of a prolonged and very public series of negotiations to which a wide range of groups contributed, and this process undoubtedly helped to generate a widespread sense of engagement with the new institutions.[23]

Third, institutional design can benefit from expertise. This is not to say that issues of institutional design are purely technical, or that the consequences of adopting particular institutions are always predictable. They are not, which is why writers as insightful as Montesquieu warned that laws should be amended "only in fear and trembling"[24] – although the luxury of such conservatism is not available to those called upon to rebuild the institutions of a disrupted state. The demand for expertise simply reflects the reality of the assumption, as Reilly and Reynolds put it, that "long-term sociopolitical stability is the nation's overarching goal; and the institutions needed to facilitate that goal may not be the same as those which provide maximum short-term gain to the negotiating actors in the transitional period".[25] This is a delicate issue, for those actors, understandably, can be extremely possessive about the processes in which they are involved. And it is indeed the case that constitutional engineers who neglect the specific context of their endeavours will likely give poor advice. In institutional design, it is a grave error to believe that "one size fits all". That said, it is equally mistaken to believe that locals can necessarily detect pitfalls which to others might be obvious. For example, in March 1993, contending Afghan groups signed an agreement that appointed two hostile party leaders to two strong executive offices – those of president and prime minister – without either delineating the responsibilities of the offices or providing a mechanism for breaking deadlocks. Within a very short time, the conflict returned to the battlefield.[26]

Moving beyond issues of process, a number of important points of substance deserve attention. Robert Goodin has identified a number of general attributes that institutions should possess if they are to be effective.[27]

- *revisability*, in recognition of the reality that human beings are fallible and that societies can change;
- *robustness* – institutions should change only in ways that are appropriate to changed circumstances;
- *sensitivity to motivational complexity*, with the individual's capacity to practise both vice and virtue kept in mind;
- *variability*, so that one can learn from experimenting with different institutional arrangements.

However, as Goodin rightly observes, none of these is "unqualified or sacrosanct".[28] In particular, one must be alert to side-effects that otherwise-attractive institutions might produce. First, one needs to be aware of the effects that new institutions might have on market relations and the private sector. Even in the most disrupted of states, markets usually continue to function, often sustaining a surprisingly large proportion of the population. This is because norms other than those ordained and enforced by the state may sustain institutions of property and contract.[29] New institutions can easily disrupt the operation of institutions such as these, with deleterious long-term consequences. This point can be broadened to address the issue of civil society more generally. There are good reasons to regard a vigorous civil society – that is, a network of groups and organisations enjoying significant autonomy from the command structures of the state and sustained by relatively high levels of face-to-face trust[30] – as a central element in what Robert Dahl has called the "social separation of powers".[31] Institutions that break down these networks can have an extremely detrimental effect on the prospects for rebuilding trust more generally.

In a deeply disrupted society, the designing of institutions can require that one address quite fundamental issues of political theory related to the role of the state. Because the issues involved are philosophical, there is scope for significant differences of opinion and perspective. Three spheres of concern are likely to be of particular importance.

1. What should be the nature and locus of political authority? Should institutional design take some notion of popular sovereignty as its point of departure, or might other considerations, such as the weight and force of tradition, merit some attention?
2. To what distributive capacity should the state aspire? Should the state be limited to providing a framework of rules for the conduct of orderly social life by other actors, or should the state itself be the principal agent of resource extraction and redistribution within a society?
3. What should be the role of military power? Should military force be used solely to defend against external threat, or should it also play a role in the maintenance of internal order?

These questions barely touch the surface of the complexities involved, but they do serve to highlight that the issues involved in institutional design are fundamentally political, and that, with the best of will, it may prove difficult to forge any consensus around proposed answers.

In any institutional design process, a key object will be to design institutions that will be legitimate, that is, will secure generalised normative support. This outcome, which might also be labelled the institutionalisation of institutions, is of central importance. As Rousseau once observed, the "strongest is never strong enough to be always master, unless he transforms strength into right, and obedience into duty".[32] Institutions that are grounded in non-legitimate bases of domination, such as coercion, are likely to be confronted at some point with a legitimacy crisis, and in any case are likely to be challenged by evolving norms in the international system, such as the nascent right to democratic governance. This is not to say, however, that legitimate institutions need necessarily have a strong democratic foundation. For example, during the Cambodian transition, the United Nations accorded a special role to the former Cambodian king, Prince Norodom Sihanouk, who resumed the throne with the adoption of the September 1993 constitution. One result of this was to blur the message about popular sovereignty that the holding of free and fair elections was designed to send. The justification was that Sihanouk was deemed to be the repository of traditional or charismatic authority, which the United Nations needed to exploit in order to bring the UNTAC mission to a successful conclusion.[33]

Legitimacy, as these last observations make clear, can have a number of different bases, and a key one is likely to be workability. If institutions operate in such a way as to satisfy the minimum requirements of potential spoilers, they are likely to take root. However, it is important to note also that institutions can benefit from receiving, and being *seen* to receive, the imprimatur of the wider world. In Afghanistan, for example, the major crisis of state disintegration that was patently exposed with the collapse of the communist regime in April 1992 was further aggravated by the unwillingness of major actors in the world community, most notably the United States and the United Nations, to take seriously the new regime that took over in Kabul. The US Embassy remained closed and, within months, the United Nations had evacuated its non-Afghan staff from Kabul as rockets from the Pakistan-backed Hezb-e Islami of Gulbuddin Hekmatyar began to rain down on the city. The signal sent was one of indifference, and Hekmatyar drew the obvious conclusion, that he could continue his rocketing with impunity.

However, if on occasion the world community errs by withholding its imprimatur, on other occasions it errs by granting it too readily. An excellent example of just such a display of indulgence came with the Cambodian elections of July 1998. These elections came in the wake of a coup by Hun Sen against First Prime Minister Prince Norodom Ranariddh, the culmination of what William Shawcross termed "a concerted attempt to nullify the results of the 1993 election",[34] and were notable for high levels of pre-poll intimidation. As Cambodia specialist Steven Heder warned in testimony to a US Congressional Committee, "[f]or the international community to come back in 1998, observe an obscene farce and then declare it on a par with 1993 is hypocrisy and duplicity on an outrageous scale".[35] Despite this warning, a number of observers adopted extravagant language to praise the polls, with former US Congressman Stephen J. Solarz terming them a "Miracle on the Mekong".[36] Expert analysis later discredited this assessment,[37] but by then the damage had been done. One of the difficulties afflicting the assessment of the Cambodian poll was that a number of international bodies involved in monitoring the election had also contributed resources for its conduct. To admit that pre-poll intimidation had nevertheless compromised the outcome of the poll would have been tantamount to an admission that the monies disbursed for the conduct of the voting had been wasted. This was a most unfortunate development, for it is vital that the criteria of freedom and fairness in assessing electoral processes not be adulterated. As Sanderson and Maley have observed, "[f]ormulations such as 'broadly representative' or 'broadly reflecting the will of the people', when used to describe elections which are not genuinely free and fair, are simply devoid of content. One cannot tell by telepathy what is the true will of the people, freely arrived at: free and fair elections are themselves the process by which that is determined."[38] Such elementary points are all too readily forgotten.

Some specific choices

A temptation for foreign ministries confronted with the challenge of reconstructing institutions is to look instead for a strong leader. Unfortunately, strong leaders are not in themselves institutions, and, when they fall, they can take other countries' foreign policies down with them.[39] There is much to be said, therefore, in favour of institutions that allow ordinary people to rule well. The following remarks are designed to explore options, related to both state and civil society, that have some claim to this character.

Some would argue that, in a disrupted state, a powerful central authority is required, with the aim, in the words of Thomas Hobbes, to keep men "all in awe".[40] But, against this, two arguments can be put. First, when the instrumentalities of the state have substantially collapsed, any attempt to rebuild a strong bureaucratic state may prompt strenuous efforts by different powerholders to capture and monopolise control of a new state because of its perceived importance in the allocation of positional or distributional goods.[41] The quest for a strong state may simply fuel further processes of disruption. Second, in disrupted states, there is rarely much to be said for institutions that depend upon heroic assumptions about individual virtue. Rather, the powers of powerholders may need to be constrained in quite specific ways. One of the key political questions, originally posed by the Roman writer Juvenal, remains "quis custodiet ipsos custodes?" – "Who will guard the guardians themselves?" The answer to this question classically came in the form of constitutionalism, and of two doctrines at its heart: the doctrines of the rule of law and of the separation of powers. The former requires that the state function in accordance with the requirements of law; the latter posits that certain functions – typically labelled legislative, executive and judicial – be exercised by different components of a political system.[42]

In the realm of the fragmentation of power, options relating to territorial fragmentation are important. John Stuart Mill defended "local administrative institutions" as "chief instrument" of the "public education of citizens",[43] and this notion has obvious appeal if one is seeking to find venues to rebuild face-to-face trust in disrupted states. Of course, such institutions need to be designed with care, so that they not become the theatre for the reinvigoration of *dis*trust. More generally, fragmentation on a federal basis may have the attraction of building on power realities already existing on the ground: this is one of the real appeals of a federal model for a state such as Afghanistan. However, the risk of a pure federal system is that it may create room for islands of brutal oppression, from which hapless civilians may have no realistic option of exit. In Afghanistan in the aftermath of the overthrow of the Taliban, there is understandable fear of a resurfacing of predatory warlordism which a federal structure could support. These considerations must be taken into account when assessing the merits of the case for federalism as a guard against repression by a central state.

Once some decision is reached on the appropriate points at which power will be concentrated, it will then be necessary to address questions of how it should be apportioned. One approach is to develop institutions that provide for power to be shared, either through a "government of national unity" or through a more formalised "consociational" model, providing not only for government by a grand coalition of political leaders, but in addition for a system of mutual vetoes, proportionality between groups in the allocation of offices, and high degrees of autonomy for groups in the running of their own affairs.[44] However, where levels of distrust are high, such approaches are hard to put into effect, for they depend upon a high level of elite cooperation; they are not actually mechanisms for generating such cooperation.[45] Another approach is to develop institutions that provide for power to be alternated between different claimants in accordance with some measure of popular sentiment. This idea lies at the heart of some conceptions of democracy, which the philosopher Karl Popper once defined as a set of institutions "which permit public control of the rulers and their dismissal by the ruled, and which make it possible for the ruled to obtain reforms without using violence, even against the will of the rulers".[46] Democracy in this sense is not simply a luxury of the affluent, as some proponents of one-party rule would maintain. On the contrary, as Sen has powerfully argued, "no famine has ever taken place in the history of the world in a functioning democracy".[47] Unaccountable power is ultimately inimical to social wellbeing.

What specific structures of office might one contemplate? An extensive, if ultimately inconclusive, literature exists on the merits of on the one hand presidential systems, and on the other parliamentary systems.[48] Pure presidential systems feature a head of state who does not depend upon the support of an elected legislature for survival, and who heads the executive government. The supporters of presidential systems welcome the possibility of strong and decisive leadership that such a system can offer, pointing to the threat vested interests can pose to the wider public – although, as the later years of the Yeltsin presidency in Russia made clear, a strong system combined with a weak incumbent can be a recipe for paralysis and the maturation of the very forces a strong presidency is intended to thwart.[49] The critics of presidentialism point to its propensity, in sharply divided societies, to add to social division because it is difficult to find a candidate with whom a wide range of groups will identify. Parliamentary systems, in which typically the executive government is drawn from an elected legislature, tend to put greater emphasis on collegiality, and can offer disparate groups at least some measure of political success, which may be important in drawing them away from more destructive patterns of behaviour. They also lend themselves to the parallel emergence of institutions of "horizontal accountability",[50] such as Ombudsmen and Auditors-General, as well as deliberative institutions[51] which not only maximise accountability between elections but provide scope for political actors to cooperate on a range of technical matters in a way that helps rebuild face-to-face trust.

Much turns, of course, on the precise method by which officeholders, either presidential or parliamentary, are to be selected. Presidents can be selected in ways that force candidates to pitch their appeal to a wide range of forces; parliaments can be selected by systems that *exclude* a wide range of forces. As Reilly and Reynolds have argued, there "is no perfect electoral system, and no 'right' way to approach the subject of electoral system design".[52] Different electoral systems have different political consequences,[53] and what is appropriate in a transitional democracy may be less appropriate in a consolidated democracy. Furthermore, diverse objectives can be entertained by architects of electoral systems – ensuring a representative parliament, making elections accessible and meaningful, providing incentives for conciliation, facilitating stable and efficient government, holding the government and representatives accountable, encouraging "cross-cutting" political parties, and promoting a parliamentary opposition[54] – and, whereas proportional representation systems may best promote some of these, plurality–majority systems may best promote others. The lesson, again, is that these issues demand careful attention and great care.

These remarks deal largely with legislative and executive institutions. But it is important also to note that the reconstitution of policing and judicial functions is vital if the rule of law is to be given any meaning.[55] Trust to a very considerable degree is built on confidence in the institutions of justice: people will embark on complex and risky games as long as they believe there are fair rules and a fair umpire. Ensuring this, it goes without saying, is a most daunting task in disrupted societies.

I wish to conclude with some brief observations about some ways in which trust can be nurtured through the institutions of civil society. As Hardin has observed, at "the most extreme change in government, such as after a major social revolution, the problem of establishing stable expectations may make trust nearly impossible for a while".[56] New state institutions are likely to be unfamiliar and to favour particular groups over others, as was patently the case after the French, Bolshevik and Iranian revolutions. In such circumstances, anonymous trust on a wide scale is likely to be heavily eroded, except amongst young people exposed to state indoctrination. The significance in social life of face-to-face trust may, however, increase. This is also the case in disrupted states that have not gone down a totalitarian path. There, trust across narrow lines can be effectively nurtured through two types of institution. One such institution is the market. The great virtue of market mechanisms is that they encourage economic agents to produce goods or services for whoever is prepared to buy them, irrespective of that person's ethnicity, religion or social location. The incentive structures of the market, although dependent on a framework of constitutive rules, reward those who take the risk of trusting their fellows anonymously.[57] Another such institution is the non-governmental organisation (NGO). NGOs, both indigenous and international, have become ubiquitous actors in disrupted states in recent years, and are usually appraised in terms of concrete costs and benefits associated with their projects. However, an additional potential benefit of their work is often overlooked, namely their capacity to provide a venue in which individuals can rediscover the virtues of trust by working cooperatively towards a specific shared goal. An excellent example of this phenomenon at work is to be found in the Mine Action Programme for Afghanistan, which is largely implemented by Afghan NGOs.[58] These bodies have mobilised the talents of young Afghans very effectively, and led to outstanding achievements in a range of mine action spheres, but have also encouraged a cooperative spirit, which contrasts sharply with some of the bitter divisions scarring Afghan society more generally.

It is wise to close this analysis on a cautious note. Prudent and careful institutional design does not put an end to often fierce political conflicts. It simply seeks to channel them into ways in which they can be conducted at lower risk. As Bertrand de Jouvenel perceptively observed, "political problems give rise to settlements, not solutions".[59] The rebuilding of trust does not lead to any kind of utopia. But it can lead to a world in which it is markedly easier to live and, for the victims of all the ills that state disruption can produce, this is unlikely to seem a negligible benefit.

Notes

1. See Dennis Wrong, *The Problem of Order: What Unites and Divides Society* (Cambridge, MA: Harvard University Press, 1994), p. 243.

2. Barbara A. Misztal, *Trust in Modern Societies* (Oxford: Polity Press, 1996), p. 24.
3. Russell Hardin, "Do We Want Trust in Government?", in Mark E. Warren (ed.), *Democracy and Trust* (Cambridge: Cambridge University Press, 1999), pp. 22–41 at p. 23.
4. See James S. Coleman, *Foundations of Social Theory* (Cambridge, MA: Harvard University Press, 1990); Robert D. Putnam, *Making Democracy Work: Civic Traditions in Modern Italy* (Princeton, NJ: Princeton University Press, 1993); Eric M. Uslaner, "Democracy and Social Capital", in Warren (ed.), *Democracy and Trust*, pp. 121–150.
5. See Russell Hardin, *One for All: The Logic of Group Conflict* (Princeton, NJ: Princeton University Press, 1995).
6. Brian Barry, *Democracy, Power and Justice: Essays in Political Theory* (Oxford: Oxford University Press, 1989), p. 134.
7. See John Higley and Richard Gunther (eds), *Elites and Democratic Consolidation in Latin America and Southern Europe* (Cambridge: Cambridge University Press, 1992); Mattei Dogan and John Higley (eds), *Elites, Crises, and the Origins of Regimes* (Lanham, MD: Rowman & Littlefield, 1998).
8. See Barnett R. Rubin, *The Fragmentation of Afghanistan: State Formation and Collapse in the International System* (New Haven, CT: Yale University Press, 1995), pp. 81–105.
9. See William Maley, "The UN and East Timor", *Pacifica Review*, vol. 12, no. 1, February 2000, pp. 63–76.
10. See Ian Ousby, *Occupation: The Ordeal of France 1940–1944* (New York: St. Martin's Press, 1997), p. 303.
11. Barbara F. Walter, "Designing Transitions from Civil War: Demobilization, Democratization, and Commitments to Peace", *International Security*, vol. 24, no. 1, Summer 1999, pp. 127–155 at p. 129. See also Barbara F. Walter, "The Critical Barrier to Civil War Settlement", *International Organization*, vol. 51, no. 3, Summer 1997, pp. 335–364; Barbara F. Walter, *Committing to Peace: The Successful Settlement of Civil Wars* (Princeton, NJ: Princeton University Press, 2002). Third parties can of course play important roles beyond the mere provision of security; see Fen Osler Hampson, *Nurturing Peace: Why Peace Settlements Succeed or Fail* (Washington DC: United States Institute of Peace Press, 1996), pp. 205–234.
12. Charles King, *Ending Civil Wars*, Adelphi Paper no. 308 (Oxford: Oxford University Press, for the International Institute for Strategic Studies, 1997), pp. 77 and 78.
13. On this mission, see Virginia Page Fortna, "Success and Failure in Southern Africa: Peacekeeping in Namibia and Angola", in Donald C. F. Daniel and Bradd C. Hayes (eds), *Beyond Traditional Peacekeeping* (New York: St Martin's Press, 1995), pp. 282–299; Margaret Joan Anstee, *Orphan of the Cold War: The Inside Story of the Collapse of the Angolan Peace Process, 1992–93* (London: Macmillan, 1996); Yvonne C. Lodico, "A Peace That Fell Apart: The United Nations and the War in Angola", in William J. Durch (ed.), *UN Peacekeeping, American Policy, and the Uncivil Wars of the 1990s* (London: Macmillan, 1997), pp. 103–133.
14. On these events, see Michael N. Barnett, "The Politics of Indifference at the United Nations and Genocide in Rwanda and Bosnia", in Thomas Cushman and Stjepan G. Mestrovic (eds), *This Time We Knew: Western Responses to Genocide in Bosnia* (New York: New York University Press, 1996), pp. 128–162; Linda Melvern, "Genocide behind the Thin Blue Line", *Security Dialogue*, vol. 28, no. 3, September 1997, pp. 333–346; Human Rights Watch, *Leave None to Tell the Tale: Genocide in Rwanda* (New York: Human Rights Watch, March 1999); *Report of the Independent Inquiry into the Actions of the United Nations during the 1994 Genocide in Rwanda* (New York: United Nations, 15 December 1999); Linda Melvern, *A People Betrayed: The Role of the West in Rwanda's Genocide* (London, Zed Books, 2000); Samantha Power, *"A Problem from Hell": America and the Age of Genocide* (New York: Basic Books, 2002), pp. 329–389;

Michael Barnett, *Eyewitness to a Genocide: The United Nations and Rwanda* (Ithaca, NY: Cornell University Press, 2002).

15. See Maley, "The UN and East Timor". For a cautious defence of the 5 May Accords, see Ian Martin, *Self-Determination in East Timor: The United Nations, the Ballot, and International Intervention* (Boulder, CO: Lynne Rienner, 2001), pp. 32–33.
16. Harry Eckstein, *Regarding Politics: Essays on Political Theory, Stability, and Change* (Berkeley: University of California Press, 1992), p. 188.
17. Jack Knight, *Institutions and Social Conflict* (Cambridge: Cambridge University Press, 1992), pp. 2–3.
18. See Jon Elster, *The Cement of Society: A Study of Social Order* (Cambridge: Cambridge University Press, 1989).
19. Michael Thompson, Richard Ellis and Aaron Wildavsky, *Cultural Theory* (Boulder, CO: Westview Press, 1990), p. 21. See also William Mishler and Richard Rose, "What Are the Origins of Political Trust? Testing Institutional and Cultural Theories in Post-Communist Societies", *Comparative Political Studies*, vol. 34, no. 1, February 2001, pp. 30–62.
20. See William Maley and Fazel Haq Saikal, *Political Order in Post-Communist Afghanistan* (Boulder, CO: Lynne Rienner, 1992).
21. For an insider's account of how it unravelled, see Giandomenico Picco, *Man without a Gun* (New York: Random House, 1999), pp. 20–39. See also William Maley, "The UN and Afghanistan: 'Doing Its best' or 'Failure of a Mission'?", in William Maley (ed.), *Fundamentalism Reborn? Afghanistan and the Taliban* (London: Hurst & Company, 1998), pp. 182–198; William Maley, *The Afghanistan Wars* (London and New York: Palgrave Macmillan, 2002), pp. 180–193.
22. See MacAlister Brown and Joseph J. Zasloff, *Cambodia Confounds the Peacemakers 1979–1998* (Ithaca, NY: Cornell University Press, 1998), pp. 287–288.
23. See Peter Harris and Ben Reilly (eds), *Democracy and Deep-Rooted Conflict: Options for Negotiators* (Stockholm: International IDEA, 1998), pp. 51–58.
24. Baron de Montesquieu, *Persian Letters* (Harmondsworth: Penguin, 1973), p. 229.
25. Ben Reilly and Andrew Reynolds, *Electoral Systems and Conflict in Divided Societies* (Washington DC: National Academy Press, 1999), p. 5. See also Chetan Kumar, "Conclusion", in Elizabeth M. Cousens and Chetan Kumar (eds), *Peacebuilding as Politics: Cultivating Peace in Fragile Societies* (Boulder, CO: Lynne Rienner, 2001), pp. 183–220.
26. See William Maley, "The Future of Islamic Afghanistan", *Security Dialogue*, vol. 24, no. 4, December 1993, pp. 383–396 at p. 390; William Maley, "The Dynamics of Regime Transition in Afghanistan", *Central Asian Survey*, vol. 16, no. 2, June 1997, pp. 167–184 at p. 174.
27. See Robert E. Goodin, "Institutions and Their Design", in Robert E. Goodin (ed.), *The Theory of Institutional Design* (Cambridge: Cambridge University Press, 1996), pp. 1–53 at pp. 39–43.
28. Ibid., p. 53.
29. See William Maley, "Realising the Minimal State: The Case of Afghanistan", *Agenda*, vol. 3, no. 2, 1996, pp. 261–264.
30. See Chandran Kukathas and David W. Lovell, "The Significance of Civil Society", in Chandran Kukathas, David W. Lovell and William Maley (eds), *The Transition from Socialism: State and Civil Society in the USSR* (Melbourne: Longman Cheshire, 1991), pp. 18–40.
31. Robert A. Dahl, *A Preface to Democratic Theory* (Chicago: University of Chicago Press, 1956), p. 83.
32. Jean-Jacques Rousseau, *The Social Contract and Discourses* (London: J. M. Dent, 1973), p. 168.

33. For further discussion of this case, see William Maley, "Peacekeeping and Peacemaking", in Ramesh Thakur and Carlyle A. Thayer (eds), *A Crisis of Expectations: UN Peacekeeping in the 1990s* (Boulder, CO: Westview Press, 1995), pp. 237–250 at p. 247.
34. William Shawcross, *Deliver Us from Evil: Peacekeepers, Warlords and a World of Endless Conflict* (New York: Simon & Schuster, 2000), p. 210.
35. Steven Heder, "Elections and Accountability for Genocide in Cambodia", Testimony before the US Senate Committee on Foreign Relations Subcommittee on East Asian and Pacific Affairs, 10 June 1998.
36. Ellen Bork, "'Miracle on the Mekong' or Orchestrated Outcome?", *Washington Post*, 5 August 1998, p. A19.
37. See John M. Sanderson and Michael Maley, "Elections and Liberal Democracy in Cambodia", *Australian Journal of International Affairs*, vol. 52, no. 3, November 1998, pp. 241–253; Sue Downie, "Cambodia's 1998 Election: Understanding Why It Was Not a 'Miracle on the Mekong'", *Australian Journal of International Affairs*, vol. 54, no. 1, April 2000, pp. 43–61.
38. Sanderson and Maley, "Elections and Liberal Democracy in Cambodia", p. 245.
39. Ibid., p. 252. This is not to suggest that exemplary leadership is not beneficial; see David W. Lovell, "Trust and the Politics of Postcommunism", *Communist and Post-Communist Studies*, vol. 34, no. 1, 2001, pp. 27–38.
40. Thomas Hobbes, *Leviathan* (London: Collins/Fontana, 1962), p. 143.
41. Hardin, *One for All: The Logic of Group Conflict*, p. 57.
42. For more detailed discussion of these principles, see M. J. C. Vile, *Constitutionalism and the Separation of Powers* (London: Oxford University Press, 1967).
43. John Stuart Mill, *Utilitarianism, Liberty and Representative Government* (London: J. M. Dent & Sons, 1910), p. 347.
44. Arend Lijphart, *Democracy in Plural Societies: A Comparative Exploration* (New Haven, CT: Yale University Press, 1977), p. 25.
45. See Timothy D. Sisk, *Power Sharing and International Mediation in Ethnic Conflicts* (Washington DC: United States Institute of Peace Press, 1996), p. 34.
46. K. R. Popper, *The Open Society and Its Enemies* (London: Routledge & Kegan Paul, 1977), vol. II, p. 151.
47. Amartya Sen, *Development as Freedom* (New York: Alfred A. Knopf, 1999), p. 16.
48. See, for example, Mathew Soberg Shugart and John M. Carey, *Presidents and Assemblies: Constitutional Design and Electoral Dynamics* (Cambridge: Cambridge University Press, 1992); Giovanni Sartori, *Comparative Constitutional Engineering: An Inquiry into Structures, Incentives, and Outcomes* (London: Macmillan, 1997).
49. See M. Steven Fish, "The Pitfalls of Russian Superpresidentialism", *Current History*, vol. 96, no. 612, October 1997, pp. 326–330.
50. See Guillermo O'Donnell, "Horizontal Accountability in New Democracies", *Journal of Democracy*, vol. 9, no. 3, July 1998, pp. 112–126.
51. For detailed discussion, see Amy Gutmann and Dennis Thompson, *Democracy and Disagreement* (Cambridge, MA: Harvard University Press, 1996); Jon Elster (ed.), *Deliberative Democracy* (Cambridge: Cambridge University Press, 1998); John Uhr, *Deliberative Democracy in Australia: The Changing Place of Parliament* (Cambridge: Cambridge University Press, 1998).
52. Reilly and Reynolds, *Electoral Systems and Conflict in Divided Societies*, p. 54. For further discussion with case studies, see Benjamin Reilly, *Democracy in Divided Societies: Electoral Engineering for Conflict Management* (Cambridge: Cambridge University Press, 2001).
53. For the classic work on this topic, see Douglas W. Rae, *The Political Consequences of Electoral Laws* (New Haven, CT: Yale University Press, 1971).

54. These objectives are elaborated in *The International IDEA Handbook of Electoral System Design* (Stockholm: International IDEA, 1998), pp. 9–13.
55. See John McFarlane and William Maley, "Civilian Police in UN Peace Operations: Some Lessons from Recent Australian Experience", in Ramesh Thakur and Albrecht Schnabel (eds), *United Nations Peacekeeping Operations: Ad Hoc Missions, Permanent Engagement* (Tokyo: United Nations University Press, 2001), pp. 182–211.
56. Russell Hardin, "Trust in Government", in Valerie Braithwaite and Margaret Levi (eds), *Trust and Governance* (New York: Russell Sage Foundation, 1998), pp. 9–27 at p. 18.
57. See Chandran Kukathas, David W. Lovell and William Maley, *The Theory of Politics: An Australian Perspective* (Melbourne: Longman Cheshire, 1990), pp. 64–68.
58. See William Maley, "Mine Action in Afghanistan", *Refuge*, vol. 17, no. 4, October 1998, pp. 12–16 at p. 15.
59. Bertrand de Jouvenel, *The Pure Theory of Politics* (Cambridge: Cambridge University Press, 1963), p. 211.

10

Democracy and democratisation

Reginald Austin

Contemporary efforts by the international community to "reconstitute political order" in disrupted states can be understood to refer to the effort to create liberal democratic orders. This is well illustrated by the assertion of the UN Commission on Human Rights in its resolution on the Promotion of the Right to Democracy that there are "indissoluble links between the principles enshrined in the Universal Declaration of Human Rights and the foundations of a democratic society".[1] The resolution was adopted with the support of 51 states, with no opposition and the abstention of only two states, China and Cuba. This is among the latest and most pointed pieces of evidence of the international community's growing conviction that a specific right – to democratic governance – has been evolving over the years, and has now matured to the point where it deserves formal recognition and hardening into at least "soft" international law. Parallel to this has been the steady articulation of a concomitant right of the international community to promote this right, even at the cost of an erosion of national sovereignty. This is evidenced by, for example, recent statements of the UN Secretary-General, and the Statement of the President of the Security Council, agreed by the Council at the end of November 1999, on its role in the prevention of conflict.[2] This has been the view of some academic and associated opinion over at least the past 20 years. The objective of liberal democracy has become more defined as the confusion over the meaning of "democracy" after the Second World War was largely resolved after 1990 and the fall of the

Berlin Wall. However, that the history of this idea has not ended is confirmed by recent events in what were beginning to be seen as "established" democracies such as Venezuela and Peru.

Nevertheless optimistic liberals can argue that the steady, sequential discrediting and disappearance of their major enemies – fascism, colonialism, minority racial supremacy and communism – have created a new era for liberal, pluralist democracy. Since Russia and most former Eastern bloc states abandoned communism,[3] and its major remaining adherent, China, has embraced at least economic "freedom", there are now very few avowed enemies of liberal-constitutional democracy. Liberal democracy has apparently vanquished all its rival forms of democracy whether "revolutionary", "peoples" or "directed". Another dimension of change in the nature of democracy involves a change from accepting democracy concentrated exclusively at the centre of the state as sufficient. A recognition is growing that pluralism may require that the freely expressed will of the people be devolved to more local levels, and that local government, autonomy or even independence are of democratic importance.

The reality, however, is more complex. Apart from the remaining absolute monarchies or overt republican dictatorships, which may be thought of as exceptions that prove the rule, there are still many states rhetorically committed to democracy but in fact either awaiting transformation to credible liberal democracy or needing a renewal of democracy where it has decayed or been corrupted into autocracy, authoritarianism or one-party rule.

The use of the term "disrupted" may be interpreted to imply that we are concerned only with states where an existing system or process of democratisation has been somehow disturbed. Disruption may arise from a military coup against an existing democracy, or be the result of the interruption of a nascent democracy by a failure to mature or of the more gradual decay of an apparently established democracy into authoritarian governance behind a facade of regular electoral form. Some of these disruptions may result in civil or even international war, but in many cases the rotting of the rule of law, civil society and other democratic institutions is accomplished without the trauma of concerted violence that can be called armed conflict. In that regard, the use of the terms "civil strife" rather than "civil war" and "disrupted" rather than "failed" states in the title of this volume is a useful correction to the debate.

International reconstitution of political order

The promoters of democracy, being in many cases sensitive and democratically correct, are understandably cautious. They often seek to avoid any appearance of imposing "their" definition of democracy as an assumed universal value. As organisations they are also restrained by a respect for sovereignty. Perhaps they are also conscious of past abuse, of alleged support for democracy being used to sustain intolerant, authoritarian and cruel forms of government. Given the continued reality of the cultural, political, economic, constitutional, social and particularly institutional diversity of societies, this may be wise. But the problem of agreed criteria for intervention to help reconstitute political order without the consent of the "assisted" state remains a major one for most unilateral, regional or multinational actors. As past and recent events in former Yugoslavia have shown, the issue of the legitimacy of international "entry" is also clearly in a state of dangerous controversy and flux.

Chapter VII of the UN Charter provides a possible mechanism for dealing with democratisation as a legitimate concern of the Security Council, through a liberal interpretation of the term "a threat to peace". However, the threat of the veto seems, after the brief euphoria following the end of the Cold War, again to have frozen the possibility of this working. Even the extreme circumstances of an ongoing genocide could not provoke a conviction that this might be such a "threat".[4]

It seems to have been forgotten that this was used to legitimise an admittedly constrained intervention against the would-be perpetuation of anti-democratic minority rule following the Rhodesian unilateral declaration of independence in 1965, which was characterised as a "threat to international peace". This was remarkable given that it happened at the height of the Cold War. It shows that this power can be used to promote democracy as an essential adjunct to peace. In the Rhodesian case the step was taken well before the "disruption" of the path to democracy had degraded to violence and armed conflict. Perhaps it should be seen as a rare case of "lessons learned" by the international community from the violence that arose in the wake of delayed decolonisation – in Vietnam, Kenya and Algeria.

An interesting example of the gradual move away from such caution can be seen within one relatively homogeneous corner of the international community: the Commonwealth. One of the essential characteristics of the modern Commonwealth is a shared constitutional history with a very specific (if originally unwritten) group of values associated with democratic governance. The 1991 Harare Declaration, building on the 1971 Singapore Declaration, reflected a consensus about what this might mean. It took at least 25 years to achieve, and asserts that "democracy, democratic processes and institutions" are among "the fundamental political values" of the organisation and its member states. However, even this "democracy" was significantly qualified by the words "which reflect national circumstances". This allowed considerable room for relativism if not contradiction.

Commonwealth practice, at the very earliest stage of this post-imperial, multiracial organisation, had managed to sharpen the meaning of this value in one specific area: racism. The Commonwealth response, first to the case of apartheid South Africa, then to Southern Rhodesia and more recently Fiji, made it clear that any government based upon overt racial discrimination, especially in relation to the franchise, would not be regarded as an acceptable democracy or a member of the modern organisation.

It was almost 30 years before the next clarification, by way of another negative definition, emerged in the Millbrook Declaration during the Commonwealth Heads of Government Meeting in New Zealand in 1995. This was accelerated by the remarkably stupid and barbaric "show" trial and rapid execution of Ken Saro-Wiwa and others by the Nigerian military regime. Henceforth the exclusion of military governments was to be applied, through an agreed procedure, to Commonwealth states. Their non-democratic basis was proof that they no longer shared the "fundamental political values" of the organisation. The Nigerian regime was excluded from membership, and the policy has been confirmed by subsequent Commonwealth action against coups d'état in the Gambia, Sierra Leone and Pakistan. To this extent, the right to democratic government has been recognised and defined, by at least part of the international community.

A right to democratic governance?

There are other important expressions of the existence of a specific conviction, in the declarations and practice of individual states and some regional and universalist organisations, that democratic governance has achieved at least "soft" normative status. In addition, its meaning has become less ambiguous and, in particular, the quality of pluralism and free choice has been emphasised. Policies, conventions and practice in Europe, the Americas, Africa and Asia reflect this trend. One recently founded and still small, but universally ambitious, organisation may be seen as further evidence of this trend.

The International Institute for Democracy and Electoral Assistance (or International IDEA, as it is generally known) is an intergovernmental organisation, founded in 1995. Its currently 20 member states have given it an important and novel mandate, dedicated specifically to the promotion of democracy and democratisation. Its Statute specifically sets out its objectives as: (1) the promotion and advance of sustainable democracy world-wide; (2) the improvement and consolidation of democratic electoral processes world-wide; (3) broadening the understanding and promotion of the implementation and dissemination of the norms, rules and guidelines that apply to multiparty pluralism and democratic processes; (4) strengthening and supporting national capacity to develop the full range of democratic instruments; (5) providing a meeting place for exchanges between those involved in electoral processes in the context of democratic institution-building; (6) increasing knowledge and enhancing learning about democratic electoral processes; and (7) promoting transparency and accountability, professionalism and efficiency in the electoral process in the context of democratic development.

IDEA as an intergovernmental organisation is authorised to engage in a range of essentially supportive activities: networking, advice and assistance, research and dissemination, and providing facilities and meeting places for the achievement of these objectives. Its current membership includes representation from the Asia-Pacific, South-East Asia, Africa, Europe, and Central, South and North America. This does not include any of the permanent five members of the Security Council. It is interesting to note that IDEA's establishment and activity owe a great deal to the initiative and ongoing support of the Nordic and other middle-level states, including India, Australia and Canada, as well as significant examples of successfully transformed states, such as Spain and Portugal, and currently seriously committed and transforming democracies, such as South Africa and Chile. Its member states are required to subscribe to and further the organisation's objectives and activities, and assist it to carry out its programme of work. A significant factor is the provision for associate membership, which is open to non-governmental organisations whose objectives complement those of IDEA. The founding states took the view that the central role of civil society in liberal democracy made such a provision both rational and necessary.

Again, it is noteworthy that the central value to which the organisation is dedicated – democracy – is not specifically, or at least not institutionally, defined.[5] The IDEA Statute and its founding Declaration use the term democracy in association with "pluralism and free and fair elections". The Statute indicates that "democracy is essential for the promotion and guaranteeing of human rights and that participation in political life, including government, is part of human rights". It expresses the "understanding that democratic and electoral processes require continuity and a long-term perspective". The more elaborated IDEA Declaration refers to "pluralistic systems of government", and to "the hopes of peoples ... for the opportunity to participate". It links "democracy and accountable government and administration ... as indispensable foundations for the realisation of social development", and proclaims that "[d]emocracy ensures that decisions are taken with the fullest participation of those who will be affected and aimed at local and participative self-governance". It states that "[i]nherent in the concept of democracy is that it grows from within and from below rather than being imposed from the outside or from above". The Declaration insists that "[a]n important institutional expression of democracy is the holding of free and fair elections in a context of pluralism". It elaborates on this "context" by reference to "[t]he rights and obligations of oppositions and governments and of the media, the functioning of parliaments, electoral laws, methods of voter registration and the methods of representation" as "central to elections".

Being a small, new organisation, International IDEA has sought to avoid duplication and to provide a service that others have not. To date its work has concentrated on developing the normative tools useful in various democratic endeavours. This includes quite mundane work: research and information gathering, seeking to combine, in straightforward language, up-to-date academic thinking and analysis with practical experience in democratisation. This has been needed especially in countries seeking to transform to democratic ways. It is most useful to those new lawmakers and practitioners "at the coal face", many of them appointed with no knowledge of the institutions they are supposed to operate and the concepts underlying them. The organisation seeks to use both its published materials and the knowledge and experience of a small but growing group of experts on deliberately long-term projects for promoting democracy at the level of specific countries. The key activities are facilitating national self-assessment of the prospects of democracy and promoting national dialogue and participation therein. The essence of the method is its being seen as a *process*, "owned" by the national partners. These would typically include government, political parties and national civil society. The process may be facilitated by actors from IDEA and regional and international specialists. One intended outcome of such a process is the establishment of a representative local democracy foundation, which should in essence take over the facilitating role and be a sustaining element in an ongoing process.

In this context, one of the most valuable services provided by the April 1999 UN Human Rights Commission resolution is its clarification of the content of the right to democracy. It repeats the right of "all peoples" to "self-determination" and recognises "that democracy is based on the freely expressed will of the people to determine their own political, economic, social and cultural systems and their full participation in all aspects of their lives". It repeats the ritual acceptance that there is no single form of democracy, referring to "the rich and diverse nature of the community of the world's democracies". But it also "affirms that the rights of democratic governance" include the following: "(1) The rights to freedom of opinion and expression, of thought, conscience and religion, and of peaceful association and assembly; (2) The right to seek, receive and impart information and ideas through any media; (3) The rule of law, including protection of citizens' rights, interests and personal security, and fairness in the administration of justice and independence of the judiciary; (4) The right of universal and equal suffrage, as well as free voting procedures and periodic and free elections; (5) The right of political participation, including the equal opportunity for all citizens to become candidates; (6) Transparent and accountable government institutions; (7) The right of citizens to choose their governmental system through constitutional or other democratic means; (8) The right to equal access to public service in one's own country".[6] This constitutes a substantial description of the conditions I believe those who seek to reconstitute political order are striving for, whether they are promoting or consolidating democracy or a democratic form of government in their own or any other country. That objective has been pursued by a variety of individuals, countries and institutions, with varying degrees of energy and various mixtures of self-interest and unselfish purpose, for decades, some might say centuries, past.

In sum, there is already considerable evidence that the majority of the international community subscribes to the notion that a "right to democracy" is either in existence or clearly evolving. This right provides increasing support for the further proposition that the international community has a parallel right to act in support of that right. However, the exact legal basis for such "entry" to help constitute or reconstitute a democratic political order, as well as the situations that might trigger that entry, require clarification. The UN Security Council has the power to do this, but the will to use this power has rarely existed, and thus it has hardly ever been exercised. The veto remains the effective and unpredictable obstacle to UN action.

Elections and reconstituting the political order

A democratic political order may have a wide variety of institutional forms and procedures, including the processes by which initial transformation from the "disrupted" (authoritarian or arbitrary) government to democracy is achieved. It also includes the institutions that enable ongoing democratic rule to manage conflicting interests and deliver the benefits of democracy, in order to consolidate and so become the society's trusted and "natural" system. If successfully managed, these make democracy the indispensable political formula for government.

One group of democratic institutions are concerned with the design, political context, planning and conduct of elections. The idea of an election goes to the heart of democracy as much as any of its other institutional pillars. It emphasises the power of the nation's citizens to "choose" to remove or retain an incumbent government at will, but in accordance with pre-ordained rules and procedures. It guarantees and institutionalises the essential uncertainty that is thought to make governments responsible and accountable to the governed.

Not surprisingly, in the wake of the widespread retreat of authoritarianism and particularly communist rule in the 1990s, the electoral tool was identified as the essential key to transformation to democracy. This was understandable but also, to say the least, naive. The lessons of the attempts to replace colonial autocracy with elected democracy from the 1960s into the 1980s had shown that the use of the electoral choice, even when it was combined with an elaborate constitution, resulted mostly in regularly "re-elected" one-party dictatorships, occasionally replaced by military regimes. The rueful phrase, repeated by disappointed democrats and cynical politicians, was that undemocratic, minority regime colonial government had been replaced by "one man, one vote, one time". The liberators had gone from "furthering the struggle, to feathering the nest".

My experience of people who enjoy governmental power (including those who are convinced democrats) suggests that their instinct is to prefer the certainty of their own continued rule, and that they need to be convinced of the benefits of uncertainty. This tendency is exaggerated when political power is also a major source of enrichment for incumbents.[7] In this sense democracy may be regarded as an "unnatural" condition. We all need to be constantly reminded of its advantages. In today's would-be transforming world, one of the main problems for those seeking to reconstruct a democratic political order is that an understanding and conviction of the value of the uncertainty of democracy, especially as a guarantee of the vulnerability of politicians to the choice of the voters, are insufficiently socialised.

The current international agenda offers a fair example of the fact that "democratising" issues continue to concern democrats in both individual nations and the international community. One candidate for the top end of the trauma and disruption scale would be Kabila's Congo. Against a historical background of one of the worst examples of a colonial regime of greed and cruelty and a disastrous decolonisation process, disruption was ongoing for decades under Mobutu. It has reached chaotic and centrifugal proportions since the civil war that brought Kabila to power.

Another contender, much more likely because of its European location to attract serious international attention, and already the subject of concerted thinking and action, is Kosovo. The differing nature of these two disrupted states more than confirms the platitude that no two democratisation problems are the same. Indonesia must also be on the list, despite the relative absence of disruption sufficient to trigger concerted international action until well into the tragedy of East Timor. In the same region, the long-standing search for democracy to replace military dictatorship in Myanmar (Burma) continues. Nigeria presents another level of military disruption of past attempts at democracy. Despite its current progress, it retains a considerable potential for further disruption. Sierra Leone is at least as challenging a case. Guatemala, where the success of a promising peace process seems to be in the balance, is yet another variant of the problem. Down the scale perhaps, but probably equally in need of the close attention of those concerned with the consolidation and long-term sustainability of "restored" democracy, are such cases as Fiji, Bougainville within Papua New Guinea, and Mindanao within the Philippines.

Less noticed but, if one takes "prevention" seriously, equally important are those countries all over the world that are still undergoing the uncertain process of democratic stabilisation.[8] They will have held, or are preparing for, their second, third or even fourth democratic elections. In some of these, essential elements of democracy as described in the UN Human Rights Commission resolution, such as the freedom of association, have been rendered meaningless. Consequently "street politics" are threatening to replace electoral politics and to disrupt what has in fact become no more than "virtual" democracy. Although the disturbances in such cases may represent civil society losing patience with the quality of such "democracies", it is probable that mechanically efficient and superficially credible elections have been and will again be held (and be internationally observed to be so) in such states. There is a danger in such situations that "reconstituting" will be delayed, because "active support and promotion" tend to be deployed only to places where disruption has actually taken place. It will in effect be limited until there is total disruption and a need for total reconstruction. There is still very limited interest in or provision for the timely shoring-up and maintenance of democracies that could be salvaged.

Limitations of electoral democratisation

It is widely recognised that it is not possible to have democracy without regular and credible elections, but that it is quite possible to have elections and yet not have democracy. It is also accepted that democracy and democratisation are both ongoing processes, with an election being a vital and regular event in the process. Faced with the task of commencing the rebuilding of democratic politics where civil strife has displaced political dialogue, one of the first questions is when and how to hold the election.

The answer must depend on the situation, and especially upon the political context. In many cases, particularly of "internationally inspired" elections in the past decade, the timing of the election has been the result of its use in post-war situations. Where a civil or perhaps international war had disrupted the pre-existing governmental system, former enemies may have agreed on a ceasefire or on peace. It has been less likely that they will have agreed (or that they will have been persuaded to agree) on who should govern the peace in the reconstituted state. If no alien occupation, Protectorate or International Transitional Authority is to be set up, this must be a national authority. If democratic government and not merely a restored state is the objective – and this has recently been the assumption where the international community has been involved – the standard expectation is that the new government must be elected. This model can be traced to the essentially peaceful, and thus in many ways very different, referendums and subsequent elections in the normally seamless, consensual and UN-managed transformations from Trusteeships to sovereign independence or incorporation.[9] It was revived in a modified form, at Commonwealth insistence and with UN endorsement, by the United Kingdom to seal the end of armed conflict and settler colonial minority rule in the transformation of Southern Rhodesia to Zimbabwe in 1980. The basis was a negotiated and sufficiently democratic universal franchise, a liberal constitution and an internationally observed "free and fair" election. In the 1990s, variations of this model of "electoral democratisation" were used in Namibia, Cambodia, South Africa and Mozambique to introduce democracy of one form or another, and with varying degrees of success.

"Success" in relation to democratisation has both a long- and a short-term dimension. Immediately satisfactory elections do not necessarily mean that a democratic government or any of the essential elements of democracy (the rule of law, an independent judiciary and a professional non-partisan civil service including the police and military, and another "free and fair" election) will be guaranteed. In fact, the long-term prospects of democracy are determined much more by the broader political context of an election than by the event itself. For example, in immediate terms, all five "transitional" elections in Southern Africa's progress from colonial to majority rule over the past 20 years can be said to have been successful. They were judged, to an acceptable degree, to have given the citizens an effectively secret vote and the facilities to cast their votes and to have them fairly counted. To this extent the essential mechanics of the elections were satisfactory. The elections provided a choice, and a reasonable opportunity for the political parties to compete for the citizens' vote, thus creating a potential basis for democratic politics to operate and grow.

Viewed in a broader context, some ostensible "successes" were in fact seriously flawed as foundations for potential democratisation. There are several possible reasons for the shortcomings. Like other transitional "peacebuilding" elections, they reveal that elections can be used for different reasons. More particularly they show that in some cases the overriding reason for the election is not the long-term achievement of democracy but the short-term avoidance of the risk of an intervening third party's indeterminate and costly involvement in the reality of transition. That problem is sometimes referred to as "mission creep". The term is revealing because the question is: What is the real mission? Is it the realisation of democracy or the cosmetic process of "going through [one of] the motions"? It is reasonable to conclude that most contemporary international democratising interventions have had a short-term, expedient and essentially domestically based purpose, rather than a thoroughgoing "missionary" zeal to ensure that democracy is not only planted (or re-planted), but also nurtured to a self-sustaining condition in the recipient state. There are good arguments for avoiding permanent dependence upon external agents for national democracy, but the balance is not yet right. One reason may be the insidious suitability of the drama of an election as a public relations exercise and an ideal "exit strategy".

The insistence upon brevity is also a product of the UN Charter's reverence for sovereignty. This has been reinforced in a world where the first wave of democratisation after decolonisation gave power to a series of "Fathers of the Nation", who found the exclusion of any further democratic intervention conducive to their determination to prolong their paternal control. On the side of the international community, the same inhibition was probably encouraged by the guilty recollection of the relatively recent historical experiences of "well- meant" colonial interventions. There was the disappointment of the apparent failure of the mission of nineteenth-century European imperialism to mould the "uncivilised world" into colonial clones, at the last possible moment hurriedly dressed for largely unplanned and unprepared independence in Westminster or equivalent West European governance habits. This disappointment may well have deepened into cynicism as most of the post-imperial "democratic" orders and constitutions that were bequeathed to those liberated from colonial or racist oppression then degenerated into militarist, intolerant or other decidedly illiberal regimes.

There is also a simpler explanation: the purpose of those international responses to disrupted democracies that have attracted attention and concern has been essentially self-interested, short-term, superficial and limited. In addition, the political management and the quality of research and information serving those planning and implementing these interventions have been, even compared with some of the past longer-term colonial interventions, dangerously ad hoc and largely unprofessional. Consequently the skills available have been very mixed and unpredictable.

That said, by the early 1990s it would appear that some lessons had been learned and could be applied. One example is the success, to date, of democratisation in Namibia. This can be attributed to the fact that the parties involved had been "working" on the transition and towards a deliberate plan for a specifically democratic outcome for decades. They included, in addition to the contending national elements, the United Nations and the UN Council for Namibia, many of whose officials, including the Head of Mission, were involved right through to the end of the UN supervision of the ceasefire and elections.[10]

Another success story is Mozambique, where the foundations of a sustainable political party system, which was critical to the 1994 election and has provided the foundation for the growth of democracy, were ironically laid by virtue of an almost exactly opposite scenario. The Special Representative of the Secretary-General (SRSG) for Mozambique, Ambassador Aldo Ajello, has stated that he was surprised and puzzled by his appointment and attributed it to the accidental coincidence of a decision to appoint an Italian with UN experience with the fact that his name commences with "A". Perhaps for this reason he applied himself to the task with unusual energy and a radical and unorthodox approach, breaking many of the UN rules and taboos in the process. He ensured that the opposing armies were disarmed and demobilised and that the Renamo insurgent leader and his colleagues were effectively tied into the electoral process and its outcome. The first test of this success was Renamo's ultimate acceptance of its defeat at the polls and engaging in its political role as the opposition in the Assembly. The continuing growth of democracy is an even more significant tribute to his work.

There is obviously a continuum – or perhaps, more accurately, a circle – between internal peace and democracy. This makes it difficult to isolate cases where the prospects of "success" can be attributed to the election as distinct from the broader political context. It is possible, with sufficient resources and an efficient and dedicated team, to conduct an election in very difficult, dangerous and improbable circumstances. The "atmosphere" makes an enormous difference to what becomes a highly theatrical event. A "peace" election is even more obviously dramatic. The stakes – the real prospect of an end to killing, destruction or repression – are very high. This enables both the electoral administrators and the potential beneficiaries to harness amazing resources of courage and patience to participate in and persist with an event that promises to mark the advent of peace. Examples include elections conducted in association with an apparent end of strife and wars in Zimbabwe, Namibia, Cambodia and Mozambique, as well as the termination of apartheid in South Africa in 1994, not to mention the East Timor consultation in August 1999. But how much then does the electoral drama and the prospect of peace distract from the more fundamental and ongoing task of building democratic politics? Since at least the adoption of the UN Charter, immediate peace has been seen as a higher priority than long-term democracy. The problem is exacerbated precisely because of the theatricality of the "peace election". The actors, who should be more responsible and aware that in the long term democracy is a better guarantee than any single election for solving the long-term problems and peace, lose their focus or deliberately concentrate attention on the immediate issue.

Democracy in the long run

Rhodesia/Zimbabwe

An early example of this problem may be seen, especially with the benefit of hindsight, in the generally praised management of the transition, largely by the British Conservative government, of the war between "Rhodesia" and Zimbabwe.

The problem of transforming the minority, settler-ruled colony of Southern Rhodesia to democracy based upon a universal, non-racial franchise preoccupied the United Kingdom and the United Nations from the early 1960s. It involved the crisis of the illegal declaration of independence (UDI) by the minority settler government in 1965, the imposition of UN sanctions, and the commencement and the gradual escalation of a War of National Liberation in the 1970s. The primary conflict was clearly between the white minority regime and the black majority nationalist movement. It was centred initially upon the basic democratic issue: the regime's refusal to accept a universal, non-racial franchise.

As the conflict evolved however, two separate nationalist political parties emerged – the Zimbabwe African People's Union (ZAPU) and the Zimbabwe African National Union (ZANU) – each with a liberation army in the field. Each was separately backed militarily, ZAPU by the Soviet Union and the German Democratic Republic, ZANU by China and North Korea. Ultimately, and increasingly as the war progressed, the two parties relied preponderantly for their support on the two main indigenous language groups in the country – ZANU on the majority Shona speakers and ZAPU on the minority (20 per cent) siNdebele speakers. There was clear evidence of tension and actual armed conflict between the two groups, despite their alliance (in the Patriotic Front) against the settler regime. Constitutional and ceasefire talks were convened by the British government, as the nominal colonial power, in Lancaster House in late 1979, following failed negotiations in 1976 and 1978. At that stage an attempt was made by Dr John Burton, a leading conflict resolution academic in Britain, to persuade the British chairman of the conference to include on the agenda the consideration of the historic, ongoing differences and more deeply rooted conflicts between these two indigenous groups. Not surprisingly, the British refused to contemplate this "diversion" from its primary goal – ridding the UK government of this albatross, ending the high-profile anti-colonial war and preventing a possible repetition of the end of the war in Mozambique where the colonial power was replaced by the installation of a victorious Marxist liberation movement government, without an election. For different reasons, involving various issues including their sense of "national sovereignty", this refusal to extend the agenda would certainly have been endorsed by the nationalist parties. The idea was rejected as being too abstract and academic. Accordingly, the constitutional discussions focused exclusively on the immediate issues: the existing war and the black/white contest for power and resources. Consequently the arguments made, the problems explored and the compromises arrived at were exclusively concerned with the "exposed" and "accepted" dispute. The constitution arising from the negotiations provided solutions only for this immediate set of problems.

One result of this approach was a constitution providing a unique and extraordinarily complex protection for white commercial farmers' land, special transitional protection for white minority political participation, a relatively weakly entrenched Bill of Rights and nothing for the democratic management of the "non-problem" of the Shona/Ndebele tensions. Also ignored in Britain's implementation of the transition and its urgent insistence upon a rapid exit from the situation was the fact that both the former liberation forces, one now augmented by the former Rhodesian military, retained considerable capacity for the use of force. All of this left a political powder keg situated in the highly inflammable geopolitical context of apartheid South Africa. The South African regime at that stage was in a high state of paranoid determination to use any means, including massive destabilisation, to protect itself against what it saw as the "total onslaught" of the combination of Die Swart Gevaar (The Black Danger) and the Red Menace.

Unhappily, the "abstract" issue did not disappear. Within months of the independence celebrations, another civil war was raging between the elected government and elements of ZIPRA, the former military wing of the electorally defeated ZAPU. Although there was some evidence of South African encouragement, the outbreak in essence revealed serious and unresolved conflict. The government responded by deploying the crack 5th Brigade, which dealt severely with the civilian population allegedly supporting the dissidents. This conflict in a widely welcomed "new democracy" was largely ignored by the international community. It raged for almost eight years, resulting in casualties and alleged atrocities that continue to infest the political dialogue in Zimbabwe. On the basis of this conflict, ZAPU was largely excluded from the government of national unity and several of its leaders were detained without trial. It was not, however, banned or nationally suppressed. The ZAPU leadership avoided the temptation to which the Angolan "opposition" had succumbed, and refused to invite or collaborate with South African destabilisation. In 1985 it won almost 20 per cent of the popular vote and returned a significant group of opposition MPs to parliament.

Zimbabwe in fact demonstrated a greater potential for plural, democratic politics than either its leaders or others had considered possible. That democratic readiness had not been suitably considered or institutionalised in the constitution, which was made in the "peacemaking" mood of 1979/80. The tragedy is that, in the confrontational atmosphere of 1985, this instinct for political restraint and survival led not to a reconsideration of the deeper issue of domestic politics in a spirit of compromise and dialogue, but to intensified military action by the government. The civilian supporters of the opposition were identified as supporters of dissidents, and continued to be subjected to severe counter-insurgency treatment. This faced the ZAPU leadership with a cruel dilemma. It could not physically protect its people and no constructive protection was available from elsewhere. It must either sacrifice its supporters or surrender its status as the opposition, and with it the growth of a healthy democracy in Zimbabwe. The upshot was a decision by the ZAPU leadership to end the killing by the only political expedient available – the least humiliating submission to the entire dominance of ZANU. This was not an easy process, as the supporters of the minority party needed to be taken along with the leadership. It was negotiated over a four-year period, ending finally in the total incorporation of the ZAPU and its leadership into ZANU in late 1989.

Zimbabwe has since been widely characterised as a one-party state. This is legally incorrect though, after the amalgamation of the two parties, opposition was in effect reduced to very few MPs, either ZANU dissenters or the representatives of a small remnant of an earlier split in ZANU. These sit in a parliament of overwhelmingly ZANU MPs, a high proportion of whom also hold ministerial posts. One can speculate as to whether constitutional discussion of the broader political issue between the major indigenous groups in 1979 would have achieved a more pluralist polity for Zimbabwe. None of the main protagonists wished to discuss it at the time. Only the "intervening" power, which controlled the process, could have raised it had it been convinced that it was critical to the long-term prospect of democracy in that country, and had that been its real concern. In a world of realpolitik it is no surprise that the issue was ignored. It does however provide an illustration of the distinction between what might become the practice of "serious democratisation" and the existing, somewhat dilettantish, approach to reconstructing a democratic political order.

What is clear is that the concentration on the settlers vs. liberation movement issue and the cut-and-dried answer – that a universal franchise election would provide democracy – meant that the deeper, longer-term issues were neglected. This not only led to a recurrence of major violence, but also influenced the long-term political order of Zimbabwe and its potential for democratisation. Thus, it is arguable that the contemporary monolithic, stagnant and autocratic style of politics that has become characteristic of Zimbabwe could have been avoided, had a more deeply considered and appropriate constitutional architecture been provided to encourage and enable a relevant and viable culture of political tolerance, interaction and opposition to survive and grow.

It is this broader political context that international promoters or "interventionists" on behalf of democratic politics should consider, particularly at the earliest stage of the reconstituting process. That unfortunately is precisely when there is the greatest temptation to deal only with the obviously urgent and relatively easy problems. It is also, sadly, when the idea that an election alone will provide a publicly satisfying and sufficient basis for democracy tends to prevail over the idea of the greater value of long-term, sustainable democracy.

Cambodia

A somewhat different problem of the use and abuse of elections to reconstitute political order is illustrated by the very ambitious plan set out in the Paris Agreement of 1991 to introduce democracy into the uniquely disrupted state that is Cambodia.[11] In common with many such cases of "disruption", there had never been a democratic government in Cambodia to be disrupted in the first place. Prior to 1991 and typically of the times, this had not prevented the existence of the closest relations between various authoritarian Cambodian regimes, in and outside the country, and several liberal democratic states.

The Paris Agreement of 1991 provided for a ceasefire and a historic comprehensive political settlement for the establishment of the foundations of a liberal democracy in Cambodia. The instrument for this transformation was the United Nations, which was granted effective sovereignty to enable it to carry out the task as the UN Transitional Authority in Cambodia (UNTAC). UNTAC illustrates many of the different problems facing the international community's efforts at the reconstruction of a democratic political order. Only some of these will be referred to here.

Perhaps the most intractable problem in such transitions, but often the most important, is the time element of the process. Like other UN efforts before and since, the UNTAC mission was to be executed within a predetermined and very specific time frame. The comprehensive nature of the mission, and the fact that the timely completion of many of the tasks was the essential pre-condition for undertaking subsequent tasks, created severe internal tensions and problems. Apart from that, the assumption that international expectations of "democracy" could be achieved in an almost totally unpredictable national environment within an arbitrarily fixed period, after which international support would be dramatically curtailed, was unrealistic.

In addition, the planning of the process neglected significant political dimensions of what was described as a "comprehensive" process. Part of the problem was connected with the planning of and the resources provided for the actual implementation of the Agreement. These included a totally inadequate and fatally delayed provision of resources to undertake preparatory activities such as creating an effective UN civil administration and control mechanism. Equally, plans and resources were hopelessly inadequate to ensure a credible level of human rights protection and a convincing start to reconstruction and rehabilitation, all of which were critical to the establishment of the "neutral political environment" within which the Agreement promised that an election would take place. The election would be an essential precursor to the new, democratic process, which would operate, first, in the constituent assembly as it debated and drafted a new constitution, and then with the formation of a government accountable to the constituent assembly, transformed into the elected parliamentary assembly. All of this should have been against a background of a reforming administration, police and judiciary and a restructured and retraining military – in effect, a credible foundation for a democratic future for Cambodia.

This failure to plan, and thus not to provide for or deliver, the vital democratising activities that the Paris Agreement foresaw before, during and after the elections is damning and dramatic evidence of the state of democratic myopia prevailing in the international community, and in particular the Security Council, at the time. The shortcomings of the provisions for civil administration, human rights, reconstruction and rehabilitation have been fully examined elsewhere.[12]

What has not been sufficiently noted was that the United Nations provided absolutely no material or other support for the setting up and operation of the constituent or parliamentary assemblies. That would have provided the elected representatives with some capacity to start to do realistic and informed work on designing and drafting a new constitution. This would have included such basics as their being able to enter into a dialogue and consultation with their provincial constituents. In other words, it would have introduced them to some of the democratic essentials of their job. It would have demonstrated and laid the foundations of their autonomy as MPs and a beginning of an understanding of democratic representation and its responsibilities. Instead they were left wondering what a democratic representative was expected to do. Those who had any idea of what they might want to do were faced with the problem of how to do anything without any resources at all. As a result they were placed immediately in a state of total dependence upon their leaders and their party, most of whom had no experience of, and even less sympathy with, the practice of democracy.

Another controversial dimension of the plan to introduce democratic politics into Cambodia became the basic question – whether or not to hold an election at all. It illustrates the dreadful dilemma that can arise when the international community engages in transitions from war to peace and democracy, as well as providing an object lesson on the consequences of how that dilemma is dealt with. (One lesson seems to be that, once an international intervention has been launched into a transitional process of this sort, and this includes the much less committed action of international election observation, it is extremely difficult to withdraw from it or abort it, unless this is forced upon it by the main national actors involved themselves.)

The problem in Cambodia, put simply, was that the planned ceasefire, cantonment and disarmament of the various Cambodian factions, planned to create the basis for an appropriate, neutral political environment and the election, never took place. This meant that there remained an unpredictable threat of violence against the election itself from the Khmer Rouge, which by the end of the voter registration period had clearly rejected the election. More seriously it meant that the parties that had accepted to take part in the election, and especially the Cambodia People's Party (CPP), were still fully armed and in control of most of the country. The CPP controlled the incumbent (state of Cambodia) instruments of power, including its army, police and secret police. Thus it was particularly able and, even more, willing to use its well-preserved and unrestrained force for what it believed would be the best electoral campaigning method, namely to intimidate the voters.

In principle this should have resulted in the cancellation of the mission. (This was precisely the position taken in 1994 by SRSG Ambassador Ajello in Mozambique, who made it clear to both the protagonists and the international community that without demobilisation there would be no election.) The dilemma faced by UNTAC at the end of 1992 was that, in spite of serious threats and killings, the process of voter registration, which had proceeded without waiting for demobilisation, had enrolled over 90 per cent of potential voters. Thus a new actor, the Khmer people, had entered the transition process, and they were demanding that their voice be heard. Intervention had created an expectation – that the UN promise of an alternative to totalitarianism (democracy) would be delivered. Could the United Nations afford to cancel the electoral part of the "show" merely because the rest of the promise was unlikely to be realised? The answer was no.

Similar situations have arisen elsewhere, in the former Yugoslavia, in Rwanda and most recently in East Timor. The international community appears to be able to delude itself and is ready to promise what it cannot, or is not prepared to, deliver. In East Timor, this included the promise of security to a population that had been more or less invited to vote for secession from the consistent military oppression of Indonesian rule, with the security to be provided by the self-same Indonesian military![13] In the same way as the promised security was not delivered in East Timor, so the elaborate promise of the foundations of democracy was not delivered in Cambodia in 1993.

Part of the problem is the failure to view democratisation as a comprehensive and ongoing process, and the treatment of its parts as separate. Thus in Cambodia the immediate question was put: Can we conduct an election in these circumstances? The answer was, "Yes, it would be possible to ensure that most voters would poll and their votes would be safely counted." Given the credibility that came with the control of the entire election machinery by UNTAC, and the fact that its voter education programme had already convinced electors of the need to register, it was clearly possible to convince voters that their vote was secret. Dealing with intimidation and threats was not a new problem, nor was it insuperable.

A major factor in this decision was the amended role of the UNTAC military component. Rather than being reduced, as planned on the assumption of a successful completion of the ceasefire and cantonment, the force was strengthened and its role redesigned. It became the defender and incidentally the logistical arm of the election. In fact, it helped create an enormously efficient and virtually unstoppable machine devoted specifically to holding the election. This originally unforeseen situation and the response to it provide a model of civil–military cooperation, and account for the effective delivery of at least the electoral dimension of democracy to Cambodia in 1993.[14]

In this situation, the CPP's continued reliance on totalitarian methods and its resort to the use of threats and force were counterproductive. Voters were sustained by a new sense of physical security provided by the military component, combined with a sense of the possibility of future peaceful methods and democratic solutions, being intensively promoted by UNTAC. This possibly explains in part the clear defeat of the CPP at the polls by the much weaker, and thus perhaps necessarily more "democratic", FUNCINPEC (Front Uni National pour un Cambodge Indépendant, Neutre, Pacifique et Coopératif). It was an election that the people believed (wrongly, and sadly for them as it turned out) would usher in a new era and see an end to repression and conflict. As the continued electoral activity of UNTAC and the enormous and confident turnout of Cambodian voters proved, the politics of fear had, at least for the time being, been overcome.

The greater and enduring problem arising from the failure to neutralise the forces of the factions, and especially of the CPP, clearly emerged later to haunt and undermine the credibility of the election and ultimately both the immediate and long-term prospects of democratic politics. Its first appearance coincided with the emerging news as the early election results were announced that the CPP was not winning the election. This resulted in the CPP insisting that the information would influence the counting of the votes. It demanded that the newly established freedom of information, in terms of which the emerging results were being reported, should be suppressed. It was an early sign of deeply entrenched totalitarian instincts.

As the election results became clear and the CPP emerged not as the winner but as the likely opposition (though by a narrow margin) to an alliance of the FUNCINPEC and the BLDP (Buddhist Liberal Democratic Party), the CPP leader Hun Sen launched a barrage of complaints and allegations of massive fraud. The only factual basis for this was that the seals on some ballot boxes had broken in the course of delivery to the counting centres. They had at all times been under UN military guard. Despite immediate investigations, which showed that this was an accidental, isolated and minor fault, the CPP persisted with the allegation of a major fraud. The United Nations, Hun Sen alleged, was guilty of serious large-scale but unspecified irregularities, and had deliberately manipulated the result. Despite the testimony of a significant international press corps, some skilled international observers and over 1,000 international poll watchers that this was not the case, not to mention the proven neutrality of an electoral machine controlled entirely by disinterested UN officials and UN volunteers, the CPP remained adamant.

More significantly, the CPP quickly backed its electoral complaints by mobilising its military forces on the eastern borders of Cambodia, adjacent to the CPP's erstwhile ally Vietnam. This, proclaimed Hun Sen, was a secessionist action by some of his commanders who were so enraged by the fraud and the CPP's defeat that they were prepared to break away from Cambodia. Hun Sen insisted that he could not control the generals unless the United Nations admitted the fraudulence of the result. The election had by then been certified "free and fair" by the Special Representative of the Secretary-General and the UN Security Council.[15] The secession and the violence continued and other unspecified dangers were threatened. It is notable that this tactic was adopted by the CPP in spite of the fact that the final results confirmed that, although it had lost the election, it had won a sufficient minority to force the FUNCINPEC–BLDP majority to seek CPP agreement to any significant resolution or decision made by the constituent assembly. Thus it was guaranteed a legislative veto and, within a democratic negotiating situation, was in a very powerful position.

Hun Sen insisted he could not end the secession unless the United Nations agreed to an independent inquiry into the irregularities. At the same time, the CPP was using the secession and individual violence against the elected victors to demand the establishment of a government of national unity. More especially, Hun Sen demanded that he should be made "the Second Prime Minister" and that the CPP should be an equal partner with FUNCINPEC in this government. Prince Sihanouk, Cambodia's once and future king, supported the idea. In the circumstances the FUNCINPEC leader, Prince Ranariddh, was forced to accept this effective annulment of their electoral victory. While the CPP demands were still being negotiated, the SRSG agreed a separate compromise in the face of the continued CPP violence, in this case on the integrity of the election. He set up an internal (UNTAC) inquiry into the "irregularities", to be conducted by the UNTAC Legal Adviser. This would report to the SRSG and the chairman of the CPP. Having thus in effect reversed the election result and put the integrity of the election in his view forever in doubt, Hun Sen ordered and immediately obtained the end of the secession.

The UNTAC Legal Office's report on the allegations of fraud and irregularities was delivered two weeks later. It confirmed what the electoral component's own immediate investigations had shown: although there had been a failure of some seals on ballot boxes, there were no deliberate irregularities, and the seal failures could not have distorted the accuracy of the result in the province where they had occurred. The report was received without comment or further protest by the CPP. It also went almost entirely unnoticed by the media. Three years later, however, it became desirable for the CPP to challenge the political compromise that had reversed the election result and kept the CPP in power. The fraudulence of the election as the basis of FUNCINPEC's legitimate authority was revived by Hun Sen. Embroidered allegations were made again to discredit and reject the result. The existence and results of the UNTAC inquiry, and their acceptance by the CPP in 1993, were not mentioned. But the fact that an inquiry had been accepted by the United Nations itself was not forgotten.

Lessons learned?

To those who are concerned to note the lessons, these cases show that the constitution or reconstitution of a democratic political order requires much more than an election – even when, as in a transition from armed conflict to an elected government, the election is a necessary and critical landmark in the process. It is important to take a broader view of democratisation. We should avoid being deluded by the neatness or the drama of an election into believing that it is or must always be the first or the most important step in the process. The question is, have we learned the lessons?

The answer seems to be: yes and no. For example, the long-term prospect of pluralist democracy in Bosnia–Herzegovina was distorted, if not permanently destroyed, by the unconsidered electoral system adopted for the election under the Dayton Agreement. Here was a fairly typical failure to think before rushing to the electoral solution. In particular, there was insufficient consideration of this fundamental issue in a highly polarised, multi-ethnic situation. It was clear in Bosnia–Herzegovina that the ethnic groups had coalesced behind their established leaders. They did not need an election to identify those who should negotiate the way out. Furthermore, the particular system chosen ensured that electoral success would go to the most nationalist candidates. Compare this with the good fortune of the South Africans between 1990 and 1994. Their leadership was able to negotiate without having the trauma of an immediate election inflicted upon it by the "wisdom" of the international community.

Of course, credit for the South African success must also go to the unique combination of leadership shown by Presidents de Klerk and Mandela. What one may for convenience sake call the "M-Factor" – leadership – is perhaps the best-kept "secret weapon" in the democratising arsenal. The very different cases of Mandela and Milosevic show the difference leaders can make. Perhaps this suggests that, when the opportunity arises to support and show solidarity with enlightened leaders and elites struggling for democracy, it should be taken more seriously than has generally been the case. The exception may again be South Africa. There the long-exiled ANC leadership, which necessarily relied for its military opposition to apartheid upon communist-supplied weapons, was consistently embraced by convinced Western democrats whose perspective was not totally distorted by Cold War paranoia. This was an important demonstration and confirmation of the core, common value being fought for: democracy. This cannot satisfactorily explain Nelson Mandela but, as his speech from the dock at the treason trial revealed, his democratic convictions were uniquely well developed from his earliest days as a politician.

Learning about the timing of electoral events is much the same mixture. Was the referendum on the Peace Agreement in Guatemala appropriate before a registration and citizenship process to include the entire people had been properly started, much less completed? The urgent demands for an immediate election in the wake of the demise of Mobutu in the Congo looked equally unwise and unrealistic. But for the almost immediate resumption of civil war, an election might well have been forced upon the unstable polity. The timing of an election, especially in the wake of conflict or such dramatic events as the crisis in Indonesia, which opened the way via "popular consultation" to possible independence for East Timor, is often not within the control of would-be supporters and promoters of democracy. Could it nevertheless be worth considering whether there are not internationally manageable alternatives to opening the Pandora's Box of an immediate electoral campaign and polling, to facilitate the democratising process? Might an alternative be to develop support for an international variation of the mechanism used, for example, at the national level in Bangladesh? There, instead of an intervention to conduct or closely supervise an election run under the control of the incumbent governing party, a temporary "caretaker" administration was set up to prepare the political context for the event. An international version of this might prove more acceptable and more effective.

The device of international election observation evolved in parallel to the democratisation process of the 1990s as a complementary international activity to the pressure on transforming states to hold elections. Though its credibility has become increasingly questioned in the light of experience, it can still be useful and remains an attractive activity – some would say recreation – for those who can afford it. It can serve several useful purposes, depending upon the circumstances of the particular stage of democratisation at which the election is conducted. It can help to build confidence among the opponents of an incumbent regime, it can provide a basis for improving the capacity of the electoral law and administration, and it can enhance the prospect of the integrity of an election. Has it helped? Again the answer is yes and no. Where it has been selective as well as comprehensive enough, or, in some cases, expensive enough, it has made a real difference. South Africa in the 1994 election is an example. The intervention and observation went well beyond the confines of the election campaign and polling. They included a long-term exercise monitoring the violence in the country, and helped to reduce it to tolerable levels in the run-up to the election. They also involved unique international support for, and indeed involvement in, the actual electoral administration by the South African Independent Electoral Commission (IEC).

Despite the fact that the international community has frequently repeated some of the mistakes of the early 1990s, there is also evidence that lessons have been learned by some of the most important "practitioners" of democratic intervention. This is equally true of certain professionally based national organisations, which have provided very focused, practical advice, assistance and training where it is called for. Among the most impressive developments have been those in the electoral field, where international support for the emergence of a new institution of governance – the IEC – has been significant. Here the pioneering work of certain national institutions has been vital: the Australian, the Canadian and the Indian Electoral Commissions have made a practical impact and indeed have inspired international organisations to follow their lead. There are of course more traditional democratic pillars of democracy, whose effectiveness and integrity have also been established, reinforced or recreated with international assistance. This process is likely to be enhanced as governance becomes recognised as a critical element of development by both intergovernmental organisations and national governments.

It may be important to recollect some of the lessons of electoral assistance during the past decade, and to guard against repeating them in new fields. The work and methods of NGOs involved in such activities as promotion of the rule of law or the independence of the judiciary should be considered before launching large-scale, heavily funded operations. Thus the activities of the longstanding International Commission of Jurists (ICJ), or of a more recent national, professional-based operation, the Australian Legal Resources International (ALRI), demonstrate the effectiveness of highly focused professional activity.

All such activities, by so many different actors, need to be appreciated and harnessed to the democratisation agenda if there is to be any real prospect of universal democracy being realised. Comprehensiveness and patience, as opposed to single or immediate solutions, should be the background against which a careful and professional approach to each case is undertaken.

Notes

1. UN Commission on Human Rights Resolution 57/1999, 27 April 1999.
2. *Presidential Statement on the Role of the Security Council in the Prevention of Armed Conflicts* (New York: United Nations, S/PRST/1999/34, 30 November 1999).
3. See J. F. Brown, *Surge to Freedom: The End of Communist Rule in Eastern Europe* (Durham, NC: Duke University Press, 1991); S. N. Eisenstadt, "The Breakdown of Communist Regimes", *Dædalus*, vol. 121, no. 2, Spring 1992, pp. 21–41; Leslie Holmes, *Post-Communism: An Introduction* (Cambridge: Polity Press, 1997); Jerry F. Hough, *Democratization and Revolution in the USSR, 1985–1991* (Washington DC: Brookings Institution, 1997); Juan J. Linz and Alfred Stepan, *Problems of Democratic Transition and Consolidation: Southern Europe, South America, and Post-Communist Europe* (Baltimore, MD: Johns Hopkins University Press, 1996).
4. Ingvar Carlsson, Han Sung-Joo and Rufus M. Kupolati, *Report of the Independent Inquiry into the Actions of the United Nations during the 1994 Genocide in Rwanda* (New York: United Nations, 15 December 1999).
5. Coming to terms with the meanings of democracy is of course a task that has challenged many authors. For a sampling of endeavours, see J. Roland Pennock, *Democratic Political Theory* (Princeton, NJ: Princeton University Press, 1979); Robert A. Dahl, *Democracy and Its Critics* (New Haven, CT: Yale University Press, 1989); Adam Przeworski et al., *Sustainable Democracy* (Cambridge: Cambridge University Press, 1995); Larry Diamond, *Developing Democracy: Toward Consolidation* (Baltimore, MD: Johns Hopkins University Press, 1999).
6. UN Commission on Human Rights Resolution 57/1999, 27 April 1999.
7. See Ronald Wintrobe, *The Political Economy of Dictatorship* (Cambridge: Cambridge University Press, 1998).
8. See Andreas Schedler, "What Is Democratic Consolidation?", *Journal of Democracy*, vol. 9, no. 2, April 1998, pp. 91–107.
9. See Lawrence T. Farley, *Plebiscites and Sovereignty: The Crisis of Political Illegitimacy* (Boulder, CO: Westview Press, 1986); Yves Beigbeder, *International Monitoring of Plebiscites, Referenda and National Elections: Self-Determination and Transition to Democracy* (Dordrecht: Martinus Nijhoff, 1994).
10. See Lionel Cliffe, Ray Bush, Jenny Lindsay, Brian Mokopakgodsi, Donna Pankhurst and Balefi Tsie, *The Transition to Independence in Namibia* (Boulder, CO: Lynne Rienner, 1994).
11. On the Cambodian process, see Janet E. Heininger, *Peacekeeping in Transition: The United Nations in Cambodia* (New York: Twentieth Century Fund Press, 1994); Trevor Findlay, *Cambodia: The Legacy and Lessons of UNTAC* (Oxford: Oxford University Press, 1995); Sorpong Peou, *Conflict Neutralization in the Cambodia War: From Battlefield to Ballot-Box* (Kuala Lumpur: Oxford University Press, 1997).
12. See Michael W. Doyle, *UN Peacekeeping in Cambodia: UNTAC's Civilian Mandate* (Boulder, CO: Lynne Rienner, 1995).
13. See William Maley, "The UN and East Timor", *Pacifica Review*, vol. 12, no. 1, February 2000, pp. 63–76.
14. See Michael Maley, "Reflections on the Electoral Process in Cambodia", in Hugh Smith (ed.), *Peacekeeping: Challenges for the Future* (Canberra: Australian Defence Studies Centre, 1993), pp. 87–99.
15. UN Security Council Resolution 835/1993, 2 June 1993.

Part 5
Reconstituting legal order

11

Rebuilding the rule of law

Mark Plunkett

Si vis pacem para pacem – "If you want peace, prepare for peace"

Following the post-referendum genocide in East Timor, the United Nations Transitional Administration in East Timor (UNTAET) peace operation will take place in an operational climate in which there is no rule of law. The international military peacekeepers of the International Force East Timor entered a rule of law vacuum in East Timor. Banditry, revenge killing and general violence may threaten not just the local populace, but also NGO workers, civilian peacekeepers and even armed military peacekeepers. Systematic, organised theft of peace operation resources may severely hamper delivery of materials and services to needy people and undermine the entire peace operation. Repression and systematic human rights abuses against the people by factional elites and their functionaries may prolong the conflict and prevent post-conflict reconciliation necessary for peace. Institutionalised official corruption, nepotism, criminalised economies (that is, the illegal sale of natural and cultural resources, narcotics and arms), racketeering and black markets could retard economic recovery and development. The expense and effort of nation rebuilding and elections by peacekeepers will be rendered nugatory if the emerging government maintains order by lawless means and in breach of fundamental human rights. Peace operations have to recognise that many of the local players, although purporting to be political factions, may be no more than sophisticated criminal organisations or crude criminal gangs that the international community has had to deal with in order to broker a peace agreement in a domestic legal void.

Unless there is an adequate mandate, a strategically planned programme and adequate resources for the restoration of the rule of law, a peacekeeping operation will fail to achieve the ultimate objective of bringing peace to people formerly deadlocked in armed conflict. True and enduring peace occurs only when there is a genuine return of the rule of law, which is the foundation for a properly functioning and legitimate state. As in any society, the peacekeepers will not be able to eliminate *all* criminal behaviour. What they must do is strive to replace a culture of violence and impunity with systems of rule observance without using violence for the management of conflicts. All armed conflicts finish some day.[1] The task of the peacemaker and peacekeeper is to bring that end-date forward in time. Peace operations are exercises in shrinking conflict time by condensing and terminating coercion activity. This is achieved by focusing on the restoration of the rule of law as the primary objective of every peace operation.

In peace operations, restoration of the rule of law must take priority over constitutional settlement. It is achieved through the delivery of specific designer-planned and implemented peace operation justice packages using the two combined techniques of (a) an enforcement model, employing legitimate minimal and lawfully sanctioned coercive measures such as arrest, prosecution, detention and trial by war crimes tribunals, and transitional peace operations courts; techniques of public shaming and office disqualification by peace operation criminal justice commissions; and the rebuilding, resourcing and training of local judges, police, prosecutors, defenders and custodial officers; and (b) a negotiation model, securing voluntary compliance by negotiating with local actors to bring about fundamental shifts in population consciousness through community participation, assessment, monitoring, evaluation, education and joint rule of law training at the elite leadership, functionary and village level to replace the culture of violence with agreed-upon management systems.

The rule of law is a precondition for the existence of a community of people who live together in a reciprocal relationship with each other and with the state. The rule of law requires that both the ruler and the ruled respect the legal rules that govern these relationships. It is the glue that holds together the web of legal relationships that forms the state. It is a notional social contract by people who consent to regulate their behaviour by rules that have the force of law, usually deriving their authority from the state.

The state has a monopoly on the legitimate use of force,[2] which can be exercised only subject to the strict requirements of the rule of law. Under the rule of law, an independent judiciary is the neutral arbiter of disputes between people themselves and between people and the state, and it determines the lawfulness of the exercise of force by a person (for example in self-defence) or by the state (for example in the execution of the law). The authority of the state is weakened when, against the rule of law, force is used by the state against its own people, by the state against another state, or by people within the state against the state or each other. If the state or its people continue to use illegitimate force in breach of the rule of law, the rule of law is eroded and may collapse completely. This will undermine the authority of the state. If unabated this will result in the collapse of the state itself.

Peace operations for people without a state or rule of law that attempt to re-create the state (for example through internationally supervised elections) without first re-creating the rule of law run the risk of slipping back to a collapsed state. Peace operations are a people-centred activity. They are first and foremost about peacemakers and peacekeepers enabling and resourcing traumatised people (whose anger and hatred may persist for generations) to make the transition from a situation in which there is no rule of law and no state, to one in which there is a rule of law, and finally to one in which there is a rule of law *and* a state.

With any group of people, the rule of law is always more starkly apparent by its non-existence than by its existence. Invariably for peace operations, the breakdown of the rule of law is essentially marked by the absence of a functioning criminal justice system (whether or not deriving its authority or its existence from the state). Genocide, wanton murder, rape and other physical attacks on ordinary people and their property are the principal human rights violations that confront peacekeepers. To measure the degree to which the rule of law exists, the questions to be answered are as follows: Are the relationships between people regulated by rules? Are the rules commonly accepted? Are the rules observed by ruler and ruled alike? Is force used to manage conflict? If force is used, is it authorised by the rules? Where a dispute exists about the rules, is there a rule that the dispute be determined by an independent umpire whose decision is accepted by all parties, and do the political elites and functionaries (military and police) observe the rule to submit themselves to the determination of the independent umpire and to abide by the decision of the independent umpire? The rule of law will finally be re-established only when most of the people are prepared to accept and freely submit themselves to it, at the level of (a) the great mass of the population; (b) the military commanders, police and local warlords; and (c) ultimately the central leadership.

War, peace and the rule of law

A harsh maxim of the law provides: "'Midst the clash of arms, the laws are silent" (*leges inter arma silent*). At the immediate place of actual fighting (the *locus belli*) the rule of law is suspended. But the rule of law may continue to function perfectly well everywhere else behind the lines. The end of the rule of law is usually clear-cut, coinciding as it does with the outbreak of hostilities at the *locus belli*. Even a small number of armed individuals can unilaterally suspend or end the rule of law with military action. The first shots of a coup or military offensive signal the outbreak of armed hostilities and with them the end of the rule of law at the *locus belli*. When the early killings go unpunished by the law, war is well under way. The rule of law thereby not just dies at the *locus belli* where it cannot operate, but also deteriorates throughout the whole territory where the law purports to extend jurisdiction, even where there is not actual fighting under way.

During war, all other disputes are submerged by the one, dominant, deadly dispute between the armed belligerents. Non-combatants are at the mercy of anyone who cares to coerce them, especially where modern military measures deliberately target civilian populations or are recklessly indifferent to them. If people are attacked by force of arms, their only recourse is to submit to their fate or to defend themselves by force of arms. The use of force of arms as the fundamental means for management of the great conflict by the military may also become the management means for subsidiary conflicts, including disputes between civilians unrelated to the war. Cheap, mass-produced but powerful weapons may soon be distributed throughout the population by guerilla groups, or fighting may leave them lying about so that they are soon acquired by civilians. In modern wars the civilians become militarised. As long as the war persists, violence becomes a currency of conflict management of non-war disputes in the war zone. Summary military discipline and expedient, indiscriminate, self-help revenge killings soon replace the ordinary peacetime judicial processes. People, particularly the young, soon learn to be proficient in the use of automatic firearms as the principal means of managing disputes as part of an entrenched culture of endemic violence.

At the end of a war in a functioning state or a well-resourced community, the rule of law may promptly recommence. But peace operations often take place where war is still being waged or is likely to break out again. And not all armed political factions or existing administrative structures are capable of becoming sovereign states within the time frame of a peace operation. An armed political faction or an existing administrative structure cannot become a sovereign state without the rule of law.

Dictators, human rights violators and warlords may have international legitimacy conferred on them under the pretence of statehood. Such fallacies hamper peace operations, as the governments of peacekeeper-contributing nations engage in the make-believe of government-to-government dealings. Peace operations require operational autonomy for peacekeepers operating on a people-to-people basis. In planning for peace, practical realities must prevail over diplomatic theoretical illusions.

The retardation of the rate of return of the rule of law is directly proportional to the ferocity of the force used against the population in the war and depends on the extent of the collapse of societal structures, both formal and informal. The strategic use of indiscriminate violence against non-combatant civilian targets is a primary cause of resistance to the return of the rule of law, and peace operations must be very careful about premature disarmament of the ordinary people. To be fair, disarmament should only be done after the rule of law has been restored. Untimely disarmament can create new sets of victims who are attacked by traditional and new enemies.

With the arrival of peacekeepers, for the non-combatant civilian population there is an air of anticipation of the rebirth of the rule of law. However, in the friction and fog of modern war, the resumption of a derelict system of the rule of law under civilian authority is often difficult. Following a war it is extremely hard to stop the momentum of possibly decades of violence and to eradicate a culture of violence in which the population remain heavily armed and kill in quick self-help retribution and deterrence of criminal warlords; in which military and police kill as the primary means to keep order; and in which the ruling elite kill as the principal means of political process.

The rule of law is usually described in the context of the relationship of the broader community (usually the state) to an individual within it. Irrespective of war and peace, some groups of people living traditional lifestyles may not recognise, or even be aware of, the primacy of a state, but nevertheless have strong but small rule of law systems. Variously described as "stateless societies" or alternatively "village-states", they nevertheless follow a sophisticated rule of law system derived from ancient legal systems (usually oral), which regulate the distribution of all resources – material, human and spiritual. Peacekeepers need constantly to question their own assumptions about what really motivates people and what rules have ascendancy over others. In peace operations, the reestablishment of the rule of law focuses on individual people and their relationship to others and to an emerging state. Where there is a micro rule of law without a state, the units of compliance consist of very small groups of people. The challenge is to bring these cohesive units of people together into a larger efficient one-unit organisation of a state whose one rule of law is compatible with the many micro rules of law. The art of re-establishing the state is to understand how to harmonise all of the micro rule of law systems into one large rule of law.

In questioning assumptions about the priority given to laws and rules and the motivation for compliance, it is important to compare the differing perspectives of the leadership elite and functionaries with the perspectives of the mass of ordinary people during war. The priority given by an individual to a rule system may be radically altered in times of war, particularly where the state is disrupted. Whereas officials will assert allegiance to the authority of "the state" or to their "group", an individual is likely to have a complete reverse of priority of rule observance, especially when the state is weakening or has collapsed.

Motivation plays an important part in a person's decision-making processes, which are activated when a gap is recognised between an ideal and actual state of affairs. A person is motivated to search for alternatives when a need exists and is not being currently satisfied, thus activating a decision-making process. Behaviour has been explained according to a hierarchy of psychology of needs of an individual, most famously by Abraham H. Maslow.[3] In order to explain human behaviour, social scientists have categorised five basic human needs and their priority. If a person's basic psychological needs (hunger and thirst) are not satisfied first, and safety second, they will not be so interested in satisfying the more advanced needs for self-esteem and self-actualisation. The prospects of satisfying all needs is radically reduced in war, so much so that most individual human effort is spent pursuing the most basic need of self-survival. During war, higher psychological needs may soon be abandoned altogether, leading to the basest of behaviour and humans' inhumanity to other humans.

The observance of the rule of law is strongly influenced by the fulfilment of basic human needs. The likelihood of detection and the prevention of punishment may be paramount. Voluntary compliance with the rule of law may also relate to convenience, or other utilitarian factors, personal morality, ethics, social relationships, and, most importantly, the legitimacy of the source of law itself.

The rule of law is like a giant wall tapestry, whose fabric is woven over time from the many threads of different laws and various rules. It is a great anthropological document that constitutes a narrative of the social history of a people. Armed conflict may tear the tapestry to shreds. The task for the peacekeeper is to see what can be done to pick up the remnant pieces, frayed ends, loose fibres and strands so as to help the people to re-weave it themselves back into their own rule of law.

The enforcement model

There is no law without a sanction, so the first objective of the enforcement model is to build legal mechanisms to redress wrongdoing. Under the enforcement model for a rule of law, a peace operation reintroduces a domestic criminal justice system to prosecute offenders for crimes committed during the currency of the peace operation. Most major human rights breaches are straightforward acts of criminal culpability, such as murder, grievous bodily harm, abduction, rape, arson and theft, which are often committed to hamper the objectives of a peace process such as the creation of a neutral political environment necessary for a free and fair election or the formation of a government of national reconciliation. This primary focus of the rule of law enforcement model is essential if one is to ensure the safe and effective conduct of all other aspects of the peace operation. A key objective of the peace operation must be to create a fair, impartial and independent judicial mechanism to provide accountability for criminal misconduct in place of the persisting culture of impunity. Under this model, the peace operation also assists any international war crimes tribunal staff in apprehending past human rights violators under international conventions dealing with torture, genocide or crimes against peace or humanity. But this is incidental and subsidiary to the rule of law enforcement model.

The enforcement model for the restoration of the rule of law is achieved by the establishment of two types of justice institution. First, there must be a functioning criminal justice system consisting of police, custodial officers, correctional officers, prosecutors, defenders and judges. The system must detect and investigate major crimes involving serious breaches of human rights such as war crimes, genocide, murder, arson and rape. It must arrest and detain accused persons. It must bring accused persons to justice by prosecuting them. It must provide fair trials by independent, competent and credible courts (and, where none exist before, transitional peace operation trial and appeal courts composed of cross-factional judges chaired by distinguished international jurists must be employed until local courts can be established). The system must also carry out any sentences imposed, including community service, fines, imprisonment and correctional supervision with probation and parole. Finally, it must provide for the paying of criminal compensation to victims.

Second, there must be a Criminal Justice Commission or Truth and Reconciliation Commission. The Commission must inquire into and report on past and continuing genocide and war crimes. It should expose official misbehaviour, including corruption, abuse of office, lack of impartiality and electoral misconduct. It should educate the people on human rights, ethics and norms, and give victims and perpetrators an opportunity to testify on record. It should have the power to grant amnesties from prosecution and civil suit, as well as to initiate prosecutions, removals from public office and prohibition of electoral candidature. Finally, it should facilitate public exposure, censure and shaming, reminders of past atrocities, payment of compensation and participation in reconciliation processes.

Prior to a peace operation, field survey missions are needed to assess the existing justice assets. Some countries can be seen as likely candidates for peace operation intervention well in advance of a peace operation. The remnants of existing justice assets may be built on, developed and improved to standards set by UN conventions. Where there is an absence of the rule of law, peace operations have to be prepared to bring their own law and to establish their own transitional criminal courts and transitional criminal justice commissions and detention centres in the short term.[4] However, the objective is to help the local people to re-create their own justice institutions, composed of their own people and using their own laws, language and culture, adjusted and improved to international standards. Where there have been exchange programmes, peacekeepers are more readily able to identify appropriate local personnel to ease the facilitation of the re-establishment of the rule of law. Potential rule of law personnel may be waiting in refugee camps to return, and can be trained in readiness to return with peacekeepers.

In peace operations, there will always be a gap in rule of law resources available to peacekeepers. This will manifest itself in an absence of legal resources (adequate laws to cover the peace operation and to empower the peacekeepers if necessary to enforce a rule of law); human resources (independent and competent judges, court administrators, prosecutors, defence lawyers, police and prison administrators and salaries); and physical resources (court houses, law libraries, police stations and detention centres).

The starting point for peacekeepers is to be unambiguous about their own source of legitimacy. Although each contributing country brings with it a body of internal legal authority governing itself, the legal authority for enforcing a rule of law will derive from international law, the domestic law of the peacekeeper's country and the host country, and consent through negotiated agreement from the host country's feuding factions and the peace operation members.

International law may make provision to enable justice reconstruction in humanitarian interventions, but the scope of direct powers is dependent on UN-authorised interventions by resolution of the UN Security Council under Chapter VII of the UN Charter, or, where there is no state, humanitarian intervention under article 39 of the UN Charter, and the laws of belligerent and non-belligerent occupation, including the Fourth Geneva Convention of 1949.

Usually there will not be any law in the host country because the state and the rule of law will have collapsed. The domestic laws of a host country usually do not make provision for peacekeepers, unless there is some special ratification by a domestic executive government already possessed of legal powers. However, where a local legislature or executive government exists, its laws and actions will not be universally accepted by the protagonists. To use the laws of one group over the other will imperil the neutrality of the peace operation. Furthermore, a peace operation can use existing local laws and local courts to enforce the law only when those laws and courts reasonably meet international standards. Usually there will be no domestic substantive or procedural law that is competent, credible and independently administered.

As a result peacekeepers frequently find themselves entering into a legal vacuum, legal chaos or at the very least considerable legal ambiguity. Treaty-makers usually fail to make sensible or adequate provision for the rule of law. It is falsely assumed that the rule of law will somehow be automatically restored at the end of war or with the arrival of peacekeepers, or held in abeyance until the formation of a new state. When peacemakers negotiate agreement for the intervention of a peace operation, they should secure agreement from the factions for comprehensive measures for the re-establishment of the rule of law. This should include full authority for the establishment and operation of transitional peace operation trial courts. Where the head agreement omits reference to enforcement mechanisms for the re-establishment of the rule of law, the peacekeepers will need to renegotiate its provision with the factions, but this will prove to be a hard task in most cases.

Hence a proper legal basis must be provided for the creation of the criminal justice system during the immediate and transitional phase. Ultimately it will be necessary to develop off-the-shelf international criminal law, practice and procedure to which peacekeepers have automatic recourse for the establishment and conduct of transitional peace operation courts. The Yugoslav and Rwanda Criminal Tribunals offer some precedents, especially on laws of evidence and rules of procedure. Soon it will be necessary for international law to recognise a peace operations criminal code, setting out criminal offences and defences, practice, procedure and evidence. An essential feature of the rule of law enforcement model is the need for a wide public dissemination of simple statements of the requirements of the law. Public education and the media must campaign to inform people of their obligations, responsibilities and rights under the law of the peace operation.

In the absence of competent, credible and independent courts, peace operations will be required to establish transitional courts. To this end peacekeepers will need to bring with them a panel of distinguished international jurists, either retired or serving judges, to chair transitional courts during the peace operation. The peace operation judges may constitute the only judicial forum for the conduct of trials where either the local courts are inadequate or will not act, or the accused, victims and witnesses are from different factions. The peace operations courts might also hear complaints and actions against the peacekeepers themselves. The distinguished international jurists will be required to sit alone or, more desirably, as chairs of benches composed of judges from each of the factions. An appeal court must also be established to hear appeals from the peace operations courts, again composed of distinguished international jurists sitting with judges from each of the factions. These courts will require proper resources, such as premises, hearing rooms, clerks, transcription services and other administrative support.

The former local judges and clerks may have grown up under authoritarian systems and have little understanding of the proper role of courts in society. Peace operation judges can provide on-the-job training and mentoring of acceptable former and new local judges who take over the criminal justice system as local courts resume their functions, or when the work of the transitional courts is over. The distinguished international jurists, prosecutors and defenders should phase themselves out with the re-establishment of a competent, independent and resourced local judiciary. A peace operation should undertake judicial training designed to provide on-site training and assistance to judges in the implementation of human rights and criminal law with a view to improving the judicial system.

After prolonged war, court houses will be destroyed or in a run-down state. Along with police stations, court houses are often the first structures to be burnt to the ground. Hence a peace operation will need to construct and resource court houses. Reconstruction and maintenance will greatly enhance the community prestige of the judiciary and working conditions of judges. The local court house should not only be a focal point for the administration of justice but also serve as a visible architectural symbol of the re-establishment of the rule of law.

After a long war there will be a complete absence of any legal texts, and a shortage of clerical materials such as filing cabinets, desks, pens and paper necessary for running a court. Courts will require copies of the existing laws that are to be interpreted and applied, as well as basic legal materials and texts. The provision of even outdated and discarded textbooks can prove invaluable for local jurists and law enforcement officials seeking assistance from the models and precedents of other jurisdictions as a solution to domestic legal problems. The courts also require adequate administrative support. The courts are assisted by clerks whose standard of education may be very basic. Modest assistance to the conditions of the clerks and the provision of filing facilities go a long way to improving the functioning of the courts; local-script word processors will be essential. In the early stages of the peace operation, when there is no effective local independent judiciary or police, the peacekeepers will be required to take on the tasks of arrest, prosecution and trial of serious offenders if the existing officials are unwilling to act or where the local officials are themselves the perpetrators of offences. If major human rights breaches are being perpetrated by the leadership of the existing factions and functionaries – as is invariably the case – this threatens the neutral political environment, putting free and fair elections at risk.

Peace operation special prosecutors will be required to conduct the initial prosecutions. They must be independent from the peace operation hierarchy. A peace operation prosecution policy should be established to guide the prosecution criteria, especially where it is decided *not* to prosecute. Political considerations and expediency on the part of the peacekeepers can play no part in these considerations. The peace operation special prosecutors are answerable to the courts for their conduct and not to any administrative hierarchy. As lawyers, prosecutors have not only a professional obligation but also an ethical duty to see that the law is respected and upheld to the best of their capability, and to prevent and rigorously oppose any violation. The peace operation should ensure that prosecutors are able to perform their professional functions without intimidation, hindrance, harassment, improper interference or unjustified exposure to civil, penal or other liability. In the performance of their duties, special prosecutors must carry out their functions impartially and avoid all political, social, religious, racial, cultural, sexual or any other kind of discrimination, protect the public interest, act with objectivity, take proper account of the position of the suspect and the victim, and pay attention to all relevant circumstances, irrespective of whether they are to the advantage or disadvantage of the suspect. A prosecutor has a heavy duty to ensure that an accused person receives a fair trial. The peacekeepers and their trained personnel must be model litigants. In the performance of their professional duties and obligations in determining whether a prosecution is to be commenced, prosecutors are independent of political considerations or directions from legislative and executive functionaries. In the final analysis, the prosecutors are not servants of government or individuals – they are servants of justice.

In the transitional phase, peace operations will be required to provide competent defence counsel for accused persons.[5] Local prosecutors and defenders obtain on-the-job training by working alongside the special prosecutors and defenders, who will phase their roles out as the local courts are established. In many peace operation theatres, there is a complete absence of a legal culture and legal profession. Law schools and Bar Associations will also be required to be established to educate and nurture a corps of professional legal practitioners, including local prosecutors and defenders.

The proper functioning of civilian police – considered elsewhere in this volume – and the construction of gaols and detention centres, consistent with the UN Minimum Standards for Prisons and environmentally and culturally sympathetic for the inmates, must be priorities of a peace operation. Also essential are prison custody diversion programmes, bail procedures and alternatives to imprisonment such as fines, community service, probation and parole where appropriate so as to reduce prison populations. A dilemma involved in the construction of detention centres is that prisoners, who are the outcasts of society, may be better housed and fed than nearby villagers, breeding resentment of the peacekeepers or, worse still, providing an incentive to be taken into custody. Further large-scale arrests and incarceration may create new human rights breaches unless custodial facilities are properly resourced and supervised.

Physical security for judges, prosecutors, defenders, police and correctional and custodial officers must be provided by the peacekeepers. This is especially important for the local judges, who will be most at risk in the early stages and especially after the departure of the peacekeepers. Hence the peace operation will need to make provision for the training of local police to protect judges, or will need to be prepared to provide reliable protection during and perhaps long after the peace operation has been completed. The peace operations must provide a proper witness-protection programme to ensure the safety of informants and their families in order to bring about successful prosecutions. This may require the permanent relocation of victims and witnesses. This is a high-cost undertaking which in some instances will involve ongoing protection for entire villages who witnessed atrocities. The offering of rewards and indemnities is also a useful tool.

Peace operations require resources to perform basic post mortems and pathology using the UN-developed model Autopsy Protocol as well as a Post Mortem Torture Detection Procedure. A corps of forensic pathologists is required for mass grave exhumations to collect evidence of genocide. Cross-cultural sensitivities and religious views may necessitate some variation of these procedures. Forensic scientific assistance, such as DNA and ballistic testing, is also required.

A peace operation must make provision for secure salaries for the judges, court staff, prosecutors, defenders, police and correctional and custodial officers. In Third World countries, the security of tenure of an entire judiciary can usually be inexpensively resourced. The cost of a justice system in these circumstances is cheap and attainable. It is certainly cheaper than the extremely high cost of the use of military hardware. The budget of the new nation must be geared to making adequate provision for sustaining the costs of the rule of law and its strengthening. Post-mission audits of the performance of local staff following the transfer of functions from UN personnel to local staff is an essential feature. Continued funding after the peacekeeping exercise may be used to ensure the continued observance of judicial decisions made during the transitional authority peacekeeping period. Post-peacekeeping enforcement of judicial decisions must be secured and monitored.

Working parallel with the courts is the peace operation's Criminal Justice Commission or Truth and Reconciliation Commission. In addition to presiding over trials, distinguished international jurists are required to sit on criminal justice commissions. The Commission acts as a commission of inquiry. Such inquiries, given lesser standards of proof, may be used to stop human rights abusers by publishing the names and misdeeds of transgressors as a deterrent, or by administratively disqualifying them from existing office or election to office. A purpose of such inquiries is to air public concerns, bring transgressors to account and embarrass wrongdoers without the need for prosecution through the courts. Further, the holding of such inquiries can be instrumental in helping in the formation of local reforms. The relatives of the victims have an opportunity to hear what happened to their loved ones and reconcile their loss, and the perpetrators are required to account publicly before any amnesty is granted by the Commission. This device is a more powerful tool for lasting and durable community reconciliation than protracted and costly prosecutions and imprisonment for offenders.

The rebirth of a new nation is often vexed by the compulsive corruption of the new leaders. This may involve bribery, nepotism and lack of impartiality. Frequently, property of the state is transferred to party political or personal use, without the peacekeepers being able to detect, stop and educate against it. National environmental and cultural assets, sometimes protected during war, begin to be looted and illegally traded with the outbreak of peace. Without adequate internal and cross-border policing, flourishing narcotics and prostitution trade can be significantly boosted by a new-born peace. Large parts of the economy become criminalised. A key area of rule of law enforcement is the adoption of anti-corruption measures. The Commission is given investigative power, using sophisticated fraud and audit detection mechanisms, especially for inquiry into allegations of abuse by officials. Anti-racketeering measures are also required. But just as important are ethics integrity training, financial and conflict of interest disclosure, and the development of codes of conduct for public officials.

The negotiation model

Whereas the enforcement model for rule of law compliance involves the use of legitimate, minimal and lawfully sanctioned force to carry out arrests, prosecutions and trials, the negotiation model seeks voluntary compliance by negotiating with the local people to bring about fundamental shifts in population consciousness, directed against tolerance of impunity for violence. The effectiveness of force and merit-review umpires (such as courts and commissions) is uncertain, risky and costly. Negotiations give greater control of outcomes and enable the parties to make their own future. People locked in intractable conflict rarely, if ever, pause maturely to reflect on possible future scenarios for enduring resolutions. The job of the peacekeeper is to road-map the conflict, draw up menus of navigable and safe pathways and, if necessary, act as a guide, walking the parties through them. Getting the local people to think of moulding their own future through negotiation is a powerful concept.

The negotiation model for the re-establishment of the rule of law is a high-intensity, people-centred activity. Nevertheless, it is low cost and low risk, with considerably higher yield for compliance with the rule of law than the enforcement model. It involves a process of direct and continuous negotiation and rule of law training by peacekeepers at three levels: the level of the great mass of the population, the level of military commanders, police and local warlords (functionaries), and the level of central leadership (ruling factional elites).

The negotiation model for the restoration of the rule of law is achieved by negotiating agreement with the host people using community consultation, public participation, stakeholder representation, mutual gains negotiation, alternative dispute resolution, and the development of work techniques, which I call Rapid Participatory Rule of Law Appraisal and Rule of Law Participatory Assessment, Monitoring and Evaluation.

In order to persuade the local people, peacekeepers need to understand that they are outsiders intervening in the internal affairs of war-traumatised people in a state of continuing unresolved conflict. Peacekeepers are both privileged and transitory. One day they will leave and have no continuing obligations to the local people. As guests in other people's country, they must behave accordingly. Although peacekeepers are "results driven", they must also be "duty oriented". Merely entering into other people's conflict will change it. Peacekeepers strive to do good for the host people, but the first ethical duty of a peacekeeper is to commit to do no harm.[6] Peacekeepers live in a fish bowl. They are under constant observation by the host community in just about everything they do. At all times they must abide by high ethical standards, because exemplary behaviour on their part can influence the behaviour of the host people around them.

Peacekeeping is not a panacea for all the conflict ills of a population. The legacy of violence will persist into future unborn generations. There may be no immediate solutions to many of the problems. For example, the demand to deal with land disputes arising from successive dispossession caused by war is usually beyond the capacity of any peace mission, because the claims will be innumerable and very resource consuming, requiring years before proper determinations can be made. Rather than trying to impose specific solutions in the short term, peacekeepers should aim to impart good *processes* for coping with conflict generally in the long term. Elegant outcomes are more likely to result from concentrating on providing fair negotiation processes rather than on substance. The job of the peacekeeper is to skill people to manage conflict. This task involves negotiation training (preferably joint factional), the provision of communication facilities, relationship-building, confidence-building, and reconciliation.

Peacekeepers themselves must be properly trained negotiators in order to negotiate effectively. The objective of the peacekeepers' negotiations is to secure agreement from the factional elite, military and police functionaries and the ordinary people to cease using violence, force, coercion and intimidation as means for managing conflicts; to accept the legitimacy and operation of a criminal justice system to umpire disputes about the use of force and the rules that govern it; to be prepared to submit disputes where they are victims and/or accused to the criminal justice system for determination and to abide by the result; and to negotiate internally within themselves, and externally with each other. The peacekeepers should demonstrate the alternatives of the transitional peace operation courts and criminal justice commissions if the locals do not develop their own criminal justice system.

In this way, the host people may come to accept that they are able to get as much from negotiations as they can get from the continued use of force. The diagnostic elements of peacekeeping negotiations are (a) weighing and costing the alternatives of *not* negotiating; (b) looking behind positions to probe for the real underlying interests of all parties; (c) forming problem-solving relationships; (d) creating genuine communications; (e) brainstorming options without commitment; (f) measuring fairness and legitimacy; and (g) making achievable commitments.

New ideas mean *change*, which is not easy for the existing exercisers of power. A peace operation means some people will have to give up military, political and economic power. The inclination to stay with the current lawlessness through fear, inaction and default decision-making may be seen as preferable to risking the unknown, even if the violence is clearly not working. Hence the negotiation for the re-establishment of the rule of law must proceed with great sensitivity and be inclusive of the whole community. Major exchanges of political power will occur because of the peace operation. Peace operations enable, and supervise, power transfers *within* each side as well as *between* each side to a conflict.

Successful power transfers also involve recognition of the gender demographics of conflict participants. In armed conflicts the leaderships of the combatants are usually (but not always) a tiny minority of older males. The armed combatants are usually males old enough to bear arms (excluding male infants and aged men). These men waging armed conflict are a minority of their total populations. In most but not all wars, women are usually non-combatants and represent the majority or at least half of the population. A peace operation must focus on demilitarising the power of the male leadership and the male combatants by civilianising them. These men must be prepared to give up the use of force through military power for both intra-group and inter-group conflicts. Civilian career paths must be created for them. Even more important is a focus on enfranchising women to access and exercise political power. Civilian career paths must also be created for women. Negotiating peace involves creating cross-factional coalitions of all the non-combatants, particularly women and aged men, so that they can be heard as well as the minority of opposing armed men.

Generally, peace operations are reliant upon culturally diverse personnel from many different countries. Inevitably peace operations are vexed by a plethora of perplexing cross-cultural conundrums, not just internal to themselves but also external to the host community. Despite the social ravages of war and persisting deep-seated hatreds, the host people will share common goals, longstanding social rules and family ties going back many generations. The multinational peacekeepers lack cultural connections and are involved with the host people for a limited period of time only. The peacekeepers do not identify themselves with the community, and are not identified by the community as belonging to them. The peacekeepers, however culturally compatible with the locals, will always be outsiders. However, they must strive to form an equal partnership in joint creative problem-solving with the host community. The negotiated compliance approach for the rule of law focuses on the formation of working relationships at a grassroots level that serves the locals. It is commonly recognised in the setting of a peace operation that one day the peacekeepers will leave. Hence, in order for their efforts to have long-term sustainability, peacekeepers must achieve self-reliance in preparation for their withdrawal.

Peacekeepers with a comparatively great abundance of resources and expertise may be enthusiastic to teach the rule of law to the local people and keen to show them how to keep the peace. However, as "outsiders", peacekeepers must try to avoid talking *at* the local people, but instead should listen and learn *from* them. The aim is to ensure that the peacekeepers – the temporary outsiders – do not impose well-meant but essentially useless, if not ridiculous, measures that have no effect in restoring the rule of law. The people of the host community, as "insiders", know a great deal, and, with the support and resources of the peacekeepers, must be full, active participants in all peacekeeping rule of law decision-making. Since the intervention will change the lives of the host people, they have a basic right to participate in the decisions that will affect them. True participation is possible only when the local people are able to determine their own goals in the negotiations about rule of law planning.

The point of entry for peacekeepers may be the moment of maximum influence, because expectations will always be unattainably high. Hence this is a time to use moral authority to persuade people to comply with sensible rule of law measures. However, by helping the locals set high goals, the peacekeepers must avoid raising undue expectations.

Peacekeepers help the insiders to identify their own rule of law issues and problems and to arrive at solutions they craft themselves. With the assistance and guidance of the peacekeepers, the locals are encouraged to set the objectives, design the activities and monitor and evaluate progress towards the re-establishment of the rule of law. This participatory approach is based primarily on understanding the rule of law needs, wants, concerns and fears of insiders, which provides a means of creating adaptive feedback to peacekeepers. These needs may be abundantly obvious to the outside peacekeepers and even starkly apparent to the community itself. The process is about getting the insiders to decide for themselves and exercise authority as a self-determining people, so as to give genuine legitimacy to rule-making and rule enforcement. *There is a time for the outside peacekeepers to intervene and a time to leave the insiders alone in this process.* Assistance by the peacekeepers comes as facilitation, as the provision of new ideas and as stimuli to discussion. If the host people have this input into rule of law projects, the results become community property and hence are more likely to become an enduring reality. Unless the locals "own" the outcome by designing it themselves, they are unlikely to observe the rule of law measures agreed upon.

In the past, peacekeepers have been woefully ignorant about local communities and social processes, and as a result some peace proposals were inappropriate and misfired. Before going into the field, peacekeepers need accurate information about the rule of law realities in order to plan. They also need to understand the social, economic and cultural context of the intervention. Many social mechanisms and complex systems of patronage are not, and may never be, apparent to outsiders. Cultural conundrums will lead to mutual bafflement between the peacekeepers and the host people.

Rapid Participatory Rule of Law Appraisal

Field survey missions are necessary to conduct a Rapid Participatory Rule of Law Appraisal to measure the extent of existence of the rule of law and to determine existing justice assets. This information is needed to plan and execute the peacekeeping rule of law intervention. This is first and foremost an exercise in anthropology and sociology. In planning for the field survey mission, the key questions to be asked are: What is not known about the area where rule of law negotiations are proposed and about the target groups? What information is already available about past and present rule of law assets, social dynamics and community practices for conflict management and dealing with violence? How do you find out what is not known? How much is it going to cost? How long is it going to take?

A considerable amount of secondary data will already be available from refugees, from people who have previously lived or worked in the subject country and from Internet search engines, libraries, research theses, survey reports, anthropological publications, learned articles and texts, commercial and business reports and assessments, land-use surveys and studies, media reports, government and non-government reports, statistics and maps, Church records and accounts, and aerial photographs and satellite imagery. The purpose of the Rapid Participatory Rule of Law Appraisal is to learn as much as possible, as quickly as possible, by collecting primary data from insiders through a process of participation by local people in the field that leads to "bottom–up" planning. It is worthwhile bringing developmental workers proficient in participatory techniques to train peacekeepers and to be part of the appraisal teams. The Rapid Participatory Rule of Law Appraisal should be conducted by multidisciplinary teams collecting information directly from the people in the field, in order to understand as much as is possible on the ground from the perspectives of different professional fields. A mix of participants such as military, police, human rights lawyers, anthropologists and other members from different institutions is helpful. By using this approach the peacekeepers engage in an exploratory analysis of on-the-ground conditions to assist both the locals and the peacekeepers in "project identification" that actually addresses the real needs and priorities of the locals as end users.

Peacekeepers are dealing with complex human catastrophes, which traumatised people themselves, let alone the peacekeepers, may not be capable of understanding, let alone explaining. The peacekeepers need constantly to update their information and question their assumptions about the host people. Outside "experts" undertaking quick visits using superficial knowledge and having limited contact run the real risk that they will reach conclusions biased by their expertise, backgrounds, prejudices and own priorities. Frequently the more qualified the experts, the more likely they are to impose their own interpretations. Some may be reluctant to hear information contrary to their beliefs. Unless they are prepared to listen to data inconsistent with their conclusions, experts can create more problems than they solve. Worse still, they can be overly territorial, suffering from a desire to own the conflict and perhaps hostile to letting others in.

Rule of Law Participatory Assessment, Monitoring and Evaluation

In carrying out the Rule of Law Participatory Assessment, Monitoring and Evaluation, the first step is for the local people and the peacekeepers to assess the current rule of law situation. Both need to understand the nature and extent of the problem. A diagnosis of the causes of the current rule of law situation (both positive and negative) is undertaken. Some general directions are determined and strategies outlined. Finally a plan of action can be devised. Facilitated by the peacekeepers, the local people identify the conditions necessary for the restoration of the rule of law, and whether, when and how these conditions can be met. Participatory assessment provides the framework for the insiders and outsiders to determine whether they want, need and can support the rule of law activities proposed. The insiders and outsiders should establish and recognise their objectives, identify the necessary conditions, draw an assessment framework, rank necessary conditions and gather and analyse relevant information.

In the Rule of Law Participatory Assessment, Monitoring and Evaluation process, the peacekeepers negotiate with host people to set baselines for crime incidents or civil conflict and management (or lack thereof), the number of police and amount of judicial resources, and the extent of human rights training and public education, measured against pre-war circumstances, current circumstances and some future desirable goals. It is important to establish criteria to measure change so the peacekeepers, factional elites, functionaries and local people can readily observe progress or regression. The steps in establishing the participatory baselines involve discussion of the purpose of the baseline, review of objectives and activities, establishment of baseline questions, choice of key indicators, both direct (measurable statistics) and indirect (anecdotal), identification of information sources and tools for baseline questions, decisions on resources in terms of skills, time and labour, and decisions about when information-gathering can be done, who will gather it and what to do with it. The baseline measurements are more than the mere gathering of crime or other statistics; they are used as a means of assessing the success or failure of responses for a rule of law adjustment to rule of law plans.

Once the peacekeepers have arrived and fanned out through the host country, incident reports will soon be generated that will begin systematically to record significant events involving violence such as ceasefire violations, massacres of civilians, large-scale criminal activity and attacks on peacekeepers. These events will trigger demand for action by the peacekeepers. Although the peacekeepers can take active measures by using their own peace operation courts and peace operation criminal justice commissions, the objective is to remove the culture of impunity by negotiating with the local people to take proper non-violent responsibility for the criminal acts of their *own* people.

The incident reports prepared by the peacekeeping military observers, civilian police, civil administration, non-government organisations and the media provide outsider observation of degrees of lawlessness. The receipt of information about, and investigation of, these incidents should be done as on-the-job training with local military and police. Independent of the peacekeepers, the locals are also asked to report and record the same and/or other incidents.

The second step of participatory monitoring is undertaken by peacekeepers and locals by broadly examining progress towards objectives and activities during the life of the peace operation. The monitoring provides information for decision makers so that adjustments can be made to rule of law plans if necessary. An ongoing picture in which problems, challenges and opportunities are identified and solutions sought early is built up over time. It serves to encourage good standards to be maintained and resources to be used effectively, as well as a complete picture of the project and information for future evaluations. The steps to participatory monitoring involve discussion of the need for monitoring, review of objectives and activities, development of monitoring questions, establishment of direct and indirect indicators, decisions on which information-gathering tools are needed, and decisions about who will do the monitoring, analysis and presentation of results.

The next step in Rule of Law Participatory Assessment, Monitoring and Evaluation is the joint undertaking of evaluation of the data collected from the monitoring. Insiders take the lead and the responsibility for the rule of law in their own community, with the outside peacekeepers facilitating the participatory evaluations using information to guide managerial decisions. Community and peacekeeper relationships are strengthened in this joint enterprise. In the participatory evaluation the community is able to make better decisions with developing evaluation skills as the peacekeepers learn from their perspectives. The community can develop culturally sympathetic options and make achievable commitments.

The final step of Rule of Law Participatory Assessment, Monitoring and Evaluation is the presentation of the results to the community by the peacekeepers in an interesting, understandable, convincing and timely manner, using written format (reports, case studies, community newsletters, newspapers, graphics and posters), oral format (drama, puppet shows, tape recordings, video, story telling, community and commercial radio, teaching lectures, public addresses and debates) and visual format (photographs, drawings, video, slides, cartoons and graphics, television).

Peacekeeping negotiations at the three local levels have to be transparent and open. Every step should be carefully taken, without surprise and in full consultation, by collaborative design of all persons concerned so that as far as possible the locals own the process and the outcomes. Rule of Law Participatory Assessment, Monitoring and Evaluation does not reduce peacekeepers to performing artists, popular theatre actors or puppeteers. Any change towards the adoption of the rule of law will be gradual and incremental. The rule of law proposals must address the grassroots needs of the host people at the three levels. Rule of law measures, while needing to be culturally appropriate, must also aspire to and be consistent with international standards. The negotiation model for the rule of law, when used in conjunction with the enforcement model for the rule of law, can deliver the foundations for the creation of a new state and ultimate peace.

Notes

1. See Fred Charles Iklé, *Every War Must End* (New York: Columbia University Press, 1991).
2. Max Weber, *Economy and Society: An Outline of Interpretive Sociology* (Berkeley & Los Angeles: University of California Press, 1978), vol. I, p. 56.
3. Abraham H. Maslow, *Motivation and Personality* (New York: Harper & Row, 1954). See also John Burton, *Deviance Terrorism and War* (Canberra: Australian National University Press, 1979).
4. For further discussion, see Mark Plunkett, "Reestablishing Law and Order in Peace-Maintenance", in Jarat Chopra (ed.), *The Politics of Peace-Maintenance* (Boulder, CO: Lynne Rienner, 1998), pp. 61–79.

5. This can be a serious problem, as some of the Nuremberg defendants discovered. See Telford Taylor, *The Anatomy of the Nuremberg Trials* (New York: Alfred A. Knopf, 1993).
6. For a wider discussion of this notion, see Mary Anderson, *Do No Harm: How Aid Can Support Peace – or War* (Boulder, CO: Lynne Rienner, 1999).

12

Military force and justice

Michael Kelly

In discussing military force and justice it is important to define what is meant by justice. In the broad context of international law, military force has often been employed in the stated cause of justice. Now that the International Criminal Court is finally established it may be that forces such as the Australian Defence Force will be committed regularly to operations dictated by the need to support the Court. In this chapter, however, the focus will be on the issue of the interim administration of justice at the communal level. In this context, the issue of military force and justice is not one that is confined to some types of peace operations. The potential for military involvement in maintaining order is present across the continuum of operations. It was an ever-present requirement in conventional operations in the Second World War, and it is even more emphasised in counter-insurgency operations and in all forms of low-intensity conflict and peace operations. The key is that it is likely to be a factor wherever civilians are present in the area of operations.

This topic is often discussed in the context of whether soldiers should perform such functions or whether these should be the exclusive preserve of civil police. The problem with this argument is that it often ignores reality. It has been the common experience to date that it is extremely difficult to mobilise civil police in anything like the numbers required and of the type required for peace operations. Often the police are from jurisdictions that do not have adequate human rights standards, or they are border police with no experience in communal policing. Mostly they are unarmed and can perform observer-type functions only. The environment is often not secure enough in the early phases of deployments for the civil police to be able to perform, usually owing to the widespread presence of arms on the streets. The bottom line is that, for the foreseeable future, soldiers will be regularly called upon to perform low-level security functions to restore communal order. The issue therefore is how to deal with this reality and identify the common factors that confront soldiers in these scenarios.

A number of key issues have proven to be common in recent peace operations. These include the primary issue of legitimacy as it relates to the action that the peace operation wishes to take in what often amounts to an intervention into areas that are usually the specific preserve of the sovereign state. An example of a legitimacy "tool" I will discuss in this respect is the law of occupation, which was employed in the context of Operation Restore Hope in Somalia in 1993 by the Australian contingent, to good effect. I contend that what often emerges in these operations is the need for a robust approach to get at fundamental problems that, if not dealt with, will serve only to constitute the seeds for further conflict or instability; Cambodia is one obvious example. The robust approach must be tempered by cultural sensitivity and the forging of an alliance with the people and their responsible leaders.

I will also highlight that in most peace operations the public security function will fall to varying degrees to the intervening military force to assume. This poses problems for the selection and preparation of the troops and the structure of the force. I will discuss a possible approach to these problems and aspects of the application of force in this context.

The context

The issue of public security in peace operations has arisen because the context in which they take place has more and more frequently been one of internal conflict. These internal conflicts have resulted in or been a product of the disintegration of a "civil society". A common feature in the cause of conflict has been the insecurity felt or attacks endured by one particular ethnic, religious or national group. This is often because the group has lost confidence in the administration of justice to secure their human rights, protect their cultural identity and guarantee their physical security. In these cases or in the case of rebellion against an authoritarian regime, the problem has been that the mechanisms of "justice" have been the instruments of repression in the first place. Addressing the issue of the administration of justice therefore goes to the heart of the conflict resolution objective in a peace operation.

In addition, the peace operation should be focused on leaving behind a viable state entity whose institutions will be self-sustaining and from which the intervening forces can depart as quickly as possible. Justice reconstruction issues are centrally tied to this objective. Having an effective public security environment encourages responsible leadership to step forward. It enables economic activity to develop, because no one will work when they know that the fruits of their labour will end up in the hands of a rapacious bandit organisation or be siphoned off by a corrupt administration. Another common feature of these conflicts is property disputes, which should be addressed by an appropriate dispute resolution forum. If this is not done the seeds will be sown for future conflict.

In order to deal with the public security function, a peace operation must be provided with a framework of legitimacy tailored to the particular circumstances of the operation. Without this legitimacy, a peace operation can rapidly lose credibility, focus, rationale and support both internationally and locally. Without a framework, the forces will be left to flounder and will be prone to descend to summary justice measures as occurred in certain notable instances in Somalia. To begin with, a mandate from the United Nations is clearly required. The UN mandate, however, is limited by certain factors. It is of necessity a brief "warrant" that establishes the basic legitimacy of the presence of the force and sets out its goals in broad terms. These bare bones ought to be provided with flesh in the form of either a detailed framework agreement, or some other international law source as a point of reference to justify actions to the international community and to the local population. The other key limiting factor is that the UN mandate cannot override the provisions of existing international law, which would be beyond its power under the UN Charter.[1]

Once the framework is settled it is then necessary to determine how the mission will be structured. Even more difficult than recruiting police is the problem of what to do about the other arms of the justice administration such as the judiciary and prisons. The judiciary in particular presents a major problem because one cannot train and employ judges and magistrates within the same time frame as one can a police force. This aspect has to be addressed, however, because a functioning police force needs a judiciary to serve.

Many important opportunities are lost in the early phases of an operation as a result of the inability to come ready to address these issues. The military offer certain institutional advantages for quickly establishing administrative and technical functions. These advantages include potential speed of mobilisation, greater logistic and equipment capability and spare capacity, as troops are often engaged in ongoing training rather than operations. Some countries are also equipped with a military capability that can be enlisted to assist in justice reconstruction. This could include military police and military judges, courts and lawyers, in either advisory or emergency and interim substitutive roles. The United States, for example, has an excellent military police and civil affairs capability that is geared for the possibility of dealing with public security and rehabilitating administrative functions of this type. If this is considered undesirable, then greater effort needs to go into establishing a call-up list of civilian volunteer specialists or a body that can coordinate the speedy recruitment of such volunteers, bearing in mind that the harshness of the operational environment or security threat may not permit this option. The reality is, however, that such an option is unlikely to meet the need.

If the military are the best source for the short term in addressing public security issues, this does not mean that they are perfectly adapted for it. This is merely to say that the potential is there. In order for that potential to be maximised, the troops must have appropriate Rules of Engagement (ROE) and operating guidelines, they must be properly trained, and the force must be properly structured with the public security function in mind. This may involve placing emphasis on military police, engineers, civil affairs, psychological operations (PSYOPS, or "Public Information" as it is often called in peace operations to avoid negative connotations) and special forces.

The legal framework

What are the possibilities in terms of legal frameworks to establish the legitimacy of the actions a peace operation may be required to take to restore an efficacious regime of public security? One regime under general international law is particularly relevant and useful in the worst-case scenarios: the law of occupation. The key embodiment of that law is the Fourth Geneva Convention of 1949.

There are 188 states party and signatory to all four Geneva Conventions of 1949, making them the most universally adopted international humanitarian law codes. The questions that arise in relation to the Convention are (a) in what circumstances will the Convention apply and in particular does it apply to peace enforcement under Chapter VII of the UN Charter; and (b) when does the Convention cease to apply?

The introduction of the Fourth Convention was to alter radically the application and shape of the legal regime regulating military presence in foreign territory. It would no longer be accurate to refer to the law of belligerent or non-belligerent occupation – a distinction based on whether the occupation occurred in the context of war or peace. This resulted from the expansion of the Convention coverage to *all* forms of non-treaty occupation, regardless of whether there was an armed conflict. The new Convention was designed to regulate the relationship between foreign military forces and a civilian population where the force exercises the sole authority or is the only agency with the capacity to exercise authority in a distinct territory. As Adam Roberts puts it:

One might hazard as a fair rule of thumb that every time the forces of a country are in control of foreign territory, and find themselves face to face with the inhabitants, some or all of the provisions of the law on occupations are applicable.[2]

How does the Convention produce this result and what did the framers have in mind when they so expanded this area of law? The answer to the first question lies in an analysis of article 2 of the Convention, where the application of the laws set out in the Convention is defined. To appreciate the Convention fully it must be understood that it has different levels of application. The four Conventions of 1949 were drafted with the object in mind of addressing all forms of armed conflict in some way, as by that time the experience of undeclared and civil wars had already been evident.[3] For example, common article 3 to all the Conventions addresses all forms of armed conflict not of an international character, while paragraph 1 of common article 2 applies the remaining provisions in the Conventions to all international armed conflicts, whether a state of war exists or not. We also can see that certain non-conflict situations were to be addressed in the Fourth Convention in particular, dealing as it does with the protection of civilian populations and their relationship with foreign armed forces. The Conventions also create certain peace-time obligations. It is important at this point to set out the exact wording of common article 2:

In addition to the provisions which shall be implemented in peacetime, the present Convention shall apply to all cases of declared war or of any other armed conflict which may arise between two or more of the High Contracting Parties, even if the state of war is not recognised by one of them.

The Convention shall also apply to all cases of partial or total occupation of the territory of a High Contracting Party, even if the said occupation meets with no armed resistance.

Paragraph 2 of the article contains the key formula, providing the expanded coverage of the provisions regulating occupations. The wording to note here is the expression, "The Convention shall also apply", meaning that it also applies to the following outlined circumstances other than a state of war or armed conflict between or among High Contracting

Parties as mentioned in paragraph 1. The additional application is to "all cases of partial or total occupation of the territory of a High Contracting Party, even if the said occupation meets with no armed resistance".[4] The form of words adopted in the 1947 *Report of the Work of the Conference of Government Experts for the Study of the Conventions for the Protection of War Victims*[5] would have made this clearer because it stated that the Convention should apply "also in the event of territorial occupation in the absence of any state of war".[6] The Report elaborated its intention in this respect by its commentary on the draft provision, stating that "[t]his Article was adopted in order to make the Convention applicable to ... every occupation of territories, even should this occupation not be forcible".[7] Nevertheless, as Pictet states regarding paragraph 2 of article 2 of the 1949 Geneva Convention:

> The sense in which the paragraph under consideration should be understood is quite clear. It does not refer to cases in which territory is occupied during hostilities; in such cases the Convention will have been in force since the outbreak of hostilities or since the time war was declared. The paragraph only refers to cases where the occupation has taken place without a declaration of war and without hostilities, and makes provision for the entry into force of the Convention in those circumstances.[8]

This general category of occupation is distinct from occupations occurring as a result of armistice or capitulation, which are covered by paragraph 1 of article 2. The Pictet commentary explains the distinction as follows:

> [S]imultaneous examination of paragraphs 1 and 2 leaves no doubt as to the latter's sense: it was intended to fill the gap left by paragraph 1. The application of the Convention to territories which are occupied at a later date, in virtue of an armistice or a capitulation, does not follow from this paragraph, but from paragraph 1. An armistice suspends hostilities and a capitulation ends them, but neither ends the state of war, and any occupation carried out in war time is covered by paragraph 1.[9]

It was clear, therefore, that the Convention was concerned not with the circumstances of the coming together of military forces and civilian populations foreign to each other in a relationship of authority and submission, but with the fact of its occurrence. As Roberts states, "[t]he broad terms of common Article 2 establish that the 1949 Geneva Conventions apply to a wide range of international armed conflicts and occupations – including occupations in time of so-called peace".[10] The practical effect is that, for the parties to it, the Convention will apply to a wide range of situations that were hitherto not within the contemplation of the formal codes or would have been covered by the less prescriptive law of non-belligerent occupation.[11]

The test is whether the force present is not just passing through, is not engaged in actual combat and is in effect the sole authority capable of exercising control over the civilian population, or any remaining authority requires the approval or sanction of the force to operate. The test is not based on whether the force has established a formal administrative framework or military government. This would be contrary to the intention of article 4 of the Convention, which defines protected persons, to whom the rights and obligations of the Convention relate, as those simply "in the hands" of the occupying power.[12] The whole thrust of this law is that the situation is temporary, seeking only the regulation of the relationship between the force and the population while the force is present.

Given the transformation that has been wrought by the Fourth Convention, it now seems possible to identify the circumstances that will attract the application of this body of law. Adam Roberts has set out four basic elements in this respect:

(i) there is a military force whose presence in a territory is not sanctioned or regulated by a valid agreement, or whose activities there involve an extensive range of contacts with the host society not adequately covered by the original agreement under which it intervened; (ii) the military force has either displaced the territory's ordinary system of public order and government, replacing it with its own command structure, or else has shown the clear physical ability to displace it; (iii) there is a difference of nationality and interest between the inhabitants on the one hand and the forces intervening and exercising power over them on the other, with the former not owing allegiance to the latter; (iv) within an overall framework of a breach of important parts of the national or international legal order, administration and the life of society have to continue on some legal basis, and there is a practical need for an emergency set of rules to reduce the dangers which can result from clashes between the military force and the inhabitants.[13]

These elements were to be found in reference to the UN Transitional Authority in Cambodia (UNTAC), in the Implementation and Stabilization Forces (IFOR/SFOR) operation in Bosnia and, in particular, in the Unified Task Force (UNITAF) and the UN Operation in Somalia (UNOSOM), the NATO operations in Kosovo and the International Force in East Timor (INTERFET) (although some of these operations were governed by formal agreements). Other recent situations that have often contained these elements are "safe haven" operations. Usually a safe haven will involve a force being deployed into a clearly demarcated area. Within the safe haven the deployed force may be required to undertake the restoration and maintenance of public order. The force may find itself the predominant authority with the varying degrees of breakdown in civil authority, including the total lack thereof, that may occur in these areas. Clearly, for example, the Convention applied to the safe haven in northern Iraq during Operation Provide Comfort and to southwest Rwanda in Operation Turquoise.

There is nothing specified or implied, in either the Fourth Geneva Convention or the customary law of occupation, that requires the force to remain. It is not, for example, a requirement that the force must remain until normal civil life or order is restored. The force is required to work towards this end only as far as it is within its capacity for the period during which it is in the territory. The force is free to depart at any time of its own pleasing and all its legal obligations with respect to that territory end with this departure.[14] The only circumstance in which the force may be obliged to remain is where a genocide is occurring, in which case there may be an obligation on the force, and indeed the international community at large, under the Genocide Convention to take preventative action.[15]

There is a gradation of application provided for in the Fourth Convention based on the changing nature of the military presence. In article 6 it specifies that, in the case of territory being occupied in a conflict situation, the general application of the Convention ceases one year after the close of military operations. While the occupation continues, however, and to the extent that the occupying power exercises the functions of government, a number of articles remain applicable. This then poses the questions of what provisions apply to a non-belligerent occupation, whether the application of the provisions changes at any point, and when they cease altogether. Pictet comments on this issue as follows:

Article 6 does not say when the Convention will cease to apply in the case of occupation where there has been no military resistance, no state of war and no armed conflict. This omission appears to be deliberate and must be taken to mean that the Convention will be fully applicable in such cases, so long as the occupation lasts.[16]

This produces the result that more provisions continue to apply for an occupation that begins as non-belligerent, whereas fewer provisions would apply in relation to an occupation begun in a conflict situation, even though it may have acquired the same character as a non-belligerent occupation one year after the cessation of military operations. This anomaly was addressed by Additional Protocol I of 1977. For those states party to it, the Protocol altered the termination provisions of article 6 of the Convention by clearly stating in article 3 (b), without qualification or elaboration, that the relevant provisions of the Protocol and Convention will cease to apply "on the termination of the occupation".

The utility of the law of occupation is extensive in relation to the public security issue, including guidelines for dealing with the local law and the parameters for departing from this law when necessary. It also provides well for the temporary administration of justice where there is no local capability. The measures for security of the force and relief operations are clearly spelled out, as is the authority for reconstructing the local justice administration.[17] Any apprehension that may be felt concerning possible obligations under this law should be dispelled by a closer reading of the manner in which the law is worded and a look at the reality of the modern operating environment. The Convention obliges the force to assume responsibilities for the population in terms of health, sustenance and welfare only to the extent that it has the spare capacity to do so, beyond what it needs to deal with operational demands, and only to the maximum extent feasible. The role of meeting the needs of the population is more than adequately met by simply allowing the array of non-governmental organisations (NGOs) to do their job in these environments because they will always be present.[18]

The United States could have relied on this law to meet the problem it had with its Foreign Assistance Act in supporting the standing up of the Somali police force during UNITAF's Operation Restore Hope. The Foreign Assistance Act prohibited the United States from supporting foreign police forces, which forced UNITAF to label the reviving Somali police force as an "Auxiliary Security Force" and limited the extent of US involvement. Citing its obligations under the law of occupation the United States could have overridden the limitations of the Foreign Assistance Act in this respect. In debates UNITAF had with aviation authorities over control of the airspace in Somalia, it could have overcome the concern these authorities felt over whether the UN mandate was suitably elastic to cover this by once again citing the force's rights and obligations under the law of occupation.[19]

The current status of non-belligerent occupation

Recent examples of pacific occupation by agreement – where the presence of a force that is assuming certain sovereign functions is regulated by a specific treaty with the host state – include the UNTAC experience in Cambodia. The Paris Agreement under which the UN forces deployed constituted the temporary transfer of key areas of sovereignty to the United Nations. However, many areas remained the source of much contention and uncertainty under the necessarily broad terms of the Agreement. The customary law of pacific occupation will fill any such voids left by an agreement of this sort, and certain fundamental principles can be applied to help clarify uncertainties.[20] One example of an area the customary law can illuminate is the right of the force to take measures for its own security.[21] Another of the principles that would also be applicable in the case of occupation by agreement relates to the aspect of control. For example, in the case of UNTAC the UN force was never able to exert its authority in the areas controlled by the Khmer Rouge. The Khmer Rouge were clearly a force exercising sole control over a part of Cambodia such as to enable them to carry out sustained and concerted military operations. The customary laws of pacific occupation therefore did not apply to that particular area of Cambodia because the occupying force had no control there.

Another recent experience of pacific occupation was that established by the Dayton Agreement involving the warring parties in the former Republic of Yugoslavia, NATO, the Organization for Security and Cooperation in Europe (OSCE) and the United Nations.[22] This Agreement provided for the deployment of a large NATO Implementation Force (IFOR) for a period of one year pursuant to UN Security Council authorisation and Chapter VII of the UN Charter.[23] IFOR was empowered to "take such actions as required, including the use of necessary force, to ensure compliance with the ... [agreement] and to ensure its own protection", a point to be emphasised throughout the document (Annex 1-A, article I (2)). There were a number of other provisions assigning authority to the IFOR commander and various agencies, approximating an occupation condition.

Of particular interest was the development of the role of an International Police Task Force building on the experience in numerous recent deployments. The management of this operation was assigned to the United Nations, and it was headed by a Commissioner appointed by the UN Secretary-General in consultation with the Security Council. It was coordinated by and came under the guidance of the High Representative. The Commissioner was permitted to receive and request personnel, resources and assistance from states as well as international and non-governmental organisations (Annex 11, article II, 2). In carrying out their functions the police were to act in accord with international standards but were to respect local laws and customs (article II, 5).

The tasks of the International Police Task Force included: monitoring, observing and inspecting law enforcement activities and facilities, including associated judicial organisations, structures and proceedings; advising law enforcement personnel and forces; training law enforcement personnel; facilitating, within the International Police Task Force's mission of assistance, the parties' law enforcement activities; assessing threats to public order and advising on the capability of law enforcement agencies to deal with such threats; advising governmental authorities in Bosnia and Herzegovina on the organisation of effective civilian law enforcement agencies; and assisting the parties' law enforcement personnel as they carried out their responsibilities, as the International Police Task Force deemed appropriate (article III).

To fulfil these tasks they were to have complete freedom of movement and be allowed access to any site, person, activity, proceeding, record or other item or event in Bosnia and Herzegovina. This was to include the right to monitor, observe and inspect any site or facility at which it believed police, law enforcement, detention or judicial activities were taking place (article IV, 3).

Far less detailed were the agreements that governed the presence of the NATO force in Kosovo and the presence of INTERFET in East Timor.[24] Both agreements raised many practical questions to which once again the law of occupation would have provided some answers.

Pacific occupation is obviously alive and well and is finding new modes of application and relevance as it is employed by the international community to meet the challenges of the diverse security crises that threaten international peace and stability. This is clearly being driven by the need to address the source of this threat, which is primarily that of tackling not cross-border invasions but internal disintegration and violence. It is important, however, that the terms of a pacific occupation be sufficient to allow a robust approach to establishing an efficacious public security administration. Both the Paris Accord in particular and to a lesser extent the Dayton process have not fully measured up to this test. It is only through action that equates to occupation that such internal strife can be effectively addressed, if addressed at all. It also requires a realisation that the process requires engagement of one form or another, depending on the circumstances, over a number of years.

The treaty approach is certainly the best option to pursue where possible. Problems that may be experienced with the treaty approach, however, include that it is sometimes not feasible to do any kind of deal with the factions, or some of them, because they may be unworthy partners, unrepresentative or too chimerical. In strictly legal terms, any agreement with an internal armed faction that cannot be described as representing "the state" has no status in international law. Such an agreement, then, can acquire such status only through its endorsement and enforcement by the UN Security Council.

The proper use of force

The dilemma that faces any peace operation is the appropriate use of force in dealing with the public security aspect. This becomes an even more complicated issue when there is no law enforcement agency of any form, or civil authority capable of enforcing a code of law. The troops will often in these circumstances be caught between the force appropriate for combat situations and something more akin to civil policing.[25] This difficult circumstance places emphasis on two aspects of military preparation: the training of the troops and the Rules of Engagement. It was clear in Somalia that some troops were better prepared for the complexity of the operation than others.[26] The Canadian Airborne Regiment Battle Group was able to achieve much good work in the Belet Weyn area, but its reputation was tarnished by the inappropriate manner in which the unit dealt with the issues of base security and crowd control. This deficiency was a consequence of disciplinary problems within one of the sub-units, poor leadership and command attitude in relation to Rules of Engagement standards, inadequate training of at least one sub-unit and the lack of a proper framework for effecting the Rules of Engagement. The Board of Inquiry into the Canadian Airborne Regiment Battle Group of 31 August 1993, a *Toronto Star* investigative story of 10 July 1994, and Canadian Television (CTV) investigative reports all revealed the extent of the disciplinary problems of 2 Commando of the Airborne Regiment. These included challenges to the authority of unit and sub-unit formal leadership, inappropriate initiation rituals, racist attitudes and practices, steroid usage and a tendency to unharnessed aggression. These problems were identified before deployment by the then Commanding Officer of the unit, Lieutenant-Colonel Paul Morneault. He recommended that 2 Commando not be sent to Somalia. Soon after passing on this advice, Lieutenant-Colonel Morneault was relieved of command and Lieutenant-Colonel Carol Mathieu was appointed Commanding Officer. The preparation of 2 Commando was not ideal. It was put through what amounted to a collective punishment exercise in an attempt to correct its discipline problems and had suffered a high turnover in junior personnel. It fell behind 1 and 3 Commandos in specific-to-mission training for Somalia as a result, focusing instead on "general purpose combat training". In an attempt to remedy the training deficiency, 2 Commando was put through a one-week crash course immediately prior to departure for Somalia. Once in Somalia, a number of training, leadership and Rules of Engagement issues arose. The troops began referring to the Somalis using derogatory epithets such as "gimmes, niggers, smufties and nig-nogs" and this was not stamped out by the unit leadership. Despite the use-of-force regime laid out by the UNITAF Rules of Engagement, the Commanding Officer on 28 January 1993 issued instructions that any Somali caught in the perimeter stealing equipment was to be shot. Major Seward, the 2 Commando Officer Commanding, wrote in his diary concerning this instruction that "he has amended the rules of engagement ordering us to open fire on individuals pilfering the camp. These individuals are teenaged Somalis. His direction ... amounts to killing children ... I will not willingly accept murdering boys stealing water, rations and even military kit." Major Seward also expressed concern over the subsequent killing of an intruder in pursuance of this policy: "I was disgusted by what seemed to be a recce [reconnaissance] platoon hunting trip. The succession of shots and the anticipatory tone of voices makes me conclude that the killing was a murder." Later instructions were issued by the sub-unit leaders, including Major Seward, physically to "abuse" captured intruders in order to deter them. This resulted in the torture and death of a Somali. On 17 February 1993 there was a demonstration by some Belet Weyn inhabitants against Lieutenant-Colonel Mathieu's selection of locals for reconstruction committees, which excluded some clans from representation. In handling the demonstration, 12-gauge shotguns were fired into the crowd by the Canadian troops, killing one Somali and critically injuring three others.[27] These disturbing events clearly show that it is not advisable to deploy assault units of this kind into a situation such as that in Somalia without careful supplementary training.

This was recognised, for example, in the preparation of the 1st Battalion, Royal Australian Regiment (1 RAR) before it deployed to Somalia. Although this unit was also trained for intense and aggressive combat, in the two years prior to the Somalia deployment it had been coming to grips with more complicated mission concepts. These revolved around low-level conflict scenarios in northern Australia and Services Protected Evacuations of Australian citizens in such circumstances as internal conflicts and the disintegration of law and order. In the course of this training the soldiers were trained to deal with varying levels of threat and the discriminating use of force. The training was in reference to two simple states of restraint based on a "red" and "amber" card respectively. The cards are plastic and carried permanently in the soldier's basic pouch. The cards themselves would be meaningless, of course, without appropriate training. This training was conducted by taking, for example, a rifle platoon and having members of the platoon play-act a scenario with props in an outdoor setting. The remainder of the platoon would observe as the scene was played out. Afterwards the soldiers would be queried as to appropriate responses and given the opportunity to ask questions and discuss the issues. The scenarios would then be varied to present gradations of the problem. In subsequent exercises the troops would be exposed to civilians, sometimes their own families, who had volunteered to participate. Also encountered would be delegates of the International Committee of the Red Cross, who have been incorporated into major Australian exercises since 1989.

This soldier-level regime of standard response is called Orders For Opening Fire, to distinguish it from higher-level Rules of Engagement reserved for commanders in control of significant weapon systems, which focus more on the strategic implications of conflict. The Orders For Opening Fire training emphasises certain key elements of the soldier's decision-making reference. The first is the clear identification of the target. This was a fundamental discipline in Somalia that the soldiers adhered to exceptionally well.[28] This concept places soldiers under the stricture that they must be able to identify the target to be fired upon as hostile or the source of a hostile act (depending on the circumstances) and not open fire indiscriminately or engage, for example, in "reconnaissance by fire" (that is, clearing an area in front of troops by massive use of firepower without regard to what may be under that fire). The element emphasised and debated most extensively in the training is the issue of self-defence and proportionate or necessary force. Here, through demonstration and discussion, the soldier is made intimately familiar with the concepts of this legal standard and the parameters set by the courts. The goal here is threefold: first, to reduce hesitation that might otherwise result in the soldier's death or the death of a person it is the soldier's duty to protect; second, to minimise the risk to innocent bystanders; and, finally, to equip soldiers with the means of explaining and accounting for their actions in any subsequent review.

In training, the concept of the proportionate use of force is carefully explored. The focus here is providing soldiers with guidelines as to the options they might use when confronted with particular situations. The first distinction that is drawn is whether the soldiers face a lethal or non-lethal threat. If they face a non-lethal threat that nevertheless has the potential to cause physical injury, then methods of responding are canvassed such as the use of batons, warning shots or riot control agents. The application of force they are instructed to apply in this circumstance must be no more than is required to neutralise the threat and not to kill or cause more bodily harm than is absolutely necessary. In response to a lethal threat, soldiers are authorised to use whatever means they can to counter the threat, including the employment of lethal force, subject only to the requirement to attempt to minimise the risk of death or injury to innocent bystanders. When 1 RAR was warned for deployment to Somalia, the troops were put through refresher Orders For Opening Fire training, modified according to the known facts about the operational environment, the specific Rules of Engagement for the mission, and the law and order role.

They were permitted to employ the level of firepower considered necessary to neutralise the threat, restricted by consideration of the proportional risk to civilians. In this respect, the training of the soldiers in the

Laws of Armed Conflict and discussion in the acted-out scenarios assisted them in judging the issue of proportionality. This training and the command philosophy of the Commanding Officer also highlighted the individual responsibility of the soldiers and the standards of behaviour expected of them when dealing with civilians. This training was validated when members of the contingent reported observed violations of these standards committed by members of another contingent, resulting in disciplinary action.[29] Any reports of an inclination to lack of respect for the local population were very quickly acted upon by the Commanding Officer. The combination of training, realistic Rules of Engagement, command philosophy, a law and order regime relying on the law of occupation, and a civic action programme explains the remarkable goodwill enjoyed by the Australian contingent with the local population. No progress in rehabilitating the public security function can be made without maintaining the goodwill of the population.

It is therefore imperative for common standards to be developed in the application of force and the Laws of Armed Conflict for all troops who are nominated to become part of a peace operation with a public security dimension. To this end it is a matter of some urgency that a training package be created and adopted by the United Nations and regional military cooperation organisations that focuses on the essential elements of behaviour and the application of force for peace operations. This package should then be provided to every prospective troop-contributing nation and a training regime commenced for those forces that have been nominated as part of the standby force arrangements between the United Nations and participating countries. The United Nations should have a permanent "Inspector General" who can advise on the implementation of this training and monitor the standards attained. The advice of this officer could then be obtained as to whether a contingent being offered for a mission had achieved a satisfactory level of training in this respect, measured against the nature of the operation. Such a package could form the basis of a general standard to apply to all armed forces, in the same manner as UN Rules relating to standards of criminal justice. Training should also be put into effect to prepare troops to operate in accord with the particular Rules of Engagement for a given mission. When Rules of Engagement are promulgated to supplement or alter original Rules of Engagement, then the onus is on commanders to ensure there is proper briefing and training for troops expected to adapt to new operating conditions.[30] As Colonel Kenneth Allard of the US Army has put it:

A single unwise tactical move by a soldier on patrol can instantly change the character of an entire operation and, when broadcast by the ever-present media pool, can also affect strategic considerations.[31]

It is a fundamental prerequisite that the military force be well disciplined and led by forceful and moral leaders. This basic soundness prevented contingents such as the US and Australian troops from experiencing the extent of the problems other contingents had in Somalia and on other operations.[32] In this respect the commanders must appreciate the differing circumstances of operations so that they will understand that most peace operations are closer in nature to what used to be termed "Counter Insurgency" operations, now given the generic term Low-Intensity Conflict.

Those commanders who are not sensitive to the subtleties of such operations should not be appointed. This was one of the major lessons to emerge from the Canadian experience in Somalia, much of the explanation for which stems from the attitude of the Airborne Regiment leadership at the time. The employment of firepower must also be highly selective and confined. The circumstances of peace-enforcing occupations and humanitarian interventions dictate a standard higher than would apply in a state of war and therefore it is incumbent on commanders to adopt tactical options that offer a more surgical approach. This once again places emphasis on the need for the assets to open up such options, including special forces and intelligence.

Justice reconstruction and interim measures

An effective justice reconstruction programme was important to the overall success the Somalia intervention hoped to achieve, but this was not reflected in the urgency, resources or efficiency with which the issue was approached. The recurrence of this central problem in peace operations requires that the international community find a way of addressing it at the outset of the contemplation of a mission. The two crucial aspects of creating an effective international response are funding and physical capability. The programme in Somalia suffered firstly because the funds to support it could not come from the peacekeeping budget for the mission. Funds had to come instead from donors. Perhaps the United Nations might have had greater success in raising funding support had it used the argument that the troop-contributing countries had obligations in this respect under the laws of occupation. In missions of this nature in the future, where it is clear that the re-establishment of a justice regime is going to be involved, an estimate should be provided of the costs involved. This cost should then be factored into the determination by the Security Council, and contributions assessed against member states in accordance with their assessed proportional contributions to the United Nations in general. In "contracted-out" operations, which appear to be the most likely for the foreseeable future, participating states should be required in the authorising resolution to organise an effective means of dealing with such reconstruction issues in tandem with UN and other agencies.

Having noted the difficulty of quickly deploying civilian experts in a peace operation, what is the interim solution? It is essential that nations that are intending to offer standby forces to UN operations develop a deployable civil affairs capability geared to addressing the restoration and maintenance of law and order. Such units could deploy rapidly, at less cost and in harsher environments than could civilian alternatives. Once circumstances permit, these units could hand over either to civilians or to local authorities that had resumed functioning. They would have the capability to establish interim measures such as military courts to hear cases involving major offenders against the force and public order. They would also be equipped and staffed to conduct investigations to support the work of international criminal tribunals or assist local prosecution efforts against major violators of international humanitarian law. These units could use as their reference the provisions of the laws of occupation and international standards established by conventions, general principles and published UN Rules. Under these authorities, a basic code could be drawn up which could serve as an interim regime in the worst case of no local code capable of application. Primarily the focus should be on rehabilitating pre-existing local codes pursuant to the obligations of the law of occupation. The world is predominantly divided into criminal law traditions derived from the Napoleonic Code, the English common law, and/or Sharia law. The nation called upon to contribute a civil affairs unit to a mission could be selected on the basis of a tradition or capability matching the assisted country so that familiarisation on deployment would be quicker. The NGO community could also be drawn into such efforts.

Such interim measures were adopted by INTERFET in East Timor, where a Detainee Management Unit (DMU) was deployed composed of military legal officers. This provided a rudimentary "pre-trial" function that enabled an assessment to be made of the evidence concerning each detainee taken by the force in terms of whether a case existed against the individual that warranted their being held for trial. This provided an essential safeguard against arbitrary detention that also met the security need to hold people for an extended period while a proper trial capability was established. This action was based on Security Council resolution 1264 authorising the operation and setting out its tasks under the Chapter VII umbrella. Using that authority the DMU process was implemented by adopting as policy the laws of occupation, so far as they were relevant to the operation. The detention and DMU processes relied on the existing Indonesian law, which was an expediency carried on by the following UN Transitional Administration in East Timor (UNTAET).[33]

In contrast, the failure in Somalia of UNOSOM II to deal effectively with justice reconstruction for reasons of funding and capability compounded the faults created during the earlier UNITAF phase regarding this issue and the restoration and maintenance of order in general.[34] This stemmed from the reluctance to recognise the need for a framework for the interim administration of justice and the rejection of the laws of occupation for this purpose. One option in this early phase, according to former Somali Police Chief Brigadier Ahmed Jama, would have been to have foreign judges come in to operate courts until a transitional government was formed and enough judges found, trained and vetted to take over. He believed this was necessary at least in Mogadishu, where it would take some time for the people to accept that a Somali judge would not be clan biased. He believed the foreign judges would have been required for at least a year.[35] This would have created problems for UNITAF and UNOSOM II because of the uncertainty both operations experienced over the authority for taking such action. This authority was clearly available under the law of occupation. This option has been partially adopted in the pacific occupation arrangements of the Dayton Agreement, under which non-nationals have been nominated to the role of Human Rights Ombudsman and to the panel of the Human Rights Chamber.

The failure to establish any form of effective law and order regime by either UNITAF or UNOSOM II led directly to the frustration that emerged among the troops of contingents where no alternative had been attempted similar to the Australian initiatives. This frustration led to incidents that would only further alienate the troops from the population and that seriously damaged the international image of the operation. The frustration of troops who have their initial motivation to help restore order checked, and the loss of faith of a population that has high expectations of what the force will do to restore security to their lives, combine to produce a tragic atmosphere of bitterness, futility and the decay of morale. There was also confusion for the commanders trying to come to grips with the complexity of the operation. In considering the detainee issue, the Canadian Board of Inquiry into the Canadian Airborne Regiment Battle Group made what was a common error in Somalia: looking for guidance on the handling of detainees from the Third Geneva Convention of 1949 Relative to the Treatment of Prisoners of War, rather than the Fourth Convention.[36] All troop-contributing governments and the United Nations have a responsibility to ensure that the men and women of their armed forces are never placed in such a position again. No mission into a failed state or to establish a safe haven should proceed without an interim administration of justice plan and a concept of operations with the appropriate resources and assets for the longer-term restoration of the local capability.

Such plans do not necessarily imply the commitment of vast sums of money and personnel. The Australian experience in Baidoa proved that much can be achieved with little, and in fact the best approach is to rely as much as possible on what can be gleaned locally. For example, it was not necessary to bring large numbers of police trainers to Somalia. In many cases the trainers who were brought in had inferior training to the formerly highly competent Somali force. This in itself was something of an insult to the locals. The Australian approach of locating survivors from the old police academy and putting them to work doing the training, in coordination with members of the former Somali CID and Somali judges, was better and would have saved much time and money. Similarly, weapons could have been issued from the confiscated stock and buildings restored from the least damaged available. The police could have been equipped with vehicles from confiscated technicals[37] or the vehicles of bandits. All that might have been needed then was some basic office equipment, stationery, communications gear, generators and uniforms to supplement what was salvaged from Somali stock in Kenya.

Another measure that should have been adopted to help finance the operation in terms of pay for the police and judges was the commencement of some form of rudimentary taxation once the markets, farms and livestock trade were functioning again in areas where councils were established. The Somali Democratic Movement council in Baidoa had wanted to commence taxation for this purpose during the later period of the Australian presence. Because the justice system was providing a secure environment for the economy to revive, the measure would have had moral logic. The authority of the laws of occupation could have been used to provide a framework for taxation. Under these provisions, the force may gather revenue for the administration of the territory and take measures necessary for the welfare of the population. As long as the taxation was applied solely for paying local personnel, it would have been easily justified. In this way the officials would be paid in accordance with what the economy could bear and there would be no difficulty of sustainability after UN departure or a lowering of expectations. One more string to the cycle of dependency could be severed. To avoid any acrimony developing among the population from the United Nations' gathering the revenue, this could have been left to the re-established councils acting in accord with UN guidelines, under UN supervision and financial monitoring.

Perhaps the key issue a law and order regime would have had to contend with had it been established was the position to be taken towards the warlords. It was advocated in some quarters that all the warlords who had been guilty of committing grave atrocities during the civil war should have been arrested en masse and placed on trial.[38] Prosecution action greatly assisted the long-term objectives of the Australian contingent in Baidoa. This poses the question of what approach should have been taken to the warlords. For the seizing of the warlords to have been effective, in the sense of being seen to be even handed and pre-empting conflict with any particular faction, all the warlords would have had to have been arrested simultaneously. Clearly this would have been extremely difficult and fraught with great risk. There is also the important consideration that, if it was intended to bring the warlords to trial, there ought to be some evidence in the possession of the force, connecting particular individuals with specific acts, that would justify every arrest. Such evidence would not have been available, if at all, until after careful investigation. More legally sustainable would have been the detention of the warlords on the grounds of the threat they represented to public safety and the safety of the force. This would still have carried grave operational risk and would have been difficult to execute.

A more feasible approach would have been the establishment, once the force was effectively and securely established, of a humanitarian law violations investigation operation to gather evidence of atrocities committed during the civil war. Initially, regional bandits, such as Gutaale in Baidoa and Jess and Morgan in the south, could have been targeted for possible prosecution (as opposed to the approach taken in the hunt for Aideed). Once sufficient evidence was available the warlords could have been arrested, when the opportunity presented, as quietly as possible, without announcing beforehand that these individuals were being sought. Targeting the lesser regional figures would have sent a powerful message to the major faction leaders to cooperate lest the same fate befall them. It would have had the added benefit of eroding the regional support for these main players. This proved to be the case with the warlord Gutaale, who was tried and executed in Baidoa and whose demise resulted in a reduction in revenue and support for Aideed. In effect this was the type of strategy that was adopted in Bosnia, which on the one hand led to accusations of inaction early in the operation but on the other led to a creeping apprehension of many of the key war criminals without provoking the scale of backlash experienced in the heavy-handed hunt for Aideed.

International tribunals

The idea of an international tribunal to try such figures is fine in theory; however, the difficulty in establishing the Rwanda and former Yugoslavia tribunals indicates that these instruments take at least a year to be rendered operable. The other problem with a tribunal in the Rwandan situation is that it focuses attention and funding on an external legal mechanism rather than on reviving the local system. The Rwandan Tribunal could prosecute at best a small number of perhaps the key figures in the 1994 genocide. In the meantime, 100,000 people languished in appalling conditions in Rwandan prisons awaiting trial. Many of these people have had accusations levelled against them that have not and will not be supported by further evidence but who were nominated on the word of a single complainant who may have had particular motives for making the accusation, such as acquiring the land of the accused.[39] Although the trial of the key figures by the Tribunal is desirable, the real problem is the ability of the system to handle the languishing thousands. An Argentinian team working in Ethiopia concentrated on enabling the Ethiopians themselves to handle the investigation and prosecutions relating to the atrocities committed by the Mengistu regime. In Somalia, priority should have been given to equipping Somalis to prosecute the bandits and warlords. Major figures beyond the capability of the locals to handle could have been tried by the domestic courts of one of the troop-contributing states where there was evidence of such persons having committed grave breaches of common article 3 of the Geneva Conventions of 1949. With no Somali sovereignty left to offend, and these figures having passed into the hands and authority of the occupying power, this would have been justifiable.

More robust action was taken by the Stabilization Force in support of the Hague Tribunal in Bosnia and by the Kosovo Force. This once again opens the question of whether such action is wise in the context of establishing the momentum of a peace process, with the hope of moving away from confrontation and recrimination. This, however, is really a question of timing, building confidence, equitable dealing and demonstrating the value of due process as opposed to summary revenge or stored grievances for a later conflict. In this respect, the apprehension and trial of offenders should be, where possible, even handed. In other words, if a Serb is to be arrested, then the force should also attempt to arrest a Croat, Muslim or Albanian suspect. In particular, focus should be on the prime instigators. Once again, however, the emphasis should be on ensuring that the internal processes of justice in Bosnia and Kosovo are efficacious and eliminate the suspicions of ethnic groups.

Now that the International Criminal Court is established, it may be possible to bring before it major violators of international humanitarian law and this will provide a useful option to deal with the major figures while also removing them from the local scene. Notwithstanding this possibility, the priority of effort should always be directed at enabling the assisted country to conduct its own trials in missions seeking to salvage and revive collapsed states. This approach is better for the long-term viability of such states.

Property disputes

Justice reconstruction should not focus solely on the issue of maintaining order. As the Australian experience in Baidoa and the operations in Haiti, Rwanda, Bosnia, Kosovo and Bougainville have demonstrated, an integral factor in laying the foundations for long-term order is the need to address the attempted supplanting of ownership of land and property. This is often accompanied, as in Baidoa, by genocidal activities.[40] It is essential to include a mechanism for resolving land and property disputes in many operations and this may include establishing a special tribunal. The same logic as was discussed in relation to criminal tribunals applies here, in that effort should be directed primarily at creating an indigenous capability to deal with these matters, albeit perhaps with close supervision. This can help take the heat out of potentially explosive situations.

The long-term view

The mission in Somalia could have achieved a great deal more had the international community been fully committed to the long-term view (finally expressed in UN Security Council resolution 814) from the first day the troops hit the beach and sent in the assets capable of carrying it out with them. In principle it is possible to restore countries or provinces such as Somalia, Rwanda, Burundi, Liberia, Sierra Leone, Ethiopia, Mozambique, Angola, Cambodia, East Timor, Bougainville, Bosnia, Kosovo, East Timor and many other situations like them. The world learned how to go about such a task in Germany and Japan after the Second World War and is relearning in Haiti, Bosnia, Kosovo and East Timor. Internal civil wars and/or social breakdown pose much greater difficulties, but they are not insurmountable. Resolution of such conflicts depends on the ability of the intervening force to manage and begin the resolution of inherent grievances, to guarantee security and to create mechanisms that will give all parties confidence that this guarantee will continue on the departure of the force.

When dealing with the public security issue in a collapsed state scenario, the idea that laboratory solutions produced in Western think tanks can be automatically and inflexibly applied should be dispelled. Similarly the concept that all developing states should be made over in the image of Western economies and societies is destructive of the social fabrics that must be built upon for long-term results, and usually cannot be sustained by the environment or resources of the assisted country. An intervention should deploy with a capability and with experienced staff in key positions but should be prepared to be flexible and imaginative, adapting the mission to the circumstances and being as inclusive of the local population and sensitive to their culture and laws as possible. It must also be prepared to remain engaged in one form or another for an extended period, with five years being a suggested conceptual planning figure.

From the perspective of the military, it is critical that the public security function in peace operations be addressed in planning for the early phases of a deployment, and force structures adjusted accordingly. Where a public security function is likely to be significant, it is advisable that a Civil Affairs Task Force be formed, which should include sizeable units of military police, engineers and civil affairs specialists in the areas of administration and law, including the three aspects of police, prisons and judiciary. Working to provide a good platform for public security from the earliest moment is the best way to achieve early redundancy for the force and therefore a quick exit and handover to civil authorities. This has been borne out by Australian experience in Somalia and East Timor. The public security function is a thorny nettle, but it is one that can be grasped if we properly equip ourselves for the task. It is worth the effort to do so, for, if the issue is dealt with effectively, the cultivation of a lasting peace has a brighter prospect.

Notes

1. See Michael J. Kelly, *Peace Operations: Tackling the Military, Legal and Policy Challenges* (Canberra: Australian Government Publishing Service, 1997), pp. 4–21, para. 434.
2. Adam Roberts, "What Is a Military Occupation?", *British Yearbook of International Law* (Oxford: Oxford University Press, 1985), vol. 55, pp. 249–305 at p. 250.
3. Denise Plattner, "Assistance to the Civilian Population: The Development and Present State of International Humanitarian Law", *International Review of the Red Cross*, no. 288, May–June 1992, pp. 249–262, at p. 258.
4. This was not intended to discourage armed resistance to an invader or to reflect a belief that it was improper to expect civilian populations to resist; such action was given legitimate belligerent status, provided certain qualifications were met, in articles 13 (2) of Geneva Convention I and 4A (2) of Geneva Convention III. The absence of the requirement for resistance reflected only the desire to simplify the de facto qualifications for the application of the Convention to ensure the protection of civilian populations in the widest range of relationships with foreign armed forces in positions of authority.
5. This Conference was convened to review draft reworkings developed by the International Committee of the Red Cross in 1937 of the earlier Geneva Conventions and was an important preliminary step towards the final drafting of the Geneva Conventions

of 1949 at the Diplomatic Conference of that year. See *Report of the Work of the Conference of Government Experts for the Study of the Conventions for the Protection of War Victims (Geneva, April 14–26, 1947)* (Geneva: International Committee of the Red Cross, 1947).
6. Ibid., p. 272. Jean S. Pictet, *The Geneva Conventions of 12 August 1949: Commentary: IV Geneva Convention Relative to the Protection of Civilian Persons in Time of War* (Geneva: International Committee of the Red Cross, 1958), p. 18.
7. *Report of the Work of the Conference of Government Experts*, p. 272.
8. Pictet, *Commentary*, pp. 21–22.
9. Ibid.
10. Roberts, "What Is a Military Occupation?", p. 253.
11. Eyal Benvenisti, *The International Law of Occupation* (Princeton, NJ: Princeton University Press, 1993), pp. 170–171, 173.
12. Pictet, *Commentary*, pp. 47, 617.
13. Roberts, "What Is a Military Occupation?", pp. 300–301.
14. "Belligerent occupation is, after all, a question of fact. It seems to the writer that an occupation would be terminated at the actual dispossession of the occupant, regardless of the source or cause of such dispossession"; Gerhard von Glahn, *The Occupation of Enemy Territory: A Commentary on the Law and Practice of Belligerent Occupation* (Minneapolis: University of Minnesota Press, 1957), p. 29.
15. For the full text of the *Convention on the Prevention and Punishment of the Crime of Genocide, 1948*, see Ian Brownlie (ed.), *Basic Documents on Human Rights* (Oxford: Oxford University Press, 1992), pp. 31–34. Article 1 of the Convention states: "The Contracting Parties confirm that genocide, whether committed in time of peace or in time of war, is a crime under international law which they undertake to prevent and to punish." The prohibition of genocide will be binding on all states, whether or not they are signatories to the Convention, because this prohibition has attained the status of *jus cogens*.
16. Pictet, *Commentary*, p. 63.
17. See Kelly, *Peace Operations*, chapter 5.
18. Ibid., paras. 518–527.
19. Ibid., pp. 7–29 to 7–36.
20. See ibid., chapter 3, paras. 343–369.
21. Ibid. See also para. 309.
22. *General Framework Agreement for Peace in Bosnia and Herzegovina*, 21 November 1995, executed in Paris, 14 December 1995.
23. UN Security Council resolution 1031 of 15 December 1995 subsequently provided full authorisation for the Agreement under Chapter VII, including UN responsibilities arising from the International Police Task Force and the High Representative for relief matters.
24. The NATO presence in Kosovo was based on the agreement with the Federal Republic of Yugoslavia on the paper presented in Belgrade on 2 June 1999 (document S/1999/649, annex 2 to UN Security Council resolution 1244 of 10 June 1999). Terms included:
    1. An immediate and verifiable end of violence and repression in Kosovo.
    2. Verifiable withdrawal from Kosovo of all military, police and paramilitary forces according to a rapid timetable.
    3. Deployment in Kosovo under United Nations auspices of effective international civil and security presences, acting as may be decided under Chapter VII of the Charter, capable of guaranteeing the achievement of common objectives.
    4. The international security presence with substantial North Atlantic Treaty Organization participation must be deployed under unified command and control and au-

thorized to establish a safe environment for all people in Kosovo and to facilitate the safe return to their homes of all displaced persons and refugees.
5. Establishment of an interim administration for Kosovo as a part of the international civil presence under which the people of Kosovo can enjoy substantial autonomy within the Federal Republic of Yugoslavia, to be decided by the Security Council of the United Nations. The interim administration to provide transitional administration while establishing and overseeing the development of provisional democratic self-governing institutions to ensure conditions for a peaceful and normal life for all inhabitants in Kosovo.
6. A political process towards the establishment of an interim political framework agreement providing for substantial self-government for Kosovo, taking full account of the Rambouillet accords and the principles of sovereignty and territorial integrity of the Federal Republic of Yugoslavia and the other countries of the region, and the demilitarization of UCK. Negotiations between the parties for a settlement should not delay or disrupt the establishment of democratic self-governing institutions.

The agreement over the deployment of INTERFET was worked out on a trilateral basis including Portugal, Indonesia and the United Nations (5 May 1999 and 28 September 1999) on the basis that there would be a UN administration that would gradually assume functions and responsibility from Indonesia and that Indonesia would continue to provide some administrative support. This was reflected also in the Diplomatic Note negotiated between Australia and Indonesia concerning the status of INTERFET forces in East Timor. As matters transpired, Indonesia withdrew all military, police and administrative personnel, leaving a total vacuum for INTERFET and UNTAET to fill.

25. Michael Maren, "The Tale of the Tape", *The Village Voice*, vol. 38 no. 34, 24 August 1993, pp. 23–24. This has been particularly so in the experience of NATO and INTERFET/UNTAET forces in Kosovo and East Timor.
26. Michael J. Mazar, "The Military Dilemmas of Humanitarian Intervention", *Security Dialogue*, vol. 24, no. 2, June 1993, pp. 151–162 at p. 158.
27. See *Canadian Airborne Regiment Battle Group Board of Inquiry Phase I* (Ottawa: National Defence Headquarters, 31 August 1993), vol. XI, pp. 3287, 3306–3310, 3313–3318, 3321, 3328–3329, 3345; Canadian Television (CTV) provided me with video recordings of all reports up to January 1995; P. Cheney, "Death and Dishonor in Somalia", *Toronto Sunday Star*, Section F, 10 July 1994.
28. Ascertained by me in reviewing all casualty-producing incidents caused by the Battalion in Somalia.
29. The Australian contingent commander, Colonel Mellor, reinforced this by writing to the soldiers concerned, commending them for their actions.
30. F. M. Lorenz, "Rules of Engagement in Somalia: Were They Effective?", unpublished paper, January 1995; Mark S. Martins, "Rules of Engagement for Land Forces: A Matter for Training, Not Lawyering", *Military Law Review*, vol. 143, Winter 1994, pp. 3–160; Kenneth Allard, *Somalia Operations: Lessons Learned* (Washington DC: National Defense University Press, 1995), pp. 37–38.
31. Allard, *Somalia Operations*, p. 6.
32. Ibid., pp. 8–9.
33. See M. J. Kelly, T. L. H. McCormack, P. Muggleton and B. Oswald, "Legal Aspects of Australia's Involvement in the International Force for East Timor", *International Review of the Red Cross*, vol. 83, no. 841, March 2001, pp. 130–136.
34. I. Alexander, "There Oughta Be a Law", *National Review*, 7 February 1994, pp. 32–33.
35. Interview with Brigadier Ahmed Jama, Washington DC, 3 January 1995.
36. *Canadian Airborne Regiment Battle Group Board of Inquiry Phase I*, p. 3332.
37. These were the vehicles adapted by Somalis by mounting crew-served and heavy

weapons of all descriptions (including the rocket pod from a former Somali Airforce fighter). Vehicle and crew became social micro-units in Somali society in their own right.
38. "The Bandits on Their Donkeys", *The Economist*, 1 May 1993, pp. 40–41.
39. Information supplied by Major Oswald and Major McConaghy, the legal officers attached to the Australian contingent in Rwanda, 1994–1995. See also the Australian ABC Television *Foreign Correspondent* investigative report "Rwanda Justice" by Jonathon Holmes on the prison situation in Rwanda and the Rwandan International Tribunal, 6 June 1995.
40. Lee V. Cassanelli, "Somali Land Resources Issues in Historical Perspective", in Walter Clarke and Jeffrey Herbst (eds), *Learning from Somalia: The Lessons of Armed Humanitarian Intervention* (Boulder, CO: Westview Press, 1997), pp. 67–76 at p. 67.

Part 6
Reconstituting social order

13
The United Nations and social reconstruction in disrupted states

Lorraine Elliott

Peace operations are increasingly complicated in a post–Cold War world, and the spectrum of action under Chapters VI and VII of the UN Charter in response to the political, humanitarian and social aspects of what are now called complex emergencies has widened considerably.[1] Peacekeeping is now as much about assisting suffering peoples as it is about untangling warring states.[2] These new forms of peacekeeping, as distinct from older, "holding-operation" forms of peacekeeping, are "characterised by a comprehensive, even holistic, proactive approach to seeking peaceful settlements".[3] The emphasis is on long-term solutions that address the root causes of extreme civil turmoil and disruption as well as the immediate humanitarian and social consequences. The complexities are exacerbated further by the array of organisations now involved in peace operations. This chapter focuses on one actor (or, more accurately, a number of actors grouped together, sometimes rather loosely, under a single label – the United Nations), and on one component of peacebuilding, that of social reconstruction.

Social reconstruction is a crucial component of peacebuilding and peace maintenance in states and societies that have been disrupted to the point of collapse as a result of civil conflict and intercommunal violence. "Controlling military violence", David Last points out, "is a defensive function which cannot win the peace".[4] The collapse of civil society is as fundamental a problem as the political and institutional fragility with which it is associated. At its most extreme, social dislocation in disrupted states engenders what Irish poet Eavan Boland calls "a nation as a community of grief".[5] However, rebuilding social order – or social justice, to be more accurate – and re-establishing an equitable civil society are some of the most difficult components of rehabilitation and often the least immediate in the face of the military, political and humanitarian dimensions of complex emergencies.

In this chapter I first consider the imperatives for and the nature of social reconstruction in the context of building sustainable peace in disrupted states. I then examine the role of the United Nations and its specialised agencies in this task and provide some assessment of their success or otherwise in meeting this challenge. The matrix of cause and consequence in civil strife is rarely straightforward, complicating attempts at finding and implementing lasting solutions. As Robert Dorff observes, the problem with "failed states is that they do not simply go away".[6] The relapse into violence and civil conflict in countries such as Cambodia, Liberia, Angola and Rwanda, for example, would suggest that negotiated settlements and UN interventions missed something crucial. At the very least it points to organisational problems of coordination, transparency and funding. At a more fundamental level, however, the missing link is a product of what Jim Whitman identifies as a central tension in the United Nations between the "enforcement of order and the enactment of values".[7]

Social reconstruction

Disrupted states are characterised by the "deterioration or disappearance of civil society"[8] and the breakdown of what might colloquially be called the "social fabric". They tend to be characterised by resentment and fear, mutual perceptions of victimisation and, often, a concomitant desire for revenge. There is a political rationale for attending to weakened or collapsed social structures. In the absence of a functioning and relatively harmonious civil society, the legitimacy and stability of political institutions is likely to be short term and fragile. Where political instability and the civil conflict that accompanies it create or exacerbate humanitarian crises and cross-border insecurities, disrupted states become cast in the role of threats to international peace and security. Indeed, some have gone so far as to claim that "disintegrating societies and failed states ... have emerged as the greatest menace to global stability".[9]

There is also a more fundamental humanitarian purpose to social reconstruction, reflected in the commitment in the UN Charter to "promote social progress and better standards of life in larger freedom". Rebuilding civil society, and all that goes with it, must be more than a means to the restoration of legitimate political authority within a "reconstructed" state. When states are disrupted, it is people who suffer. Therefore social reconstruction – or "normalisation" as Mary Kaldor prefers to call it[10] – must address human security, restoring and enhancing individual and community well-being for those whose lives and livelihoods have been undermined or destroyed by conflict and for whom future security remains uncertain and contingent. This is, as Sophie Albert puts it, "peacekeeping with the people".[11]

Emergency humanitarian relief, directed towards preserving life and reducing suffering in the short to medium term, is a necessary but rarely sufficient condition for moving from civil strife to the re-establishment of civil society. Social reconstruction builds on the idea of humanitarian space, the "access that must be secured and maintained if humanitarian activities are to have integrity and effectiveness".[12] For long-term peacebuilding to be effective, humanitarian space must be integrated with social or civil space characterised by "a public pressure for cosmopolitan right".[13] Social reconstruction is reactive, restorative and preventive, although the components are often difficult to separate. It is directed towards individuals, towards the rehabilitation of communities and towards the rebuilding of civil society. The three are mutually reinforcing and synergistic but the indicators for operational success are subjective and frequently elusive.

Repatriation of refugees and displaced persons is central to stabilisation and social reconstruction. This task in itself can be overwhelming. Statistics show, for example, that over half the population in disrupted states and societies in Africa (Angola, Eritrea, Liberia, Mozambique, Rwanda, Somalia and Sudan) have fled their homes at some stage during extended civil conflict.[14] Those who are required or encouraged to return should be able to do so without fear of retaliation or intimidation and with a general feeling of continued physical security. Disarmament is therefore an important component of post-conflict security. In many countries, the laborious, expensive and dangerous task of demining is also often a key to the ease or otherwise of repatriation and physical re-establishment of communities.

Repatriation is, however, more than an exercise in logistics, particularly in situations where territory has changed hands, or houses and other belongings have been destroyed or appropriated by those who have stayed behind or moved in after a community has dispersed. Communities need to be re-established in more than a physical sense. Strategies for rebuilding social order and rehabilitating civil society must respond to the social and psychological consequences of conflict and violence for individuals within communities. Civil society cannot function where there are individual insecurities and continuing enmities among groups of people. Simply removing weapons from warring factions or militia groups makes little sense unless attention is also given to the feelings of insecurity, however valid or not they might be, that might otherwise encourage continued acquisition and use of arms. As Antonio Donini, former chief of the Lessons Learned Unit of the UN Department of Humanitarian Affairs has observed, "we have little experience in dealing with fifteen year olds who have never been to school but are proficient in using assault rifles as a coping mechanism".[15] Social reconstruction, therefore, is a conflict-resolution and confidence-building measure. It involves "rebuilding the trust and mutual confidence of erstwhile enemies ... ending ... mutual hate and fear"[16] and re-establishing respect for human rights and the rights of others.

Although the popular representation of disrupted states is often that of "ancient ethnic hatreds" that have, for reasons not always clear, "boiled over",[17] many disrupted states have enjoyed a range of mechanisms to facilitate peaceful intercommunal relationships. In many cases, these have been destroyed.[18] Social reconstruction must recognise and address this. This burden cannot be borne by the communities alone. As Albert suggests in her discussion of Bosnia and Herzegovina, it is too much to expect that refugees and displaced persons, simply "by returning to their previous homes ... [will] erase all the consequences of ethnic cleansing and contribute to [the] rebirth of multi-ethnicity".[19]

Humanitarian and social normalisation strategies also involve counselling and assistance for vulnerable members of the society, including unaccompanied and traumatised children, sexually abused women (and, increasingly it would seem, men), as well as former combatants. It requires assistance to re-establish agriculture and to find employment and, in many countries, particular assistance to women who are often now required to take on the unfamiliar role of head of household. It may well demand rebuilding of health, education and welfare services.[20] Rebuilding civil society as part of the social fabric of communities also has institutional and associational dimensions. It can include capacity-building and training programmes to strengthen local political, civil and humanitarian institutions, including "NGOs, ... cooperatives, religious organisations, women's movements, green groups and ... the media".[21] A robust civil society, based on norms of participation and autonomy, is better placed to "demand accountability from those who rule them".[22]

Equity and justice, including a "more equitable distribution of goods and services",[23] are fundamental to all these processes. As Michael Dziedzic argues, "the objective of sustainable security will only be assured when impunity is no longer the norm and justice is perceived to be available to all ... achieving this aim entails mobilisation and strengthening of civil society". "At the end of the day", he continues, "civil society is the constituency that stands to gain if justice and order become the norm."[24]

Despite the importance of social reconstruction to peacebuilding, the inclusion of social reconstruction in the typology of peace operations is often uncertain and its conceptual and operational content assumed rather than articulated with any clarity.[25] It is most often categorised as part of post-conflict peacebuilding. Pirnie and Simons, for example, include "more ambitious operations" designed to "change the condition and status of a country"[26] in the transition phase of peace operations. This phase includes facilitating reconstruction and cooperating closely with civilian components and NGOs within the country itself. David Last identifies post-conflict peacebuilding as the *final* stage in a process of de-escalation with the "ultimate aim of restoring a peace acceptable to all parties".[27] This linear approach is unsatisfactory and the process is rarely so easily compartmentalised. Social reconstruction usually takes place against the background of more general agreements to end conflict and (re-)establish political order along with humanitarian relief to meet a range of emergency needs. But it is also fundamental to bringing conflict to an end. The "relief–rehabilitation–development" continuum that has characterised much of the humanitarian literature and that tends to locate rebuilding civil society within programmes for rehabilitation and long-term development serves further to separate peacebuilding from development programmes and muddies the place of social reconstruction in both.

The United Nations and social peacebuilding

The United Nations remains the lead international agency in responding to complex emergencies and in mandating peace operations, in accordance with the provisions of the UN Charter on peaceful settlement of disputes and collective security arrangements in response to threats to international peace and security. However the UN role in restoring peace to disrupted states is split between the political interests of the Security Council and the more humanitarian and social interests of a range of programmes and specialised agencies. The roles and responsibilities are increasingly blurred but are nevertheless often pursued either in isolation from each other, or in the midst of confusion about how they should be coordinated or integrated.

Mandates for peacekeeping interventions, expressed in resolutions of the Security Council, have begun to include "social reconstruction" as one purpose (among many). The mandate for the 100-Day Action Programme for Accelerated Humanitarian Assistance in Somalia (underwritten by the Unified Task Force) included the "rehabilitation of civil society".[28] Security Council resolution 814 specifically mandated the second UN Operation in Somali (UNOSOM II) to "assist the people of Somalia to promote and advance political reconciliation through broad participation ... [and] to create conditions under which Somali civil society may have a role, at every level, in the process of reconciliation".[29] The mandate for UNTAC, the United Nations Transitional Authority in Cambodia, included a requirement for general programmes on human rights education, remedial action for human rights violations and "rebuilding the basic institutions of civil society".[30] Security Council resolution 1272 establishing the United Nations Transitional Administration in East Timor (UNTAET) stressed the importance of reconciliation and included "social services" and "rehabilitation" in the list of mandated elements. It called for the UN Mission to "cooperate closely with the East Timorese people ... in the development of local democratic institutions and human rights institutions", although neither this resolution nor resolution 1338 extending the life of UNTAET makes specific reference to civil society.[31]

A mandate, however, is not a mission and it carries with it no guarantee of success. Responsibility for operationalising a Security Council decision on peace operations passes to the Secretary-General and the Secretariat. As with all components of a UN mission, the central questions for social reconstruction are not just what repertoire of expertise is required, but who should provide it and, equally important, who should fund it.

The key United Nations agencies with a role to play in responding to complex emergencies and in the long-term construction of sustainable peace are the United Nations Children's Fund (UNICEF), the United Nations High Commissioner for Refugees (UNHCR), the World Food Programme (WFP), the World Health Organization (WHO) and the United Nations Development Programme (UNDP).[32] They have no official peacekeeping mandate but functionally and organisationally they have become enmeshed increasingly in peacekeeping, or peacebuilding in the broadest sense. Their tasks include providing emergency response to the humanitarian dimensions of civil conflict and contributing (albeit not always effectively) to the process of reconstruction and rehabilitation of disrupted states and societies. Their emergency response work in the field often precedes Security Council-mandated peace operations and may continue in the absence of such operations. Not all situations of complex emergency – civil conflict and humanitarian disaster – elicit a Security Council peacekeeping response.

Responsibilities for refugees and for children are obvious as the missions for UNHCR and UNICEF. Even then, each has been required to adjust to the demands of complex emergencies in disrupted states, with their work focusing as much on short- and medium-term relief in peacekeeping situations as on longer-term reconstruction. UNHCR, as Newland and Waller Meyers observe, now "more often finds itself involved with UN and regional peacekeeping forces"[33] as well as working with internally displaced persons who do not, technically, come under the definition of refugees in international law. UNICEF dropped "Emergency" from its title (although not from its acronym), but an increasing proportion of its funds are directed towards exactly that kind of relief work. The same applies to the World Food Programme, which has shifted from "mainly development to mainly humanitarian relief",[34] with up to 80 per cent of its annual budget resulting from appeals for emergency food relief, according to Weiss.[35]

The World Health Organization also has no mandate for peacekeeping. Its statute does, however, make a connection between the "health of all peoples" and the attainment of peace and security,[36] and the Organization has become increasingly politicised on issues particularly related to instruments of war. WHO's work in complex emergencies in disrupted states encompasses the provision of technical expertise and assessment, including working to enhance protection of non-combatants, dealing with mental and physical injuries and re-establishing local health facilities, including community-based care. The Organization's preference for working, wherever possible, with local health professionals has a specific peace and social reconstruction component, with an emphasis on strengthening professional ethics and encouraging reconciliation through its "Health as a Bridge for Peace" programmes.

The UNDP, with its extensive in-country representation and experience, is perhaps best placed, in theory at least, to take a lead role in social reconstruction in the context of development as a process of peacebuilding (although it has often been accused of getting out rather too quickly when things get tough). Its sustainable human development framework and its emphasis on human security give voice to the concerns of people and communities as well as, and sometimes rather than, those of states, even though UNDP is tasked to work with governments. The Programme's record of activity in disrupted states includes assistance for resettlement and reintegration of displaced persons and combatants, restoration of health and education services, analysis of civil reform needs, coordination of capacity-building and support for human rights initiatives.[37]

Despite this capacity and attention, it is difficult to find anything other than criticism of the United Nations and its agencies with respect to operational efficiency, coordination, accountability, transparency and competence in peacebuilding and social reconstruction. In one of the more trenchant observations, Findlay elaborates the "failings of the UN in planning and managing peacekeeping operations, both at UN headquarters and in the field ... the ad hoc, amateurish, almost casual methods of the past", which, he argues, "simply could not keep pace, resulting in disorganisation, mismanagement and waste".[38] In a presentation to the Fifth Committee of the General Assembly (Administrative and Budgetary) in November 2000, Secretary-General Kofi Annan characterised the United Nations as "too slow, too tied up in red tape, too weak or too fragmented to deal effectively with conflicts".[39] Four problems are explored here: the nature of intervention and consent; integration of political and military goals with social and humanitarian ones; coordination among UN programmes and agencies; and long-term support for the development components of peacebuilding.

Intervention/intrusion and consent

Humanitarian concerns have clearly invoked a reassessment of non-intervention as a correlate of the principle of state sovereignty.[40] The subject is complex and fuel for much intellectual and academic debate. Complex emergencies often throw into disarray the formal requirements of consent. There is often no actual sovereign government or single acknowledged political authority to provide that consent. Indeed, Secretary-General Annan has argued that in such circumstances "the old dictum of 'consent of the parties' will be neither right [nor] wrong; it will be, quite simply, irrelevant".[41] Humanitarian situations raise normative tensions between the protection of "oppressed peoples and innocent bystanders"[42] and the legal claims of states or the alleged value of non-intervention as fundamental to the continuing functioning of the international system. Interventions on humanitarian grounds have therefore tended to be finessed through the judgement that threats to peace and security are involved. Recent Security Council resolutions might lead one to conclude, in fact, that "any serious humanitarian crisis has the potential of being defined as a threat to international peace and security".[43] Others are less concerned about state-centric legal niceties or philosophies. As Minear and Weiss argue, "when sovereignty and suffering clash, the latter should prevail".[44] Reconstruction, Ramsbotham argues, "is the most positive demonstration of the commitment of the world community to resolving a particular crisis and thus a justification for intervention".[45]

In disrupted states and humanitarian emergencies, however, the consent of people is just as important as that of political entities such as governments or would-be governments. As Ramsbotham and Woodhouse ask, "does the outcome converge with the wishes of those in whose name it is carried out?"[46] Repatriation programmes must involve consultation with intended beneficiaries.[47] Social reconstruction programmes must work with local communities.[48] This requires knowledge of the social and cultural foundations of those communities and the establishment of mutual trust. This is not always an easy process in times of civil disruption, especially if it proceeds against a background of political and military intervention. UN agencies (and non-governmental organisations) are increasingly susceptible to the imputation that "if you are not for us you are against us",[49] particularly since the proscription on participation in peace operations by Security Council permanent members has been lifted.

Rebuilding social order requires bottom–up approaches. Yet grassroots initiatives do not always feature high on the agenda of military and political planners, who are often more concerned with re-establishing the institutions of government and administration and working with elites. Indeed, the failure of UN programmes to work effectively with local communities has been identified as one of the biggest problems in recent peacekeeping and peacebuilding operations. Somalia and the failure of UNOSOM II provide one such example. The United Nations, Menkhaus argues, "lacked an understanding of the nature of Somali political culture".[50] The decision to deal primarily with factional leaders and warlords to the exclusion of "more traditional leaders and structures"[51] has been much criticised.[52] Although traditional "clan" forms of organisation were a key factor in the deep divisions that beset Somalia, marginalising them also contributed to UNOSOM II's problems. Attempts to establish district and regional councils floundered because traditional elders responsible for local community governance were not always included and because funding for leadership and management training under UNOSOM II was erratic.[53] Malaquias identifies similar difficulties in Angola, arguing that the failure of the United Nations Angola Verification Mission (UNAVEM) to prevent further conflict arose because civil society was not involved in the process of political renewal.[54] Concerns have already been raised that the UN/World Bank reconstruction programme in East Timor "lacks the comprehensive strategic framework" to ensure real community participation in anything other than an ad hoc fashion.[55]

Long-term rehabilitation and reconstruction programmes also raise the spectre of "western cultural intrusion" and the dangers of social engineering in pursuit of political goals defined predominantly by Western liberal democracies.[56] Social reconstruction is, or should be, a process of *participatory* development: democratic constitutions and multiparty elections reflect a neoliberal consensus that may do little to encourage "local decision-making and the facilitation of an increasingly heterogeneous civil society".[57] However, although social reconstruction programmes should be "carefully crafted so as to be compatible with local culture and tradition",[58] problems can also arise if those traditions are the source of inequities and injustices.

There is a gender dimension here as well. "Relief and rehabilitation operations", Whaley writes, "have tended to be dominated by men"[59] or designed without adequate consultation with or acknowledgement of the needs and contributions of women. In countries or regions as different as Cambodia and Kosovo, women are more than "victims" of civil conflict. They are central to the processes of social reconstruction and participation, often required to take up the burden of providing for both the elderly and the young, and re-establishing agriculture and other forms of economic infrastructure. Whaley's discussion of the African Women in Crisis Programme, sponsored by UNIFEM (United Nations Fund for Women), demonstrates that peace operations and social reconstruction are still failing in their attempts to engage with local communities and civil societies.

Integration and coordination

The peace process in disrupted states requires the integration of military, political, social and humanitarian objectives and yet this has proven immensely difficult. Jarat Chopra uses the term "peace maintenance" to describe this framework within which "diplomatic activities, humanitarian assistance, military forces and civilian elements are ... coordinated and harmonised".[60] However, the United Nations' attempts at establishing peace maintenance frameworks (or what the Department of Political Affairs calls "preventive peacebuilding"[61]) have tended to be "hurried [and] improvised"[62] in individual cases and faced with "demonstrated lack of political and bureaucratic will"[63] in the general case.

The direction of peace missions is usually the responsibility of political and military leadership and is more likely, therefore, to be directed towards political and military goals, with a primary concern for order rather than justice.[64] This reflects, in part, a normative problem, characterised by competing views about security, the relationship between order and justice, and conflicts between the United Nations' mandate for "peace and security" defined by its member states and its mandate for "fundamental human rights, social progress and better standards of life *in larger freedom*" for "we the peoples". Opinions differ on whether peace/security (order) or justice (values) should prevail when choices have to be made.[65]

These normative tensions contribute to operational and policy difficulties. Military objectives and culture sit uncomfortably with humanitarian and social purposes and the operations required to give effect to them. These tensions have become more apparent as traditional peacekeeping has given way to (or at least been required to accommodate) military support for humanitarian relief and establishing the foundations for long-term peacebuilding. Most military officers, as Michael Dziedzic observes, are in "uncharted territory" when dealing with social and humanitarian problems, particularly "when thrown into this complex task with a host of other international actors with whom they are largely unfamiliar".[66] Their tasks increasingly require skills in diplomacy, negotiation and conflict resolution, although uncertain and volatile situations might also require the use of force along with careful judgements about how much and when. The resolution establishing UNTAET, in which military personnel remain the dominant component, specifically called for personnel with "appropriate training in international humanitarian, human rights and refugee law, including child and gender-related provisions, negotiation and communication skills, cultural awareness and civilian–military coordination".[67]

Civil–military relations can often go "horribly wrong", Cousens argues, with "confusion caused by a foggy chain of command, competition and military forces preferring to operate in isolation".[68] In northern Iraq, for example, observers have argued that "military officials were ... unfamiliar with relief organisations, lacked knowledge of relevant international humanitarian law and showed little interest in local customs and institutions".[69] Relations between UNHCR and the UN Protection Force (UNPROFOR) in the former Yugoslavia have been characterised as "very testing".[70]

Ending conflict and bloodshed are important goals but, without a more comprehensive integration of purpose (and monitoring of that purpose), the pursuit of those objectives can clash with long-term goals of building a just and sustainable peace.[71] Humanitarian objectives and social restoration, and the work of UN agencies in pursuit of those goals, can be compromised in the face of economic sanctions mandated for political reasons. Examples include Iraq (where UNICEF, the WFP and WHO have been active) or statements by NATO leaders that aid for infrastructure and economic repair in Serbia would not be forthcoming while Milosevic remained leader.[72] Whitman argues (and he is not alone) that the "UN-mandated sanctions against Iraq are causing much suffering which is an affront to humane decency".[73] At times, UN peace operations, particularly the political–military components, can undermine attempts at social reconstruction and rehabilitation through their impact on local economies and continued patterns of exploitation, making life more difficult for the humanitarian and development agencies. The increase in prostitution in Cambodia (UNTAC), Mozambique (ONUMOZ) and the former Yugoslavia (UNPROFOR) is a case in point.[74] In its resolution extending the life of the transitional administration in East Timor, the Security Council saw fit to refer to the need to sensitise peacekeeping personnel in the prevention and control of HIV/AIDS. The inflow of hard currency associated with UN missions and transitional arrangements can distort local economies, jobs are lost when the United Nations finally pulls out, and locals who work for the United Nations can be left vulnerable to social and political retaliation. The imperatives of integration can also encounter what one commentator calls "serious structural flaws", noting that in Mozambique and El Salvador long-term social and economic reconstruction was made more difficult by the impact of World Bank and IMF policies which served to "increase hardship and dislocation".[75]

Despite attempts to make UN missions more holistic and integrated, it has proved difficult to implement longer-term reconstruction and development mandates in support of peacebuilding. Peace missions established by the Security Council are country specific and ad hoc. They must work *with* the permanent UN programmes and agencies, rather than subsuming or appropriating them. The United Nations remains vulnerable to "institutional competition, overlaps and poor coordination among key organisations".[76] Although the UNHCR, UNICEF and the UNDP are technically under the legal authority of the United Nations, each has its own governing body, funding and mandate. They remain jealous of their reputations and autonomy. Within the Secretariat, peacekeeping missions are the responsibility of the Department of Peacekeeping Operations (DPKO); humanitarian relief is the responsibility of the Office for the Coordination of Humanitarian Affairs (OCHA); and peacemaking and peacebuilding (including electoral assistance and outreach to NGOs and civil society) are the mandate of the Department of Political Affairs.

The United Nations has sought to overcome these problems of demarcation and coordination through a series of reforms. In 1992, the General Assembly approved the establishment of a Department of Humanitarian Affairs (DHA) to improve humanitarian coordination among UN agencies in the field and to ensure that emergency relief was embedded in programmes to address the causes of conflict.[77] DHA was not an operational body. It was intended to function with technical and operational support from an Inter-Agency Standing Committee (IASC), which includes non-governmental organisations. DHA was the subject of much criticism in terms of its mandate and the limited resources provided to it.[78] Its problems were little different from those of its predecessor, the United Nations Disaster Relief Organisation (UNDRO), about which Griffiths and his colleagues say: "its mandate significantly outstripped its capacity and it never had the political clout to achieve its aims ... it was beset by many problems including an uncertain mandate, inadequate staffing and funding, lack of in-country capacity, lack of support from other UN agencies [and] a long-running dispute over whether it should be operational".[79]

In the 1997 round of UN reform, Kofi Annan replaced the DHA with the Office for the Coordination of Humanitarian Affairs (OCHA).[80] The Under-Secretary-General who heads OCHA also doubles as the United Nations' Emergency Relief Coordinator and chairs IASC. IASC is designed to ensure inter-agency decision-making on needs assessment, consolidated appeals, field coordination and the development of humanitarian policies. OCHA also chairs the Executive Committee for Humanitarian Affairs (ECHA), which provides a forum for the humanitarian community and the Political Affairs and Peacekeeping Departments within the Secretariat to share perspectives. The Disaster Response Branch of OCHA oversees a UN Disaster and Assessment Coordination Team (UNDAC), a Field Coordination Support Unit (FCSU) and a Military and Civilian Defence Unit (MCDU) to coordinate the use of Military and Civilian Defence Assets in Emergency Response (MCDA). In order to improve coordination and integration among departments within the Secretariat as well as among funds and agencies in the field, OCHA worked to develop Strategic Frameworks and Common Programmes to cover the range of in-country UN activities in times of complex crises and peacebuilding. Where UNDP's Resident Coordinator, usually responsible for officially coordinating all other UN activities within a country, takes on the task of Resident Humanitarian Coordinator, she or he will report to UNDP and to OCHA.

The August 2000 report of the Panel on United Nations Peacekeeping Operations (the Brahimi Committee) called for more reform. The Panel recommended the restructuring of the DPKO and the establishment of a new information and strategic analysis unit, under the auspices of the Executive Committee on Peace and Security, to service all UN departments concerned with peace and security. Yet more coordination does not overcome inter-agency jealousies. Indeed, as Weiss points out, those jealousies can often limit the possibilities for coordination.[81]

Funding

Social reconstruction requires not only immediate funds directed towards various aspects of humanitarian assistance and relief, but continuing financial support for rehabilitation and development as crucial to long-term security-building. If it is to be effective, funding for peacebuilding has to be "sustained and predictable" as well as "flexible".[82] It is none of these things. Whereas peacekeeping missions are funded out of assessed contributions, the UNDP, the UNHCR and UNICEF rely on voluntary contributions supported by country-specific consolidated appeals for humanitarian assistance programmes. In the mid-1990s the United Nations' annual peacekeeping and humanitarian assistance budgets amounted to just over US$4 billion each.[83]

The record of the international community – publics and governments – is not good once the commitment to short-term peacekeeping and humanitarian relief translates into a requirement to commit to long-term reconstruction and development. Indeed, public support for peacekeeping generally remains ambivalent, illuminating the tension between the "do something" imperative (particularly in the face of mass death from starvation or violence) and the "do nothing" imperative, particularly if military casualties among peacekeeping "troops" are likely to be involved. As Stedman and Rothchild put it, "attention wanes and resources vanish".[84] What is promised by governments through the Consolidated Appeals Process, now managed by OCHA, is often not delivered, and what is delivered is not enough to meet emergency and peacebuilding needs.[85] This reluctance to commit resources to reconstructive peace operations is but one component of the more general decline in development assistance as measured by the Development Assistance Committee of the Organisation for Economic Co-operation and Development or the UNDP in its annual Human Development Report. Although the Consolidated Appeals Process is intended to provide better opportunities for coordination, it also runs the risk that agency claims become something of a "shopping list". Indeed, individual agencies often prefer to manage their own appeals in order to maintain their "brand image" in the public mind. Dangers arise that financial contributions will be tied to the political interests of donor countries or to high-profile projects that might or might not be the most crucial to humanitarian assistance or to long-term peacebuilding.[86] One recent example of tensions between military and social–humanitarian goals is the funding difficulties that UNHCR has faced in Kosovo. UNHCR's Special Envoy, Dennis McNamara, publicly expressed his concern that the NATO allies could find billions of dollars for the military campaign but no such funds for repatriation of refugees and long-term reconstruction.[87]

Lessons learned?

Quite how these problems are to be overcome is unclear. The Lessons Learned Unit of the Department of Peacekeeping Operations has identified a number of areas of what it calls "multidisciplinary peacekeeping" in which, based on recent experience, operational practice could be improved.[88] Although the report says what should be done, and identifies essential elements for success, it does little to suggest how it could be

THE UNITED NATIONS AND SOCIAL RECONSTRUCTION 271

done. It suggests, for example, that the "planning process has to be as comprehensive as possible", that "adequate means and resources" must be made available to "implement the mandate", and that "effective coordination ... [and] clearly defined common goals [within a] coherent framework" are essential to the success of a mission. It calls for guidelines to be developed and frameworks for cooperation to be strengthened. It identifies "peacebuilding" as an integral part of peacekeeping missions, to ensure that a "foundation of peace and development" upon which a country can build is left behind once a mission departs. It talks about restoring basic civic services, demobilisation, counselling and social infrastructure as fundamental to that long-term foundation. However, in the absence of a commitment to put these lessons into practice, they remain in effect insubstantial. As Whaley points out with respect to the reports of the Lessons Learned Unit on Somalia, although there was "unequivocal ... commitment to the integration of development into complex peace operations" there were no modalities to ensure "the effective participation of development specialists and development cooperation managers in the process".[89] In something of an understatement, Ross Mountain, Assistant Emergency Relief Coordinator and Director, OCHA-Geneva, observed at a presentation at NATO headquarters in 1998 that "I think the absence of profound insight and our poor ability to use the lessons which have been learned is ... unsettling".[90]

On the need for better integration of civilian and military components, Dziedzic calls for "planning for coordinated actions by both military and civilian elements of the peace missions to strengthen civil society as well as promot[ing] good communication with local authorities".[91] Yet what kind of pre-mission briefing and training should be given to the military and civilian elements of peacekeeping missions if their work is, at minimum, not to undermine the options for long-term social reconstruction? What skills should military forces and observers have to engage in the "hearts and minds campaign" that Findlay argues is one of their first tasks in order to build credibility and trust with the civilian population,[92] which are, in turn, crucial to social reconstruction? How easy is this if peacekeeping training has been marginalised within the force structures and military doctrine of individual contributing UN members?

Who should have responsibility for overall coordination of peace operations in all its phases? The Security Council? David Ramsbotham argues, for example, that post-conflict reconstruction strategies should be mandated by the Security Council.[93] Or should coordination and responsibility for reconstruction, including social reconstruction, be more firmly mandated to the Secretariat? Should coordination be turned over to UNDP Resident Coordinators once political settlements are reached and/or implemented? Should the device of appointing a Special Representative of the Secretary-General (SRSG) be the vehicle for coordination? In Kosovo, for example, the SRSG coordinates under one operation not only the relevant UN bodies but also the Organization for Security and Co-operation in Europe, which directs democratisation and institution-building, and the European Union, which has responsibility for economic reconstruction, tasks that are more directly relevant to social reconstruction and longer-term peacebuilding.[94]

Childers and Urquhart have suggested that the Trusteeship Council be revived to oversee peace operations and the rebuilding of disrupted or failed states,[95] a suggestion that, regardless of its intent, cannot help but echo the colonial past of that body. Other suggestions[96] include giving the task as permanent lead agency to UNHCR, revamping the International Committee of the Red Cross to fulfil this role or establishing a new, unitary humanitarian agency within the United Nations (a proposal made by former US Secretary of State Warren Christopher). Chopra calls for some kind of political directorate or joint political authority as the best mechanism for "operational political direction and ongoing decision-making in the field".[97] On the other hand, should one accept that the necessary degree of intra-UN coordination is simply unachievable?[98]

Conclusion

Social reconstruction or normalisation, and the rebuilding of a just and equitable civil society, are essential components of long-term peacebuilding. Social reconstruction is short and long term, restorative and preventive. It spans the spectrum of relief, rehabilitation and development. Its constituents are individuals, communities and societies. It requires long-term commitment and support from the international community but it must be guided by local needs and practices, not the interests of the donors. Without it, sustainable peace is not possible.

The United Nations' record in facilitating social reconstruction and encouraging an emergent civil society in disrupted states is somewhat shaky, with some success in Mozambique and even Cambodia perhaps, despite some setbacks, but with little to claim elsewhere. Some of that failure must be attributed to problems within the United Nations. It has been difficult to operationalise the reconstitution of social (as opposed to political) order as part of peacebuilding rather than as a development process that cuts in once "peace" has been restored and the peacekeepers (and the media) have gone home. It has been difficult to overcome inter-agency turf battles. Despite the commitment of many people within the United Nations, it seems unlikely that this will change in the near future. However the organisation also faces an insuperable

THE UNITED NATIONS AND SOCIAL RECONSTRUCTION 273

achievement dilemma. Once peace operations are UN mandated, governments can "pass the buck", particularly once the specialised agencies are involved. Although governments (on the grounds of responsible expenditure of taxpayers' funds) are reluctant to provide the United Nations with the financial and operational wherewithal to support long-term peacebuilding – one Special Representative of the Secretary-General was moved to characterise funding arrangements as a "pattern of utmost parsimony"[99] – they are quick to blame it when success is minimal or non-existent. As Mackinlay and Kent point out, "once public pressure has been mollified, the long-term problems of the post-crisis phase are often left to the UN's civil elements and the NGOs".[100] Yet at some point, as Blechman argues, "the world community itself is accountable".[101] The choice is clear. Ginifer argues that the international community "can either choose to abandon substantive attempts to reconstitute war-torn societies and resort to minimalist forms of intervention ... or it will need to become more long-term in its approach".[102] For people and communities in disrupted states, only the latter option is any real option at all.

Notes

1. The struggle to comprehend and label "peacekeeping" has expanded the lexicon to include "Chapter six-and-a-half" operations, wider peacekeeping, multidimensional peacekeeping, extended peacekeeping, second-generation peacekeeping, indirect peacekeeping and a range of other terms. The discussion here does not distinguish between specific peace enforcement operations and other missions that had a broader mandate or purpose under the Charter.
2. See William J. Durch, cited in Oliver Ramsbotham and Tom Woodhouse, *Humanitarian Intervention in Contemporary Conflict: A Reconceptualization* (Cambridge: Polity Press, 1996), p. xii.
3. Trevor Findlay, "The New Peacekeepers and the New Peacekeeping", in Trevor Findlay (ed.), *Challenges for the New Peacekeepers*, SIPRI Research Report no. 12 (Oxford: Oxford University Press, 1996), pp. 1–31 at p. 12.
4. David M. Last, *Theory, Doctrine and Practice of Conflict De-escalation in Peacekeeping Operations* (Clementsport: Canadian Peacekeeping Press, 1997), p. 119.
5. Eavan Boland, *Object Lessons* (London: Vintage Press, 1996), p. 149.
6. Robert H. Dorff, "The Future of Peace Support Operations", *Small Wars and Insurgencies*, vol. 9, no. 1, Spring 1998, pp. 160–178 at p. 164.
7. Jim Whitman, "The UN Specialised Agencies, Peacekeeping and the Enactment of Values", *International Peacekeeping*, vol. 5. no. 4, Winter 1998, pp. 120–137 at p. 121. The issue of the relationship between the United Nations and non-UN actors is not addressed here, although it is an important dimension of social reconstruction and peacebuilding. Nor does this chapter delve into the difficulties raised by recent NATO interventions into peace enforcement and humanitarian relief. However, it is important to note that UN agencies are rarely the only actors in peace operations and in post-conflict peace reconstruction. The United Nations and its agencies work (or should work) in conjunction with a more or less formalised peacebuilding network which will

include political actors and authorities within the country, the World Bank and the IMF, other international donors, non-governmental organisations (both humanitarian and development) and the private sector; see David Ramsbotham, *The Changing Nature of Intervention: The Role of UN Peacekeeping* (London: Research Institute for the Study of Conflict and Terrorism, 1995), pp. 21–22.
8. Larry Minear and Thomas G. Weiss, *Mercy under Fire: War and the Global Humanitarian Community* (Boulder, CO: Westview Press, 1995), p. 2.
9. Brian Atwood, cited in Dorff, "The Future of Peace Support Operations", p. 165.
10. Mary Kaldor, "A Cosmopolitan Response to New Wars", *Peace Review*, vol. 8, no. 4, December 1996, pp. 505–514.
11. Sophie Albert, "The Return of Refugees to Bosnia and Herzegovina: Peacebuilding with the People", *International Peacekeeping*, vol. 4, no. 3, Autumn 1997, pp. 1–23.
12. Minear and Weiss, *Mercy under Fire*, p. 38.
13. Kaldor, "A Cosmopolitan Response to New Wars", p. 509.
14. Ramsbotham and Woodhouse, *Humanitarian Intervention in Contemporary Conflict*, p. 103.
15. Antonio Donini, "Asserting Humanitarianism in Peace-Maintenance", *Global Governance*, vol. 4, no. 1, January–March 1998, pp. 81–96 at p. 93.
16. Last, *Theory, Doctrine and Practice of Conflict De-escalation in Peacekeeping Operations*, p. 119.
17. The characterisation of conflict as "ethnic" can also construct certain images of how social rehabilitation should proceed. Ramsbotham and Woodhouse, *Humanitarian Intervention in Contemporary Conflict*, p. 98, note in the Bosnian case, for example, that, although "there are few ethnic differences, the competing parties became Bosnian Muslim, Bosnian Croat and Bosnian Serb", making interests and needs "progressively more difficult to negotiate".
18. Albert, "The Return of Refugees to Bosnia and Herzegovina", p. 4, identifies "good neighbourliness" (*komsiluk*) as a "deeply-rooted social tradition" in Bosnia upon which "peaceful relationships between different ethnic groups at grass-roots level and in daily life" were based.
19. Ibid., p. 2.
20. In Rwanda, for example, over 80 per cent of health care workers and educators either were killed or fled: Krishna Kumar, "The Nature and Focus of International Assistance for Rebuilding War-torn Societies", in Krishna Kumar (ed.), *Rebuilding Societies after Civil War: Critical Roles for International Assistance* (Boulder, CO: Lynne Rienner, 1997), p. 19.
21. Timothy M. Shaw, "Beyond Post-conflict Peacebuilding: What Links Sustainable Development to Human Security", *International Peacekeeping*, vol. 3, no. 2, Summer 1996, pp. 36–48 at p. 42.
22. Martin Griffiths, Iain Levine and Mark Weller, "Sovereignty and Suffering", in John Harriss (ed.), *The Politics of Humanitarian Intervention* (London: Pinter, 1995), pp. 33–90 at p. 69.
23. Minear and Weiss, *Mercy under Fire*, p. 138.
24. Michael J. Dziedzic, "Policing the New World Disorder: Addressing Gaps in Public Security during Peace Operations", *Small Wars and Insurgencies*, vol. 9, no. 1, Spring 1998, pp. 132–159 at p. 155.
25. A survey of the literature on post–Cold War peacekeeping and peacebuilding reveals that restoring social order is addressed much less frequently than the military and humanitarian dimensions.
26. Bruce R. Pirnie and William E. Simons, *Soldiers for Peace: Critical Operational Issues* (Santa Monica, CA: RAND/National Defense Research Institute, 1996), pp. xii, xiv.

27. Last, *Theory, Doctrine and Practice of Conflict De-escalation in Peacekeeping Operations*, p. 3.
28. See Omar Halim, "A Peace-Keeper's Perspective of Peace-Building in Somalia", *International Peacekeeping*, vol. 3, no. 2, Summer 1996, pp. 70–86 at p. 80.
29. Cited in Ken Menkhaus, "International Peacebuilding and the Dynamics of Local and National Reconciliation in Somalia", *International Peacekeeping*, vol. 3, no. 1, Spring 1996, pp. 42–67 at p. 42.
30. See Nicholas Hopkinson, *Humanitarian Intervention*, Wilton Park Paper no. 110 (London: Her Majesty's Stationery Office, 1996), p. 58.
31. United Nations Security Council Resolution 1272 (1999), S/RES/1272, 25 October 1999; United Nations Security Council Resolution 1338 (2001), S/RES/1338, 31 January 2001.
32. Regional intergovernmental organisations have sought to develop their capacities for responding to political and humanitarian emergencies in disrupted states, sometimes on a fairly ad hoc basis. This group includes the European Union, which established the EC Humanitarian Office (ECHO) in April 1992, the Organization of American States, the Organization of African Unity and IGADD, the Horn of Africa's Intergovernmental Authority on Drought and Development.
33. Kathleen Newland and Deborah Waller Meyers, "Peacekeeping and Refugee Relief", *International Peacekeeping*, vol. 5, no. 4, Winter 1998, pp. 15–30 at p. 15.
34. Leon Gordenker, "Clash and Harmony in Promoting Peace: Overview", *International Peacekeeping*, vol. 5, no. 4, Winter 1998, pp. 1–14 at p. 12.
35. Thomas G. Weiss, "Civilian–Military Interactions and Ongoing UN Reforms: DHA's Past and OCHA's Remaining Challenges", *Global Governance*, vol. 5, no. 4, Winter 1998, pp. 49–70 at p. 53.
36. See Yves Beigbeder, "The World Health Organisation and Peacekeeping", *International Peacekeeping*, vol. 5, no. 3, Winter 1998, pp. 31–48 at p. 31.
37. See Dennis Dijkzeul, "The United Nations Development Programme: The Development of Peace?", *International Peacekeeping*, vol. 5, no. 4, Winter 1998, pp. 92–119 at p. 102.
38. Findlay, "The New Peacekeepers and the New Peacekeeping", p. 18.
39. United Nations General Assembly, Press Release GA/AB/3414, 27 November 2000.
40. For more on this debate see, *inter alia*, Barry M. Blechman, "The Intervention Dilemma", *Washington Quarterly*, vol. 18, no. 3, Summer 1995, pp. 63–73; Adam Roberts, "Humanitarian War: Military Intervention and Human Rights", *International Affairs*, vol. 69, no. 3, 1993, pp. 429–449; Tonny Brems Knudson, "Humanitarian Intervention Revisited: Post–Cold War Responses to Classical Problems", in Michael Pugh (ed.), *The UN, Peace and Force* (London: Frank Cass, 1997); and Nicholas J. Wheeler and Justin Morris, "Humanitarian Intervention and State Practice at the End of the Cold War", in Rick Fawn and Jeremy Larkins (eds), *International Society after the Cold War: Anarchy and Order Revisited* (London: Macmillan, 1996).
41. Cited in David Jablonsky and James S. McCallum, "Peace Implementation and the Concept of Induced Consent in Peace Operations", *Parameters*, vol. 29, no. 1, Spring 1999, pp. 54–70 at p. 62.
42. Blechman, "The Intervention Dilemma", p. 64.
43. Knudson, "Humanitarian Intervention Revisited", p. 155.
44. Minear and Weiss, *Mercy under Fire*, p. 96.
45. Ramsbotham, *The Changing Nature of Intervention: The Role of UN Peacekeeping*, p. 22.
46. Ramsbotham and Woodhouse, *Humanitarian Intervention in Contemporary Conflict*, p. 76.
47. See Kumar, "The Nature and Focus of International Assistance for Rebuilding War-torn Societies"; and Albert, "The Return of Refugees to Bosnia and Herzegovina".

48. See J. David Whaley, "Improving UN Developmental Co-ordination within Peace Missions", *International Peacekeeping*, vol. 3, no. 2, Summer 1996, pp. 107–122; Griffiths, Levine and Weller, 'Sovereignty and Suffering'.
49. Ramsbotham and Woodhouse, *Humanitarian Intervention in Contemporary Conflict*, p. 99.
50. Menkhaus, "International Peacebuilding and the Dynamics of Local and National Reconciliation in Somalia", p. 57.
51. See Jeremy Ginifer, "Development and the UN Peace Mission: A New Interface Required", *International Peacekeeping*, vol. 3, no. 2, Summer 1996, pp. 3–13 at p. 9.
52. See also Halim, "A Peace-Keeper's Perspective of Peace-Building in Somalia"; Menkhaus, "International Peacebuilding and the Dynamics of Local and National Reconciliation in Somalia".
53. See Halim, "A Peace-Keeper's Perspective of Peace-Building in Somalia".
54. See Assis Malaquias, "The UN in Mozambique and Angola: Lessons Learned", *International Peacekeeping*, vol. 3, no. 2, Summer 1996, pp. 87–103.
55. Patrick Candio and Roland Bleiker, "Peacebuilding in East Timor", *Pacific Review*, vol. 14, no. 1, 2001, p. 72.
56. Hugo Slim, "The Stretcher and the Drum: Civil–Military Relations in Peace Support Operations", *International Peacekeeping*, vol. 3, no. 2, Summer 1996, pp. 123–140 at p. 137, identifies concerns about "Western military forces, using military humanitarian operations as rehearsals for the projecting of power into developing world settings at short notice". Ramsbotham and Woodhouse, *Humanitarian Intervention in Contemporary Conflict*, p. 96, also draw attention to perceptions "in the South" that humanitarian assistance is "a substitute for addressing the structural causes of conflict, if not ... a means of reinforcing the system of power and dependency from which the North profits so much".
57. Shaw, "Beyond Post-conflict Peacebuilding", p. 39.
58. Dziedzic, "Policing the New World Disorder", p. 155.
59. Whaley, "Improving UN Developmental Co-ordination within Peace Missions", p. 118.
60. Jarat Chopra, "Introducing Peace Maintenance", *Global Governance*, vol. 4, no. 1, January–March 1998, pp. 1–18 at p. 7.
61. United Nations Department of Political Affairs, *Preventive Action and Peacemaking*, June 2001, http://www.un/org/Depts/dpa/docs/peacemak.htm.
62. Gordenker, "Clash and Harmony in Promoting Peace", p. 7.
63. Weiss, "Civilian–Military Interactions and Ongoing UN Reforms", p. 50.
64. See, for example, the analyses provided in Ginifer, "Development and the UN Peace Mission", and Slim, "The Stretcher and the Drum".
65. See Duane C. Bratt, "Explaining Peacekeeping Performance: The UN in Internal Conflicts", *International Peacekeeping*, vol. 4, no. 3, Autumn 1997, pp. 45–70; compare Whitman, "The UN Specialised Agencies, Peacekeeping and the Enactment of Values".
66. Dziedzic, "Policing the New World Disorder", p. 134.
67. United Nations Security Council Resolution 1272 (1999), S/RES/1272, 25 October 1999.
68. Richard P. Cousens, "Providing Military Security in Peace Maintenance", *Global Governance*, vol. 4, no. 1, January–March 1998, pp. 97–105 at p. 102.
69. Minear and Weiss, *Mercy under Fire*, p. 177.
70. Ramsbotham and Woodhouse, *Humanitarian Intervention in Contemporary Conflict*, p. 154.
71. Ramsbotham and Woodhouse, *Humanitarian Intervention in Contemporary Conflict*, p. 75, raise the controversial issue of whether "a failure to address the underlying polit-

ical conditions which stimulated the humanitarian concern [in Iraq]" might mean that "the situation in the end is worse than it would have been without the intervention".
72. This leverage has been acknowledged as one reason the new government in Serbia was willing to hand Milosevic over to the Tribunal in The Hague.
73. Whitman, "The UN Specialised Agencies, Peacekeeping and the Enactment of Values", p. 120.
74. See Slim, "The Stretcher and the Drum".
75. Ginifer, "Development and the UN Peace Mission", p. 7; see also Stephen John Stedman and Donald Rothchild, "Peace Operations: From Short-term to Long-term Commitment", *International Peackeeping*, vol. 3, no. 2, Summer 1996, pp. 17–35. Although it is beyond the scope of this chapter, this embeds problems of social and political disruption and civil strife in the broader context of debates about global inequities between rich and poor and the causes and consequences of underdevelopment or mal-development.
76. Ginifer, "Development and the UN Peace Mission", p. 8.
77. Even so, it was not until 1995 that the UNDP Administrator became a regular participant in the weekly meeting of the Under-Secretaries-General for Peacekeeping, Political Affairs and Humanitarian Affairs, which was established in 1993 to enhance integration of the various components of peace operations (see Whaley, "Improving UN Developmental Co-ordination within Peace Missions").
78. See, for example, Whaley, "Improving UN Developmental Co-ordination within Peace Missions"; Paul Taylor, "Options for the Reform of the International System for Humanitarian Assistance", in Harriss (ed.), *The Politics of Humanitarian Intervention*, pp. 91–143; Weiss, "Civilian–Military Interactions and Ongoing UN Reforms".
79. Griffiths, Levine and Weller, "Sovereignty and Suffering", p. 70.
80. See David B. Steele, "Securing Peace for Humanitarian Aid?", *International Peacekeeping*, vol. 5, no. 1, Spring 1998, pp. 66–88 at p. 81; UN Doc A/51/1950, 16 July 1997.
81. Dijkzeul, "The United Nations Development Programme", and Weiss, "Civilian–Military Interactions and Ongoing UN Reforms", attempt to make some sense of the latest round of UN reform and reorganisation as it might relate to humanitarian peacekeeping and social reconstruction.
82. Whaley, "Improving UN Developmental Co-ordination within Peace Missions", p. 112.
83. Ramsbotham and Woodhouse, *Humanitarian Intervention in Contemporary Conflict*, pp. 159–160.
84. Stedman and Rothchild, "Peace Operations: From Short-term to Long-term Commitment", p. 28.
85. Stedman and Rothchild, "Peace Operations: From Short-term to Long-term Commitment", p. 28, note that, between 1991 and 1994, donors pledged nearly US$1.7 billion to the Cambodian peacebuilding effort but that only US$300–500 million was actually delivered.
86. See, for example, Hopkinson's discussion of the situation in Cambodia: Hopkinson, *Humanitarian Intervention*, pp. 59–60.
87. United Nations High Commissioner for Refugees, "Kosovo Crisis Update", *UNHCR News*, 2 July 1999. At the same time, Secretary-General Kofi Annan expressed concern at the US position that it would only fund food and medicine assistance in humanitarian aid for Greater Yugoslavia, questioning its usefulness when people were still forced to drink unsafe water ("Billions on Bombs but Not on People: UN", *The Weekend Australian*, 3–4 July 1999, p. 17).
88. See Department of Peacekeeping Operations, *Multidisciplinary Peacekeeping: Lessons from Recent Experience* (New York: DPKO Lessons Learned Unit, n.d.), http://www.un.org/Depts/dpko/lessons/handbuk.htm.

89. Whaley, "Improving UN Developmental Co-ordination within Peace Missions", p. 112.
90. Ross Mountain, "Humanitarian–Military Cooperation", Statement to the Ad Hoc Group on Cooperation in Peacekeeping, NATO HQ, Brussels, 24 April 1998, http://www.reliefweb.int/ocha_ol/programs/response/mcdunet/0rmount.html.
91. Dziedzic, "Policing the New World Disorder", p. 155.
92. Findlay, "The New Peacekeepers and the New Peacekeeping", pp. 24–25.
93. Ramsbotham, *The Changing Nature of Intervention: The Role of UN Peacekeeping*, p. 21.
94. In other UN-mandated interventions, the role of regional organisations such as the Organization of African Unity (OAU) or the Economic Community of West African States (ECOWAS), or even NATO, has been confined primarily to peacekeeping or peace enforcement rather than social reconstruction.
95. Cited in Ramsbotham and Woodhouse, *Humanitarian Intervention in Contemporary Conflict*, p. 160.
96. See Weiss, "Civilian–Military Interactions and Ongoing UN Reforms", pp. 51–52.
97. Chopra, "Introducing Peace Maintenance", p. 9.
98. Dorff, "The Future of Peace Support Operations", p. 161, raises the possibility that it may not be possible to find solutions to all the problems confronting us in the context of peace support operations. He suggests that, "despite our Enlightenment-based enthusiasm for applying human skills to the successful solution of problems, there are limits on what we can do, and the limits are considerable in some of these conflicts".
99. Dame Margaret Anstee, cited in Whitman, "The UN Specialised Agencies, Peacekeeping and the Enactment of Values", p. 132.
100. John Mackinlay and Randolph Kent, "A New Approach to Complex Emergencies", *International Peacekeeping*, vol. 4, no. 4, Winter 1997, pp. 31–49 at p. 34.
101. Blechman, "The Intervention Dilemma", p. 64.
102. Ginifer, "Development and the UN Peace Mission", p. 6.

14

Reconstituting whose social order? NGOs in disrupted states

Fiona Terry

The images of NATO troops establishing camps for Kosovar refugees in Albania and Macedonia raise several questions about civil–military cooperation in disrupted states.[1] What does it mean for humanitarian principles when a belligerent party to the conflict assumes primary responsibility for refugees? Have the military, by virtue of their logistical capacity and reaction speed, carved out a new niche for themselves in the humanitarian milieu? Has refugee law, which arguably bestows responsibility for the protection of refugees on the United Nations High Commissioner for Refugees (UNHCR), become obsolete? Is this the end of humanitarianism, as some observers have suggested?[2]

The developments in the Balkans came in the wake of a period of unprecedented criticism of humanitarian action in general, and of non-governmental organisations (NGOs) in particular. The limit of humanitarian action as a remedy for human suffering has been dramatically demonstrated in the Great Lakes region of Central Africa since 1994. Although the stated purpose of humanitarian aid is to alleviate the humanitarian symptoms of crises, not to address the political causes, aid organisations have been inculpated in the failure of this endeavour and, in some cases, accused of exacerbating the problem. In response to perceived failures – and a tarnished image – NGOs, UN agencies and government donors have reappraised many facets of humanitarian aid operations and the application of humanitarian principles. One of the recurring themes that has emerged is that a uniform set of standards should be applied to the provision of humanitarian relief, and that coordination and cooperation should be enhanced among the various actors to assuage some of the difficulties posed by "complex emergencies" in the post–Cold War world.

In this chapter, I argue that increased conformity and coordination in the response to crises, although sound in intention, are not a panacea for the problems inherent in providing humanitarian assistance in disrupted states. Much of the analysis that informs the current discourse of humanitarian assistance is premised on flawed assumptions about the role of NGOs and the context in which they operate. Although there are several genuine changes in the nature of conflict in the post–Cold War period that impact upon the provision of aid, the dilemmas confronting aid today are essentially the same as in the past. It is the international response that is more "complex"; proliferation in the number and type of actors in the field has exacerbated inherent dilemmas in the provision of humanitarian assistance. The convoluted nature of the response warrants re-analysis of the roles and objectives of humanitarian aid, but the proposed solution of closer collaboration among NGOs, UN agencies, governments and military forces is likely to direct aid towards politically expedient outcomes and away from its initial purpose. There is, in fact, a need for greater independence in the actions of NGOs from government donors and military forces.

The chapter is divided into four sections. The first briefly discusses the purpose of humanitarian aid organisations, and explores the paradox at the heart of humanitarian action in war. The second section examines some of the ways in which aid organisations reacted to the moral dilemmas of the Cold War period, when aid was used by donor governments and beneficiaries alike to pursue political agendas. Having shown that the moral dilemmas and complexity associated with the provision of humanitarian aid are not a 1990s phenomenon, the third section identifies some of the additional complications that have arisen with the advent of military forces alongside aid organisations in the response to the human consequences of disrupted states. The fourth section offers some brief conclusions.

NGO diversity in purpose and principles

The fact that no better term has appeared in the English or French languages to describe a "non-government organisation" (NGO), other than by what it is not, says a great deal about the disparate nature of these associations. Differentiated from business by the absence of a motive to make and distribute profits among shareholders,[3] and generally professing a single purpose as opposed to the multiple purposes of governments and the United Nations, NGOs are supposed to be anchored in and reflect the concerns of civil society. NGOs are generally established to fill a perceived void in government activity or responsibility; to lobby government and inform public opinion about an issue; or to advance a combination of these pursuits. NGOs are typically viewed as having a "voluntary" and non-bureaucratic nature, and being free from the sovereignty constraints of states, albeit within the confines of domestic national legislation.

The origins of Western humanitarian NGO activity[4] are embedded in two main traditions: religion and eighteenth-century European Enlightenment philosophies. The distinction between these approaches is still evident today: some NGOs profess a charitable "duty" to assist the less fortunate, whereas others base their action on the "rights" of individuals to certain minimum standards by virtue of their membership of humanity. The earliest ancestors of modern NGOs were established in the twelfth century, when Christian organisations such as the Order of the Knights of St John of Jerusalem (later the Order of Malta) formed to take care of the sick and wounded on an international basis.[5] The first human rights NGO was established in 1839 to fight the slave trade. In 1847 the first secular medical voluntary organisation was established, the American Medical Association, but it was a few years later, in 1863, that the first universal secular organisation, the International Committee of the Red Cross (ICRC), was formed in Geneva. Although not an NGO, since its mandate is conferred under international law, the ideals and principles underpinning the work of the ICRC became the foundation for the generations of NGOs that subsequently developed in the area of international humanitarian relief.

Humanitarian NGOs profess a common objective to alleviate the suffering of victims of conflict, marginalisation, discrimination or oppression around the globe, and profess to put the concerns of humanity above other considerations. But, beyond this objective, humanitarian NGOs exhibit as many differences as similarities in ideology and approaches to the provision of assistance to vulnerable populations. Beyond the "charity" versus "rights" distinction above, aid organisations also differ in the importance they place on proximity to government institutions; on adherence to the principles of neutrality and impartiality of humanitarian action; and on whether pragmatism should be favoured over a principled approach to the provision of aid. Contemporary approaches invariably reflect the basis on which each agency was formed. Oxfam, for example, was created in 1942 to lobby against the starvation caused by the British government blockade of Greece, and has continued to argue for justice in its subsequent operations. Similarly, Médecins Sans Frontières (MSF) was created by doctors frustrated by delays in Nigerian government approval for access to starving civilians in Biafra, and has continued to put the right of all people to medical assistance above concerns of state sovereignty. Other NGOs such as CARE were created with a more technical than political bent, providing CARE packages to Europe in the wake of the Second World War, and have continued to focus on the technical aspects of the provision of aid.

NGO attitudes concerning relationships with government represent one of the areas in which they differ most. European NGOs generally guard greater independence than those of the United States. It is interesting to note that, whereas many important figures from NGOs in France have become senior figures in the French government,[6] in the United States, and to a lesser extent in Australia, personnel have also moved the other way. Julia Taft, for example, was the director of the Office of US Foreign Disaster Assistance in the US Agency for International Development before becoming the head of InterAction, the NGO coalition body in the United States in 1993. In 1997 she was reappointed to the US government, as Assistant Secretary of State for Population, Refugees and Migration Affairs. Similarly, Andrew Natsios became the vice-president of World Vision after serving in a senior position in the US government, and the former prime minister of Australia, Malcolm Fraser, was chair of CARE Australia from 1987 to 2001. His 1999 mission to the Federal Republic of Yugoslavia as the special envoy of the Australian government raises interesting questions about the distinction between NGOs and governments, as does the level of funding that some NGOs receive from government coffers. If an NGO receives 90 per cent, or even more than 50 per cent, of its funding from government sources, can it be legitimately called "non-governmental"? Most NGOs do not consider this to be of concern, rejecting the idea that government funding necessarily ties humanitarian action to the foreign policy interests of governments. After all, the US intervention in Somalia is widely cited as an example of US government altruism in the face of massive human suffering.[7] Furthermore, many NGOs claim that, by lobbying for and spending government funding in humanitarian crises, NGOs are ensuring that governments uphold commitments to the broader international community and reflect the concerns of their tax-paying constituents.

The diversity of NGO opinions and approaches is a reflection of the variety of concerns expressed by the civil society in which NGOs are anchored. But the diversity is also a reflection of the inherent paradox at the core of humanitarian action, and how individual aid organisations try to reconcile competing moral principles. The fundamental aim of humanitarian action is to save lives and alleviate suffering, but, from its inception, this humanitarian act has had the potential to prolong conflict and hence the suffering of its victims. A common question unites humanitarian, political and military actors: is it better to have a brief, decisive war that ignores humanitarian principles, or a conflict prolonged by the respect of humanitarian demands? The noble idea of providing protection and assistance to wounded soldiers on the battlefield was at the heart of the birth of modern humanitarian activity, proposed by the founder of the Red Cross, Jean-Henri Dunant, after he witnessed the carnage of the Battle of Solferino in 1859. But, in the subsequent intergovernmental agreement to implement Dunant's dream, no provision was made to prevent the return of the wounded to combat. This paradox was illustrated vividly in Afghanistan every time a mujahid wearing a prosthesis appeared at a health post with a fresh war wound. The potential role of aid in war is also recognised in the Geneva Conventions of 1949. Article 23 of the Fourth Convention permits a belligerent party to refuse passage of humanitarian aid if there are reasons for fearing that the consignment may be diverted, that control may not be effective, or that a definite advantage may accrue to the military efforts or economy of the enemy.

This central dilemma of humanitarian action has become prominent in the past few years as the end of the Cold War thrust humanitarian issues to centre stage. The early optimism of a new world order with a humanitarian cornerstone was tempered by the US and UN failure in Somalia, but humanitarian issues remained on the agenda as the "lowest common denominator"[8] in deliberations by the United Nations and member states about the best way to respond to the increasing incidence of state disruption. This expanded role was accompanied by deeper scrutiny of humanitarian endeavours, as aid failed to achieve the ambition it was set and was even accused of being part of the problem. Influential observers began asserting that "a new reality has emerged which recognised that humanitarian action does not occur in a political vacuum"[9] in the post–Cold War environment, emphasising "how much more complex humanitarian work was now than it had been in the past".[10] An even more recent assertion is that this has led to "a collective identity crisis among aid workers in war zones as well as among those that analyse such efforts".[11] This "identity crisis", however, has been ongoing for the past 30 years as aid organisations have struggled simultaneously to reflect the volition of their members; to adhere to the mandate of their organisation, whether self-imposed in the case of NGOs or conferred under law for the ICRC; to alleviate the suffering of victims, however defined; and to negotiate a path between conflicting priorities and principles in the highly political and complex environment of the Cold War period.

The permanence of moral dilemmas in humanitarian action

Far from working within the "crisp and simple concepts of the Cold War era",[12] humanitarian aid organisations were confronted with profound dilemmas during the 1960s, 1970s and 1980s as images of human suffering and the provision of aid were used by donors and recipients alike to pursue political objectives. In the late 1960s, many NGOs came to the aid of Biafrans starved by the Nigerian blockade of the secessionist territory, only to find that their actions increased the intransigence of the secessionist leadership for whom famine was an important propaganda tool with which to gain international legitimacy. The Biafran leader, Colonel Ojukwu, chose to print new legal tender and stamps at the height of the famine which claimed the lives of 1 million people, and only when he fled the country did the fighting stop. In Ethiopia in 1985, famine and the aid that it attracted were also used as weapons of war, this time to facilitate the deportation to the south of the country of northerners accused of sympathising with rebel forces, provoking the death of up to 100,000 of them.[13] Aid was used as a lure; the Mengistu regime restricted the entry of children to many feeding centres until their parents agreed to be resettled.

In refugee camps throughout the Third World, guerilla movements received protection, sustenance and a dependent population from which to draw legitimacy and new recruits. Refugee camps in Pakistan harboured mujahidin fighting the Soviet-backed regime in Kabul; the United States sent "humanitarian aid" to Honduras to assist the Contras in their war against the Sandinista regime in Nicaragua; and the United States dominated the financial contributions to the Cambodian refugee camps in Thailand, preferring to support the revival of the Khmer Rouge than to allow the Vietnamese government to remain unopposed in its support of Phnom Penh.

Retaining the neutrality, impartiality and independence of humanitarian action in the highly political context was difficult, and the approach adopted by the aid organisations was far from uniform. The International Committee of the Red Cross applied strict neutrality to its operations, which facilitated access to the heart of conflicts in some instances, and restricted access altogether in others if consent from both sides was not forthcoming. In the Cambodian crisis, for example, the ICRC's insistence on a presence on both sides of the conflict successfully overcame the prohibition placed on other agencies, whereas strict adherence to the same principles in Afghanistan curtailed its access to war victims. In some circumstances, organisations such as MSF and Oxfam prioritised principles of proportionality over concerns of neutrality, judging that the needs on one side were greater than on the other, or that the nature of a regime precluded the possibility of aid effectively reaching the people. Thus Oxfam's abhorrence of the Khmer Rouge and concerns of justice for the Cambodian people directed its decision to work inside Cambodia and not with the refugees along the Thai–Cambodian border. MSF similarly chose not to work with the Khmer Rouge, but considered that the nature of the Vietnamese-backed regime in Phnom Penh obviated the possibility of aiding civilians inside Cambodia, so limited its assistance to the non-Khmer Rouge refugee camps. In the Afghan conflict, MSF worked inside Afghanistan with the mujahidin, judging that the indiscriminate and disproportionate force employed by Soviet troops warranted aiding the victims of these atrocities, regardless of the violation of state sovereignty and of strict neutrality. In Honduras, by contrast, MSF made a concerted effort to assist refugees fleeing the right-wing government of El Salvador and the left-wing government of Nicaragua, recognising that there were victims of atrocities on both sides.

Some NGOs operating at this time expressed overtly political agendas according to ideological belief. In Honduras, for example, a spate of American NGOs, including the United States Council for World Freedom, Friends of the Americas and the Nicaraguan Freedom Fund, assisted the Contras in the Nicaraguan refugee camp, while, at the other end of the country, left-wing European organisations worked in the camps containing Salvadoran refugees who had fled the right-wing dictatorship in San Salvador. Other NGOs chose to ignore the political context surrounding the aid operation, instead focusing on the technical provision of assistance. After the Biafran famine, NGOs began to professionalise their delivery capacities, developing pre-packaged kits, contingency stocks and standardised guidelines to facilitate rapid responses to political and natural disasters. However, ignoring the dilemmas did not make them disappear; in the highly political contexts the choice was rarely "between a political position and a neutral position but between two political positions: one active and the other by default".[14] Whether they openly acknowledged it or not, humanitarian aid was often an extension of the foreign policy of the donor governments or used by host governments for political ends.

Obtaining access to vulnerable populations during this period involved protracted negotiations with governments, rebel authorities and local leaders. An "ideal" environment in which to work was one characterised by respect for humanitarian principles and their practical application in operational standards (otherwise known as humanitarian space). Such standards include the freedom to assess the needs of the population independently; to retain unhindered access to the population; to conduct, monitor and evaluate the distribution of aid commodities; and to obtain security guarantees for expatriate and local personnel and for property. Obtaining all these guarantees was rare in conflict zones, and thus aid organisations were required to prioritise the importance of each and fix a bottom line of acceptable compromise. In the early 1980s in Cambodia, Oxfam staff considered that opposing the international isolation of Cambodia was more important than monitoring and evaluating the impact of their aid, and Oxfam accepted the conditionality imposed by Phnom Penh.[15] MSF's bottom line, by contrast, was ensuring that aid reached the intended beneficiaries and, since this could not be verified, MSF, as noted earlier, chose not to intervene. Compromises were constantly made when weighing up the need for, and effectiveness of, humanitarian aid against the potential harm that the aid might do. Some negative consequences may be "acceptable" if the overall objective of saving lives that would otherwise have been lost can be achieved. MSF draws the line when aid is turned against the very people it is trying to assist. MSF denounced such practices in Ethiopia in 1985 and in the Rwandan refugee camps in Zaire and Tanzania in 1994. Other agencies decided otherwise.

The preceding discussion illustrates that the divergence of opinions and approaches of humanitarian actors to the dilemmas posed by contemporary crises is not new. The collective amnesia of past difficulties reinforces the prevailing discourse of "complex emergencies", which tends to depict contemporary crises as more dramatic. Claims, for example, that the scale of the Rwandan refugee flow had not been seen "since biblical times" ignored precedents such as the exodus of up to 100,000 refugees per day from Pakistan to India in one eight-week period in 1971, eventually creating a refugee population of 9–10 million.[16] The 1990s environment was also supposedly characterised by a disregard for international humanitarian law by combatants and the direct targeting of relief personnel: "shooting at the Red Cross used to be unthinkable."[17] Disregarding the deliberate targeting and destruction of ICRC ambulance units by Italian planes in Ethiopia in 1935–1936,[18] it is true that aid workers were increasingly targeted in the mid-1990s compared with the past. But there are more lucid explanations for this, elaborated below, than increased barbarism.[19] Moreover, international humanitarian law was not uppermost in the minds of combatants during the wars in Vietnam or Central America. Perhaps because they were "freedom fighters" and not "barbarians" it was different. Or perhaps because aid workers were not present beside CNN to witness the atrocities, they did not occur. Civilians were the primary casualty of war long before the 1990s: guerilla strategies, if they were to be successful, necessarily implicated the civilian population. An effective way to catch the fish was to drain the sea.

Contrary to this dominant trend of identifying causal factors to explain increased complexity, it is predominantly the reaction that is complicated as competing agendas of the different actors come into contact. The most profound change in humanitarian action in the 1990s was the proliferation of actors from NGOs, the United Nations, donor governments and the military reacting to the humanitarian consequences of conflict, genocide or state disruption. Few NGOs ventured into the heart of conflicts prior to the advent of "negotiated access" in Sudan in 1989, but the "new world order" opened the door to the vast new array of "humanitarians". The injection of aid into the heart of disintegrating states in which authority and the state's monopoly of violence are contested gives aid greater prominence as a potential source of exploitation. The end of superpower patronage of militant factions contributed to their fragmentation, and has led to increased competition among them for control of resources. Some of the fiercest battles are no longer over the spoils of government but around gold and diamond mines in Sierre Leone, Liberia and the Democratic Republic of the Congo (formerly Zaire). Aid is also a target of this wave of criminalisation of legal and illegal economic commodities, both directly and indirectly.[20] The diversion of aid supplies has contributed to the revenue of numerous armed movements, most recently in south Sudan, and the indirect exploitation of aid through taxation and protection rackets was particularly prominent in Somalia and Liberia.

The fragmentation of structures of authority has also left aid organisations with few reliable interlocutors in the field to ensure their safety. Acceptable conditions and security guarantees may be successfully negotiated with faction leaders, traditional elders and local government representatives, but their control may not extend to all armed elements. These changes legitimately cause new concerns for aid agencies in the field. But pursuing the discourse associated with "complex emergencies" confuses the specificities of war, famine, epidemics, drought, population displacement, massacres and genocide, and renders irrelevant the precedents from the "simple" past. One observer has remarked that the vogue for labelling crises "complex emergencies" is a means with which to conceal "that one does not know what is going on".[21] But, more insidious than this, the term actually distorts understanding, making no distinction between the causes of suffering, instead defining the crisis in terms of the required "multifaceted response". How often has the Rwandan crisis been described as a "complex emergency"? The causes of crises are political; some *consequences* may be humanitarian. But labelling them "complex emergencies" and "humanitarian crises" disconnects the consequences from the causes and permits the international response to be assigned to the humanitarian domain.

The dilemmas confronting humanitarian agencies from the unintended consequences of aid gained prominence in the 1990s because they are now genuinely unintended. The same "side-effects" that sustained the "good" anti-Vietnamese factions in the refugee camps in Thailand, or the anti-Soviet fighters in the Afghan refugee camps, also supported the genocidal former Rwandan regime in the refugee camps in Zaire in the 1990s. No longer in the name of a "just" cause, the inherent paradoxes of aid have attracted unprecedented criticism and have been accused of being part of the problem. Government donors, particularly the United States, have capitalised on this as a reason to review the rationale for aid, suggesting that in future it should be tied more closely to foreign policy interests. Senior officials from the US Agency for International Development wrote in the *International Herald Tribune*:

> It now seems clear that in those camps more than a million people were controlled against their will by the perpetrators of genocide in Rwanda ... Shocking but true, the provision of humanitarian assistance by the United States, the European Union and others helped those who committed genocide to control these people for more than two years ... The future course seems clear: Humanitarian aid must be linked more closely to our foreign policy.[22]

Feigning prior ignorance of the militarised nature of the Rwandan refugee camps and blaming aid for the problem were shameless attempts to shed responsibility for the failure of political leaders to address the causes of the problem. Fears of "another Somalia" paralysed the political and military machinery of the United Nations and member states in January 1994, when allegations of plans to "exterminate the Tutsi" were first transmitted to New York by General Dallaire, the Commander of the UN peacekeeping force in Rwanda (UNAMIR).[23] According to Dallaire, only 5,000 troops with an appropriate mandate would have been sufficient to stop the genocide once it began in April,[24] but the bulk of the UN force was withdrawn. Having made a concerted effort to avoid American engagement to stop the genocide, even ordering US officials to avoid the use of the word "genocide" because of the moral obligations it invokes, the United States was at the helm of the military engagement to fight the war against cholera in the refugee camps in Goma. Following boasting that "the US Government response so far has been massive, aggressive, and immediate as possible",[25] the cholera vibrio was defeated while the Rwandan leaders and army who orchestrated the genocide and the population exodus to Zaire regrouped and settled in the refugee camps, in full view of the US, Israeli, French, Japanese, Canadian and Dutch military contingents. Bestowed with a humanitarian mandate, the military forces could participate in the dramatic rescue without risking protracted and potentially dangerous engagement in the political arena, which might have generated adverse domestic repercussions.

Humanitarian action has thus been transformed from a tool with which governments pursue foreign policy objectives to a tool with which to avoid foreign policy engagement. Furthermore, it has now also become a convenient scapegoat for failures in resolving crises that are misleadingly labelled "humanitarian". The situations that create a need for humanitarian assistance, the context in which this aid is provided and the resolution of the causes of human distress are all determined in the political sphere. Unless the political parameters of crises are addressed, humanitarian action is doomed to failure. The purpose of humanitarian action is to put the concerns of humanity first, and aid organisations prioritise the humanitarian imperative to alleviate suffering, particularly in the critical phase of a relief operation. International military contingents and humanitarian organisations suffer from the same fate if either are deployed in isolation of an overall diplomatic strategy to address the causes of the conflict.

Military–NGO cooperation in disrupted states

The end of the Cold War, it was hoped, would usher in a new era of stability and justice. No longer would Western leaders need to support authoritarian regimes as bulwarks against the spread of communism, and humanitarian aid could be deployed in accordance with its original purpose. Appeals to the inviolability of state sovereignty were no longer going to protect brutal regimes from external scrutiny, and military forces were to be deployed in support of humanitarian ideals. The first test of the "new humanitarian world order" came with Operation Provide Comfort in 1991 in defence of Iraqi Kurds who were oppressed by the forces of Saddam Hussein. Bernard Kouchner, the staunchest humanitarian advocate of the *droit d'ingérence* (the right to intervene), celebrated this "extraordinary development in our century of horrors and massacres[:] for the first time the international community prevented a genocide, for the first time it permitted a population which was expelled to return to their villages and their land".[26] Other successes followed in which the roles of the military complemented those of the aid agencies. From August 1992 to February 1993, for example, the US military conducted Operation Provide Relief, an airlift that delivered food from Mombasa to aid organisations on the ground in Somalia.

Aid organisations have also publicly called for military intervention when confronted with massive human rights abuses, most vocally in Rwanda during the 1994 genocide. But the absence of any response in Rwanda reversed the last vestiges of aid organisations' optimism about the new humanitarian world order, already tarnished by setbacks in Somalia and Bosnia. Rather than alleviating the dilemmas confronting humanitarian aid organisations through creating a humanitarian space in which aid organisations could operate, the military have been increasingly deployed in duplicitous circumstances with ambiguous and restrictive mandates. Furthermore, the appearance of the military in the disaster zone has added another, invariably louder, voice to the array of actors responding to the crisis. Having a different fundamental purpose from that of the humanitarian organisations, inevitable clashes and misunderstandings have ensued. Two major sources of frustration have been the preference of UN Security Council members for limiting the mandates of military forces to a "humanitarian" role, and the dominance of the military "end-state" that accompanies military deployment. Naturally, military forces need a goal and direction, but the high financial and political investment by politicians in such ventures often leads to a politically expedient outcome, to the detriment of longer-term solutions.

A first problem is that of mandates. As highlighted in the example from Goma above, limiting military engagement to humanitarian tasks imbues it with the same shortcomings as humanitarian aid: the efforts are addressing only the symptoms, not the causes of the problem. The cholera epidemic in Goma was arrested, but the more profound problem of the presence of the former Rwandan government and army in the refugee camps, which only a military or police presence could have averted, was ignored, resulting in the prolongation of the Rwandan conflict to the present day. The failure of the UN member states to contribute military or police personnel to the refugee camps left humanitarian aid organisations with a terrible dilemma. Should they prioritise the humanitarian imperative to provide aid to the camps, thereby strengthening the power of the former Rwandan regime residing therein, or prioritise the consequences of the aid and withdraw from the camps, thereby abandoning the *bona fide* refugees to their fate? Unlike other contexts in which remaining neutral in the conflict is an important precondition for the legitimacy of peacekeeping forces, international law condemning genocide and providing for the exclusively civilian nature of refugee camps caused no such constraints. There was no clearer case for intervention than during the Rwandan genocide and in the refugee camps: the United Nations and member states cannot be neutral when confronted with preventing and punishing genocide.

More muscular mandates were given to the military forces in Somalia and Bosnia than to those in Goma, with the military tasked with providing protection, not just material assistance. But the object of protection was humanitarian convoys and personnel, not the local people. The provision of humanitarian aid is a means to an end, the end being the preservation of life and dignity. Although insecurity can prevent aid reaching vulnerable populations, the deployment of military forces to protect the means in isolation of the ends is a dangerous travesty. A full belly does not provide civilians with protection. What is the point of protecting the aid supplies when the civilians the aid is intended to assist are in greater danger of losing their lives to violence? The most appalling consequence of the limited mandate is the false sense of security it provides to civilian populations. In Kigali, Kibeho and Srebrenica, troops have stood helplessly by and witnessed the slaughter of civilians because their mandate did not extend to such a role. And, to compound the tragedy, the lesson learned by the UN system is not that the abandonment was, in the words of General Dallaire, *"inexcusable by any human criteria"*,[27] but that efforts should be made in future to reduce the expectations:

> Many Rwandese believed that the United Nations was there to stop the genocide and were bitterly disappointed when this was not the case ... UNAMIR should have done more to inform the public about its limited role and mandate early on, particularly for the protection of civilians at risk, so as not to give the people a false sense of security. This might have also averted disasters such as the Kibeho massacre, where internally displaced people in the Kibeho camp believed that UNAMIR soldiers would protect them from the RPA [Rwandan Patriotic Army].[28]

This enormous travesty begs the question of the purpose of military intervention. In whose interests are the armed forces intervening?

A second problem relates to end-states and political expediency. The fanfare that accompanies military forays to address the humanitarian consequences of state disruption contributes greatly to the mobilisation of funds for the entire programme. One only needs to glance at the tins of chicken pâté, foil-wrapped cheeses and fresh fruit and milk provided to the Kosovar refugees to realise that budget allocations are greater there than in forgotten tragedies away from the media spotlight. But just as politicians can gain domestic kudos from the public show of compassion – as George Bush did through sending troops to Somalia in his final days in office – so they can rapidly lose support when casualties appear, as changes in American attitudes to Somalia and in Belgian attitudes to Rwanda attest.

One of the most important lessons to come from the mistakes of Somalia is that strict objectives must be set in advance of the military deployment and an "end-state" identified that, when reached, signals the successful completion of the mission. Even as American troops landed in Somalia, no agreement had been reached between the United Nations and the US administration regarding crucial details of the mission such as the disarmament of factions. Unclear objectives led to a swing from under-engagement to over-engagement[29] as the operation faced increasing opposition from the factions and the Somali people. Subsequent peace operations have been more firmly aligned to specific objectives, such as the facilitation of free and fair elections in Cambodia.

The establishment of an end-state is not, in itself, problematic because all external interveners need to identify the point at which their assistance is no longer required. However, the huge investment of money and political reputation inherent in multifaceted responses tends to sway donors and politicians towards the most politically expedient result, often to the detriment of longer-term solutions, particularly when the agenda of the interveners is not shared by the people in whose name they intervened. One of the first effects of the US intervention in Somalia, for example, was the recognition of General Aideed and Ali Mahdi as the legitimate representatives of the Somali people with whom to negotiate. With this one move, the US Special Envoy, Robert Oakley, undid months of thoughtful negotiation by the former representative of the UN Secretary-General, Mohamed Sahnoun, who had gained the respect and trust of the traditional elders and grassroots associations, which he was promoting as alternative sources of power to that of the warlords. Relations with Aideed fell apart, and the United Nations Operation in Somalia (UNOSOM) tried to re-establish links with the traditional leadership in order to forge a civilian government. But, again, political expediency undermined efforts to reconstitute political and social order, as the UNOSOM political leadership imposed Western notions of democracy and rigid timetables on the Somali elders. The push for an outcome neglected the importance of the process and doomed the expensive efforts to failure.

The push towards the end-state invariably prioritises the achievement of short-term stability over issues of reconciliation and justice, to the obvious detriment of longer-term issues of governance and legitimacy. Experiences from Rwanda are particularly pertinent. The solution to the Rwandan crisis was associated with the return of the refugees and the stability of the governing regime; thus, when a report suggested that the RPA had killed up to 40,000 civilians on its march to Kigali, Boutros-Ghali, at the request of the US government, suppressed the report, claiming that "it does not exist".[30] Naturally the United Nations was reluctant to criticise human rights abuses against the new government when it had done nothing to prevent genocide and was protecting the perpetrators of the genocide in UN-sponsored refugee camps. But the lack of condemnation of these initial killings and subsequent ones, such as occurred at the Kibeho camp for the displaced in April 1995, condoned such acts and assisted in the rise of Tutsi hardliners to power at the expense of the moderate members of government.[31] This, in turn, reduced the possibilities for refugee repatriation. Although most observers emphasise the influence of the *génocidaires* in the camps in preventing the return of the refugees, the insecurity inside Rwanda was also to blame for the stalemate in the refugee crisis. As the Special Envoy of the UNHCR, Carol Faubert, said in an interview with *Le Monde* in July 1995: "The violence has disappeared in the camps, but it could recur. For the moment, three months after the Kibeho massacre, the camp extremists have no need to discourage the refugees from returning."[32]

The Kibeho massacre highlights another dimension of the clash between humanitarian objectives and political objectives which comes to the fore in the push for an end-state. Members of UNAMIR and the Independent International Commission of Inquiry[33] into the massacre have apportioned some of the blame to the NGOs operating in Kibeho for not having cooperated more fully with attempts to close the camp and return the people to their communes of origin. The Rwandan government had legitimate reasons for wanting to close the camps, arising in particular from strong suspicions that the camps sheltered *génocidaires* who were responsible for continuing instability in the south. But the innocent inhabitants of the camp also had legitimate fears of returning to their homes, based on widespread incidents of violence and insecurity throughout the country, the growing number of arrests of genocide suspects, many of whom even the government admitted were innocent,[34] and the illegal occupation of houses by returnees from the Tutsi diaspora, complaints against whom could result in false accusations of guilt and hence imprisonment. Moreover, even the report of the Commission of Inquiry noted that in March 1995 only 60 per cent of the 37,000 internally displaced persons who had returned to their home communes had stayed there.[35] When the internally displaced persons resisted the camp closure, between 300 persons (according to the Rwandan government) and 4,000 persons (UN and MSF estimates)[36] were killed.

Apportioning some blame to the NGOs for the slaughter illustrates the depth of misunderstanding of the purpose of humanitarian aid organisations and the priority they attach to the concerns of humanity. Forcibly to repatriate refugees to their country of origin when they have well-founded fears of persecution on recognised grounds is a violation of refugee law. Refugee asylum is premised on the principle that, if the state cannot uphold its responsibility to provide protection to its nationals, then a country of asylum, with the assistance of the UNHCR if requested, will provide such protection. The same law does not extend to people who have not crossed an international border, but the principle is the same. For a humanitarian aid organisation to have assisted in the return of people against their will and in fear of their lives would have been contrary to its commitment to put the concerns of this population before other considerations. The NGOs may have agreed to participate in the closure of the camps during the planning stages of the operation but, when it became clear that the camp inhabitants did not want to return home, the NGOs were right to object to their forced removal. To accuse NGOs of responsibility for the killing through their non-cooperation is absurd. The men who ordered and carried out the killings are to blame for the massacre. The refusal to participate in such a process is a legitimate ethical choice. As Rony Brauman has articulated in reference to other situations, "deciding to act means knowing, at least approximately, why action is preferable to abstention".[37] Had international personnel been aware that the Rwandan Patriotic Army would open fire on the displaced population if they did not leave the camps, then they would have been obliged to pressure the Rwandan government to prevent human rights abuses, rather than participate in the violation of one set of rights to achieve another. The donors' preoccupation with stability at all costs undermined crucial considerations of justice and helped set the stage for the Rwandan army and Zairean rebel attacks on the Rwandan refugee camps in Zaire in late 1996, which resulted in further massive loss of human life.

Thus some of the constraints on effective military–NGO cooperation in disrupted states derive from the limited mandate bestowed on military forces, which, although useful logistically, does little to address the crux of the crisis. Further complications arise when a rigid end-state is imposed, with which all aid agency activities are expected to conform. Aid organisations that express concerns at the attachment of humanitarian aid to the political goals of the peace process are branded uncooperative and obstinate. But the use of aid as a tool of peace violates the humanitarian principle of impartiality, which maintains that aid be given according to need as the only criterion. Similarly, accepting armed escort and permitting the military to negotiate on behalf of aid organisations jeopardise the future of aid activities if the peace operation turns sour. The intervention of the military in a disrupted state is bound to generate some winners and some losers: neutrality is only as valid as the local perception. Thus aid organisations are often better off establishing their own relationships with local authorities and building relationships of trust independent of the political and military structures. The dilemmas that frequently confront humanitarian aid organisations have no obviously right and wrong response, and aid organisations must weigh up the pros and cons of their action irrespective of the "quick fix" priorities associated with military intervention.

Conclusion

This chapter has attempted to shed some light on the diversity of ways in which NGOs have responded over the past 30 years to the difficulties and ethical dilemmas inherent in the provision of humanitarian assistance. The prevailing discourse of the 1990s emphasised changes in the global environment, but the dichotomy between the Cold War period and the post–Cold War period is overstated. Labels such as "complex emergency" blur rather than illuminate the causes of crises and the most appropriate response, and they undervalue genuine changes in the nature of conflict that impact upon the provision of aid, such as the fragmentation of combatant groups and the criminalisation of economic activity. The proliferation of actors and the insertion of aid into the heart of conflicts have increased the stakes of humanitarian aid in disrupted states, but the fundamental ethical dilemmas and the choices they impose remain the same. Were aid organisations right to provide food aid inside Bosnia, thereby encouraging people to stay and risk violence at the hands of the Bosnian Serbs, or was it better to transport them to safety, thereby contributing to the policy of ethnic expulsion? Were organisations right to protest against the Taliban's prohibition on the employment of women and withdraw their assistance from the country, or would it have been better to ignore this issue in favour of continued assistance to the Afghan population, thereby risking condoning the policy through acquiescence? Should NGOs have agreed to Charles Taylor's demands for 15 per cent of all aid entering his territory in 1995 in order to access the severely malnourished Liberian inhabitants, or should concerns about fuelling the war economy have taken precedence?

The prominence of humanitarian issues in the 1990s was due to the appeal of humanitarian aid as a highly visible yet low-risk remedy to human suffering. It serves to mollify the intense, but short-lived, concern of the general public at images of suffering conveyed to their lounge rooms by CNN, without necessitating a potentially protracted engagement in the affairs of a distant land. In recent years, however, it has become increasingly apparent that aid is not a solution to political crises and may exacerbate the problem when deployed in isolation from diplomatic and political engagement. However, instead of committing to a more robust political policy, statements such as that of Atwood and Rogers suggest that governments prefer to divert humanitarian aid away from its primary objective of alleviating suffering, to fulfil instead a similar role to that of the Cold War as a tool of foreign policy. But, lacking the strong direction of the Cold War, foreign policy is today promoting minimalist goals of "stability" and low-cost, quick-fix solutions, rather than engagement in more profound issues of justice and human rights.

Cooperation and coordination became the panacea for difficulties in responding to "complex emergencies" in the 1990s, and the activities of all aid organisations are expected to conform to the prevailing perspective, particularly when the high-cost military are deployed. Aid organisations, the United Nations and government donors have increasingly engaged in discussions about regulating the activities of NGOs. Many donors have made adherence to the codes of conduct and minimum standards in the provision of relief[38] – established by NGOs to improve accountability to donors and beneficiaries – a condition for funding, thus turning them from general guidelines to tools of regulation. These standards, however, do not reflect the ethical dimensions of the provision of assistance and, by enforcing conformity in operations, potentially deny the possibility of differing priorities. The technical standards were met in the Rwandan refugee camps, for example, but that did not protect the refugees from attack in late 1996. MSF withdrew from the refugee camps, prioritising considerations of the consequences of the camps over the "humanitarian imperative" to remain, but this legitimate choice went against the prevailing view and the desire of the major donors. Organisations that espouse different views, based on past experience or differing priorities, are viewed as adversarial in the current climate of consensus. Will NGOs that engage in advocacy or decisions that conflict with the dominant view be excluded from certain fields of activity in the future?

Coordination among the various actors in the field is obviously vital to ensure that the needs of vulnerable populations are covered and that duplication of activities is avoided, and to minimise the extent to which the actions of some agencies compromise the actions of others, particularly when negotiating for access and security guarantees. Coordinating NGOs may be like herding cats, but this is preferable to having controls imposed over NGO activity. Who should set the rules and under whose authority should they be enforced? The largest donors are the United States and the European Union, but are their agendas and plans for the reconstitution of social order the same ones desired by the citizens on the ground? The divergence of views among humanitarian actors reflects the lack of clear solutions to ethical dilemmas, and active debate is crucial to a deeper understanding of the issues and choices. The increasing influence of government donors in humanitarian crises, facilitated largely by the acquiescence of quasi-NGOs, risks eroding humanitarian principles in favour of politically expedient objectives, to the detriment of populations in need of unconditional assistance.

Notes

1. The term "disrupted states" refers to states that are disintegrating through the erosion of government authority and structures, and states that, through committing crimes against their own people, forfeit their right to legitimacy. This term is preferable to "collapsed" or "weak" states because these preclude crises provoked by the strength of the state, such as the Rwandan genocide in 1994 and the Kosovo crisis in 1999.
2. David Rieff, "The Death of a Good Idea", *Newsweek*, 10 May 1999, p. 65.
3. NGOs are often described as non-profit organisations although this label is not strictly

accurate. NGOs often do make profits on investments, but these are reinvested in the organisation rather than distributed among shareholders. Hence not-for-profit is a more accurate term.
4. Acts of charity and benevolence are identifiable in all cultures and societies, but this discussion is limited to the evolution of Western NGOs and humanitarian thought. For a discussion of the universality of such sentiments, see Iphraim Isaac, "Humanitarianism across Religion and Cultures", in Thomas Weiss and Larry Minear (eds), *Humanitarianism across Borders: Sustaining Civilians in Times of War* (Boulder, CO: Lynne Rienner, 1993), pp. 13–22.
5. Yves Beigbeder, *The Role and Status of International Humanitarian Volunteers and Organisations: The Right and Duty to Humanitarian Assistance* (Dordrecht: Martinus Nijhoff, 1991), p. 8.
6. The most famous example in France is Bernard Kouchner, one of the founders of MSF and Médecins du Monde, who became the first Secretary of State for Humanitarian Action. Claude Malhuret and Xavier Emmanuelli, both former presidents of MSF, also became senior French government officials after leaving MSF, Malhuret as Secretary of State for Human Rights, and Emmanuelli as Secretary of State for Humanitarian Action.
7. See, for example, Martha Finnemore, "Constructing Norms of Humanitarian Intervention", in Peter Katzenstein (ed.), *The Culture of National Security: Norms and Identity in World Politics* (New York: Columbia University Press, 1996), pp. 153–185 at p. 156.
8. Adam Roberts, *Humanitarian Action in War: Aid, Protection and Impartiality in a Policy Vacuum*, Adelphi Paper no. 305 (Oxford: Oxford University Press, for the International Institute for Strategic Studies, 1996), pp. 15–16.
9. Thomas Weiss, "Military–Civilian Humanitarianism: The 'Age of Innocence' Is Over", *International Peacekeeping*, vol. 2, no. 2, Summer 1995, pp. 157–174 at p. 157.
10. Emma Bonino, comments attributed in the Final Report from an ECHO–ICRC seminar, "Humanitarian Action: Perceptions and Security", Lisbon, 27–28 March 1998, p. 6.
11. Thomas Weiss, "Principles, Politics and Humanitarian Action", *Ethics and International Affairs*, vol. 13, 1999, pp. 1–22 at p. 1.
12. Antonio Donini, "Beyond Neutrality: On the Compatibility of Military Intervention and Humanitarian Assistance", *The Fletcher Forum*, 1995, pp. 31–45 at p. 31.
13. Alain Destexhe, *L'humanitaire impossible ou deux siècles d'ambiguïté* (Paris: Armand Colin, 1993), p. 119.
14. Rony Brauman, "Refugee Camps, Population Transfers, and NGOs", in Jonathan Moore (ed.), *Hard Choices: Moral Dilemmas in Humanitarian Intervention* (Oxford: Rowman & Littlefield, 1998), pp. 177–194 at p. 181.
15. For a discussion of the inability of all aid organisations to monitor the distribution of relief in Cambodia in the early 1980s, see William Shawcross, *The Quality of Mercy: Cambodia, Holocaust and Modern Conscience* (New York: Simon & Schuster, 1984), pp. 365–370.
16. Destexhe, *L'humanitaire impossible*, p. 73.
17. Bonino, Final Report of ECHO-ICRC seminar, p. 6.
18. See Marcel Junod, *Warrior without Weapons* (Geneva: International Committee of the Red Cross, 1982), pp. 22–83.
19. Robert Kaplan's article "The Coming Anarchy", *Atlantic Monthly*, no. 273, 1994, pp. 44–76, initiated a popular trend which suggests that barbarism was on the rise in many parts of the world, particularly Africa, leading a descent into anarchy. For more lucid explanations of the violence associated with contemporary conflict, see Paul Richards, *Fighting for the Rainforest: War, Youth and Resources in Sierra Leone* (Oxford: James Currey, 1996); David Keen, "A Rational Kind of Madness", *Oxford Develop-*

ment Studies, vol. 25, no. 1, 1997, pp. 67–75; and Jean-François Bayart, Stephen Ellis & Béatrice Hibou, *The Criminalisation of the State in Africa* (Oxford: James Currey, 1999).
20. François Jean, "Aide humanitaire et économie de guerre", in François Jean and Jean Christophe Rufin (eds), *Économie des guerres civiles* (Paris: Hachette, 1996), pp. 543–589 at pp. 571–576.
21. Gwyn Prins, "Modern Warfare and Humanitarian Action", Final Report of ECHO–ICRC seminar, p. 13.
22. J. Brian Atwood and Leonard Rogers, "Rethinking Humanitarian Aid in the New Era", *International Herald Tribune*, 12 March 1997, p. 10. The authors were the administrator of the US Agency for International Development and the acting administrator of its Bureau for Humanitarian Response, respectively.
23. Interview with Iqbal Riza, former deputy head of the Department of Peacekeeping Operations (DPKO) under Kofi Annan and currently Chief of Staff to the UN Secretary-General, Annan; http://www.pbs.org/wgbh/pages/frontline/shows/evil/interviews/riza.html, accessed 8 April 1999.
24. See Scott Feil, *Preventing Genocide: How the Early Use of Force Might have Succeeded in Rwanda* (New York: Report to the Carnegie Commission on Preventing Deadly Conflict, 1998).
25. Prepared statement of Brian Atwood to the "Crisis in Central Africa" Hearing before the Subcommittee on African Affairs of the Committee of Foreign Relations, US Senate, 26 July 1994, p. 9.
26. Bernard Kouchner, "Sauver les corps", Action Humanitaire Devoir d'Ingérence: Naissance d'un nouveau droit, *Les Cahiers de l'Express*, March 1993, p. 6.
27. Romeo Dallaire, "The End of Innocence: Rwanda 1994", in Jonathan Moore (ed.), *Hard Choices: Moral Dilemmas in Humanitarian Intervention* (Oxford: Rowman & Littlefield, 1998), pp. 71–86 at p. 79 (emphasis in original).
28. Lessons Learned Unit, Department of Peacekeeping Operations, *Comprehensive Report on Lessons Learned from United Nations Assistance Mission for Rwanda (UNAMIR), October 1993–April 1996* (New York: DPKO, 1996), p. 42.
29. John Sommer, *Hope Restored? Humanitarian Aid in Somalia 1990–1994* (Washington DC: Refugee Policy Group, 1994), p. 117.
30. For a discussion of the Gersony Report, see Alison Des Forges, *Leave None to Tell the Story: Genocide in Rwanda* (New York: Human Rights Watch, March 1999).
31. In August 1995 two senior Hutu members of the government, Prime Minister Faustin Twagiramungu and Minister of the Interior Seth Sendashonga, were sacked for being critical of the extremist measures employed by elements of the armed forces. The hardening of the regime was also associated with the rise of the "Ugandan Colonels" to power within the RPA and the reshuffling of government posts, which sidelined the more moderate ministers and empowered people close to the regime leaders and those who were considered to be compliant. See Gérard Prunier, *Rwanda: The Social, Political and Economic Situation in June 1997* (Geneva: Writenet, July 1997).
32. Jean Hélène, "Des organisations humanitaires reprochent aux autorités rwandaises de ne pas favoriser le retour des exilés", *Le Monde*, 30–31 July 1995, p. 4 (my translation).
33. Marc Brissel-Foucault et al., *Report of the Independent International Commission of Inquiry on the Events at Kibeho, April 1995. Submitted to the Government of Rwanda*, 18 May 1995.
34. Howard Adelman and Astri Suhrke, "Early Warning and Conflict Management", *The International Response to Conflict and Genocide: Lessons from the Rwanda Experience*, Study no. 2 (Copenhagen: Steering Committee of the Joint Evaluation of Emergency Assistance to Rwanda, 1996), p. 94, note 132.
35. Brissel-Foucault et al., *Report of the Independent International Commission of Inquiry*, p. 6.

36. United Nations Human Rights Field Operations Rwanda, *Report Kibeho IDP Camp, Gikongoro Prefecture from 17 April to 24 April 1995* (Kigali: UNHRFOR, 1995), p. 16, and Médecins Sans Frontières, "Rapport Kibeho" (Amsterdam, Barcelona, Brussels, Geneva and Paris: unpublished report, May 1995), as cited in Jean-Hervé Bradol and Anne Guibert, "Le temps des assassins et l'espace humanitaire, Rwanda, Kivu, 1994–1997", *Hérodote*, nos. 86–87, 1997, pp. 116–149 at pp. 128–129.
37. Brauman, "Refugee Camps, Population Transfers, and NGOs", p. 192.
38. See the Sphere Project, http://www.sphereproject.org.

15
Comprehensive security partnerships for refugees

Sadako Ogata

Wars and refugees have never been so inextricably linked as in recent years. As the United Nations High Commissioner for Refugees (UNHCR) until the end of December 2000, I have reached the conclusion that an agency such as the UNHCR will remain relevant not only as an essential player in the international community's response to humanitarian crises, but also as an advocate for early and effective conflict prevention and resolution. Conflicts produce massive human displacement of refugees, internally displaced persons and war-affected civilians.

First of all, we should understand the nature of contemporary wars, which are primarily internal and intercommunal. We should take note of their intensity and objectives, especially the brutal expulsion of entire communities from specific areas. Conflicts today are inevitably the main cause of mass exodus but, in turn, internal conflicts and refugee flows threaten peace and security across borders in many areas.

Over the years, I have observed the interface between the political and humanitarian spheres grow and evolve. I have not ceased calling for political support for humanitarian crises. I have repeated, countless times, that humanitarian action can only address – but cannot resolve – political problems. I have given much thought to the relationship of humanitarian and political bodies. Bridging the gap between the pressing, often dramatic, interests of the most vulnerable and deprived people in the world and the legitimate concerns of states was the crucial theme of my decade at UNHCR.

I would like to elaborate and concentrate on two main areas: peace operations and peacebuilding.

Peace operations in a changing security environment

As has been said many times, the nature of war has changed. But the concept of peace operations may still be based on the assumption that wars are fought across clear-cut front-lines. And, in spite of discussions on wider approaches, peace operations continue to be country based, and reflect neither the internal nor the regional nature of many of today's wars. At UNHCR we asked ourselves such questions as an agency dealing – precisely – with forced population movements across blurred conflict lines and across borders.

UNHCR deploys its own staff – unarmed humanitarian workers – to dangerous and isolated duty stations; they are increasingly targeted and – as in the terrible September incidents of Atambua and Macenta – attacked and brutally killed; the gap in time between the beginning of humanitarian activities and that of peace operations continues to widen; last, but certainly not least, in many places, such as West Timor, Guinea and Liberia, forced population movements have become the cause and conduit of grave insecurity and instability, and little is done to address the problem – as if we had learned nothing from the lessons of the former Eastern Zaire.

In most parts of the world where UNHCR and its humanitarian partners are called upon to operate, mechanisms to address security problems are slow moving, unwieldy and not adapted to the new type of conflicts. In many places, they simply do not exist. Among my most vivid memories is the rescue operation that UNHCR set up in the former Zaire in 1996; when all deployment of international forces failed, UNHCR staff had to go and search for scattered, hungry and terrified refugees in the rainforest of that vast country, sometimes even on foot.

I am aware of the difficulties – in political terms, in military terms and in terms of resources. But let me insist first of all on the need to initiate and implement peace operations much more rapidly. The issue of timing has not yet been satisfactorily addressed by governments. UNHCR knows that peace operations will inevitably be slower than the humanitarian response. In refugee emergencies, UNHCR, other UN front-line agencies (especially the United Nations Children's Fund and the World Food Programme), the Red Cross movement and non-governmental organisations (NGOs) will continue to be the first ones on the ground. But if there has to be complementarity in this endeavour, UNHCR must do all that it can to reduce the gap between the deployment of humanitarian personnel and the implementation of some security support measures. Otherwise, the cost is simply unbearable, as proven by the catastrophic consequences of inaction in the successive Great Lakes crises, for example; or by the recent murders in Indonesia and Guinea.

UNHCR has become used to being called to confront refugee emergencies literally at a few hours' notice. It has no choice: delays in its work inevitably mean that lives are lost. Since 1992, it has therefore progressively built systems to respond quickly to sudden, massive population movements. These systems are based, essentially, on the concept of stand-by resources that can be mobilised and sent to the field within 72 hours – staff, equipment, goods and money.

Since 1992, however, the environment has changed rapidly. Political pressure for quick solutions to refugee problems has increased, and there is a growing number of humanitarian actors, including governments themselves. The Kosovo refugee crisis in 2000 proved that UNHCR had to adapt its existing emergency response systems to a new and more crowded humanitarian space, and the area on which it is focusing in particular is to upgrade its surge capacity to address refugee emergencies at a very short notice.

But, no matter how rapidly and effectively humanitarian agencies mobilise, their response will be inadequate unless the environment in which they operate is secure. I am speaking both of staff security and, from UNHCR's point of view, of the security of refugees and of the communities hosting them.

There is today an increased awareness that humanitarian agencies should not be left alone to confront difficult and dangerous situations. The question is, how do we ensure that? I have often spoken – sometimes in the UN Security Council – of the need to look at different options: not only full-fledged peacekeeping, but also and especially measures intended to *support* local law enforcement capacity.

I insist on the word *support*; this is the key concept, and it implies working together, as opposed to straightforward intervention. I am also referring to very specific situations – especially insecure border areas in and around refugee sites. And I am thinking of relatively simple measures: assisting the judiciary; training the police and military; supporting the police with logistics and communication; deploying, if necessary, liaison officers to work as coordinators and advisers. UNHCR has some such programmes – and they are working reasonably well – in western Tanzania in the area hosting refugees from Burundi, Rwanda and the Democratic Republic of the Congo. UNHCR needs the Security Council's support for similar programmes in other critical spots – in Guinea, for example, whose government has requested international cooperation in addressing security problems in the areas bordering Liberia and Sierra Leone.

The response of governments to the concept of a "ladder of options" to improve local security in refugee-inhabited areas has been very positive, but has remained, so far, in the realm of theory! It is urgent that UNHCR takes steps to operationalise it and to implement concrete, predictable measures, for example the deployment of "humanitarian security" staff. UNHCR needs to know what contributions may be forthcoming – in human, material and financial terms – and, again, how quickly they will be available.

I have insisted so far on "intermediate" security measures because I know that in most situations peacekeeping is simply an unrealistic option, but I also believe that the transition that started with the end of the Cold War has not yet ended, that new (or renewed) conflicts will flare up in different regions and that the international community will have to maintain peace after very fragile ceasefire agreements are signed. Peacekeeping, therefore, will continue to remain necessary, but, to remain relevant, it will have to adapt to the new environment and become speedier in deployment and more effective in output.

The humanitarian community has welcomed the initiative of Secretary-General Kofi Annan of an in-depth review of peace operations. UNHCR has been among the most eager supporters of the Brahimi Panel report, and is participating very actively in the discussions on its implementation.

The report is very important and courageous in its attempt to discuss comprehensively, and in a broader context, how the United Nations can fulfil its key function to help maintain peace and security. But, from a more specific, operational, humanitarian perspective, the report is also extremely relevant to UNHCR and its partners, particularly because it sets out a few objectives that, if achieved, would provide crucial support to humanitarian action. It stresses the need for quick decisions in responding to crises; it gives priority to quick fact-finding missions to the field; it underlines the importance of identifying, and pursuing, early solutions; and it places great emphasis on *presence* in the field. These are crucial aspects, whose importance UNHCR has advocated for years. They are also, by the way, basic elements of any humanitarian deployment. They clearly show the affinity, if I may call it that, between humanitarian action and peace operations, and the need to refine their relationship and mutual support.

UNHCR and other humanitarian agencies have large programmes in post-conflict areas, where peacekeeping is vital – Bosnia, Kosovo and East Timor, just to mention a few. Without peacekeepers, these agencies could not have worked, or continue to work, effectively in those areas. On the other hand, it is pleasing that, in discussing the concept of preliminary assessments, the role that is played (and can be played) by humanitarian, field-based agencies has been recognised. It is very important that these agencies are seen as complementary to peace operations, and not just as other actors who happen to work in the same areas.

Having said that, and speaking from not only a humanitarian but also a refugee perspective, I would like to take this opportunity to go beyond the conclusions of the Brahimi Panel report. In West Africa, for example, there have been cross-border attacks in both Guinea and Liberia, in areas hosting refugees and indeed *because* of the presence of refugees. Beyond Sierra Leone's borders, however, the only presence of the international community, amidst half a million refugees, is humanitarian, because the mandate of the UN Mission in Sierra Leone (UNAMSIL) is of course limited to that country. Yet, not only are humanitarian workers seriously at risk in border areas of Liberia and Guinea, but there is also a very real danger that the Sierra Leone conflict will spread and that refugee flows will be one of the conduits of this propagation. The conflict, in simple words, may become regional, but the response, as I have said, continues to be country based.

I understand of course that to expand peacekeeping beyond a country's borders presents many political hurdles and problems of resources. Sierra Leone is itself a good example of the difficulties encountered by a large operation in an area of relatively low strategic interest, with uncertain prospects and high risks. However, the issue of insecurity spilling across borders from countries in conflict, and affecting areas hosting refugees in particular, should be examined and factored into strategies for such operations.

West Africa is a case in point, but the matter is broader and particularly serious in Africa – the Burundi, Congo and Angola conflicts, for instance, pose similar problems. Could peacekeepers in situations of refugee flows that might become "carriers" of instability be given a special, cross-border observatory mandate – in a word, to monitor areas hosting refugees *beyond* the borders of the country in which those peacekeepers operate? Refugee-hosting countries, of course, would have to agree, but it would be in their interest because this "expanded" concept of peacekeeping could address some of their own concerns in terms of security and stability.

Had this form of support been available in, say, West Timor, the events of September 2000 could perhaps have been avoided. Such an arrangement would also have been useful in the former Eastern Zaire in 1994–1996; and some of the subsequent violence and instability could possibly have been prevented.

Peacebuilding needs more attention

Let me now turn to the second important area – peacebuilding. For years UNHCR has been saying that, unless more attention is devoted to the consolidation of institutions and communities after conflict, peace will not hold. UNHCR, of course, has a very special interest in this process because of its mission to ensure that refugees return home and settle down in safety and dignity. And it has had very difficult experiences in countries emerging from conflict, with large numbers of people returning and resources rapidly dwindling after emergencies have subsided – as in Rwanda, Liberia and Bosnia, just to mention a few examples.

The focus on peacebuilding truly makes the Brahimi Panel report very complete. Once more, however, we should shift into operational mode and look at how we can be as comprehensive in action as we are on paper. From the perspective of the UN refugee agency, the problem, as I have said many times, is that it does not have the resources, or indeed the expertise, to run development programmes; and yet development agencies are slow to come once emergencies have ended. There is a gap between emergency, short-term humanitarian activities and the implementation of medium- to long-term development and reconstruction programmes. During this gap, societies can unravel again very easily and conflicts re-start.

I have personally made efforts to coordinate a joint initiative with two key international development partners of UNHCR – the World Bank and the UN Development Programme (UNDP). This initiative, which was launched in January 1999 under the auspices of the Brookings Institution, has become known as the "Brookings process". UNHCR aimed in particular at filling the gap in funding and the gap in responsibilities and operations. In some countries the agency has initiated interesting and creative projects, for example with the World Bank in war-affected areas of Sri Lanka. In others, such as Sierra Leone, it has made proposals for pilot projects involving all three agencies. UNHCR is now examining opportunities elsewhere – Burundi would be a possibility if a peace agreement is eventually implemented. For its part, UNHCR has made great efforts. But the response by governments and organisations has been very timid, and raising funds for post-conflict activities is still a very difficult and uncertain exercise. I remain disappointed by the limited response to UNHCR's work in this area.

For UNHCR, peacebuilding is not an abstract concept. It sees the concrete, sometimes desperate needs of returnees in devastated areas or in areas where communities continue to be deeply divided. It is doing its part to address these needs. In the 1980s, UNHCR initiated "quick impact projects" for emergency rehabilitation in areas of return. In some places, it was criticised for having gone beyond its mission; but in countries such as Rwanda, for example, could it have afforded to withdraw when returnees still lived under plastic sheeting or when schools had no roofs, books or teachers?

UNHCR is now going further and exploring new avenues, particularly in the promotion of community coexistence as a first step towards reconciliation. It has launched a pilot project in returnee areas of Rwanda and Bosnia, called "Imagine Coexistence". The project consists essentially of support to small, community-based inter-ethnic income-generating activities, around which UNHCR would like to build clusters of other activities branching off into the community – sports, theatre, culture, dialogue. This is one of the innovative approaches that UNHCR is taking. But its impact, once again, will be limited, unless there are more rapid and comprehensive efforts towards peacebuilding at various levels.

One crucial issue, which I would like to mention before concluding, is that of disarmament, demobilisation and reintegration (DDR). UNHCR is particularly anxious that effective DDR contributes to the creation of a safe environment for refugees returning home. Without any doubt, DDR is also one of the areas in which UNHCR expects more decisive action by the Security Council. In their great potential and in the obstacles that undermine them, DDR programmes reflect all the contradictions of peacebuilding.

Two problems need to be addressed in particular. First, the roles and responsibilities of all actors involved in DDR-related activities must be clarified. Second, there must be a stronger focus on reintegration, because disarmed and demobilised soldiers, if they are not given opportunities for a future, will go back to more lucrative military activities. These are not small matters, and, unless they are addressed seriously, little progress will be achieved in this important area.

Establishing security partnerships for refugees

The past 10 years have proven that, if humanitarian operations are not part of a comprehensive political and security approach, they are less effective, or even risk aggravating humanitarian crises and exposing the workers to dangers. What must be established, at different levels, are what UNHCR would call "security partnerships for refugees" – joint ventures among states hosting refugees, those ready to provide resources, and international humanitarian organisations and NGOs. Through active dialogue among a wide range of partners, we must find practical ways to contain insecurity linked to refugee crises, improve peace operations and focus more decisively on peacebuilding.

Part 7
Transition to civil order

16
Disarmament and reintegration of combatants

Samuel M. Makinda

The "compleat diplomat" of the future should remain cognizant of realism's emphasis on the inescapable role of power, keep liberalism's awareness of domestic forces in mind, and occasionally reflect on constructivism's vision of change – *Stephen M. Walt*[1]

In recent years, policy makers and commentators concerned with managing intrastate conflicts or "repairing" the so-called disrupted states have suggested formulas that involve the disarmament, demobilisation and reintegration of combatants. These measures have been considered vital not only for helping to settle internal armed conflicts, but also for significantly reducing military expenditures and allowing scarce resources to be redirected towards civil projects. In other words, it has been assumed that disarmament, demobilisation and reintegration are important for state-building, economic reconstruction, the conversion of "swords into ploughshares", the reduction of religious or ethnic tensions, peacebuilding and development in general. Ultimately, these processes are considered necessary for security. In this chapter, I define security as the protection of the people and the preservation of their norms, values, institutions, interests and resources in the face of military and non-military threats.[2]

Stephen Walt's statement above, which calls for an eclectic or pluralist theoretical approach to understanding world problems, appears to have some relevance for the policies and strategies that incorporate the disarmament, demobilisation and reintegration of ex-combatants in civil wars or disrupted states. There is no clinical definition of a disrupted, failed or collapsed state. However, policy makers and commentators often use these terms interchangeably to refer to countries that have experienced or may be experiencing different levels of governance problems.[3] Although I recognise that the international community has a moral responsibility to help its poorer members, these terms partly stem from the mistaken belief that all states, regardless of time and geographical region, are expected to exhibit similar characteristics.

In this chapter, I critique the logic, assumptions and methodologies that have been used since the 1990s to justify disarmament and reintegration of combatants in civil strife, and provide a framework for rethinking these measures. To do so I have divided the rest of this chapter into four sections. In the first section, I address theoretical issues, pointing out that realists, liberals, constructivists and feminists view disarmament and reintegration differently. In the second, I outline the conventional approach to disarmament and reintegration, using Somalia and Cambodia as case studies. I argue that very often the international community does not ask the right questions before undertaking these measures. In the third section I use Robert Cox's ideas on problem-solving and critical theories to make observations about what has often been underestimated or ignored by those charged with the responsibility of managing disarmament and reintegration. In the fourth section, I conclude by suggesting what I believe needs to be done, pointing out that disarmament and reintegration processes would have yielded significantly different results if they had been centred around the norms, values, interests and institutions of the peoples and the societies in question. The message of this chapter is that there is no magic formula for disarmament and reintegration, and that those charged with implementing this process have to keep asking questions that will enable them to understand better the societies that they have the responsibility to serve.

Theoretical perspectives

The four theoretical perspectives employed in this chapter – realism, liberalism, constructivism and feminism – consist of competing research programmes, but here I will treat them as if they represented one tradition each.[4]

From the realist perspective, the need for disarmament stems from the significance of military power and the use of force in settling political and other disputes. Realist accounts of world politics are predicated on war and its consequences. They emphasise state power, territorial integrity, national interests and state survival. Realism posits that the most important global actors are sovereign states, which are rational and operate in a competitive, anarchic and self-help environment.[5] However, applying realism to a civil war somewhat overstretches the realists' conception of military power. The realism that Stephen Walt and other international relations realists have in mind deals specifically with problems of anarchy and military force outside, not inside, the state.[6] Nevertheless, the disarming of freelance or unattached militias and other subnational groups, in particular, highlights an important normative principle of realism. It helps portray the state not only as the dominant actor on the world stage, but also as a unitary actor that has, or should have, a monopoly of legitimate violence within its territory. It is mainly as a unitary actor that the state can best pursue its "national" interest in an anarchic and self-help international system. Thus the pursuit of disarmament and reintegration in disrupted states, to a certain extent, may help reinforce the state-centrism inherent in the realist conception of international affairs.

Contrary to realist claims, liberals posit that anarchy can be mediated and the "heterogeneous state of peace and war" can "become a state of global peace, in which the expectation of war disappears".[7] Indeed, from the liberal point of view, disarmament, demobilisation and reintegration suggest that progress and change are always possible. The fact that former enemies can integrate or reintegrate and cooperate suggests that it is always useful to emphasise the positive or optimistic view of human motivations and interests. Moreover, reintegration creates the possibility of former enemies engaging in "collaborative and cooperative social action", which may result "in greater benefits for everybody".[8] These measures are considered vital in the attainment of peace, the reconstruction of political communities and the spread of desirable values such as democracy and the rule of law. The disarmament and reintegration of combatants suggest that war and conflict in society are not inevitable, and that human reason can triumph over fear. Disarmament, demobilisation and reintegration may also facilitate humanitarian intervention.[9] Moreover, the integration or reintegration of ex-combatants demonstrates both the acceptance of the existing structures and institutions of law, order and power within a society, and the resolution of problems of cooperation at the national level.

Whereas realists and liberals privilege material forces, with the liberals tacking ideas onto the material base, constructivists argue that structures of human association "are determined primarily by shared ideas rather than material forces".[10] From the constructivist perspective, disarmament, demobilisation and reintegration are primarily ideas and only secondarily material forces. Disarmament and reintegration therefore touch on what constructivists see as the vital causal and constitutive questions in the reconstruction of society. It is assumed that they impinge on interests, identities, social structures and processes, and thus impact on societal change.[11] For instance, constructivists would be interested in the two-way process demonstrating how the Khmer Rouge have helped create the social structures in which their friends, competitors and enemies are embedded, and how these friends, competitors and enemies have, in turn, constituted the identity of the Khmer Rouge. They would, for instance, emphasise the fact that the name "Khmer Rouge" conjures up the image of terror, genocide and obstruction to the UN authorities. In other words, constructivists would assume that, in a conflict such as that which obtained in Cambodia from the early 1980s to the early 1990s, there is likely to be a structure of understandings between the main protagonists, such as between the Khmer Rouge and their competitors and rivals. It is also assumed that this social structure was constructed by – and continues to reproduce the identities and interests of – both sides. Therefore, for constructivists, the relationship between social structures, actors or agents and social processes is extremely important.

Disarmament, demobilisation and reintegration are also seen differently from a feminist perspective. Feminist thinkers are interested in shedding light on how gender issues have been understood, calculated and configured in disarmament, demobilisation and reintegration.[12] For instance, following UN Security Council resolution 1325 on women, peace and security, women's groups convened several meetings in Berne, London, Nairobi and other places to work out strategies for gender-sensitive early warning of conflicts. Feminists believe that a gender perspective is useful in providing a better understanding of unequal social hierarchies and identifying ways in which violent conflict, disarmament and reintegration affect men and women differently.

Although those who design strategies for peacebuilding or for international intervention of one kind or another do not pose and ask themselves what theoretical approach they should adopt, they very often non-self-consciously apply theory. I have no reason to assume that one theoretical framework is better than the other, but I believe that a team of peacebuilders, equipped with insights from all the major theoretical frameworks, would make a great difference. Such a team is likely to be more prepared to listen to and accommodate the interests of those they are required to serve. Accommodating the perspectives and interests of those who need help is the best way to approach disarmament and reintegration in failing or failed states.[13]

Conventional approaches

Disarmament, demobilisation and reintegration measures have been attempted in different countries, with varying degrees of success. In conventional literature, disarmament refers to the reduction, elimination or surrender of weapons and ammunitions. Demobilisation is described as a form of disarmament, because, as Mats Berdal suggests, it refers to "the formal disbanding of military formations", including "the process of releasing combatants from a mobilised state".[14] Integration and reintegration, on the other hand, refer to the process of retraining and social absorption of ex-combatants and their families into non-military, and especially income-generating, activities; it is basically a return to civilian life. However, there is so much overlap among the three processes that in this chapter I will refer mainly to disarmament and reintegration.

Using standard or "conventional" approaches, disarmament and reintegration measures have been tried, for example, in Bosnia, Cambodia, Eritrea, Ethiopia, Kosovo, Mozambique, Namibia, Northern Ireland and Somalia, among others. The reasons for the failure or success of these measures have been partly specific factors in the disrupted or "failing" states themselves, but they have also included the misguided perspectives as well as the poor policies and strategies of the international community. The existence of a "comprehensive political settlement" did not determine or guarantee success. For example, the parties in Cambodia, Mozambique, Namibia and Northern Ireland reached what the international community described as comprehensive political settlements. However, the fates of disarmament and reintegration differed widely in these theatres. In the case of Bosnia, Kosovo and Somalia, disarmament was imposed by external powers,[15] but the end result was not the same. What has been clear is that different ways of bringing about an end to hostilities appear to have given rise to different expectations.

In the majority of cases of civil war or disrupted states, the international community, usually led by Western powers, has expected to achieve a wide range of goals and objectives through the processes of disarmament and reintegration. These objectives have included the reduction of the sizes of armed forces and of weapons in circulation; the amalgamation of some of the ex-combatants into a single and "legitimate" military force structure; and the delegitimation of the militias and other armed groups in the state. The ultimate goal of disarmament and reintegration has been the reduction of military expenditures, the reallocation of scarce resources more "rationally" and the forging of new and "legitimate" social structures and processes.

The process of addressing disrupted or failed states is one in which the West has assumed the "responsibility" of reconstructing some developing countries.[16] As I have already indicated, in some cases disarmament and reintegration were proposed in Western capitals without their proponents asking vital questions about the states or societies in question. This was the hallmark of conventional approaches. It was as if the international community or the United Nations had not given much thought to how armaments determine, and are, in turn, determined by, the shape, intensity and durability of political conflicts. Let me illustrate this by explaining briefly how disarmament and reintegration strategies were designed and implemented in the early 1990s in two different situations: Somalia and Cambodia.[17] In Somalia, what appeared like "peace" was merely a charade imposed by the international community prior to the main parties reaching an agreement, whereas in Cambodia the warring parties themselves (and their sponsors) reached a political settlement after nearly a decade of negotiations. The integration or reintegration of ex-combatants in these countries was not accomplished because the disarmament process, which would have led to integration, did not succeed.

Case study 1: Somalia

Following the fall from power of former dictator Siad Barre in January 1991, Somalia was immediately plunged into chaos. Most clans and their institutions remained intact. However, in the space between clans (at the bottom) and the international community (at the top) there was no peace, order or security. Instead, there was widespread anarchy throughout Somalia, with armed militias killing their perceived competitors or rivals, terrorising everyone else, looting and extorting international relief agencies. The violence was widespread largely because there were huge amounts of weapons in the country, which had originated in the 1970s and 1980s from the Soviet Union, the United States and Europe. The United Nations and all diplomatic missions closed shop in 1991 and fled, but some non-governmental agencies remained behind to provide relief. By 1992, when the United Nations decided to return to Somalia on humanitarian grounds, the armed militias and clan-based political factions had made it extremely hard for international relief agencies to reach those in need of help. There was no government, no national army, no police force, no national currency, and no functioning public institutions such as banks, hospitals and schools. In other words, Somalia was not even a "disrupted" state. It had lost any semblance of a state.

By the late 1990s, one could argue that anarchy within the country and the militias had in effect "killed" Somalia, preventing it from participating in the affairs of international society. If we were to define a state as "an organizational actor embedded in an institutional-legal order that constitutes it with sovereignty and a monopoly on the legitimate use of organized violence over a society in a territory",[18] Somalia has lost the main characteristics of a state. It has no capacity to protect its people or territory. It has no institutional structure through which it can act either domestically or internationally as a unitary actor. It has no capacity to send out or receive diplomats. And many of "its" people, who have tried to establish their own "new" states on "its" territory, do not see themselves as belonging to an entity called Somalia. The self-declared "republics" of Somaliland and Puntland are an indication of how difficult it will be to re-establish a united Somalia along the 1960 boundary lines. However, the international society continues to recognise Somalia as a sovereign state. Indeed, Somalia has illustrated that a state does not "exist", "die" or "disappear" unless the hegemonic states, which claim to speak on behalf of international society, say so. All that Somalia, as an entity, represented in 2001 were lines on a map. The United Nations and the international community in general made three attempts to resuscitate the Somali state in the 1990s, but they failed.

The first UN Operation in Somalia (UNOSOM I) was a lightly armed traditional peacekeeping force. It lasted from May 1992 to November 1992, but it was largely ineffective in the face of opposition from well-armed militias. The militias and the leaders of the more than 14 organised factions or subnational military formations prevented UNOSOM I from operating because they were benefiting from the chaos in the country. The first Special Representative of the UN Secretary-General, Mohamed Sahnoun, did not entertain any idea of disarming factions, so the UN Secretary-General Boutros Boutros-Ghali did not insist on it.

However, stung by the opposition UNOSOM I faced from the militias, and in the face of large numbers of Somalis dying from disease and starvation (the so-called CNN effect), Boutros-Ghali persuaded US President George Bush to help. After all, it was President Bush who had earlier described the immediate post–Cold War era as a new world order "where the rule of law supplants the rule of the jungle, a world in which nations recognize the shared responsibility for freedom and justice".[19] President Bush agreed to lend a hand, and this resulted in a US-led Unified Task Force (UNITAF) or Operation Restore Hope. UNITAF, which lasted from December 1992 to April 1993, was an enforcement operation established under Chapter VII of the UN Charter. With the mandate to use all necessary means to open relief supply routes and create a safe environment for humanitarian activities, UNITAF brought some calm to about 40 per cent of Somalia.[20]

In a letter to President Bush on 8 December 1992, Boutros-Ghali suggested that UNITAF should ensure that, before it withdrew, it had neutralised and brought under international control all the heavy weapons of the organised factions. He also urged it to disarm gangs and freelance militias. However, the US commander of UNITAF, Lieutenant-General Roger Johnston, refused to undertake comprehensive disarmament, arguing that it was not part of his mission.[21] Some contingents within UNITAF attempted disarmament, but it was only partial. Berdal argues that such "efforts ... remained patchy in scope, poorly organized and confused in implementation".[22] Boutros-Ghali believed that, since Security Council resolution 794, which authorised UNITAF, had called for the establishment of a "secure environment", it envisaged comprehensive disarmament. There was indeed an expectation that UNITAF would try to control or confine the Somali military formations and militias. However, as Berdal observes, there is "no automatic or inherent relationship between the process of disarmament and the creation of a secure environment".[23] While the UN Secretary-General and the UNITAF commander were debating the efficacy of disarmament, the Somali militias, who understood UNITAF to be a temporary operation, hid their weapons until after it had left. This disagreement over disarmament delayed the transfer of power from UNITAF to UNOSOM II.

After UNITAF's departure, the second UN Operation in Somalia (UNOSOM II) was deployed from May 1993 to March 1995. UNOSOM II was the first ever enforcement operation to be directed and commanded by the office of the UN Secretary-General. Security Council resolution 814 of March 1993, which authorised UNOSOM II, recognised the "fundamental importance of a comprehensive and effective programme for disarming Somali parties, including movements and factions". As expected, UNOSOM II attempted some disarmament measures, but they were undertaken in a haphazard manner, with the result that there was no comprehensive disarmament. Indeed, it was UNOSOM II's attempt to disarm one faction, led by General Mohamed Farah Aideed, in June 1993 that led to military clashes in Mogadishu in which 23 UNOSOM II soldiers and hundreds of Somalis were killed. I argued then, and still believe, that "UNITAF's failure to disarm factions and gunmen [was] largely to blame for the military clashes between UNOSOM II forces and Somalis".[24] However, the haphazard disarmament measures that UNOSOM II undertook meant that some groups, which were disarmed, faced great danger from those groups that were still armed. The disarmed groups increasingly found it hard to secure food and other supplies for their people. Although widespread anarchy in Somalia was to blame for most of the problems that UNOSOM II faced, the UN force was also mismanaged. When UNOSOM II was withdrawn in March 1995, it had not attained its primary objectives.[25]

Disarmament efforts in Somalia raised important questions, which the United Nations did not address. Without the minimum conditions for peace, order and security, it was not clear who was to benefit from the haphazard disarmament undertaken. Disarmament was pursued without consent from the parties involved, and this immediately raised doubts about their cooperation with UN authorities. Given the fact that the state in Somalia did not exist, it was not clear what the disarmed groups were expected to do. Indeed, without a resolution to the issue of Somalia's statehood, disarmament appears to have been misplaced.

Case study 2: Cambodia

Compared with Somalia, the Cambodian state remained far more intact despite the protracted civil war. All four political/military factions of the civil war signed the 1991 Paris Peace Agreement: the State of Cambodia (SOC)/Cambodian People's Party (CPP), with Hun Sen as Prime Minister and Heng Samrin as President; the royalist FUNCINPEC, led by Prince Norodom Ranariddh; Son Sann's Khmer People's National Liberation Front (KPNLF); and the Khmer Rouge (Cambodian Reds) or the Party of Democratic Kampuchea (PDK), nominally led by Khieu Samphan, but in reality controlled by Pol Pot. An estimated 1.7 million Cambodians died during the rule of the fanatical Khmer Rouge from 1975 until January 1979, when an invading Vietnamese force drove them out and installed the Heng Samrin regime. For more than a decade the surviving Khmer Rouge and the two non-communist factions (FUNCINPEC and KPNLF) had fought against the Heng Samrin regime, which, officially until 1989, was supported by Vietnamese troops, advisers and financing.

The four factions, which have sometimes existed under different names, had unequal armed forces, in number of personnel and weapons. The largest military formation was SOC/CPP's, which far outnumbered the second largest, the Khmer Rouge. While SOC/CPP controlled the largest portion of the country, the Khmer Rouge and non-communist factions had full or partial control of the west, north-west and northern areas, which border Thailand from where they received their supplies.

The United Nations Transitional Authority in Cambodia (UNTAC) arrived in Phnom Penh in March 1992, mandated by the Security Council to disarm the soldiers, repatriate the refugees, control the administration and run an election. UNTAC had to repatriate an estimated 360,000 refugees from camps in Thailand and help resettle 700,000 refugees, internally displaced persons and demobilised soldiers. The difficulties of resettlement were compounded by the wide spread of landmines and by SOC/CPP's reluctance to hand over arable, non-mined land to the returning refugees.

UNTAC was required to disarm more than 200,000 soldiers of the four factions and 250,000 SOC/CPP militia members. UNTAC was to assemble the soldiers in 82 pre-designated cantonment sites throughout the country, disarm them all and demobilise at least 70 per cent of them.

The Khmer Rouge incrementally reneged on its undertakings under the Paris Peace Agreement, beginning with its refusal to disarm, mark mine fields and disclose troop details. Hoping the Khmer Rouge would eventually comply, UNTAC proceeded with cantoning and disarming the forces of the other three factions, and in the first month more than 50,000 soldiers, plus SOC's navy and airforce, had been surrendered to the United Nations.[26] However, the intransigence deepened: the Khmer Rouge refused the United Nations access to areas under its control, fired at UN aircraft and held hostage UN personnel and equipment. In the face of the Khmer Rouge's continued non-cooperation, UNTAC suspended the disarming process and later authorised the armies of the other three factions to protect polling stations against expected Khmer Rouge attacks on the electoral process.

The Khmer Rouge's two most ardent demands were that UNTAC guarantee that no Vietnamese soldiers or advisers remained in Cambodia masquerading as civilians, and that UNTAC dismantle the SOC administration. UNTAC did its best to address the Khmer Rouge's concerns on the first point, but said the second was inconsistent with the Paris Agreement and to act on it could cause "chaos".[27] The Khmer Rouge had a valid point: that UNTAC was mandated to control the five key areas that could influence the election (defence, interior, finance, foreign affairs and information) and failed to control these spheres fully. UNTAC could not get on top of the political, military, institutional and "knowledge" power of SOC/CPP, partly because it did not understand the SOC/CPP system. The SOC/CPP, which had established administrative control over much of the country with the help of its Vietnamese backers and had consolidated its power base in the subsequent 13 years, was simply too powerful for UNTAC and for the other factions.[28] UNTAC comprised foreigners who came into the country, most for the first time and for a short period, and who had little knowledge or comprehension of the complex sociocultural aspects of the country, least of all the political structures of SOC, a deficiency subsequently noted by the then UN Secretary-General.[29]

The SOC/CPP, which ruled by fear and favour, the latter being an element of patronage that remained entrenched in the Cambodian culture, was able to manipulate, cohere, obstruct and sometimes intimidate the administration officials, other groups and UNTAC personnel.[30] The starting point for the SOC/CPP was its adherence to sharing political and military power with its rivals. From that starting point, the SOC/CPP then used its pervasive power to maintain as much of its administrative control as possible.

The ultimate objective of UNTAC was to introduce a democratic system that would effect power-sharing in a peaceful environment. Disarmament and the building of a new armed force with ex-combatants of the four factions were envisaged as part of the peaceful, power-sharing strategies.

The key obstacle to the disarmament and reintegration of ex-combatants in Cambodia was the Khmer Rouge's refusal to cooperate with the peace process. The basis for the Khmer Rouge's non-compliance was its perceived failure of UNTAC to control the SOC/CPP administration. UNTAC's inability to control the SOC/CPP administration stems from its failure to understand fast enough the structures, processes and implications of that power and the extent to which the SOC/CPP controlled the structures of society, from the government in Phnom Penh, through the provinces and districts, to the village level.[31]

The Khmer Rouge's refusal to disarm and demobilise made them the main obstructors to the peace process. It also provided UNTAC with something to blame for its weaknesses. Lee Kim and Metrikas have blamed the Khmer Rouge's refusal to cooperate with UNTAC partly on the delayed deployment of the UN operation.[32] The Khmer Rouge used slow deployment as an *excuse* not to cooperate. From there on, the influence and power of the Khmer Rouge lay in its knowledge of how to generate fear among the Cambodians, and particularly among the ethnic Vietnamese in Cambodia.

UNTAC's failure to disarm Cambodian military formations in accordance with the UN resolution reflected the power equation that UNTAC was not able to alter. This indirectly gave the Khmer Rouge an opportunity not to comply; hence disarmament had to be abandoned. CPP's undented power has continued to be a dominant feature of Cambodian politics. As Sue Downie argues, the 1998 Cambodian elections were largely influenced by the problems that the United Nations had left unresolved in 1993.[33]

Observations

The Somali and Cambodian cases illustrate that the conventional approach to disarmament has been pursued mainly from what Robert Cox has described as a "problem-solving" rather than a "critical" perspective. A problem-solving perspective corresponds with the realist and liberal theories, whereas the critical perspective corresponds with some aspects of constructivist and feminist theories, which I discussed earlier in this chapter. Cox has argued that a problem-solving formula generally "takes the world as it finds it, with the prevailing social and power relationships and the institutions into which they are organized, as the given framework for action".[34] That is largely how the mandates of UNITAF, UNOSOM II and UNTAC envisaged the process of disarmament in Somalia and Cambodia.

Cox has further argued that the "aim of problem-solving is to make [the existing power] relationships and institutions work smoothly by dealing effectively with particular sources of trouble".[35] The problem-solving approach can be useful in some circumstances, especially because it can "fix limits or parameters to a problem area". However, part of its weakness is that it fails to take account of the interconnections between different spheres of public life, and may therefore fall short of providing a viable solution to a problem. In Somalia, and to a certain extent in Cambodia, the UN mandates did not envisage disarmament as an integral part of the whole process of peacebuilding or state-building. That is why, for instance, the UNITAF commander in Somalia could argue that disarmament was not a part of the requirement to establish a "secure environment" in the country.

To deal with some of the problems of disarmament effectively, a peacebuilding operation would need to combine insights from problem-solving and critical perspectives. A critical perspective, according to Cox, "does not take institutions and social and power relations for granted but calls them into question by concerning itself with their origins and how and whether they might be in the process of changing".[36] A critical perspective can open up extra possibilities for action in the processes of disarmament because it "is directed to the social and political complex as a whole rather than to the separate parts".[37] Comparing the problem-solving and critical perspectives, Cox has argued:

[W]hereas the problem-solving approach leads to further analytical subdivision and limitation of the issue to be dealt with, the critical approach leads toward the construction of a larger picture of the whole of which the initially contemplated part is just one component, and seeks to understand the processes of change in which both parts and whole are involved.[38]

It is by combining insights from the two perspectives that a peacebuilding or peacemaking operation can appreciate more clearly the important fact that disarmament is essentially a social and political process, not a technical or managerial issue. In Somalia, for example, a critical perspective would have called into question the idea of imposing a centralised state structure on a fragmented society. Unlike Cambodia, Somalia, with its boundaries as they were in 1991, had existed only since 1960. A critical perspective would have led to considerations of alternative political communities in Somalia.[39] In Cambodia, the problem-solving formula gave rise to the assumption that, once the political settlement had been reached and agreements signed, implementation would follow logically. A critical perspective would have led to a more serious consideration of the workings and implications of the SOC/CPP power structures vis-à-vis the power of other factions. A critical perspective would, for instance, have anticipated the wider implications of the Khmer Rouge's refusal to cooperate with UNTAC, which meant peace and four-party power-sharing did not eventuate. Indeed, the civil war continued, in that the post-UNTAC government had to fight against Khmer Rouge for several years before persuading the remnants to defect. Unfortunately, peacekeeping planners and those implementing the mandates often take a best-case scenario attitude and do not sufficiently plan for the actions of non-compliant parties or belligerents.

A combination of insights from problem-solving and critical perspectives would enable those involved in the process of disarmament to appreciate the fact that this process is predicated on simultaneous and parallel political, social and economic reconstruction. The two perspectives would help us understand that implementation of a peace process is not merely a matter of financial resources and technical arrangements. Financial resources and technical arrangements are vital, but they are second-order priorities. The relationship or interplay between disarmament, on one side, and political, social and economic reconstruction, on the other, is at the core of any successful peacebuilding or peacemaking project.

By combining the two perspectives, peacebuilders and disarmament advocates can best appreciate why disarmament requires the climate of trust and confidence that it does. Generating trust and confidence among former enemies is a long-term process that is anchored in political, social, economic and psychological factors. It requires the transformation of political and military enemies and rivals into friends and partners, of outsiders into insiders, and of "them" into "us". It requires the complex redefinition of the political and security environment, so that actions previously associated with fear can generate hope and confidence. This perspective was virtually absent in attempts to achieve disarmament in Somalia. Although ardent attempts were made to bring the factions together in Cambodia, through the four-party Supreme National Council and Mixed Military Working Group, ultimately they were not sufficient to persuade the Khmer Rouge to join the peace process. Moreover, any attempt to achieve disarmament should be done at the same time as efforts are made to address the root causes of conflict. Indeed, it is essential that disarmament and reintegration be incorporated in the overall process of resolving the root causes of conflict. The consequences of failure to do this include resumption of conflict.

This is largely because the problems that caused conflict or war do not go away simply because the parties in question have agreed on a political settlement. The differences between the Khmer Rouge and SOC/CPP could not disappear overnight because of a political settlement, although the two non-communist parties were able to join CPP in a coalition "government of national reconciliation". However, grievances and conflicts of interest between the two main factions persisted long after the formal settlement was reached, and these continued to exert pressure on the politics and the process of peacebuilding, including disarmament.

Another important factor that has often been underestimated or ignored is the legacy of war and conflict. Those charged with the responsibility of achieving disarmament have sometimes failed to take into consideration the fact that civil war and strife, and the concomitant arms, leave behind significant and complex socio-psychological and economic legacies, which need to be addressed. For example, Somalia and Cambodia have many people whose lives have been dominated by fighting, looting, extorting or defying formal authority. Problems such as these can be addressed effectively only if the approach to disarmament takes account of other aspects of society. Hence the need to draw insights from both the problem-solving and critical perspectives.

Those involved in the peacebuilding, peacemaking and disarmament processes would also do well not to see the soldiers and other fighters as atomistic individuals seeking their own glory or satisfaction in isolation. These fighters see themselves as belonging to particular communities. They give loyalty to these communities and define themselves and their goals by the rules, values and codes of these communities. Anyone familiar with the political terrain in Somalia would know that the parties to the conflict were often driven by deep clan ties and other social identities and the interests that underpin them, and these interests and identities could not be swept away overnight.

Conclusion

In dealing with disarmament and reintegration, we are constantly required to address several questions almost simultaneously. For example, are we dealing with ideas such as identities, interests and institutions, or only material factors such as weapons and soldiers, or both? Soldiers and weapons are material factors, and we can approach them as such if we utilise a problem-solving perspective, but this will not yield sufficient information, in some situations, to enable us to take meaningful action vis-à-vis long-term peace and development. Soldiers and armed formations may be regarded as agents or actors, but these agents are constituted by social structures and processes. From a critical perspective, we should regard soldiers and weapons as part of the processes and institutions in which they are embedded. If we separate them from the structures, processes, interests, values and institutions that constitute them, we isolate them and ultimately mislead ourselves. If we isolate or reify them, we may canton them, confine them or remove them from particular locations, but we shall still leave the structures and values that constituted them intact.

Another question that we may ask ourselves is: what do we want to achieve? Do we want to achieve security, democracy or development? In many Third World states, these three are inseparable. If we want to attain security, then what constitutes security for the individuals, organisations and societies in a particular situation? Let us assume that, for the people of Cambodia or East Timor, security at the beginning of the twenty-first century simply means their own protection as a people, and the preservation of their norms, rules, interests, institutions and values in the face of military and non-military threats. This view of security is consistent with the need to preserve the state, as well as the structures, principles and institutions on which the state is anchored, but only to the extent that protection of the boundaries and governing structures is not privileged over the people. Defined in this manner, security may be diminished or enhanced by disarmament, depending on the particular circumstances.

Therefore, any effort to design disarmament and reintegration strategies needs to take account of the fact that this process is a part of a wider long-term attempt to create the necessary political, economic, social and psychological environment for decent life. Disarmament and reintegration touch not only on the identities and interests of individuals, but also on politics, the economy and social life. We need to recognise that for individual combatants, disarmament requires the abandonment of both their professions and ways of life. For some people, a weapon is not just a means for attaining security. Weapons have economic, political and social dimensions.[40]

Finally, weapons and soldiers have significance and effect largely, but not exclusively, because of the meanings, values and understandings that we attach to them. The East Timorese in 1999, for example, were frightened of weapons in the hands of Indonesian troops; but the same, or similar, weapons in the hands of Australian troops reassured them and inspired hope and confidence in them. Therefore, in designing strategies for the disarmament and reintegration of ex-combatants, we should always bear in mind the fact that we are dealing with ideas, culture and identity, in addition to material objects.

Acknowledgements

I am grateful to Ian Cook, Melissa Curley, Sue Downie, Stuart Latter and an anonymous referee for useful comments on earlier versions of this chapter. Sue Downie's ideas were especially critical in the section on Cambodia.

Notes

1. Stephen M. Walt, "International Relations: One World, Many Theories", *Foreign Policy*, no. 110, Spring 1998, pp. 29–46 at p. 44.
2. See Samuel M. Makinda, *From Natural Resources to National Wealth: Ethical, National Interest and Policy Issues for Africa in the New Millennium* (Tokyo and Accra: United Nations University Institute for Natural Resources in Africa, 2001), p. 50; and Robert Jackson, *The Global Covenant* (Oxford: Oxford University Press, 2000), pp. 185–215.
3. For an interesting and insightful explanation of disrupted, failed and dysfunctional states, see Nii Lante Wallace-Bruce, "Of Collapsed, Dysfunctional and Disoriented States: Challenges to International Law", *Netherlands International Law Review*, vol. 47, no. 1, 2000, pp. 53–73; and Amin Saikal's chapter in this book.
4. Other theoretical perspectives such as critical social theory, International Society (or English School), postmodernism and poststructuralism would also have something to say about disarmament and reintegration, but owing to space constraints I cannot address them in this essay.
5. Michael Mastanduno, "Preserving the Unipolar Moment: Realist Theories and US Grand Strategy after the Cold War", *International Security*, vol. 21, no. 4, Spring 1997, pp. 49–88; and Kenneth W. Waltz, *Theory of International Politics* (Reading, MA: Addison-Wesley, 1979).
6. See also John J. Mearsheimer, "The False Promise of International Institutions", *International Security*, vol. 19, no. 3, Winter 1994–95, pp. 5–49; and Stephen M. Walt, "The Renaissance of Security Studies", *International Studies Quarterly*, vol. 35, no. 2, June 1991, pp. 211–239.
7. Michael W. Doyle, *Ways of War and Peace* (New York: W. W. Norton and Co., 1997), p. 210.
8. Robert Jackson and Georg Sorensen, *Introduction to International Relations* (Oxford: Oxford University Press, 1999), p. 109.
9. For some of the best literature on humanitarian action, see N. J. Wheeler, *Saving Strangers: Humanitarian Intervention in International Society* (Oxford: Oxford University Press, 2000); F. K. Abiew, *The Evolution of the Doctrine and Practice of Humanitarian Intervention* (The Hague: Kluwer Law International, 1999); Larry Minear and Thomas G. Weiss, *Mercy under Fire: War and the Global Humanitarian Community* (Boulder, CO: Westview Press, 1995); Oliver Ramsbotham and Tom Woodhouse, *Humanitarian Intervention in Contemporary Conflict: A Reconceptualization* (Cambridge: Polity Press, 1996); and Adam Roberts, *Humanitarian Action in War*, Adelphi Paper no. 305 (Oxford: Oxford University Press for the International Institute for Strategic Studies, 1996).
10. Alexander Wendt, *Social Theory of International Politics* (Cambridge: Cambridge University Press, 1999), p. 1.
11. Wendt, *Social Theory of International Politics*; and John G. Ruggie, *Constructing the World Polity* (London: Routledge, 1998).
12. For interesting perspectives on feminism, see, for instance, Christine Sylvester, "The Contributions of Feminist Theory to International Relations" in S. Smith, K. Booth and M. Zalewski (eds), *International Theory: Positivism and Beyond* (Cambridge: Cambridge University Press, 1996); Heidi Hudson, "Mainstreaming Gender in Peacekeeping Operations in Africa", paper presented at the International Conference on New African Perspectives, University of Western Australia, Perth, 26–28 November 1999; and J. Ann Tickner, "Re-visioning Security", in Ken Booth and Steve Smith (eds), *International Relations Theory Today* (Cambridge: Polity Press, 1995), pp. 175–197.
13. For more on "failed" states see, for example, I. William Zartman (ed.), *Collapsed*

States: The Disintegration and Restoration of Legitimate Authority (Boulder, CO: Lynne Rienner, 1995).
14. Mats Berdal, *Disarmament and Demobilisation after Civil Wars*, Adelphi Paper no. 303 (Oxford: Oxford University Press for the International Institute for Strategic Studies, 1996), p. 39.
15. Berdal, *Disarmament and Demobilisation after Civil Wars*.
16. See Jackson, *The Global Covenant*, pp. 294–315.
17. A referee of this book would have liked me to discuss a case where disarmament was successful. I know of two cases where it succeeded – Mozambique and Namibia – but their successes are not attributable to better strategies by the international community. Showing a case where there was success despite misguided international policies will not alter my thesis.
18. Wendt, *Social Theory of International Politics*, p. 213.
19. George Bush, "Toward a New World Order", US Department of State Dispatch, 17 September 1990, p. 91. See also Ramesh Thakur, "UN Peacekeeping in the New World Disorder", in R. Thakur and C. A. Thayer (eds), *A Crisis of Expectations: UN Peacekeeping in the 1990s* (Boulder, CO: Westview Press, 1995), pp. 3–22.
20. Kevin M. Kennedy, "The Relationship between the Military and Humanitarian Organizations in Operation Restore Hope", in Walter Clarke and Jeffrey Herbst (eds), *Learning from Somalia: The Lessons of Armed Humanitarian Intervention* (Boulder, CO: Westview Press, 1997), pp. 99–117.
21. Samuel M. Makinda, *Seeking Peace from Chaos: Humanitarian Intervention in Somalia* (Boulder, CO: Lynne Rienner, 1993), p. 71.
22. Berdal, *Disarmament and Demobilisation after Civil Wars*, p. 26.
23. Ibid., p. 24.
24. Makinda, *Seeking Peace from Chaos*, p. 72.
25. Jonathan T. Howe, "The United States and United Nations in Somalia: The Limits of Involvement", *Washington Quarterly*, vol. 18, no. 3, Summer 1995, pp. 49–62.
26. "Second Progress Report of the Secretary-General on UNTAC, 21 September 1992", reprinted in *The United Nations and Cambodia 1991–1995* (New York: UN Department of Public Information, 1995), p. 213; also UNTAC press briefings, Phnom Penh, 13 June and 27 June 1992.
27. "Second Progress Report of the Secretary-General on UNTAC, 21 September 1992"; also "Letter Dated 27 July 1992 from the SRSG for Cambodia to the Secretary-General Concerning the Situation in Cambodia", both reprinted in *The United Nations and Cambodia 1991–1995*, p. 211 and p. 206, respectively.
28. Sue Downie, "Cambodia's 1998 Election: Understanding Why It Was Not a 'Miracle on the Mekong'", *Australian Journal of International Affairs*, vol. 54, no. 1, April 2000, pp. 43–61.
29. Sue Downie, "The United Nations in East Timor: Comparisons with Cambodia", in Damien Kingsbury (ed.), *Guns and Ballot Boxes: East Timor's Vote for Independence* (Melbourne: Monash Asia Institute, 2000), p. 123.
30. Downie, "Cambodia's 1998 Election".
31. Downie, "The United Nations in East Timor", p. 123.
32. Cheryl M. Lee Kim and Mark Metrikas, "Holding a Fragile Peace: The Military and Civilian Components of UNTAC", in Michael W. Doyle, Ian Johnstone and Robert C. Orr (eds), *Keeping the Peace: Multidimensional UN Operations in Cambodia and El Salvador* (Cambridge: Cambridge University Press, 1997), pp. 107–133 at p. 124.
33. Downie, "Cambodia's 1998 Election".
34. Robert W. Cox, "Social Forces, States and World Orders: Beyond International Relations Theory", in Robert O. Keohane (ed.), *Neorealism and Its Critics* (New York: Columbia University Press, 1986), pp. 204–254 at p. 208.

35. Ibid.
36. Ibid.
37. Ibid.
38. Ibid., p. 209.
39. See also Samuel M. Makinda, "Clan Conflict and Factionalism in Somalia", in Paul B. Rich (ed.), *Warlords in International Relations* (London: Macmillan, 1999), pp. 120–139.
40. Berdal, *Disarmament and Demobilisation after Civil Wars*.
41. For a concise analysis of security in East Timor, see, for example, James Cotton, "Against the Grain: The East Timor Intervention", *Survival*, vol. 43, no. 1, Spring 2001, pp. 127–142.

17
Policing civil order

Adrien Whiddett

In essence there are two kinds of police: kin police, who exercise an authority bestowed by a consenting majority, and ruler-appointed police, who exercise an authority bestowed by a minority over the majority. Policing in Australia derives from kin police and its refinement organisationally since the founding in Great Britain in 1829 of the so-called "Modern Police".

Policing is one of the few vocations whose membership is required to swear an oath of office. In liberal societies the oath of office differs, but in effect police swear that they will do their duty without fear or favour, malice or ill-will. The intention is to put the rule of law and its impartial enforcement above any and all other interests, public or private. Thus, in the proper execution of their duty, police are independent officeholders. A number of important cases uphold this distinction and the Commonwealth Parliament has endorsed it.[1] Otherwise, however, police are accountable to the government and to the community in whose name consent to police is granted. Significantly, the Australian Federal Police Act 1979 draws out the distinction between operational and administrative responsibilities and accountability consistent with the principles outlined.

A former Commissioner of the Metropolitan Police, London, and architect of the Australian Federal Police, Sir Robert Mark, coined the phrase "policing by consent"[2] when referring to the philosophy of impartial and unobtrusive policing in a free society. This very apt phrase captures the crucial principle that police must maintain a relationship with the public which reaffirms that the police and the public are one and the same – that police are only members of the public who are paid to give their full attention to duties that are largely incumbent on every citizen. This last important principle is pivotal in the context of successful peacekeeping.

Policing a democracy is infinitely more demanding than policing a totalitarian state. In the liberal state it is a fundamental right that citizens may go about their lives and lawful affairs free from the undue interference of the state or its agents. The question of what are lawful and unlawful affairs is ultimately one for citizens and their elected representatives to decide; it is not a question for police, even though police may contribute to the development of public policy and law. There is also a rightful expectation that, where intrusion by the state in the lives of citizens occurs, it should be lawful, minimal and accountable to the very citizens in whose affairs the state has intruded. Because the more intrusive interference in the affairs of citizens is usually manifested by police, the authority and power to do so are finely balanced against the higher, inalienable rights and freedoms of the citizenry, and the lawful, independent police function should always be exercised exclusively for and on behalf of those citizens. The powers and responsibilities exercised by police are conditional and may be withdrawn more easily than they are granted. It is said that the best law is less law, and less law means less erosion of civil liberties. Therefore, although police often seek new law to deal more effectively with crime, this is not freely granted even if the arguments in favour are soundly based. The abuse of power by police, of course, is a singularly persuasive disincentive for governments to confer additional powers.

It is against this historical and constitutional background that Australian police, including the Australian Federal Police, discharge their duties to the law, government and the people. However, not all in the world are seized by the aforementioned high-minded ideal of consensual policing. The reality is that not all of the world's "police" are as Australians know them, nor are their actions as Australians would rightly demand and expect. In many countries the police and military are indistinguishable. Even the titles that describe function and suggest impartial, minimum force policing such as "security" or "public safety" have, in a grotesque Orwellian fashion, come to be synonymous with the oppression and sometimes butchery of the very people from whom these "policing" elements are drawn and whom they have undertaken to protect. I personally find it offensive that the word "police" is often used by the international media and other commentators to describe the various rag-tag militia and assortment of murderous rabble who are increasingly emerging in disrupted states and are exacting a terrible toll on ordinary citizens.

The rule of law and the contemporary global criminal environment

More communities have perished by their inability to enforce laws than have been destroyed by nature or hostile aggression. In the history of communities, absence or weakness of effective law enforcement machinery can be seen to be, very frequently, the true cause of failure in battle.[3]

The rapid growth and spread globally of major organised crime are increasingly a barometer in assessing both the moral and the practical preparedness of a state to maintain the rule of law, as well as civil order in a peacekeeping context. Thus the unwillingness or inability of a state to deal with the growing economic and political power and pervasiveness of organised crime ought to be viewed as an emerging significant factor which will complicate peacekeeping and the early return of civil order. Moreover, a state that is already severely weakened by systemic organised crime, and the corruption it breeds, may prove intractable to reform.

Crime adapts to changing environments, with traditional street-level crimes of violence, theft and damage being influenced by prevailing societal standards and conditions. More complex organised and economic crime, however, actually thrive on upheaval and on the uncertainties, vulnerabilities and opportunities manifested by the freer flow globally of people, money, goods, services and ideas. The criminal environment is part of, not distinct from, the more causal and influential political, social and economic environments. It is caught up in greater global phenomena: the revolution in modern technology, particularly communications and transport; the development and spread of global markets, associated with the deregulation of financial systems and the gradual weakening and disappearance of sovereign borders and their controls; the breakdown of old totalitarian regimes and the emergence of new regimes with market-oriented economies; the growing, illicit mass migration of humanity; the extreme changes to social structures, including the steady disappearance of unskilled jobs and widening social inequalities; and the substantial increase in the economic power, political influence and transnational pervasiveness of highly organised, sophisticated and exploitative criminals. If, in addition, a state, through internal or external events, has become dysfunctional, then the effect of organised crime will be magnified.

The dire effects of the global crime phenomenon will become more apparent in the next few years as differentiation between legitimate and illegitimate political and economic power becomes more difficult. Accordingly the distinction between national security and law enforcement interests is blurring. Increasingly, criminal threats have national security implications. Crime now has the means to undermine the very foundations of the state; organised crime amasses significant reserves of undeclared, untaxed wealth to rival the economies of small countries and threatens not only the rule of law but the very primacy of the state. Thus traditional precepts as to what distinguishes or separates national security, military and law and order threats are themselves under challenge by global events.

It was gratifying to note that, quite recently, the then Chief of the Australian Defence Force, Admiral Barrie, acknowledged the significant shift in thinking on the phenomena that constitute threats to national security.[4]

World disorder

The former President of the United States, George Bush, addressing the US Congress after the liberation of Kuwait, opined that the Gulf War was the first test for "a new world coming into view, a world in which there is the very real prospect of a new world order".[5] In fact there appears to be a new world disorder. At the start of a new millennium, the world is experiencing dramatic upheavals and even greater uncertainty. With the collapse and continuing fragmentation of the once seemingly immovable bipolar world order of the Cold War period, hope for a better global future at first seemed well founded. Yet, if anything, the world is more unstable, more unpredictable. Most of the planet's people face grinding poverty, chronic health and welfare problems, shrinking access to clean air and water, and high mortality rates. Disputation between states and communities over ecological issues is on the increase as the depleted and degraded natural resources of the planet are contested, and the rise of nationalism, tribalism, and racial and religious intolerance add to this volatility. Increasingly, it is civilians who are being killed and displaced by war and conflict. At the beginning of the twentieth century civilians constituted 5 per cent of war casualties; at century's end they constituted around 90 per cent.[6] It seems that the rules, such as they were, on the treatment of non-combatants have been swept away and all are fair game.

The world stands at new crossroads where conventional perspectives on what constitutes war and what may be termed public violence have been blurred. Moreover, the beginnings and endings of conflicts are frequently difficult to discern. They tend to wax and wane, and often they are undeclared and have vague and deeply historical origins, reignited suddenly by seemingly incoherent developments. It is clear that, although humankind has advanced technically, we have not advanced morally, and that the unevenness globally of the social condition, the widening gap between the haves and have-nots, is increasing the volatility of an already volatile world.

It is in this context that peacekeeping attempts to assuage the planet's many affrays.

The thin blue wedge

I have no doubt that the world should eventually have an international police force which will be accepted as an integral and essential part of life in the same way as national police forces are accepted.[7]

Peacekeeping is said to be the "grey zone between pacific settlement and military enforcement ... given concrete expression by inserting the thin blue wedge [UN peacekeeping force] between combatants".[8] In the first place, it is reasonable to ask why a country such as Australia, a middle-ranking country in geopolitical terms, should become involved in UN peacekeeping operations, particularly when operations are not resoundingly successful, are costly and put operatives at risk.

Of considerable importance are Australia's already established credentials as a "good international citizen". Australia also has obligations as a responsible nation to the principles of the United Nations and as a middle power contributor to the Western alliance. Nevertheless, peacekeeping is a double-edged sword, in that costs may be exacted in adverse foreign policy and in commerce and trade action on the part of those countries whose displeasure Australia may incur owing to its involvement in peacekeeping. Even traditional allies, such as the United States, are not necessarily aligned with Australia in all its expressions of support for UN commitments (for example geo-environmental resolutions). A true commitment by Australia to the principles of justice and equity moves it away from necessarily being in the "camp" of one side or the other, even when the "camp" may be that of a traditional ally. Australia's assistance in the fight against apartheid and against colonialism in the case of Namibia are examples. The opportunity for Australia to participate in the Second UN Emergency Force (Sinai), 1973–1977 (UNEF II) gave Australia an opportunity to demonstrate its even-handed approach to the Middle East.[9]

The nature and scope of peacekeeping operations have evolved over the decades and there is debate about what should be classed as an international peacekeeping operation, because some operations, such as the UN involvement in the Korean War, 1950–1953, are seen as too warlike to be considered "peacekeeping".[10] The close-quarter battle is a task for the most sophisticated soldiering, not for police, whose role should be that of containment until military aid arrives. The high degree of training, more sophisticated weaponry, experience and fitness of specialist troops are likely to reduce rather than increase the possible loss of life in a close-quarter battle.[11] In the main, UN peacekeeping operations involve personnel drawn from armed service elements of participating nations. Australia's contribution has been no different, yet the involvement of conventional police elements is likely to escalate if present trends continue.

Globocop

The Australian Federal Police (AFP) has three distinct international roles: a liaison officer network in 15 countries; an adviser/training role in the region; and peacekeeping. The first role involves cooperating with foreign law enforcement agencies to combat major transnational crime, particularly the drug traffic and other organised crime. The second role is undertaken through two programmes: the Law Enforcement Cooperation Program and the Law Enforcement Assistance Program. The reach of the programmes is confined to the Asia-Pacific region and involves the delivery of training in investigations (fraud, drugs and sexual assault), forensic and technical skills, intelligence and the management of major investigations. The third role, peacekeeping, has also served to define a gratifyingly positive reputation for the Australian Federal Police overseas.

Australian police first became exposed to international peacekeeping in 1964 when the First Contingent (1964–65), comprising 40 civilian police from all states and territories and of the Commonwealth, joined civilian police from Austria, Denmark, New Zealand and Sweden to embark on a peacekeeping operation in Cyprus that continues to this day. Since the First Contingent, Australia has contributed between 20 and 35 police from federal, state and territory police forces. From 1976 (the 13th Contingent) the Australian contingents comprised solely Commonwealth and, from 1979, Federal police. Cyprus, its geography, history and politics, shaped a state of affairs which epitomises the circumstances that call for police, rather than military, action, yet has involved both over the years. The absence of a formal peace agreement between the opposing sides means the situation remains volatile, with occasional flare-ups and much diplomacy, ingenuity and plain good police work employed to permit some semblance of normalcy. As Harbottle states,[12] the decision to raise a small multinational civilian police component to form part of the UN Peace-keeping Force in Cyprus (UNFICYP) was a novel and experimental departure from usual practice, acknowledging that, as useful as military police are, they are limited in dealing with a usually resentful citizenry. Harbottle, a former Brigadier and Chief of Staff of UNFICYP from June 1966 to August 1968, came to realise that the insinuation of impartial civilian police into what now is a largely civil situation was indeed one of the "unqualified successes"[13] of the UN action in Cyprus. Fursdon, too, noted that the gradually improving situation in Cyprus called for a rise in UNFICYP's civilian profile and a reduction of its military one.[14]

Making the transfer from military to police supervision in peacekeeping is a matter of crucial timing and judgement. Nevertheless, once there is an opportunity to reimpose the rule of civil law, it ought to be taken, even if the truce or peace is uneasy. An early return to some semblance of civil normalcy can be expected to have a salutary effect in calming the populace.

At one point, in 1992, the Australian government considered sending the Australian Federal Police to Yugoslavia during its dismemberment, as part of the United Nations' efforts to halt the conflict. Clearly, the time was not right for UN civilian police in what had become a brutish war zone where the most base atrocities were commonplace. In Cambodia, however, where the political and military position was also anything but ideal, an Australian Federal Police contingent of 10 was despatched in May 1992 to form part of the United Nations Transitional Authority in Cambodia (UNTAC). Stationed in Thmar Puok, in the north-west of Cambodia, the Australian contingent's patrol area extended some 2,500 square kilometres and had a population of about 78,000. The area was reportedly controlled by the Khmer People's National Liberation Front; however, there were substantial numbers of Khmer Rouge (DK) soldiers in the region. The contingent was not far from the operations of the UN High Commissioner for Refugees, formerly the UN Border Relief Organisation (UNBRO), in Aranyaprathet, Thailand, where a one-man Australian Federal Police contingent, a Superintendent, had been serving the United Nations for more than three years as an adviser.

The Australian Federal Police contingent's role was to supervise, monitor and control local Cambodian police in their designated area, investigate human rights violations and report on such to the UN command, provide training and development to Cambodian police, and assist in bringing an environment of calm and confidence conducive to the holding of free elections. Although the Australian Federal Police contingent was but a small cog in the peacekeeping machine in Cambodia, its successes were laudable and quite disproportionate to its size. A firm, but cheerful, professional approach to "community policing" duties won the respect and support of the villagers. Extra-curricular activities, such as the building and equipping of a children's playground and the teaching of English, were rewarded with greater acceptance of Australian police by the people and undoubtedly improved their security. The AFP contingent's efforts received high praise from the then UNTAC Force Commander, Lieutenant-General John Sanderson and from visitors to the region, such as the then Australian Prime Minister, Paul Keating, and the then Minister for Foreign Affairs and Trade, Senator Gareth Evans. Of the Australian Federal Police's efforts, General Sanderson said:

[T]he very small AFP contingent did a remarkable job in Cambodia. Its members numbered 10 out of a total civil police force of 3,600. If there had been 360 groups of that potency, I think we would have had a much more significant impact on the outcomes in Cambodia because the law is the key issue in this. While we were not the sovereign authority in Cambodia, the process of taking the law down to the grassroots and getting it implemented there ... was the key process, and the AFP contingent did that ... [T]he contingent actually wrote the body of law, established the school and the police station and supervised the activity.[15]

The Report of the Senate Standing Committee on Foreign Affairs, Defence and Trade[16] touched lightly – in Recommendation 18 – on a change of direction in peacekeeping for Australia when it urged the Australian government to develop a comprehensive reference list of factors that ought to be taken into account in formulating policy advice on participation by Australia in future peacekeeping operations. Included in the points that followed, mention is made of the "evaluation of the different kinds of contributions Australia might make (military, police, electoral etc)"; yet the report refrains from considering a fundamental review of the differing roles of police and military as they relate to the achievement and maintenance of law and order. Nevertheless, the report exposed for public comment the importance, relevance and extent of Australia's past and potential peacekeeping commitments. The report also foreshadowed the means for a heightened role for civilian and non-government organisations,[17] which would place the emphasis for the execution of many tasks now performed by the military (for example, medical services, transport, catering, communications, and engineering and technical assistance) on civilian contractors and non-government agencies. In passing reference to the role of police in this critical chapter, the report asserted that it was "useful in the UN context to preserve the distinction between police serving in a non-military capacity and the more usual military police units", and later briefly acknowledged: "Depending on the tasks to be performed, the United Nations may have a need for civilian police personnel in the future, as operations become less exclusively military ... [I]t may also be that some of the tasks that have traditionally been carried out by military personnel would be performed by

UN civilian police."[18] In its 1994 report, the Committee devoted more space to the increasing part played by civilian organisations, including the Australian Federal Police, in peacekeeping and touched on the concept of "justice packages", which will be addressed further in this chapter.[19]

Strategies and plans for conflict intervention must be integrated and graduated, running from khaki to blue on the critical planning spectrum. The timely relief of UN military forces by UN police ought to be one of the key objectives of any peacekeeping operation once sustained armed conflict has ceased. Experience in Cyprus shows that the early reinstatement of civil authority was critical in establishing a peace of sorts, even if completely harmonious civil affairs are elusive. It is likely that events globally will compel the United Nations and national governments, including Australia, to review peacekeeping operations to see how best they can be constructed with economy and success, particularly given that dispatch will be an elusive part of the equation. The work of the United Nations Transition Assistance Group (UNTAG) in Namibia, for example, broke new ground in using civilian personnel to assist in the process of political change in that country, and again to assist in the conduct of the election process. At the UN level, more police and civilian planners ought to be used to develop strategies for the deployment and use of non-military personnel once more or less normal relations in a trouble spot have been achieved. In that regard, the Australian Federal Police assisted in the second UN Operation in Somalia (UNOSOM II) to provide advice on monitoring and training civilian police in Somalia; and, in 1994, 16 AFP members were attached to the United Nations Operation in Mozambique (ONUMOZ) to undertake a similar role.

As touched on earlier, civil order is in a finely balanced state even in liberal societies. How much more difficult is it, then, to impose or maintain civil order in a society whose basic social fabric and infrastructure have broken down. How much do the rule of law and the concept of civil obedience count when the most basic amenities are non-existent or hopelessly degraded? Policing cannot occur satisfactorily in a vacuum. Having a justice framework, or "package", in place is crucial to the success of individual elements of the framework – of which policing is one – and to the success of the whole. Clearly, adequate food, water and shelter and other basic communal services are fundamental requisites if the rule of law is to be reinstated successfully in a state that has long been reduced to brutal existence. The successful restoration of the rule of law is dependent on the willingness of a society to restore and maintain civil order in all its forms; one cannot be had without the other. Peacekeeping is not possible if there is no prospect of a peace to be kept. There has to be a critical mass, in terms of the readiness and willingness of citizens to accept, at the most rudimentary level, the rule of law. Otherwise police will be ineffective and military intervention the only course.

The Australian Federal Police has had considerable experience in foreign lands as peacekeepers and advisers, and has learnt many lessons over the years. Principal among these lessons is to assume nothing but heed much about the history, culture and mores of the society in which it is to work. Police peacekeepers need to understand the structure of the society and of the government (if there is one) and the way the significant societal elements function and interact. A mistake to avoid is to assume there is an understanding and acceptance of – or a preparedness to understand or accept by the host community – an "Australian" (liberal) approach to policing. Another lesson is not to assume that all proven remedies are easily transportable elsewhere. In short, police peacekeepers have to be adaptable and receptive to the realities and challenges of the foreign environment; to accept that they may not "know what is best" for a particular society. One very indispensable lesson, however, is that peacekeepers need optimism, patience and a heavy-duty sense of humour.

When law and order have broken down, there follow the most dire consequences. Anarchy prevails; people revert to taking the law into their own hands, using extreme violence in asserting their will or defending what they perceive as their rights. The encircling disorder is also often used as a convenient cover to exact reprisals against those involved in unconnected disputation, often over quite trivial issues. Such "order" as there may be will often be enforced by those with superior weaponry, or by soldiers who are merely resting from the main fighting. There will be no courts to dispense justice, or gaols or prisons to hold offenders. It is instructive that, in some societies where anarchy has ruled, court houses, police stations and prisons have long been destroyed, literally, so that even the symbols of order have been vanquished. In the slow and painful return to order, there will be an understandable reluctance on the part of people to accept roles as members of courts, police and prison systems, because injury or death might be the price of such service in restoring the rule of law. There is also the serious issue of certain functions, including those of a police officer, being viewed in some cultures with a negativity bordering on loathing. Additionally, indigenous people who first assist the UN mission may incur the wrath of their brethren, and more so once the United Nations has withdrawn.

Lastly, the AFP participates in a poignant but inescapable endgame of the United Nations' work: it has investigators in the International Criminal Tribunal in The Hague who are actively involved in bringing war criminals to justice.

The training of police

The training of foreign police also requires the positive attributes described earlier, especially patience. And this is not being patronising. UN police have found over the years that where they have failed to sustain a long-term commitment to training and the reinforcement of programmes, the ground gained is quickly eroded. In some cultures, the Western-style "quick fix" approach is seen as puzzling and sends a negative message as to the peacekeepers' true interest in, and commitment to, the host's plight. Training is also much assisted if there is already a history of working together collegiately with foreign police in conventional crime areas, where trust and cooperation have been built up, and particularly where a number of officers have previously been participants on Australian courses. For example, the Australian Federal Police offers a small number of courses, held both in Australia and abroad, to international participants, and the value is not only in the courses themselves but in the mutual cooperation and networks such programmes engender. In the longer term, of course, the hope is that the liberal philosophies and substance of the programmes have a positive and lasting influence on the policies, practices and procedures of recipient agencies, and perhaps more widely in the community. There is likely to be a need to instil unfamiliar doctrine: the use of minimum as opposed to maximum force in executing police duties; emphasising service to the law rather than to the ruler; and acting independently and impartially in the performance of duty.

In tense conflict situations, the Australian Federal Police stresses the importance of commencing from a minimum-force position. It teaches and practises the principles of defensive skills. In short, the "use of force continuum" approach is a comprehensive technique in applying graduated measures to deal with violence or the threat of violence, the starting point being the use of refined communication skills to de-escalate an incident, the extreme end point – the act of absolute last resort – being the use of deadly force. Even in the most extreme situations in foreign places, the AFP prefers its peacekeepers to be unarmed. This may seem paradoxical given that police in Australia are invariably armed; however, long experience in peacekeeping and similar operations over some 35 years has confirmed that an armed peacekeeper is potentially more at risk than one who is unarmed. There are several reasons for this: first, the unarmed peacekeeper is seen to be of no personal threat to those with whom he or she deals and they become more at ease in his or her presence; secondly, a principal purpose, and indeed symbolism, of such operations is to restore confidence in the general populace that a change for the better is in prospect and is not dependent on the continuance of violence and armed rule by any protagonist; and, thirdly, sidearms are quite useless against (usually) superior and overwhelming weaponry. It is also impossible to lead by example toward the restoration of peace if you bear the accoutrements of war.

Although the military play a vital role in the rebuilding of societies, their strength is in delivering infrastructure services and logistical, technical and overall organisational competencies. Military training is not conducive to training civilian police. The mission of each is different, therefore the philosophies and tradecraft of each are equally different. A colleague and veteran of a number of UN missions, Bill Kirk, provided an indelible practical example of this difference:

[I]n Thailand in Site 2 one evening, I moved about the camp with my Swedish colleague and interpreter to observe the police we were about to train patrolling the camp. There was no lighting. They moved about in a military fashion, taking cover in the shadows cast by the moon between the buildings. The Swede and I did what policemen normally do. We walked between the huts using the interpreter and talking to the people asking them about their problems and life generally.

Although the transference of technical and procedural knowhow may seem relatively straightforward, it can be complicated by reason of UN police coming from contributing countries with quite different legal systems. For instance, police officers trained to work within the adversary system will have a different approach to their duties from colleagues who are used to the inquisitorial system. Unless these differences are worked through, they have the potential to confuse those the UN police are to train. More important, however, is the sharing of the same positive attitude and sense of purpose in fraught situations. A calm (at least outwardly!) demeanour, coupled with firm determination, on the part of the police peacekeeper can defuse tense situations, and these traits and techniques need to be transferred to those new to police work.

Another factor, on which much has been said and written by others, is the variable standard of the personal qualities and professional skills of some peacekeepers sent by some countries, even when the United Nations' specifications are quite clear. Put bluntly, the presence of ill-equipped personnel simply adds, quite disproportionately, to the difficulties of the task, inflicting on colleagues the burden of additional responsibilities so as to compensate.

Although it is clear that, for the foreseeable future, military force, judiciously employed and intelligently controlled, will need to be readily available to the United Nations, the earnest objective of policy ought to be the graduated replacement of military by civil means at the earliest possible time. If world peace is humankind's ultimate prize, then the new world order must be clothed in blue, not khaki.

Notes

1. *Enever* v. R. (1906) 3 CLR 969; *R. v. Commissioner of Police of the Metropolis; ex parte Blackburn* [1968] 2 QB 118 at 135; *Parliamentary Debates (Hansard)*, vol. S.45, 24 September 1970, p. 865; *Parliamentary Debates (Hansard)*, vol. H. of R. 208, 9 September 1996, p. 3703.
2. Sir Robert Mark, *In the Office of Constable* (London: Collins, 1979).
3. Charles Reith, *The Blind Eye of History* (London: Faber & Faber, 1952), p. 15.
4. Admiral C. A. Barrie, "Change, People and Australia's Defence Capability for the New Century", *Australian Defence Force Journal*, no. 134, January–February 1999, pp. 5–15.
5. *Time Magazine*, 1 April 1991, p. 21.
6. Michael Kidron and Ronald Segal, *The New State of the World Atlas* (London: Simon & Schuster, 1992), p. 120.
7. UN Secretary-General U Thant, 13 June 1963.
8. Ramesh Thakur, "From Great Power Collective Security to Middle Power Peacekeeping", in Hugh Smith (ed.), *Australia and Peacekeeping* (Canberra: Australian Defence Studies Centre, 1990), pp. 1–21 at p. 8.
9. See *United Nations Peacekeeping and Australia* (Canberra: Australian Government Publishing Service, May 1991), p. 80.
10. See Smith (ed.), *Australia and Peacekeeping*, p. 125.
11. Sir Robert Mark, *Report to the Minister for Administrative Services on the Organisation of Police Resources in the Commonwealth Area and Other Related Matters* (Canberra: Australian Government Publishing Service, 1978), p. 16.
12. Michael Harbottle, *The Impartial Soldier* (London: Oxford University Press, 1990), p. 176.
13. Ibid.
14. Edward Fursdon, "UN Peacekeeping in Cyprus", *Conflict Studies*, no. 232, June 1990, pp. 11–18 at p. 18.
15. Cited in *Australia's Participation in Peacekeeping* (Canberra: Australian Government Publishing Service, 1994), pp. 92–93.
16. See *United Nations Peacekeeping and Australia*.
17. Ibid., pp. 87–108.
18. Ibid., p. 90.
19. *Australia's Participation in Peacekeeping*, pp. 87–102.

18

Afterword: Rebuilding the rule of law in the Horn of Africa

Martin P. Ganzglass

I have never been in the police or military and have not served with a non-governmental organisation (NGO) in the field. I have been a union labour lawyer for most of my professional life. I am particularly in awe of those who have devoted their lives to restoring the rule of law in what might politely be termed disrupted states, and which I prefer to call failed or collapsed states. However, for better or for worse, I have also spent a good part of my life involved with East Africa, first as legal adviser to the Somali National Police Force, then for some time as a lawyer for various ministries of the Somali government, and more recently as a lawyer for Eritrea.

Somalia is the epitome of a failed state. It holds the record as the modern nation-state that has gone for the longest time without a central government – almost nine years since the overthrow of Mohammad Siad Barre. On the other hand, the newly independent country of Eritrea holds the record for the longest continuous war for independence in Africa, if not the world. After emerging from a 30-year war for independence, it is as much of a success story as Somalia is a failure.

Eritrea also is no stranger to Australians. Thomas Kenneally, the author of *Schindler's List*, has written a marvellous novel of the Eritrean struggle for independence, entitled *To Asmara*. Professor Fred Hollows, an Australian ophthalmologist, devoted himself during the later years of the struggle to training Eritreans in eye surgery and providing medical supplies to the Eritrean People's Liberation Front (EPLF). Today, as part of his legacy, almost every regional hospital has an ophthalmological unit to take care of the most common eye diseases in Eritrea. During his lifetime, Dr Hollows was made an honorary Eritrean citizen. After he died, the Eritreans honoured his memory by naming a kindergarten in the capital for him.

I propose in these remarks to cover four areas: first, Somalia and the unsuccessful efforts of the international community to restore the rule of law there; second, Eritrea and the development of a civil society under law, after 30 years of armed struggle; third, the advantages and disadvantages of justice-based NGOs and whether a new justice-oriented NGO would be desirable; and, fourth, how the approaches used in Somalia and Eritrea and those of justice-based NGOs could be applied in other situations, such as Kosovo.

Somalia

First Somalia and a brief thumbnail history. Somalia became independent in 1960. A coup in 1969 by Army General Mohammad Siad Barre overthrew the democratically elected government and led to 20 years of dictatorship, before Siad Barre was himself overthrown in 1991. After a brief period of euphoria, and the hope of restoration of democracy for the nation, Somalia disintegrated into chaos and lawlessness. Clan-based warlords, with heavily armed young men from their clan, governed territorial fiefdoms. They engaged in a brutal campaign of looting, rape and murder against members of other clans and tribes. Somalia, which in the 1960s was the most unified country in all of Africa, bound together by one language, one culture, one history and one religion, became a series of warring mini-states. The historian Barbara Tuchman described the effects of such chaos in her book on Europe entitled *A Distant Mirror* and subtitled *The Calamitous 14th Century*. In Somalia in 1993, like Western Europe in the 1300s, armed bands brought commerce and farming to a complete halt. This in turn produced famine and disease.

In Somalia, when NGOs attempted to provide food, medicine and shelter for the hundreds of thousands of destitute and starving Somalis, the warlords extorted protection money to allow NGOs to deliver a portion of the food to starving women and children. One estimate is that more than 70 per cent of all Somali children under the age of 5 in the southern part of the country died of starvation or disease from 1991 to 1993.

The United Nations mounted a feeble effort, the first UN Operation in Somalia (UNOSOM I), to break the cycle of extortion and starvation. It failed because the lightly armed Pakistani troops were quickly bottled up at the Mogadishu airport by one of the warlords, Mohamed Farah Aideed. In November 1992 President Bush initiated Operation Restore Hope, known to Australians as Operation Solace. It was a multinational, armed humanitarian intervention, with most of the troops being supplied by the United States, but with Australian, French, Belgian, Italian, Indian, Pakistani, Botswanan and Nigerian units as well. It was designated as UNITAF, for Unified Task Force. It occupied about 40 per cent of the entire country, including the capital, Mogadishu, and the central and southern regions of Somalia, where most of the violence and starvation were occurring.

When Operation Restore Hope began, extortion was the order of the day and relief supplies were not reaching the starving population in the interior. As a result of this anarchy, Somalia had become divided, de facto along clan lines. The only place a Somali was safe was among those of his or her own clan. However, the de facto clan division and the reappearance of tribalism had the unforeseen advantage of establishing a sense of trust between the population in one particular area and the people who would later serve as judges and police, because they were all of the same clan or subclan. This same phenomenon appears to be happening today in Kosovo.

The Australians were assigned the Bay Region and the main city of Baidoa in the south-west part of the country. At the time, Baidoa was controlled by a faction of Mohamed Farah Aideed. Prior to the arrival of the Australian troops, this faction, using force and terror, ruled the local, indigenous population of Baidoa, who were from a different tribal grouping.

The Australian Defence Force (ADF) incorporates restoration of civil society as part of its military mission. The US forces in Somalia had no civil affairs programme. This difference in approach had significant practical consequences on the ground. For example, in February 1993, the ADF in the Bay Region declared the Somali Penal Code the law of the region. The US military never did so in its zones. The Marines generally did what they could to rebuild the police in and around Mogadishu but it was an ad hoc effort. The US Military Command, fearful of mission creep, that is, moving from a humanitarian relief effort to so-called nation-building, avoided the obvious need to rebuild the institutions necessary to re-establish the rule of law.

In Baidoa, the Australians rebuilt the Regional Court and Police Station complex. The ADF used armed force to break the warlords' gangs and bring the worst offenders to justice. This meant using Somali judges, police and court administrators, and applying the Somali Penal Code to charge, try and convict those arrested. The ADF provided protection to those Somalis who participated in the judicial process – the judges, police and witnesses. The end result was that the Australians were the most successful of all UNITAF forces in restoring the rule of law in their part of Somalia. The use of the Somali police, including a CID unit, also lessened the Australians' security burdens in the region. Unfortunately, in the US sector, security meant force protection rather than security for the non-combatants. The initial reports from Kosovo indicated that once again NATO was emphasising force protection, that is, arresting those who attacked NATO troops but not establishing a rule of law to protect the general population.

Admittedly, Mogadishu was a more difficult situation than the Australian zone: the two major warlords continued to struggle for power. But the Australian approach should have been made part of the Operation, and applied wherever else in Somalia it was possible to do so. One of the tragedies of Operation Restore Hope is that UNITAF failed to build on the Australian success in the Bay Region. The ADF proved that aggressive intervention to rebuild the court system and re-establish the police could work, while the rest of UNITAF squandered the invaluable resource of the professional, apolitical Somali National Police.

The failure rapidly to reconstitute the Somali police on a regional basis led the US military under the second UN Operation in Somalia (UNOSOM II) to assume police functions. In June 1993, after the takeover by UNOSOM II, Mohamed Farah Aideed's forces attacked a UN Pakistani unit in Mogadishu. This was followed by UNOSOM issuing an arrest warrant for Aideed and the injection of US Rangers into the rabbit warren of the back alleys of Mogadishu and the death of 18 Rangers in October 1993. This in turn led to the US pullout from Somalia and the end of UNOSOM II in failure. Today, conditions in Somalia, although not quite as bad as in 1992, are much the same. Somalis are dying from hunger and disease and NGOs are unable to operate freely without paying extortion to one warlord or another.

A veritable cottage industry of Lessons Learned conferences sprang up after Operation Restore Hope and UNOSOM II. But the most obvious lesson for the US military – using civil affairs units in conjunction with armed forces to restore the justice system – did not have to be learned. The United States had such units in Kuwait after its liberation from Iraqi occupation in the Gulf War, that is before Operation Restore Hope. When the United States intervened in Haiti, in September 1994, that is after Operation Restore Hope, it provided advisory teams to the Haitian Ministry of Justice. There were also about 800 Civilian Police (CIVPOL) advisers in Haiti. The basic lesson to be drawn from the Somali situation is to confirm what the Australians did and what the United States and its allies did in Kuwait and Haiti: make it a top priority to restore the system of justice and the rule of law. This means applying a body of law acceptable to the population; rebuilding judicial institutions and the police; and using armed force to support the courts and police and initially to protect civilians associated with the justice system.

I want to digress for a moment, because Operation Restore Hope also raised some interesting issues about the relationship between NGOs and the military. In Mogadishu, the NGOs continued to employ armed guards hired from one warlord's faction or another to provide protection, despite the presence of 36,000 UNITAF troops in country. This led to a complex and, in my opinion, basically unworkable system of permits from UNITAF to these armed guards to carry weapons. Frequently, guards during the day became bandits at night.

In Baidoa, the Australians did not permit NGOs to hire armed guards. The ADF, together with the reconstituted Somali police, took responsibility for protecting NGO personnel, property and cash. Without a functioning Somali police force in Mogadishu, the Australian model might not have worked. I would leave some room for flexibility depending upon local circumstances, but in general I believe there is no need for NGOs to hire their own armed security guards in situations of military humanitarian intervention. This is especially true if the intervening military force actively engages in disarmament.

Eritrea

In comparison with Somalia as a failed state and ultimately unsuccessful armed humanitarian intervention, Eritrea is a success story. Again let me set the stage with a very brief summary of Eritrea's history. In the late 1890s, when East Africa was divided by Britain, France, Italy and Ethiopia, Eritrea became an Italian colony. The Italians maintained it as a separate colony even after they conquered Ethiopia in the 1930s. When the Italians were defeated, Eritrea was administered separately by the British from the spring of 1941 until 1952. The United States, for its own Cold War security reasons, ignored the Eritrean wishes for self-determination. In 1952 the United Nations, on the initiative of the United States, passed a resolution establishing Eritrean autonomy but federated with Ethiopia under Emperor Haile Selassie. This arrangement was patently unworkable. It grafted a democratic Eritrean entity onto a feudal Ethiopian empire. In 1962, the Eritrean assembly was forced, virtually at gunpoint, to terminate the federal status of Eritrea and make it part of the Ethiopian empire. Thus began the 30-year war for independence. This had a curious echo in East Timor where the Indonesian government claimed that in 1976 East Timor accepted the arrangement with Indonesia, meaning the invasion in 1975.

The Eritreans first fought against the Ethiopian military, who were armed principally by the United States. Following the overthrow of the emperor in 1974 and the establishment of a Marxist government, the Soviets began supplying massive amounts of weapons to Ethiopia, reportedly over US$1 billion worth. The Ethiopian army became the second largest in Africa. From 1977 on, the Eritreans fought against a Soviet equipped and trained Ethiopian military, who were assisted at various times by Cuban troops, Yemeni, North Korean and Libyan pilots, and internal security forces advised by East Germans. For 30 years, the Eritreans relied only on themselves, using captured and refurbished weapons. They integrated their armed forces, with men and women serving in combat. The highest rank held by women was Lieutenant-Colonel, and women frequently commanded company-sized units in combat. The Eritreans won the war in 1991 and voted overwhelmingly for independence in a democratic referendum in 1993. Incidentally, as was proposed for East Timor, Eritreans residing outside of Eritrea were encouraged to vote in the referendum for independence, and did so in large numbers.

With a population of only 3.5 million, Eritrea today is like Israel in 1948, Denmark and Holland at the time of the two world wars, and Finland in the late 1930s. It is a small country in a tough neighbourhood.

So how does a newly independent nation, emerging from an armed struggle and with the country in ruins, re-establish the rule of law? Shortly after gaining independence, Eritrea adopted the existing Ethiopian Penal Code, with some modifications. Eritrea could make do with a transitional Ethiopian law, but it was obvious that adopting the law of the country it had fought against for 30 years was politically unacceptable. And the 1957 Ethiopian Penal Code was out of date. This same concept – of temporarily accepting a modified law of the oppressor nation because it is serviceable and familiar – may also apply to East Timor.

Eritrea at the time of independence had fewer than 60 qualified lawyers and judges, who were already overextended. The Eritreans' approach was to use foreigners to assist in code drafting, financed by the United Nations Development Programme (UNDP), but to retain control of the process and content. In other words, they did not opt for simply having foreign experts draft a modern code and present it to the government. First, under the direction of the Ministry of Justice, they formed search committees to select people to draft four main codes: the Commercial Code, the Civil Code, the Penal Code, and the Code of Criminal Procedure. Eritreans gave the Commercial Code priority because they regarded it as essential for attracting private investment and rebuilding the economy. When the search committee came up short on candidates for drafting the Penal Code and the Criminal Procedure Code, I was asked to join the team of one American and one Canadian law professor.

The Eritreans' approach was the same for each code. They convened a conference in Asmara of the lawyers, judges, government officials and representatives of civic organisations to begin an exchange of ideas. The initial conference on the Penal Code produced several clear directives from the Eritrean side. First, the Code was to have strong anti-corruption provisions and new and expanded sections on narcotics, air piracy and modern financial crimes such as money laundering. The reason for the emphasis on anti-corruption provisions is in part the fact that most Eritreans living abroad remit a percentage of their income to Eritrea. It is the greatest source of foreign revenue, exceeding export earnings. Thus, it is imperative for the government to have the ability to punish corruption severely in order to maintain the confidence of the Eritrean population. Second, Eritrean culture clearly emphasises community solutions and is very protective of children. This translates into the concept of community work as a punishment for lesser offences, and an emphasis on punishing adults for either targeting minors or using them in the commission of crimes. Third, Eritrea is a country of nine ethnic groups. The total population is approximately equally divided between Muslims and Coptic Christians. Therefore, crimes that attempt to set one group against another, or that are committed to incite racial or religious hatred, must be severely punished. Kosovo appears to be in great need of such a provision today.

As the foreign part of the drafting team, we made it clear that the Penal Code, more than any other law of a nation, embodies its cultural and moral values. Therefore, it was up to the Eritreans to make sure that the draft expressed these values. First, we firmly indicated that, although we would divide the crimes up into six classes of offences (three serious and three petty), we would not recommend specific penalties for specific crimes. The Eritreans had to decide, consistent with their cultural values, which crimes deserved to be punished more severely than others. Second, we also indicated that our draft would include commentary for each article so that the Code, when adopted and published, would serve as a guide for judges, prosecutors and lawyers in the future.

The first draft we produced adopted many of the provisions of the Singapore Prevention of Corruption Act; the section on offences involving narcotics came from the Australian Model Penal Code, which focuses on the commercial motivation of illegal drug trade, and severely punishes supplying drugs to children or using children to traffic in drugs; other provisions came from the codes of Canada, Greece, Israel, Germany, Great Britain and Ethiopia.

We forwarded the draft, some time passed while the Eritreans reviewed it, and we then attended a second Penal Code conference in Asmara. The Eritreans had gone through all of the offences and designated the punishment for each crime. They decided to allow the imposition of the death penalty in a few instances, including aggravated murder, which includes murder committed for reasons of ethnic or religious bias or hatred.

We had an interesting discussion on kidnapping and abduction. During the conference, many of the male delegates supported the provision in the old Ethiopian Penal Code that permitted a young man to abduct a young woman, have sex with her and avoid prosecution for kidnapping and rape if he consented to marry the woman. The representative from the National Union of Eritrean Women spoke in opposition, hesitantly and timidly in English. She then apologised to us for her poor English and switched into Tigrinean. Her voice took on the tone of steel and her sentences cracked like a whip. The gist of what she said was that women had fought alongside men for 30 years and made the same sacrifices in the struggle and they were not now going to be subjected to feudal laws. A free and independent Eritrea meant equality for all. There was no further debate, and the President of the High Court, who was chairing the meeting, simply said that it was the consensus of the group, after hearing the views expressed by the representative of Eritrean women, that kidnapping and rape were crimes that were not absolved by any consent to marriage.

The point of this anecdote is to underscore that, by including as part of the process not only the legal community but also representatives of the society to be governed by the laws, the draft truly became Eritrean law. The draft was placed in the hands of the Ministry of Justice, to go thence to the cabinet and then to the parliament for debate and passage.

In sum, the Eritrean approach to reconstituting the legal order following the war for independence was: (a) to adopt a modified code from the colonial power to serve in the interim; (b) to get UNDP funding for code drafting but to keep control of the process; and (c) to utilise foreign experts as part of an overall Eritrean team to develop a draft law acceptable to a broad base of the population.

Justice-based NGOs

The third area I want to cover is the role of justice-based NGOs. There are two main advantages to justice-based NGOs. First, they are independent; that is, they are not governmental or international agencies. They thus offer both expertise and neutrality. Governmental or international agencies may be unacceptable in some situations. For example, in Rwanda, after the slaughter of an estimated 500,000 people and the establishment of a new government, the Rwandans distrusted France for supporting the Hutu regime and harbouring former government officials accused of crimes of genocide. Secondly, NGOs are likely to be more efficient and to intervene more quickly than national or international groups. For example, the UN Department of Peacekeeping Operations (DPKO) in Somalia deliberately delayed re-establishing the Somali Police Force while it pursued the unrealistic political objective of a national Somali coalition government.

Justice-based NGOs have two main disadvantages. First, the provision of justice is seen as political. Justice-based NGOs are also tied to the quality of justice dispensed by the government they are aiding. An organisation called Justice Without Borders would not be viewed the same way as Doctors Without Borders. Assistance in restoring the rule of law may be seen as a determination that the government receiving the assistance is legitimate. The decision to treat a starving child makes no judgement about the government. Secondly, many NGOs, such as the American Bar Association, that have provided assistance in drafting codes in many of the countries from the former Soviet Union are in fact national based.

Why not create a new NGO which will be international in scope while avoiding the disadvantage of a slow-functioning international agency? Call it Justice Without Borders, consisting of experts in every category involved with a justice system – judges, lawyers, court administrators, prosecutors, police, and so on. Assume that this NGO has a roster of volunteers from all around the world, representing most of the legal systems and speaking enough different languages to be able to serve virtually anywhere. Could it work and, if so, in what types of situations?

Lessons for Kosovo

Let me now try to apply these three models – the Australian approach in Somalia as part of an armed humanitarian effort, the Eritrean code-drafting approach, and the hypothetical Justice Without Borders-type NGO – to Kosovo.

Kosovo is a classic case of armed humanitarian intervention. There is a NATO and UN approved force in Kosovo to protect the Kosovars from the Serbs, and the remaining Serbs from the Kosovo Liberation Army (KLA) and ethnic Albanians. What law should apply to the civilian population? What entity should vet former police and judges? This is tricky because the law must protect both the majority ethnic Albanians who have been brutalised by the Serbs, and the Serb minority who remain in Kosovo. In Somalia, the people accepted the police and judges because of de facto tribal segregation. It appears that there has been such de facto division between Serbs and ethnic Albanians in much of Kosovo. Could Serb police be employed in Serb neighbourhoods or villages and ethnic Albanian police in Albanian areas? Can NATO institute separate Serb and Albanian courts? Would this undercut NATO's policy that there will be no partition of Kosovo? In Somalia it was recognised that the clan-based justice system broke down when it dealt with members of minority clans. One proposal was to have foreign judges sit as the third non-tribal judge on a three-judge panel, with jurisdiction in serious and capital cases. It might be possible to have three-judge panels in Kosovo, consisting of a Serb, an ethnic Albanian and a foreign judge to ensure fairness.

Serbia ended Kosovo's autonomy in 1989. If there was a penal code familiar and acceptable to Kosovars from that autonomous period, that should be the law declared by NATO to be in effect in Kosovo today. If there was no such law and the Serbian Penal Code was on its face fair, but unfairly applied or circumvented by some Serbian national security Act, then that Penal Code could be used. The point is that a determination on the law to be applied should be made early and publicised to the Kosovars.

Kosovo today is much like Kuwait after the Iraqi occupation, like Somalia prior to Operation Restore Hope and like Haiti during its period of chaos. Judges, police and court personnel have fled into exile, been killed or gone into hiding, and the judicial infrastructure has been destroyed. Obviously, a major civil affairs effort as part of the military intervention is necessary to rebuild the judicial system. As in Somalia in the Australian sector, such an effort must begin by locating Kosovo members of the judiciary and police, re-establishing the courts and police stations and protecting them, if necessary, from Serb or KLA attacks. Justice-based NGOs could provide supplemental support, particularly in training new judges and court personnel. Given the security situation in Kosovo, re-training of the police might best be left to NATO, their civil affairs units, and a UN CIVPOL programme, which at this time is slated to have 3,000 civilian police advisers.

There is no one hard and fast rule, no one-suit-off-the-rack-fits-all-customers approach. I am sure there are other models. Certainly, there are other permutations to these three models. The overall goal is to develop and implement a system of justice that is accepted as just and fair by the people subject to that system. As in Eritrea, this will require substantial local input and, eventually, approval by elected officials.

I want to conclude with a short poem by Wislawa Szmborska, the Polish Nobel Prize Poet, which is relevant to the underlying subject of this book. It is entitled *Breughel's Two Monkeys*:

This is what I see in my dreams about final exams:
two monkeys, chained to the floor, sit on the windowsill,
the sky behind them flutters,
the sea is taking its bath.

The exam is the History of Mankind.
I stammer and hedge.

One monkey stares and listens with mocking disdain,
the other seems to be dreaming away –
but when it's clear I don't know what to say
he prompts me with a gentle
clinking of his chain.[1]

People are truly free only when they live under the rule of law in a just society. It gives them the opportunity, as human beings, to achieve their full intellectual capabilities.

Note

1. Wislawa Szmborska, "Breughel's Two Monkeys", translated by Stanislaw Barancyal and Clare Cavanagh, *The New Yorker*, 22 March 1993, p. 61.

Contributors

Reginald Austin is Director of the Rules and Guidelines Programme of the International Institute for Democracy and Electoral Assistance (International IDEA). He was previously Director of the Legal and Constitutional Affairs Division of the Commonwealth Secretariat in London, Head of the Electoral Component and Chief Electoral Officer of UNTAC in Cambodia, Head of the Electoral Division of UNOMSA in South Africa, and Professor of Law at the University of Zimbabwe.

Frederick M. Burkle, Jr, is Senior Scholar, Scientist and Visiting Professor at the Centre for International Emergency, Disaster and Refugee Studies, Schools of Medicine and Public Health, The Johns Hopkins University Medical Institutions. He was previously Professor of Pediatrics, Surgery and Public Health and Chairman, Division of Emergency Medicine, Department of Surgery, University of Hawaii Schools of Medicine and Public Health. A Captain in the US Naval Reserve, he served as joint military liaison for the Humanitarian Assistance Coordination Center in southern Turkey, northern Iraq, Baghdad and Somalia. He has also served as Director, Center of Excellence in Disaster Management and Humanitarian Assistance, Hawaii.

Simon Chesterman is an Associate at the International Peace Academy in New York, and author of *Just War or Just Peace? Humanitarian Intervention and International Law* (2001).

Cees De Rover is the former Senior Adviser on Law Enforcement and Security Issues to the Special Representative of the UN Secretary-General in Burundi, former Deputy Director of the Police Institute for Public Order and Safety of the Netherlands, and a former Dutch police official with the rank of Commissioner of Police. He is author of *To Serve and to Protect: Human Rights and Humanitarian Law for Police and Security Forces* (1998).

Paul F. Diehl is Professor of Political Science at the University of Illinois at Urbana-Champaign, author of *International Peacekeeping* (1994), and co-author of *War and Peace in International Rivalry* (2000), *Territorial Changes and International Conflict* (1992) and *Enhancing Organizational Performance* (1997).

Helen Durham is a Barrister and Solicitor of the Supreme Court of Victoria and the High Court of Australia, and has served as the National Manager of International Humanitarian Law (IHL) for Australian Red Cross. Currently working for the International Committee of the Red Cross, she received her SJD degree from Melbourne University. Dr Durham has co-edited *The Changing Face of Conflict and the Efficacy of International Humanitarian Law* (1999).

Lorraine Elliott is a Fellow in the Department of International Relations at the Australian National University. Her most recent book in this field is *Global Politics of the Environment* (1998). Dr Elliott is a member of the Australian Committee of the Council for Security Cooperation in the Asia Pacific (CSCAP) and the Australian National Committee of the International Human Dimensions Programme.

Martin P. Ganzglass is a partner in O'Donnell, Schwartz & Anderson in Washington, DC. He graduated from the City College of New York and the Harvard Law School. He is the author of *The Somali Penal Code: Cases, Commentary and Examples* (1971) and *Constitutions of the World: Somalia* (1971, 1979 and 1981). He has served as Legal Counsel to the Government of Eritrea and as part of the team drafting the Penal Code and Code of Criminal Procedure.

Michael Kelly is a Lieutenant Colonel in the Australian Army, presently serving in the Directorate of Operations and International Law at the Defence Legal Office. He holds a PhD in international law from the University of New South Wales. His areas of speciality are operations law, counter-terrorism, peace operations, counter-insurgency, and peacebuilding, and he is author of *Peace Operations: Tackling the Military, Legal and Policy Challenges* (1997).

Samuel M. Makinda is Associate Professor and Head of the School of Politics and International Studies at Murdoch University in Perth. He is author of *Superpower Diplomacy in the Horn of Africa* (1987), *Security in the Horn of Africa* (1992) and *Seeking Peace from Chaos: Humanitarian Intervention in Somalia* (1993).

William Maley is Professor and Foundation Director of the Asia-Pacific College of Diplomacy at the Australian National University, having taught for many years in the School of Politics, University College, University of New South Wales. He is author of The Afghanistan Wars (2002), co-authored Regime Change in Afghanistan: Foreign Intervention and the Politics of Legitimacy (1991) and Political Order in Post-Communist Afghanistan (1992), and edited Fundamentalism Reborn? Afghanistan and the Taliban (1998).

David M. Malone, a career Canadian Foreign Service Officer currently on leave, is President of the International Peace Academy, New York, and author of *Decision-Making in the UN Security Council: The Case of Haiti* (1998).

Sadako Ogata served from 1991 to 2001 as the United Nations High Commissioner for Refugees. A graduate of Georgetown University and the University of California at Berkeley, she has served as Professor of International Relations at Sophia University, as well as Chair of the Board of UNICEF, and as a Special Rapporteur to the UN Human Rights Commission.

Mark Plunkett is a Barrister-at-law. In 1993 was appointed the first UN Special Prosecutor investigating war crimes, crimes of genocide, and major human rights violations in Cambodia. His specialist area of study has been the re-establishment of the rule of law in post-conflict peacekeeping, and he has served as a Director of Paxiquest Consulting.

Amin Saikal is Director of the Centre for Arab and Islamic Studies (The Middle East and Central Asia) and Professor of Political Science at the Australian National University. He has held visiting appointments at Princeton and Cambridge and is author of *The Rise and Fall of the Shah* (1980) and *Islam and the West* (2002), and co-author of *Regime Change in Afghanistan: Foreign Intervention and the Politics of Legitimacy* (1991).

Charles Sampford is Foundation Professor of Law and Director of the Key Centre for Ethics, Law, Justice and Governance at Griffith University. He is author of *The Disorder of Law: A Critique of Legal Theory* (1989), and has edited or co-edited *Interpreting Constitutions* (1996), *Legal Education: New Foundations* (1998) and *Public Sector Ethics: Finding and Implementing Values* (1998).

Thomas E. Seal is a Colonel in the United States Marine Corps, presently serving as Deputy Director of the Humanitarian Demining Programs Office in the US Department of State. He has been Director of the Concepts Division at Marine Corps Combat Development Command, Quantico, Virginia, and served as Senior United Nations Military Observer in Observer Group Egypt. He holds Masters Degrees in US Diplomatic History, from Purdue University, and in National Security Studies, from the United States Naval War College.

Fiona Terry is a Researcher at the Médecins Sans Frontières (MSF) Foundation in Paris. She participated in the emergency response for the Kurdish population in northern Iraq after the Gulf War; in Somalia during the famine and civil war in 1992–1993; in the

Rwandan refugee camps in Tanzania following the genocide and mass exodus of the Hutu population; in Liberia throughout 1995; and in Rwanda following the return of refugees from Zaire and Tanzania in late 1996. Dr Terry received her PhD in International Relations from the Australian National University and is author of *Condemned to Repeat? The Paradox of Humanitarian Action* (2002).

Ramesh Thakur is Vice Rector of the United Nations University. In 2002 he served as Senior Adviser and Principal Writer of the Report of the Secretary-General on UN reform. Educated in India and Canada, he was formerly Professor and Head of the Peace Research Centre at the Australian National University in Canberra and Professor of International Relations and Director of Asian Studies at the University of Otago in New Zealand. A member of the International Commission on Intervention and State Sovereignty (ICISS), he also serves on several advisory boards around the world. The author and editor of 17 books and some 150 journal articles and book chapters, Dr Thakur is also a regular contributor to the opinion pages of the quality press.

Raimo Väyrynen is Professor of Government and International Studies and Senior Fellow at the Joan B. Kroc Institute for International Peace Studies at the University of Notre Dame. He was previously Professor of International Relations at the University of Helsinki and Secretary-General of the International Peace Research Association. He has recently co-edited *War, Hunger and Displacement: The Origins of Humanitarian Emergencies* (2000).

Adrien Whiddett is an officer of Australia's National Crime Authority, having earlier served as Deputy Commissioner of the Australian Federal Police. He is a graduate of Monash University, Melbourne, and of the US Federal Bureau of Investigation (FBI) National Executive Institute, a Foundation member of the Society of Police Futurists International and a Fellow of the Australian Institute of Management.

Index

Aartsen, Jozias van, 68
ACRI (African Crisis Response Initiative), 44
ADF (Australian Defence Force), 229, 342–343, 344
Afghanistan
 collapse of revenue base in, 21
 as disrupted state, 19
 ideological struggle disruption in, 21
 institutional design building in, 168, 173
 loss of trust in, 165
 sectarian roots of disruption in, 21
 September 11th triggering US intervention in, 23, 125
 Soviet invasion of, 22
 tracing causes of disruption in, 22–23
AFP (Australian Federal Police), 331–339
African regional conflicts, 115–116
Aideed, Mohamed Farah, 316, 342, 343
Ajello, Aldo, 191, 198
Albert, Sophie, 259, 260
Allard, Kenneth, 243
ALRI (Australian Legal Resources International), 203
American Bar Association, 348
American Medical Association, 281

Angola
 lack of adequate neutral security force in, 166
 UNAVEM II (United Nations Angola Verification Mission II) in, 166, 265
Annan, Kofi, 57, 264, 269, 303
anonymous trust, 164
armed conflict
 causes of violence and, 133–135
 civil war
  history of 20th century, 111–113
  impact of external intervention in, 123–126
  institutionalisation of national sovereignty and, 118–123
  negotiations during, 126–128
  outside forces involved in Lebanon, 36
  regional cases of, 113–118
 disarmament/reintegration of combatants
  conclusions on, 322–323
  conventional approaches to, 312–319
  observations on, 319–322
  theoretical perspectives of, 310–312
 genocide during
  examining root causes of, 133–135
  international criminal tribunals for crime of, 148–149

355

armed conflict (cont.)
  genocide during (cont.)
    UN failure to stop Bosnia and Rwanda, 45
    UN Group of Experts to investigate Cambodian, 149–151
  international law/security and, 135–138
  Orders For Opening Fire response during, 242
  ROE (Rules of Engagement) during, 232, 240, 243
  Rule of Law destroyed during, 210–212
  waging peace to end, 142–143
  See also intervention; military
arms control verification, 42
ASEAN (Association of South East Asian Nations), 114, 115
Austin, Reginald, 168, 180
Australian Defence Force (ADF), 229, 342–343, 344
Australian Federal Police (AFP)
  globocop role by, 332–334
  report on direction of, 334–337
  training of, 337–339
Australian Model Penal Code, 346
Autopsy Protocol, 218

Baidoa (Somalia), 248, 250, 342–343, 344
Balkans
  Dayton Accords to end conflict in, 40, 45, 201, 238
  International Police Task Force in, 238–239
  Kosovo, 22, 24, 119
  Macedonia, 36, 62, 66
  regional conflicts in, 118, 121–122
  See also Bosnia; former Yugoslavia; Kosovo intervention
Barre, Mohammad Siad, 19, 314, 341
Barry, Brian, 165
Berdal, Mats, 313, 315–316
Biafran humanitarian aid, 283–284, 285
Blechman, 273
Boland, Eavan, 258
Bosnia
  Dayton Accords for, 40, 45, 201
  effect of delay in international action in, 124
  international protective services for Muslims in, 41
  NATO intervention in, 44, 45
  property disputes in, 250
  UN failure to stop genocide in, 45
  UN peacekeeping in, 38
  See also Balkans
Bosnia–Herzegovina, 201
Bougainville, 250
Bousquet, René, 165
Boutros-Ghali, Boutros, 47, 315, 316
Brahimi Report (Report of the Panel on UN Peace Operations), 63, 269, 304
Brauman, Rony, 294
Brecht, Berthold, 135
Breughel's Two Monkeys (Szmborska), 349–350
Burkle, Frederick M., Jr., 6, 96
Burton, John, 193
Burundi, 133–134
Bush, George, 315, 330

Cambodia
  democratisation progress in, 195–201
  disarmament/reintegration of combatants in, 317–322
  end of strife and wars in, 192
  farce of elections (1998) in, 171
  humanitarian aid to, 284–286
  ideological struggle disruption in, 21
  interventions leading to free elections in, 40
  Khmer Rouge of, 312, 317–322, 333
  lack of institutional design building in, 168
  Paris Agreement of 1991 on, 195–196, 237, 239, 317
  UN Group of Experts to investigate war crimes in, 149–151
  UNTAC in, 168, 196, 198, 199, 237, 238, 262, 317, 318–319, 333
Canadian Airborne Regiment Battle Group, 240
Canadian Television (CTV), 240
CAR (Central African Republic), 62
CARE, 282
CBIRF (Chemical/Biological Incident Response Force) [USMC], 90–91
ceasefires
  as intervention stage, 39–40
  repeated violations of Lebanon, 45
"Chapter Six-and-a-half Operations", 4
Chesterman, Simon, 5, 57
Childers, 272

Chopra, Jarat, 266
Churchill, Winston, 6
CIMIC (UN Civil–Military Co-operation), 104–105
Civil Affairs Task Force, 251
civil society
   addressing issues of transition between civil strife and, 5–11
   humanitarian intervention as condition for rebuilding, 259
   peacekeeping operations to preserve, 4–5
   Rule of Law required for, 5
   trust requirement for, 163
civil war
   history of 20th century, 111–113
   impact of external intervention in, 123–126
   institutionalisation of national sovereignty and, 118–123
   negotiations during, 126–128
   outside forces involved in Lebanon, 36
   regional cases of, 113–118
Clinton, Bill, 44
coercive territorial revisionism, 119–120
cohesive states, 18–19
Cold War
   UN as forum during, 58–59
   UN Security Council vetoes during, 97
   Western success during, 92
   See also post–Cold War era
Commonwealth Heads of Government Meeting (New Zealand, 1995), 183
Commonwealth practice, 182–183
complex emergencies
   factors influencing future
      environmental security, 99–100
      examining importance of, 97–98
      political and legal, 98–99
      socioeconomic, 99
   need for civil–military responses, 102–106
   prevailing discourse of, 286, 287, 295
   public health responses, 101–102
   research issues of, 100–101
Conflict Prevention and Peace Forum (2000), 66
Congo. *See* DRC (Democratic Republic of the Congo)
Cook, Ian, 323
Cook, Robin, 67
Cousens, Richard P., 267

Cox, Robert, 319–320
CPP (Cambodia People's Party), 197, 199–200, 201
crisis management diplomacy, 65
Curley, Melissa, 323

Dahl, Robert, 169
Dallaire, Roméo, 166, 291
Dandeker, Christopher, 42
Darmos, Zoe, 158
Dayton Accords, 40, 45, 201, 238
DDR (disarmament, demobilisation and reintegration), 306
Declaration on Friendly RElations (1970), 71
democracy/democratisation
   Cambodian experience with, 195–201
   debate over right to governance and efforts toward, 183–186
   international community objections regarding, 180–181
   international reconstitution of political order and, 181–183
   policing civil order in
      Australian Federal Police peacekeeping role in, 331–339
      globocop activities, 332–336
      historic/constitutional background of, 327–328
      Rule of Law/global criminal environment and, 329–330
   reconstituting political order
      elections and, 186–188
      lessons learned from, 201–203
      limitations of electoral democratisation, 188–192
   Rhodesia/Zimbabwe experience with, 192–195
   UN Charter provisions on dealing with, 182
DHA (Department of Humanitarian Affairs), 268
Diehl, Paul F., 5, 31
diplomacy
   crisis management, 65
   strategic sanctions as tool of, 65–66
disarmament/reintegration of combatants
   conventional approaches to
      case study 1: Somalia, 314–317
      case study 2: Cambodia, 317–319
      overview of, 312–314

disarmament/reintegration of combatants (cont.)
    East Timora and, 323
    observations on, 319–322
    theoretical perspectives of, 310–312
disrupted states
    authoritarian or concealed authoritarian rule of, 21–22
    being punished for international law violations, 19–20
    defining, 3–4, 181, 296n.1
    forms of disruption in, 20–24
    institutional design to rebuild trust in, 167–175
    international community
        actions by, 41–44
        humanitarian interests in, 33–34
        human rights interests in, 34–35
        organisations involved in responses by, 44–46
        risks, problems, and barriers to responses by, 46–53
        security interests in, 35–36
        timing of responses to, 36–41
    key dimensions defining international responses to, 32–33
    military response to, USMC role in, 83–95
    rebuilding Rule of Law in
        enforcement model for, 213–219
        Eritrea and, 344–347
        impact of war and, 210–212
        justice-based NGOs and, 347–348
        lessons for Kosovo, 348–350
        necessity/requirements of, 207–209
        negotiation model for, 220–227
        Somalia and, 341–344
    social reconstruction in
        overview of, 258–261
        UN role in, 261–270
    suffering from degrees of incapacity, 19
    trust in
        institutional design to rebuild, 167–175
        loss of, 164–167
    See also state disruption
A Distant Mirror: The Calamitous 14th Century (Tuchman), 341
DMU (Detainee Management Unit), 245–246
Documentation Center of Cambodia, 150
Donini, Antonio, 260
Dorff, Robert, 258

Downie, Sue, 319, 323
DPA (UN Department of Political Affairs), 62
DPKO (UN Department of Peacekeeping Operations), 63, 268, 348
Draft Statute (1994), 151–153
DRC (Democratic Republic of the Congo)
    conflict over resources of, 287
    determination to fight by factions in, 125
    elections and reconstituting political order in, 187–188
    international security interests in, 35
    international state-building actions in, 42
    negotiations used as diversion in, 127
    outside intervention in, 23–24, 125
    proliferation of civil war parties in, 127
Drummond, Sir Eric, 2
Dubuet, Fabien, 155
Dunant, Jean-Henri, 283
Durant, Ariel, 84, 85
Durant, Will, 84, 85
Durham, Helen, 7–8, 145
Dziedzic, Michael, 260–261, 267, 271

East Timor
    disarmament in, 323
    domestic prosecutions in, 147
    as embryonic state, 19
    INTERFET (International Force for East Timor) forces in, 104, 105–106, 239, 245
    international state-building actions in, 42
    lack of adequate neutral security force in, 166
    lost of trust in, 165
    national self-determination progress in, 119
    UN Security Council decisions on, 104
    UNTAET (UN Transitional Administration in East Timor) in, 207, 246, 262, 267
ECHA (Executive Committee for Humanitarian Affairs) [UN], 269
Eckstein, Harry, 167
ECOWAS (Economic Community of West African States), 45, 46, 68, 74
Elaraby, Nabil, 59
elections
    farce of Cambodian 1998, 171
    IEC administration of South African (1994), 203
    interventions leading to free, 40

limitations of democratisation through, 188–192
reconstituting political order through, 186–188
supervision of, 42
electoral democratisation, 188–192
Elliott, Lorraine, 10, 257
Elmquist, M., 105
embryonic states, 19
empirical (or internal) sovereignty, 3
end-state, 291–292, 293
enforcement model, 213–219
environmental security issues, 99–100
EPLF (Eritrean People's Liberation Front), 340
Eritrea, 340–341, 344–347
Ethiopia, 22, 344–345
Ethiopia-Eritrea border war (1998–2000), 59, 344–345
EU (European Union), military/humanitarian capabilities of, 125
Evans, Gareth, 334
external sovereignty, 2

face-to-face trust, 164–165, 169
Falk, Richard, 26
Faubert, Carol, 292–293
Fiji, 188
Findlay, 271
1st Battalion, royal Australian Regiment (1 RAR), 241–243
former Yugoslavia
International Criminal Tribunal for, 148, 149, 248–249
legitimacy crisis in, 22
preventive deployment to, 36, 62, 66
UNPROFOR (UN Protection Force in former Yugoslavia) in, 102–104, 267
See also Balkans
Fraser, Malcolm, 282
Friedman, Thomas, 86
Friends of the Americas, 285
Fromkin, David, 85
FUNCINPEC, 199, 200, 210

Ganzglass, Martin P., 11, 340
Gardner, Anne Marie, 64
Geneva Conventions, 102, 140, 148, 153, 155–156, 215, 232–236, 283
genocide
examining root causes of, 133–135
international criminal tribunals for crime of, 148–149
UN failure to stop Bosnia and Rwanda, 45
UN Group of Experts to investigate Cambodian, 149–151
See also Rwanda genocide
Ginifer, 273
globalisation
criminal environment and, 329–330
six key areas of, 86
See also international community; world order
Goodin, Robert, 169
Goulding, Sir Marrack, 62–63
Gow, James, 42
Griffiths, 268
Group of Experts (UN), 149–151

Hammarskjöld, Dag, 4
Harare Declaration (1991), 182
Hardin, Russell, 164, 174
Harvard University-UN joint initiative (2000), 66
"Health as a Bridge for Peace" programmes (WHO), 263
Heder, Steven, 171
Helprin, Mark, 84
Hollows, Fred, 340, 341
Honduras, 285
humanitarian intervention
avoiding foreign policy engagement using, 288–289
Biafran, 283–284, 285
in Cambodia, 284–286
community interest in, 33–34
as condition for rebuilding civil society, 259
end-state identification during, 291–292, 293
gathering war crime evidence during, 154–156
limitations of, 279–280
NATO's Kosovo action framed as, 72, 73
NGOs
assistance actions of, 41
cooperation between military and, 289–294
origins and traditions of, 281–282
permanence of moral dilemmas of, 283–289

humanitarian intervention (cont.)
  post–Cold War focus on, 283, 295–296
  problems faced by indigenous healthcare providers during, 97
  "public health" capacity of countries for, 98
  relief–rehabilitation–development continuum during, 261
  repositioning debate on, 72–73
  shifting concepts of sovereignty/human rights and, 68–69, 264–266
  social reconstruction role of, 258–261
  See also intervention
human rights
  gathering evidence of abuse of, 156–157
  international community interests in, 34–35
  intervention and shifting concepts of sovereignty and, 68–69, 264–266
  military intervention to defend, 289–290
  research on documenting abuses of, 100–101
  Un Security Council resolutions on sovereignty and, 103–104
Hun Sen, 199, 200, 201
Hussein, Saddam, 289

ICC (International Criminal Court), 151–153
ICRC (International Committee of the Red Cross), 146, 154, 155, 157, 241, 272, 281, 284, 286
IFOR (NATO Implementation Force), 238
IGOs (international governmental organisations)
  coordination of international action and, 48–49
  coordination problems between NGOs and, 49–50
  disrupted states depending on help by, 47, 48
  international community responses and role of, 36
IMF (International Monetary Fund)
  information on financial issues of disruption on, 37
  preventive measures recommended by, 60, 76n.15
  social reconstruction made more difficult by, 268

Independent International Commission of Inquiry, 293
institutional design
  legitimacy of, 171
  principles of, 167–172
  role of NGOs in, 175
  "social separation of powers" in, 169–170
  specific choices in, 172–175
INTERFET (International Force for East Timor) forces, 104, 105–106, 239, 245
international community
  democracy/democratisation and, objections regarding, 180–181
  rule of law, human security issues guiding the, 1–3
  state disruption and
    humanitarian interests in, 33–34
    human rights interests in, 34–35
    response to, 24–27
    security interests in, 35–36
  See also globalisation; world order
International Criminal Court, 151–153
international criminal tribunals
  ad hoc, 148–149
  alternatives to prosecution by, 147–148
  interim justice measures using, 248–250
  rebuilding Rule of Law using, 215–219
International Herald Tribune, 288
International IDEA
  described, 183–184
  Statute and Declaration of, 184–185
international intervention coordination, 48–51
international law
  armed conflict and rules of, 135–138
  international community guided by, 1–3
  required for civil society, 5
  See also Rule of Law
International Law Commission, 151
International Police Task Force, 238–239
intervention
  complex emergencies and
    factors influencing future, 97–100
    need for civil–military responses, 102–106
    prevailing discourse of, 286, 287, 295
    public health responses, 101–102
    research issues of, 100–101
  Cook speech (2000) on principles of, 67–68

in Democratic Republic of the Congo, 23–24, 125
doctrine vs. exception approaches to, 69–72
impact on civil war by outside, 123–126
key dimensions defining responses to disrupted states by, 32–33
Kosovo
"immaculate coercion" notion coming out of, 85
legal considerations of, 70
NATO role in, 44, 72–73
questions raised by, 136–137
UN Security Council Resolution 1244 (1999) on, 4
organisations involved in, 44–46
repositioning the debate on, 72–73
response barriers/risks/problems of
lack of necessary interest, 46–48
perils of internal conflict, 51–52
problems of coordination, 48–51
sustaining action vs. developing exit strategy, 52–53
responses by
actions of, 41–44
ceasefire stage of, 39–40
organisations involved in, 44–46
role of USMC in military responses, 83–95
timing of, 36–41
shifting concepts of sovereignty/human rights and, 68–69
United Nations
armed force intervention by, 139–142
UN Charter criteria permitting intervention, 120, 136
See also armed conflict; humanitarian intervention; prevention actions; UN peacekeeping operations
IOs (international organisations)
cooperation between US and, 87
operating with US Marine forces, 93
IPA (International Peace Academy), 63, 64
Iraq
collapse of revenue base in, 21
Operation Provide Comfort, 41, 289
Iraqi Oil-for-Food sanctions, 66

Johnston, Roger, 315
Jouvenel, Bertrand de, 175
juridical (or external) sovereignty, 2, 3

justice
alternative to prosecution, 147–148
defining, 145
domestic prosecutions and, 147
gathering evidence for
by humanitarian actors, 154–156
by human rights actors, 156–157
importance of, 153–154
military force and
context of, 230–232
justice reconstruction and, 244–250
legal framework of, 232–237
long-term view of, 250–251
non-belligerent occupation status and, 237–239
proper use of, 239–244
Rule of Law
rebuilding, 207–227, 244–250
supported by, 145–158
See also Rule of Law
justice institutions
ad hoc international criminal tribunal, 148–149, 215–216
Draft Statute establishing international criminal, 151–153
enforcement model, 213–214
International Criminal Court (ICC), 151–153
UN Charter provisions on reconstruction of, 214–215
Justice Without Borders (hypothetical NGO), 348
Juvenal, 172

Kaldor, Mary, 259
Kashmir, 19
Kaufmann, Chaim D., 122
Keating, Paul, 334
Kelly, Michael, 9, 229
Kenneally, Thomas, 340
Kent, Randolph, 273
Khmer Rouge (Cambodia), 312, 317–322, 333
Kibeho massacre, 292–294
King, Charles, 166
Kirk, Bill, 338
Kosovo
elections and reconstituting political order in, 188
international intervention in disruption of, 24

Kosovo (cont.)
  national self-determination progress in, 119
  property disputes in, 250
  rebuilding Rule of Law in, 348–350
  separatism in, 22
  terms of NATO presence in, 252n.24–253n.24
Kosovo intervention
  "immaculate coercion" notion coming out of, 85
  legal considerations of, 70
  NATO role in, 44, 72–73
  questions raised by, 136–137
  UN Security Council decisions on, 4, 104
Kosovo Liberation Army (KLA), 348, 349
Kosovo refugee crisis (2000), 302
Kouchner, Bernard, 289
Krasner, Stephen D., 2
Kratochwil, Friedrich, 120
Kurdish secessionism movement, 22
Kuwait invasion (1990), 21

"ladder of options" concept, 303
Last, David, 257
Latter, Stuart, 323
Leader, Nicholas, 157
Lebanon
  as disrupted state, 19
  outside forces causing conflict in, 36
  outside intervention in, 23
  repeated ceasefire violations in, 45
  sectarian roots of disruption in, 21
legitimacy issues
  Ethiopian and Yugoslavian crises over, 22
  of institutional design, 171
  of military force and justice, 230–232
  UN Charter on legal intervention, 71, 120, 136
  See also Rule of Law
Lessons Learned Unit (UN Department of Humanitarian Affairs), 260, 270–272, 343–344

Macedonia, 36, 62, 66
Macfarlane Burnet Centre for Medical Research (Melbourne), 100
Mackinlay, John, 273
McNamara, Dennis, 270
Maginot Line concept, 92

MAGTFs (Marine Air–Ground Task Forces) [US], 89–90
Mahdi, Ali, 292
Makinda, Samuel M., 11, 309
Maley, William, 8, 163, 171
Malone, David M., 5, 57
Maslow, Abraham H., 133, 212
Mathieu, Carol, 240, 241
Mearsheimer, 121
mercy vs. justice, 145
MEU(SOC)s Marine Expeditionary Unit (Special Operations Capable), 89–90
MFO (Multinational Force and Observers), 45–46
migration trends, 86
military
  cooperation between NGOs and, 289–294
  disarmament/reintegration of combatants
    conclusions on, 322–323
    conventional approaches to, 312–319
    observations on, 319–322
    theoretical perspectives of, 310–312
  ROE (Rules of Engagement) followed by, 232, 240, 243
  USMC (United States Marine Corps), 83–94
  See also armed conflict; UN peacekeeping operations
Millbrook Declaration, 183
Mill, John Stuart, 172
Mine Action Programme for Afghanistan, 175
Minear, 264
MINURCA (Central African Republic), 62, 66
"Miracle on the Mekong", 171
"mission creep", 190
"Modern Police" (Great Britain), 327
Montesquieu, Baron de, 168
Morneault, Paul, 240
MoU (memorandum of understanding), 151
Mountain, Ross, 271
Mozambique
  democratisation progress in, 191
  end of strife and wars in, 192
  ONUMOZ (United Nations Operation in Mozambique) in, 335
MPF (Maritime Prepositioning Force), 90
MSF (Médecins sans Frontières), 154, 281–282, 284, 285, 286, 296

Namibia
  democratisation progress in, 191
  as embryonic state, 19
  end of strife and wars in, 192
  interventions leading to free elections in, 40
NAM (Non-Aligned Movement), 72
national self-determination, 118–119
National Union of Eritrean Women, 347
nation-state, 118
NATO
  evolving international roles of, 44, 46
  Kosovo intervention by
    agreement terms for, 252n.24–253n.24
    debate over "humanitarian", 72, 73
    lessons for, 348–349
    loss of anonymous trust following, 165
    peacekeeping role in Bosnia following, 45
    questions raised by, 136–137
Natsios, Andrew, 282
negotiation model
  overview of, 220–224
  Rapid Participatory Rule of Law Appraisal of, 220, 224–225
  Rule of Law Participatory Assessment, Monitoring and Evaluation of, 220, 225–227
Newland, Kathleen, 263
NGOs (nongovernmental organizations)
  cooperation between US and, 87
  coordination problems between IGOs and, 49–50
  diversity in purpose and principles of, 280–283
  humanitarian interventions
    assistance by, 41
    cooperation between military and, 289–294
    origins and traditions of, 281–282
    permanence of moral dilemmas in, 283–289
  human rights violations documented by, 156–157
  international community responses and role of, 36, 43–44
  operating with US Marine forces, 93
  pre-disruption action warnings from, 38
  rebuilding Rule of Law and justice-based, 347–348
  response to state disruption by, 24–25
  role in institutional design by, 175
  role in reconstruction of justice, 237
Nicaraguan Freedom Fund, 285
"no fly" zones, 41
non-belligerent occupation, 237–239
Nuremberg, 149

Oakley, Robert, 292
OAS (Organization of American States), 44, 79n.62
OAU (Organization of African Unity), 44, 45
OCHA (Office for the Coordination of Humanitarian Affairs) [UN], 104, 268, 269, 270
OECD (Development Assistance committee of the Organisation for Economic Co-operation and Development), 61
OEO (Other Expeditionary Operations) [USMC], 91–92
Ogata, Sadako, 10, 300
OMFTS (Operational Maneuver From the Sea) [USMC], 91
100-Day Action Programme for Accelerated Humanitarian Assistance in Somalia, 261–262
ONUMOZ (United Nations Operation in Mozambique), 335
Operation Provide Comfort (Iraq), 41, 289
Operation Provide Relief (Somalia), 289
Operation Restore Hope (Somalia), 230, 237, 315, 342, 343, 344
Order of the Knights of St. John of Jerusalem (later Order of Malta), 281
Orders For Opening Fire, 242
OSCE (Organization for Security and Cooperation in Europe), 238
Oxfam, 281, 284, 285–286

pacification actions, 41
Pakistan
  challenges of international intervention in, 24
  disruption due to instability of, 20
Papon, Maurice, 165
Paris Agreement of 1991, 195–196, 237, 239, 317

peacebuilding
  rebuilding Rule of Law as, 207–227, 244–250
  rebuilding trust as, 163–175
  social reconstruction as, 261–270
  UNHCR role in, 304–306
peacekeeping operations. *See* UN peacekeeping operations
Peace of Westphalia (1648), 2
Penal Code conference (Asmara), 346–347
"People of War" project (ICRC), 146
Persian Gulf crisis (1990–1991), 88
Pirnie, Bruce R., 261
Plunkett, Mark, 9
policing civil order
  Australian Federal Police peacekeeping role in, 331–339
  globocop activities, 332–336
  historic/constitutional background of, 327–328
  Rule of Law/global criminal environment and, 329–330
  world disorder and, 330–331
political order
  institutional design to restore trust and, 167–175
  international reconstitution of, 181–183
  limitations of electoral democratisation, 188–192
  reconstituting
    Cambodian, 195–201
    elections and, 186–188
    lessons learned from, 201–203
    limitations of electoral democratisation, 188–192
    Rhodesia/Zimbabwe, 192–195
  right to democratic government and, 183–186
Ponte, Carla del, 149
Popper, Karl, 173
post–Cold War era
  central role of humanitarian aid in, 283, 295–296
  conflict trends and causes during, 63–64
  forms of state in, 17–20
  increase in state disruption during, 17
  international intervention and "myth" of, 27
  similar characteristics of 38 major conflicts during, 96
  UN and disputes during, 59–63
  See also Cold War

Post Mortem Torture Detection Procedure, 218
Prendergast, Sir Kieran, 63
prevention actions
  conflict prevention strategies, 64–67
  conflict trends, causes and, 63–64
  IMF recommended, 60, 76n.15
  time lag between funding-action as weakness of, 67
  United Nations strategies for, 58–63
  See also intervention
preventive deployment
  conflict prevention through, 66
  described, 41
  to Former Yugoslav Republic of Macedonia, 36, 62, 66
property disputes, 250
protective services, 41
"public health" capacity, 98
public health responses, 101–102
Pugh, Michael, 103, 104
PVOs (private voluntary organisations)
  cooperation between US and, 87
  operating with US Marine forces, 93

Rainsy, Sam, 168
Ramsbotham, David, 264, 271
Rapid Participatory Rule of Law Appraisal, 220, 224–225
Red Cross (ICRC), 146, 154, 155, 157, 241, 272, 281, 284, 286
refugee asylum, 293–294
refugee camps
  controlling violence in, 292–293
  Kibeho massacre in, 292–294
  "ladder of options" concept and, 303
  moral dilemmas involved in aid to, 284, 286
refugees
  Commission of Inquiry report (1995) on placement of, 293
  destablisation of neighboring states by, 35, 62
  international humanitarian interests in, 33–34
  public health issues regarding, 101–102
  repatriation of, 259–260, 292
  UNHCR establishing security partnerships for, 306
  See also UNHCR (UN High Commissioner for Refugees)
regional conflicts. *See* civil war

Reilly, Ben, 169, 174
relief rehabilitation–development continuum, 261
Report of the Panel on UN Peace Operations (Brahimi Report), 63, 269, 304
Report of the Senate Standing Committee on Foreign Affairs, Defence and Trade (1994), 334–335
Resolution 1244 (UN), 4, 74, 142
Reynolds, Andrew, 169, 174
Rhodesia
  declaration of independence (1965) by, 182
  democratisation progress in, 192–195
Roberts, Adam, 233
ROE (Rules of Engagement), 232, 240, 243
Roosevelt, Franklin D., 2
Rover, Cees de, 7, 132
Rule of Law
  armed conflict and, 135–138
  international community guided by, 1–3
  mercy and justice and, 145–158
  policing civil order and, 329–330
  rebuilding in disrupted states
    enforcement model for, 213–219
    in Eritrea, 344–347
    impact of war and, 210–212
    interim measures for, 244–250
    justice-based NGOs and, 347–348
    lessons for Kosovo, 348–350
    necessity/requirements of, 207–209
    negotiation model for, 220–227
    in Somalia, 341–344
  required for civil society, 5
  See also international law; justice; legitimacy issues; the state
Rule of Law Participatory Assessment, Monitoring and Evaluation, 220, 225–227
Rwanda
  disruption due to ethnic antagonisms, 20–21
  international impact of refugees from, 34
  international lack of interest in, 47
  lack of adequate neutral security force in, 166
  property disputes in, 250
  UNAMIR (United Nations Assistance Mission for Rwanda) in, 166, 288, 293

Rwanda genocide
  causes of violence during, 133–134
  International Criminal tribunal for, 148, 149, 248–249
  public calls for military intervention of, 289–290, 291
  UN failure to stop, 45
  See also genocide
Rwandan Patriotic Army, 294

Saikal, Amin, 5, 17
sanctions, enforcement of, 42
Sanderson, John, 171, 334
Saro-Wiwa, Ken, 183
Schindler's List (Kenneally), 340
Seal, Thomas E., 6, 83
security environment
  international community interests in, 35–36
  UNHCR peace operations in changing, 301–304
Selassie, Emperor Haile, 344
Selassie, Haile, 22
September 11th (2001), 23, 26, 125
Shakespeare, William, 145
Shawcross, William, 171
Siad, Mohammad, 340
Sierra Leone
  conflict over resources of, 287
  negotiations used as diversion in, 127
  potential for further disruption in, 188
  regional conflicts involving, 116
Sihanouk Norodom, 170
Simons, William E., 261
Sinapore Declaration (1971), 182
Sinapore Prevention of Corruption Act, 346
Slim, Hugo, 50
Small Wars Manual (USMC), 84, 88–89, 91
social reconstruction
  gender issues of, 266
  overview of, 258–261
  United Nations and
    funding, 269–270
    integration and coordination, 266–269
    intervention/intrusion and consent, 264–266
  responses by, 261–264
"social separation of powers", 169–170
Solarz, Stephen J., 171

Somalia
  Canadian investigative reports on military disciplinary problems in, 240–241
  disarmament/reintegration of combatants in, 314–317, 320
  internal disruption of, 20
  international lack of interest in, 47
  100-Day Action Programme for, 261–262
  Operation Provide Relief in, 289
  Operation Restore Hope in, 230, 237, 315, 342, 343, 344
  proliferation of civil war parties in, 127
  rebuilding Rule of Law in, 341–344
  unclear objectives of intervention in, 291–292
  UN intervention in, 38, 139, 140
  UNOSOM II in, 246–247, 262, 265, 316, 335, 343
  UNOSOM I in, 292, 315, 341–342
Somali National Police Force, 340
Sørensen, Georg, 18, 19
South Africa
  democratisation process in, 201–202
  electoral administration by IEC in, 203
South African Commission on Truth and Reconciliation, 148
South African Independent Electoral Commission (IEC), 203
South American regional conflicts, 113–114
South-East Asian regional conflicts, 114–115, 123
sovereign state system, Peace of Westphalia as framework for, 2
sovereignty
  defining various meanings of, 2–3
  dynastic vs. civic, 120
  institutionalisation of national, 118–123
  intervention and shifting concepts of human rights and, 68–69, 264–266
  UN Charter provisions on, 102–103, 104
  Un Security Council resolutions on human rights over, 103–104
  violation of UN Universal Declaration of Human Rights and, 98–99
  See also Westphalian ideal
SRSG (Special Representative of the Secretary-General), 271–272
the state
  forms of, 17–20
  mercy and justice in transition period, 145–158

  sovereignty as exercised by, 2–3
  See also Rule of Law
state disruption
  attempts by UN to address, 3
  described, 3–4, 181
  forms of, 20–24
  international response to, 24–27
  post–Cold War increase in, 17
  See also disrupted states
Status of Armed Forces Agreement (UN), 140–141
Stroun, Jacques, 155
Szmborska, Wislawa, 349

Taft, Julia, 282
Taliban (Afghanistan), 21
Taylor, Charles, 116
terrorism
  domestic vs. international, 111–112
  September 11th (2001) attack as, 23, 26, 125
Terry, Fiona, 10, 279
"Three Block War", 90
Tito, Josip Broz, 22
To Asmara (Hollows), 340
Touvier, Paul, 165
transitional states
  ad hoc international criminal tribunals, 148–149
  alternatives to prosecution in, 147–148
  domestic prosecutions, 147
  mercy vs. justice of, 146–147
trust
  anonymous vs. face-to-face, 164–165, 169
  as civil society requirement, 163
  institutional design to build, 167–175
  politics and, 164–167
  three steps to restoring, 165–166
Tuchman, Barbara, 341

UNAMIR (United Nations Assistance Mission for Rwanda), 166, 288, 293
UNAVEM II (United Nations Angola Verification Mission II), 166, 265
UNBRO (UN Border Relief Organisation), 333
UN Charter
  international criminal tribunals under, 148–149
  intervention in accordance with, 71, 120, 136

peacekeeping operations under, 102–103, 104
prevention of conflict statement in, 58
provisions on dealing with democratisation, 182
provisions enabling justice reconstruction under, 214–215
resolution on Cambodian tribunals under, 150–151
on state sovereignty, 68, 190
UN CIMIC (Civil–Military Co-operation), 104–105
UN Commission on Human Rights, 180
UN Department of Humanitarian Affairs, 49
UN Department of Humanitarian Affairs Lessons Learned Unit, 260, 270–272, 343–344
UN Department of Peacekeeping Operations (DPKO), 63, 268, 348
UN DHA (Department of Humanitarian Affairs), 268
UNDPA (Department of Political Affairs), 62, 268, 269–270, 345
UNDP (United Nations Development Programme), 262, 263
UNDRO (United Nations Disaster Relief Organisataion), 268
UN ECHA (Executive Committee for Humanitarian Affairs), 269
UNEF II (Second UN Emergency Force), 331
UNFICYP (UN Peace-keeping Force in Cyrus), 332–333
UN Group of Experts, 149–151
UNHCR (UN High Commissioner for Refugees)
  complex emergency/sustainable peace role by, 262–263
  DDR (disarmament, demobilisation and reintegration) efforts by, 306
  early actions in Kosovo by, 103
  establishing security partnerships for refugees, 306
  as humanitarian actor, 154
  independent governing body, funding and mandate of, 268, 269–270
  peacebuilding role by, 304–306
  peace operations by, 301–304
  protection of refugees responsibility of, 279

"quick impact projects" initiated by, 305
See also refugees
UN Human Rights Commission, 185–186, 188
UNICEF (United Nations Children's Fund), 262–263, 268, 269–270
UNIFEM (United Nations Fund for Women), 266
UN INTERFET (International Force for East Timor) forces, 104, 105–106
Unita in Angola sanctions (2000–2001), 66
UNITAF, 237, 342, 343
United Nations
  armed intervention by
    debate over legality of, 69–72
    historic outcomes of, 139–142
    UN Charter criteria permitting, 120, 136
  attempts to address state disruption by, 3
  Cold War forum provided by, 58–59
  Draft Statute (1994) of, 151–153
  economic sanctions against Iraq, 21
  ICC (International Criminal Court) established by, 151–153
  joint initiative between Harvard University and, 66
  post–Cold War disputes and, 59–63
  reforms required for stable world order, 138
  social reconstruction role of
    funding, 269–270
    integration and coordination, 266–269
    intervention/intrusion and consent, 264–266
    responses by, 261–264
  time lag between funding and action as weakness of, 67
  "Uniting for Peace" formula of, 58–59
  See also UN peacekeeping operations
United States
  cooperation between IOs, NGOs, PVOs and, 87
  international intervention role by, 26
  intervention in Afghanistan by, 23
  national character influencing future actions by, 85–86
  non-intervention doctrine trend in, 124–125
  September 11th (2001) terrorist attack on, 23, 26, 125

United States (cont.)
  social reconstruction role of, overview of, 258–261
  See also USMC (United States Marine Corps)
United States Council for World Freedom, 285
"Uniting for Peace" formula, 58–59
UN Minimum Standards for Prisons, 218
UN OCHA (Office for the Coordination of Humanitarian Affairs), 104, 268, 269, 270
UNOSOM II (United Nations Operation in Somalia II), 246–247, 262, 265, 316, 335, 343
UNOSOM I (United Nations Operation in Somalia I), 292, 315, 341–342
UN Peace-keeping Force in Cyprus (UNFICYP), 39
UN peacekeeping operations
  Australian role in, 331–339
  Brahimi Report on, 63, 269, 304
  distinctions between collective security force and, 38–39
  expansion and reformulation of, 31–32
  as intervention alternative, 126
  in Macedonia, 36, 62, 66
  mixed results of, 44–45
  NATO's role in Bosnia, 45
  policing civil order through, 331–332
  to preserve civil society, 4–5
  preventive deployment and, 41
  risks/problems/barriers of
    ambivalent mission statements/weak rules of engagement, 102–103
    lack of necessary interest, 46–48
    perils of internal conflict, 51–52
    perils of internal conflict and, 51–52
    problems of coordination, 48–51
    sustaining action vs. developing exit strategy, 52–53
  Rule of Law rebuilding
    enforcement model for, 213–219
    negotiation model for, 220–227
  in Somalia, 38, 139, 140
  strategic, 42–43
  timing issues of, 36–41
  traditional, 41–42
  traditional vs. complex, 4
  UN Charter requirements for, 102–103, 104

  See also intervention; military; United Nations
UNPREDEP (UN Preventive Deployment Force) [Macedonia], 62, 66
UNPROFOR (UN Protection Force in former Yugoslavia), 102–104, 267
UN Security Council
  Cold War forum provided by, 58–59
  Kosovo intervention decisions by, 4, 104
  Resolution 1244 (1999) by, 4, 74, 142
  resolution 1325 on women, 312
  resolutions favouring human rights over sovereignty, 103–104
  Status of Armed Forces Agreement of, 140–141
  vetoes on action during Cold War by, 97
UN Standby Arrangements programme, 103
UN Status of Armed Forces Agreement, 140–141
UNTAC (UN Transitional Authority in Cambodia), 168, 196, 198, 199, 237, 238, 262, 317, 318–319, 333
UNTAET (UN Transitional Administration in East Timor), 207, 246, 262, 267
UNTAG (United Nations Transition Assistance Group), 335
UN Universal Declaration of Human Rights, 98–99, 180
urbanisation trends, 86
Urquhart, 272
US AGency for International Development, 288
US Foreign Disaster Assistance, 282
US Foreign Policy for Peace Conference, 146
US MAGTFs (Marine Air–Ground Task Forces), 89–90
USMC CBIRF (Chemical/Biological Incident Response Force), 90–91
USMC OEO (Other Expeditionary Operations), 91–92
USMC OMFTS (Operational Maneuver From the Sea), 91
USMC *Small Wars Manual*, 84, 88–89, 91
USMC (United States Marine Corps)
  limitations on innovation by, 92–93
  as model in civil–military equation, 83–84
  obstacles to civil–military cooperation by, 93–94
  world view of, 87–92
  See also United States

Van Evera, 122
Väyrynen, Raimo, 7, 111
Vietnam, 85

Waller Meyers, Deborah, 263
Walt, Stephen M., 309, 311
war. *See* armed conflict
Weiss, Thomas G., 263, 264
Westphalian ideal, 2
  See also sovereignty
WFP (World Food Programme), 262, 263
Whaley, 266, 271
Whiddett, Adrien, 11, 327
Whitman, Jim, 258, 267
WHO (World Health Organization), 100, 262, 263
Wiesenthal, Simon, 153
Wieviorka, Michel, 111
Woodhouse, 264
World Bank
  focus on social capital development by, 61
  information on financial issues of disruption by, 37
  peacebuilding partnership between UNHCR, UNDP and, 305
  social reconstruction made more difficult by, 268
world order
  basic requirements of stable, 138
  policing civil, 327–339
  UN reforms needed for stable, 138
  See also globalisation; international community
World Vision, 282

Zacher, Mark W., 119, 120
ZAPU (Zimbabwe African People's Union), 192–193, 194
Zartman, William, 127
Zimbabwe
  democratisation progress in, 192–195
  end of strife and wars in, 192
Zuroff, Efraim, 146